Fundamentals of Polygraph Practice

Dedication*

D.J.K.: To Lisa, Don III, Jennifer, John, and Matthew.
P.K.S.: To Richard, Judy, Julie, Marla, Tony, Brenda, and Larry.

*For the text Fundamentals of Polygraph Practice.

Fundamentals of Polygraph Practice

Donald J. Krapohl
National Center for Credibility Assessment (ret), Columbia, SC, USA

Pamela K. Shaw
National Polygraph Academy, Lexington, KY, USA
Shaw Polygraph Services, Inc., Lexington, KY, USA

AMSTERDAM • BOSTON • HEIDELBERG • LONDON
NEW YORK • OXFORD • PARIS • SAN DIEGO
SAN FRANCISCO • SINGAPORE • SYDNEY • TOKYO
Academic Press is an imprint of Elsevier

Academic Press is an imprint of Elsevier
525 B Street, Suite 1800, San Diego, CA 92101-4495, USA
The Boulevard, Langford Lane, Kidlington, Oxford OX5 1GB, UK

© 2015 Elsevier Inc. All rights reserved.

No part of this publication may be reproduced or transmitted in any form or by any means, electronic or mechanical, including photocopying, recording, or any information storage and retrieval system, without permission in writing from the publisher. Details on how to seek permission, further information about the Publisher's permissions policies and our arrangements with organizations such as the Copyright Clearance Center and the Copyright Licensing Agency, can be found at our website: www.elsevier.com/permissions.

This book and the individual contributions contained in it are protected under copyright by the Publisher (other than as may be noted herein).

Notices
Knowledge and best practice in this field are constantly changing. As new research and experience broaden our understanding, changes in research methods, professional practices, or medical treatment may become necessary.

Practitioners and researchers must always rely on their own experience and knowledge in evaluating and using any information, methods, compounds, or experiments described herein. In using such information or methods they should be mindful of their own safety and the safety of others, including parties for whom they have a professional responsibility.

To the fullest extent of the law, neither the Publisher nor the authors, contributors, or editors, assume any liability for any injury and/or damage to persons or property as a matter of products liability, negligence or otherwise, or from any use or operation of any methods, products, instructions, or ideas contained in the material herein.

British Library Cataloguing in Publication Data
A catalogue record for this book is available from the British Library

Library of Congress Cataloging-in-Publication Data
A catalog record for this book is available from the Library of Congress

ISBN: 978-0-12-802924-4

For information on all Academic Press publications
visit our website at http://store.elsevier.com/

Disclaimer:
All contents of this book were developed and written by Donald Krapohl and Pamela Shaw, except those sections listing other authors. All statements of fact, opinion, or analysis expressed are those of the authors and do not reflect the official positions or views of any U.S. Government agency. Nothing in the contents should be construed as asserting or implying U.S. Government authentication of information or endorsement of the authors' views. The material authored by Donald Krapohl has been reviewed by the Central Intelligence Agency and the Defense Intelligence Agency to prevent the disclosure of classified information.

Publisher: Shirley Decker-Lucke
Acquisitions Editor: Elizabeth Brown
Editorial Project Manager: Joslyn Chaiprasert-Paguio
Production Project Manager: Lisa Jones
Designer: Matthew Limbert

Cover designed by Marla J. Rhine

Contents

Foreword xiii
Preface xv

Chapter 1 **A History of Lie Detection** 1
    Ancient Traditions 2
    Observations of Behavior 4
    Observations of Physiology 6
    Modern Developments 8
        Instrumentation 8
        Cardiovascular Measures 8
        Breathing 12
        Electrodermal 13
    First Precedent in Law 15
    The Advent of Multiple Recordings 17
    Modern Instrumentation 18
    Evolution of Techniques 20
    Evolution of Analytic Methods 23
    Final Comment 25
    References 25

Chapter 2 **Anatomy and Physiology for Polygraph Examiners** 29
    Joel M. Reicherter
    Background 29
    Organization 30
    Integumentary System 32
    Nervous System 34
    Cardiovascular System 46
    Respiratory System 53
    Conclusion 60
    About the Author 60
    References 60

Chapter 3 **Test Question Construction** 61
    Irrelevant Questions 64
        Examples of Irrelevant Questions 64
    Relevant Questions 65
        Primary Relevant Questions 66
        Secondary Relevant Questions 68

	Probable-Lie Comparison Questions	68
	Exclusionary Phrases	70
	Examples of PLCs	70
	Directed Lie Comparison Questions	73
	Examples of DLCs	74
	Other Common Questions	75
	Sacrifice Relevant Question	75
	Symptomatic Questions	75
	Introductory Question	76
	Less Common Questions	76
	Countermeasure Question	76
	Guilt Complex Question	77
	Hope/Fear Questions	77
	Overall Truth	78
	Positive Control	78
	Conclusion	78
	References	78
Chapter 4	**Data Collection**	**81**
	Explaining Sensors to the Examinee	81
	General Introduction	82
	Pneumographs	82
	Electrodermal	82
	Photoplethysmograph	83
	Cardiovascular	83
	Motion Sensor	83
	Sensor Placement	83
	Pneumograph Sensors	83
	Electrodermal Sensors	84
	Photoplethysmograph Sensor	86
	Blood pressure Cuff	86
	Motion Sensor	88
	Tracing Appearance	88
	Pneumograph	88
	Electrodermal	89
	Photoplethysmograph	90
	Motion Sensor	90
	Cardiovascular	91
	Appearance of the Chart	93

	Final Comment	94
	Reference	94
	Recommended Readings	94
Chapter 5	**Analysis of Polygraph Data**	**95**
	Definitions	95
	Other Definitions	96
	How to Approach Chart Interpretation	97
	Features	97
	Electrodermal	98
	EDR Exemplars	99
	Amplitude	99
	Cardiovascular	100
	Cardiovascular Exemplars	101
	Artifacts in the Cardiovascular Channel	101
	Vasomotor	103
	Pneumograph	103
	Suppression	104
	Slowing	104
	Baseline Rise	104
	Movement Sensor	106
	Scoring Systems	107
	About 7-Position Scoring	108
	About 3-Position Scoring	108
	About the ESS	108
	Scoring Rules	109
	Response Windows	109
	Scoring the Pneumograph	110
	Scoring the Electrodermal Channel	112
	Scoring the Cardiograph	113
	Scoring the PPG	115
	Rank Order Scoring	115
	Decision Rules	117
	Multiple-Issue and Multiple-Facet Examinations	117
	7- and 3-Position Scoring	118
	Empirical Scoring System	118
	Single-Issue Examinations: Investigative	119
	Federal Zone Comparison Technique	119

"You Phase" 120
Utah Probable-Lie Test 121
Single-Issue Examinations: Evidentiary 121
Global Analysis 122
Purposeful Non-cooperation 123
References 123

Chapter 6   **Polygraph Screening 127**
Overview 128
Successive Hurdles 129
Test Topics 130
Adjudications 132
Recording 133
Surveys 133
Significant Case Tracking 133
Results 133
General Suggestions for Pretest Interviews 134
Directed-Lie Screening Test 136
DLST Pretest Interview 137
Introduction of the Directed Lies 137
DLST Test Phase 138
DLST Scoring 139
DLST Decision Rules 139
Next Steps 140
Air Force Modified General Question Technique 141
AFMGQT Pretest 142
AFMGQT Test Phase 142
AFMGQT Scoring 144
AFMGQT Decision Rules 145
Relevant/Irrelevant Screening Test 145
RI Pretest 146
RI Test Phase 146
RI Scoring Rules 147
RI Decision Rules 147
Screening Examination Reports 148
References 148

Chapter 7   **Specific-Issue Testing Techniques 151**
Case Preparation 152
Pretest Interview 153
The Introduction 153
Overview of the Process 154

  Consent Form, Rights Advisement 154
  Gathering Biographic Information 154
  Explaining the Polygraph 155
  Discussion of Test Issues 155
  Question Introduction 156
  Acquaintance Test 156
 Federal Zone Comparison Technique 156
  FZCT Test Phase 158
  FZCT Scoring Rules 159
  FZCT Decision Rules 159
 Utah Probable Lie Test 159
  UPLT Test Phase 160
  UPLT Scoring 162
  UPLT Decision Rules 162
 Air Force Modified General Question Technique 163
  Versions of the AFMGQT 164
  AFMGQT Scoring 164
  AFMGQT Decision Rules 165
 References 166

Chapter 8   **Recognition Tests 167**
 Peak of Tension 167
  Constructing KSPOTs 168
  Constructing SPOTs 170
  Analyzing the POT 171
 Concealed Information Test 172
  CIT Instrumentation 177
  CIT Testing 178
  Analyzing the CIT 180
  Summary of Best CIT Practices 182
 References 184

Chapter 9   **Scientific Issues 185**
 Validity 185
 Reliability 188
 Types of Validity Studies 189
  Field Studies 189
  Laboratory Studies 190
 Effect of Decision Rules 191
 Effects of Base Rates 194
 Polygraph Theories 201
  Psychological Set 201
  Relevant Issue Gravity 203

	Differential Salience 203
	Preliminary Process Theory..204
	References 204
Chapter 10	**Polygraph Legal Issues 207**
	Gordon L. Vaughan
	Admissibility of Evidence of Polygraph Examination Results........ 207
	From *Frye* to *Daubert* 207
	Post-Daubert Admissibility of Polygraph Evidence...............212
	Stipulated Polygraph Evidence 217
	Polygraph Evidence in Sentencing 219
	Polygraph Admissibility in Other Proceedings 221
	Use of Polygraph in Interrogation 221
	General Rule 221
	Miranda Considerations 222
	Postconviction Sex Offender Testing...223
	Polygraph in the Workplace 225
	Licensing of Polygraph Examiners...227
	The Future of Polygraph and the Law 227
	Acknowledgments 229
	About the Author 229
Chapter 11	**Advanced Topics 231**
	Physical Conditions Requiring Accommodation..........................231
	Amputations/Injuries 231
	Blindness..233
	Cardiovascular Disorders...233
	Dwarfism 235
	Hearing Impairment...235
	Obesity 237
	Pregnancy..238
	Stuttering...238
	Ethics 239
	Reasons for Ethical Lapses 240
	Ethical Principles 241
	Conclusion 242
	Report Writing 243
	Identification 243
	Background 243
	Purpose 244
	The Examination...244

Pretest 244
Test Phase 245
Analyses and Results 245
Posttest Statements 247
Other Information 247
Postconviction Sex Offender Testing (PCSOT).........................247
Instant Offense 249
Instant Offense Investigative..249
Prior Allegation..249
Sexual History (I & II)..249
Sex Offense Monitoring...250
Maintenance 250
Asset Forfeiture Testing...251
Conclusion 254
Working with Foreign Language Interpreters..........................254
Step 1: The Interpreter 254
Step 2: Preparation..255
Step 3: Pretest 257
Step 4: Testing 258
Conclusion 259
Silent Answer Test..260
Yes Test...262
Case 1..263
Case 2..264
Case 3..265
Case 4..266
Paired Testing: The "Marin Protocol" 266
Requirements 268
Conclusion 271
Testing Victims of Traumatic Events..271
Recommendations...272
References...273

Chapter 12 Alternate Technologies 275
Event-Related Potentials..278
How It Works..278
Potential in Lie Detection 279
Functional Magnetic Resonance Imaging 280
How It Works..280
Potential in Lie Detection 281
Thermal Imaging 281

    How It Works 281
    Potential in Lie Detection 282
  Saccadic Eye Movement 283
    How It Works 283
    Potential in Lie Detection 284
  Oculomotor Deception Test 285
    How It Works 285
    Potential in Lie Detection 285
  Laser Doppler Vibrometry 286
    How It Works 287
    Potential in Lie Detection 287
  Voice-Based Systems 288
  Autobiographical Implicit Association Test 289
  References 290

Glossary 293
Appendix A: Public Law 100 – 347 309
Appendix B: 2015 Update to the APA 2011 Meta-Analytic Survey of Validated Polygraph Techniques 319
Appendix C1: Confidential Report 335
Appendix C2: Polygraph Examination Report 339
Index 343

Foreword

Some years ago, we were camped at the base of a glacier on Mt. Adams in southwestern Washington State, preparing for early morning bid for the summit. While I melted snow to make instant mashed potatoes for dinner, Don Krapohl regaled us with stories of fantastic new German-Chinese restaurant that had opened near his home. The food was great. There was only one problem—an hour after dinner, you were hungry for power.

I have heard Don speak on a number of occasions, often about topics covered in this book, and he always started his talk with a joke. You can imagine my disappointment when his book did not start that way. To remedy the situation, I started the Foreword with one of Don's better jokes.

Now, *Fundamentals of Polygraph Practice* is a great book. It covers a lot of ground and should be of interest to any student of the polygraph. The book was written by Don Krapohl and Pam Shaw with a few invited chapters by other authorities. I met Pam Shaw a few years ago at a meeting of the New Jersey Polygraph Association. Pam was President of the American Polygraph Association at that time. Everyone appreciated that she agreed to do most of the instruction at those meetings, especially I.

I met Don Krapohl at David Raskin's workshops on the polygraph at the University of Utah in the late 1970s. I was a new graduate student in David's lab at the time, and during the workshop, David had me teach a unit on psychophysiology. I thought that was fitting because I was a student of psychophysiology, not the polygraph. I was interested in the polygraph only because it produced many channels of physiological data that could be related to psychological processes. Whereas most psychophysiologists spend many years investigating a single physiological measure, Raskin had set up his Beckman Dynograph to record eight channels of physiological activity. It was a gold mine of data for someone interested in the relationship between physiological activity and psychological processes. As far as I was concerned, the observed changes in physiology could be associated with almost any emotion or any form of cognitive activity. It just happened to be deception. I came to learn, as most of you already know, that deception during polygraph tests is tightly linked to changes in electrodermal, cardiovascular, electrophysiological, respiratory, and oculomotor activity. In psychology, it is extremely rare to see correlations between two variables as large as those obtained between deception and physiology. We benefited greatly from the strong and stable relationships between deception and physiology in our efforts to develop computer programs to measure physiological changes that discriminate well between truthful and deceptive people. In a report to the Air Force in 1962, Joseph Kubis, a psychologist at Fordham University, concluded that it was not feasible to develop computer programs to extract diagnostic information from polygraph charts. By 1980, we had demonstrated not only that it could be done but also that any idiot can do it.

Thirty-five years ago, Don attended Raskin's workshops because he was, and continues to be, a dedicated student of polygraph technology. Technology is the study of the practical use of scientific discoveries. *Fundamentals of Polygraph Practice* seeks to apply the results of scientific research to the practice of psychophysiological detection of deception. It describes evidence-based, best practices for polygraph professionals. Best practices are not based on proclamations by polygraph gurus, however clever and charismatic they might be. They are not built on opinions expressed by uninformed and arrogant members of the scientific community with antipolygraph biases and no apparent interest in data that conflict with their prejudices. They are not well served by selective and misleading reviews of the existing scientific literature by other scientists who find value in only their own preferred polygraph technique. Best practices are not shaped by political interests, bureaucratic expediency, or compromise. Best practices are those for which there is good empirical support. They are data-based methods that have consistently produced results superior to those achieved by other approaches. Best practice also implies a commitment to be open to change and adapt as new findings show a conceptual or practical advantage of one method over another.

Over the years, advocates for various polygraph techniques have come and gone. Critics of the polygraph have come and gone. Program managers and directors have come and gone. Alternatives to the polygraph have been proposed and found lacking (see Chapter 12). Funding for research on the polygraph has come and gone. One thing that has not changed is the need for valid credibility assessments. Another thing that has not changed has been the unwavering commitment of these authors to the advancement of validated polygraph techniques. The authors have acquired funding to support research on polygraph techniques. Under their leadership, the quality of research published in the journal *Polygraph* has improved significantly. The primary author developed the OSS-2 scoring system, which outperformed all other scoring methods in recent comparisons of manual and automated polygraph scoring techniques, and he has published numerous other research reports, reviews, and book chapters related to the polygraph. *Fundamentals of Polygraph Practice* is just the latest in a long line of substantive contributions to the field.

No one in the polygraph community is better qualified to write a book on evidence-based practice than these authors. Don and Pam are poster children for evidence-based practice, and their book falls squarely at the interface between science and practice. The writing is clear and contains many good examples of best practice. I highly recommend this lucid and authoritative practitioner-oriented text on polygraph techniques.

Douglas Adams once said, "Solutions nearly always come from the direction you least expect, which means there's no point trying to look in that direction because it won't be coming from there." Hoping Adams is wrong, I will be looking in my mailbox for a copy of this book.

John C. Kircher, Ph.D.
Professor of Educational Psychology and Adjunct Professor of Psychology
Author of the Computerized Polygraph System and the Ocular-motor Deception Test
Recipient of the John E. Reid Memorial Award for Distinguished Achievement
in Polygraph Research, Teaching or Writing

Preface

For those with an interest in the fields of psychology and criminal justice, there are few careers more fascinating, or more consequential, than that of a polygraph examiner. On any given day, professional examiners can be found resolving high-profile crimes, helping assess candidates for jobs, supporting treatment providers in offender management, working to protect national secrets, validating intelligence information, and assisting attorneys, judges, government leaders, and the average citizen. Each case presents a unique opportunity to resolve problems in a way that no other method can.

Because polygraph results always have consequences for someone, and often profound consequences, those who choose to practice in this field must be properly prepared. That preparation entails a good educational foundation, a commitment to excellence, and uncompromising integrity. This book strives to capture and organize best practices for students of polygraphy. We believe that they will find it to be a beneficial supplement to a formal and accredited polygraph education program.

It was not our goal merely to provide a learning text for polygraph students, however. There are many more who are curious about polygraphy. With so much public over- and underestimation about what polygraphy really is and what it can do, we thought it important to make the content accessible to nonpractitioner communities as well. It is our hope to resolve some of the general misconceptions of the polygraph, with the twin goals of managing public expectations and improving the services polygraph examiners provide. Consumers of polygraph services, such as law enforcement agencies, courts, sex offender treatment providers, government screening programs, and the general public can come to learn what the limits and possibilities of the polygraph are, what conditions are necessary for accurate polygraph results, and to expect examiners to perform according to professional standards. In ways that legislation and professional associations cannot accomplish alone, the raising of consumer awareness can create an even greater professional orientation to the use of best practices.

Undertaking this project has been a revelation to us in that we discovered how much assistance we would need from our many professional friends and colleagues to help us get our facts right. We owe a debt of gratitude to the best and brightest examiners we know. We sincerely appreciate the technical suggestions from Donnie Dutton, Bill Norris, and Mark Handler. We owe a special thanks to Ben Blalock, who spent countless hours correcting our drafts. Without their comments, criticisms, and suggestions, this volume would have suffered. We are very grateful to Skip Webb and Ray Nelson for their contribution of the very informative appendices, and for the admin and library support from Louane Powers and Katie Baldwin. Thanks also go to Cholan V. for permission to reprint many of the illuminating images appearing in the book.

Early on, we recognized the wisdom of using specialized experts in two essential topic areas for a well-rounded polygraph instruction book. Those topic areas were Law, and Anatomy and Physiology, and fortunately, two of our profession's best experts stepped up to help us: Professor Joel Reicherter who produced perhaps the best anatomy and physiology chapter for polygraph examiners to be found, and Gordon Vaughan, Esq., General Counsel for the American Polygraph Association and easily one of the best-known experts in polygraph law. Polygraph students will benefit immensely from their chapters, and we are indebted to these gentlemen for contributing them.

We also received unhesitant support from the manufacturers of polygraphs in providing images for the Data Collection chapter. We would like to express our sincere appreciation to our friends Jamie Brown of Limestone Technologies, Chris Fausett and Sue Luttrell from Lafayette Instruments, and Ben Blalock of Stoelting Instruments.

We also thank Joslyn Chaiprasert-Paguio of Elsevier Publishing for deftly handling the uncountable details that allowed our ideas to come to print.

We would be remiss if we did not give credit to the thought leaders of science who, over the many years, have helped illuminate the practitioner's path, and in doing so help establish a specialized new field, polygraphy: Drs. Hugo Munsterberg, John Larson, John Kircher, David Raskin, Charles Honts, John Podlesny, Joseph Kubis, Frank Horvath, Gordon Barland, Lou Rovner, Stuart Senter, Avital Ginton, David Lykken, Akihiro Suzuki, Eitan Elaad, Stanley Abrams, Gershon Ben-Shakhar, Michael Bradley, Vance MacLaren, Ronald Craig, and our recently departed good friend Andrew Dollins. Through data and debate they have forced us to reconcile our practices with empirical evidence, and in doing so, have moved polygraphy toward more defensible methods. In addition, the polygraph field has benefited from the work of researcher/practitioners who expanded our practical knowledge: Leonarde Keeler, Clarence D. Lee, John Reid, Norman Ansley, Mark Handler, Raymond Nelson, James Matte, and Nathan Gordon. These, and others we may have missed, have been immensely impactful to the practice of polygraphy in its various forms, and each has left a mark on the daily work of the many thousands of polygraph examiners around the world.

And as a final thought, we offer a wish to our fellow practitioners. To polygraph examiners everywhere, whatever the mission, who remain steadfast unbiased seekers of the truth, who fight the good fight every day, we wish you Godspeed.

The material authored by Donald Krapohl has been reviewed by the U.S. Defense Intelligence Agency and the Central Intelligence Agency to prevent the disclosure of classified information. All statements of fact, opinion, or analysis expressed are those of the authors and do not reflect the official positions or views of the U.S. Government. Nothing in the contents should be construed as asserting or implying U.S. Government authentication of information or US Government endorsement of the author's views.

A portion of royalties from this book are donated to the Andrew Dollins Memorial fund at the University of Utah College of Education to honor the memory of our good friend and an exceptional polygraph researcher.

# CHAPTER 1

A history of lie detection

> *And then shall he tremble, and shall look pale, even as if death had come upon him. And then shall ye say: Because of this fear and this paleness which has come upon your face, behold, we know that thou art guilty.*
> **Helaman 9: 33–34, Book of Mormon**

It may come as a surprise to some that deception is a universal quality of this world. It is not new, it is not isolated, and there is no reason to conclude that there is more or less of it than there has been in the past. Deception is neither an aberration nor a departure from the laws of nature. Rather, it is intricately woven into the fabric of life on earth. It surrounds us, is part of us, and has been here before there was an "us." One powerful reason for deception's ubiquity is that it can have immense survival value to living things: it can improve the chances of avoiding predators, of winning a mate, in securing a meal, and of confounding a competitor. It appears throughout the spectrum of biology. Insects do it all the time, and well. So do fish and birds. Deceptive strategies are found among crustaceans, lizards, mammals, snakes, invertebrates, many plants, and even bacteria. One might be tempted to conclude that where there is life, there is deception.

Humans deceive perhaps more often, more nuanced, and for more reasons than any other species. It seems to be part of a collective psychology, or perhaps it is simply more available to that species with the biggest relative brain size. Nonetheless, deception is very much a part of us, so much so that the English language offers no fewer than 20 synonyms for it. And while lying among humans can be socially accepted occasionally, expected at times, and even demanded in others, there are conditions where it is destructive to the legitimate interests of individuals and society. Here lies the critical importance of lie detection, as a defense against those who would use deception to do harm.

From the historical perspective, the use of a polygraph for lie detection is quite new; however, the quest for a method for verifying statements is very old. Virtually every culture across history with a system of writing has given comment to it, offering various and sundry methods to ferret out the deceiver. Given the many obvious advantages it might afford the person who knows when others are lying, it is not unreasonable to suspect that human interest in lie detection emerged right along with the human capacity for telling lies, which most certainly predates written history.

In this chapter, we cover historical antecedents to the modern field of "lie detection" leading up to the polygraph. It is divided into sections that generally correspond with significant trends and milestones over the course of history leading to the polygraph. It begins first with ancient traditions in lie detection.

ANCIENT TRADITIONS

Frequently in early societies, it was believed that goodness could be differentiated from evil simply because goodness was stronger, or that divine intervention would protect the truth speaker (Larson, 1932). Tests were devised based on the assumption that a magical force would come into play to identify or rescue the truth speaker. For example, one such test was an ordeal involving bread and cheese (Trovillo, 1939). The practice, called "Corsnaed," was used by Roman Catholic priests during the Inquisition to detect the guilt of a member of the priesthood. First, bread and cheese were placed on the altar. The priests would then offer prayers to Gabriel, asking him to make it impossible for a suspected priest to swallow the bread and cheese if he were guilty of the offense in question. After the prayers were completed, they would require the suspected priest to eat the bread and cheese in their presence. If the priest could not swallow these items, it was a sign of guilt. However, reports of a priest unable to do so are difficult to find.

In India a similar notion of divine intervention in the ordeal prevailed. A'li Ibra'hi'm Kha'n (1806)[1] describes nine ways in which the ordeal may be conducted. They include the balance, fire, water, poison, Cófha (or water in which an idol has been washed), rice, boiling oil, red-hot iron, and images. They are briefly described here:

> *The balance*: The accused fasts the entire day and is then bathed in sacred water. After worshipping the deities, the accused is placed on a balance and weighed. There is more prayer, and the accusation is written on a piece of paper and bound to the head of the accused. Six minutes later he is reweighed. If he weighs more, he is pronounced guilty. If he lost weight, he is judged innocent. If his weight is unchanged, he is weighed again. It is expected that his weight will change in this third weighing. Finally, if the balance device on which he is weighed was to break, this is a sign of guilt.
>
> *The fire*: A hole "nine hands long, two hands broad, and one hand deep is made in the ground, and filled with a fire of pippal wood." The accused is compelled to walk barefoot across the flames. If he is unhurt, he is innocent: if burned he is guilty.
>
> *The water*: The accused is placed in water up to his navel. Hindu instructions take care to say of the water that "no ravenous animal be in it." A Bráhman enters the water holding a staff. A soldier shoots three arrows into the air, and

---

[1] Similar reports were made by the French missionary Dubois (1817).

another man is sent to pick up the arrow that has traveled the farthest. A second man near the water is also sent to this arrow. At that moment the accused must submerge under the water holding to the Bráhman's foot or staff, and remain under the water until the two men return with the arrow. Failure to remain completely under water until the arrow is retrieved is an evidence of guilt.
The poison: Here there are two versions. One involves a mixture of barley-corn, butter, and poison eaten from the hand of the Bráhman. A lack of effect of the poison signifies innocence, but illness indicates guilt. In the second, the accused must reach his hand into a deep pot which contains a poisonous snake in addition to a ring, seal, or coin. He must take out the object without getting bitten by the snake. If he is successful, he is deemed innocent. A snake bite indicates guilt.
The Cófha: The accused drinks three draughts of water in which images of deities have been washed. Illness within 2 weeks is a sign of guilt.
The rice: This ordeal is used when there are several suspects in a theft. Dry rice is brought forth. Sometimes it is weighed with a sacred stone, other times special incantations are read. The suspects are then made to chew a portion of the dry rice, and then place it on leaves of the pippal or the bark of certain trees. Rice that has remained dry, or has blood in it, is an indication that it came from the guilty person.
The hot oil: Oil is heated, and the accused places his hand into it. Burns on the hands show guilt, whereas the lack of burns is expected from the innocent.
The red-hot iron: Metal, in the form of an iron ball or the head of a lance, is heated red hot and placed on the hands of the accused. As with the ordeal of the hot oil, burns indicate guilt, and a lack of burns signifies innocence.
The images: The image of one of the deities (Dharma) is made of silver and another image is made of clay or iron of a second deity (Adharma). The images are placed in a large jar, and the accused is compelled to place his hand in the jar and draw out one of them. If he draws the silver image, he is considered innocent, but he is guilty if he draws out the other image. In an alternate form, images of the deities are rendered on two pieces of cloth, one white and one black. Both pieces of cloth are "rolled up in cow-dung, and thrown into a jar, without having ever been shown to the accused." Again, the accused draws one of the pieces of cloth from the jar, with white representing Dharma and innocence.

In the first modern scholarly book on deception detection, Larson (1932) examined the history of this field. He listed the major approaches as trial by combat, ordeal, torture, benefit of clergy, sanctuary, and compurgation (i.e., multiple sworn endorsements of innocence). Larson draws heavily from Lea's (1892) expansive exploration of these categories, three of the most popular of which are briefly discussed below:

Trials by combat: This method had several forms, most commonly the duel wherein two adversaries faced off in physical combat. Variations were introduced in many countries, including the hiring of surrogates to do the fighting. Special consideration was given in some countries for women, children, and the handicapped who were to contest against able-bodied men. In those cases, instead of the weaker contestant hiring a surrogate, the rules of the combat were adjusted to offset the inequality in physical strength. Lea's (1892) extensive coverage of the subject reveals a very wide range of trials by combat across cultures.

Ordeals: This category of truth test abounds with examples, with the most frequent among them involving water and heat/fire (Lea, 1892; Matthews, 1791). Water has been used for guilt detection through processes such as immersion of the suspect (e.g., witch hunts in the United States in the seventeenth century), sanctification of icons that the suspect must touch, adding of objects or impurities to water that the suspect must drink, or suspects plunging an arm into water to retrieve an unseen object that would signify their innocence or guilt. The ordeals by heat/fire could include walking across hot coals, placing hot metal against the tongue, carrying a hot metal objects, or placing the suspect's arm in boiling oil or water. Typically, the suspect who survived these ordeals uninjured was judged innocent.

Torture: This method of guilt detection is found in virtually all cultures and throughout most of history. It has been used to force confessions to crimes and to antireligious beliefs. Torturers have shown a peculiarly innovative streak and have been successful in extracting admissions to whatever matter they wished. However pervasive torture has proven over the centuries, the earliest as well as the most recent writers of this approach have observed that it is highly flawed in that it develops confessions from both the innocent and the guilty. Moreover, the growth of the concept of human rights, especially in the second half of the twentieth century, has moved many nations away from torture and toward more discriminative methods of truth verification, including forensic science and the polygraph.

OBSERVATIONS OF BEHAVIOR

One of the prominent methods of olden times was based on observations of the behavior of truth tellers and liars. In the well-known account, King Solomon displayed a remarkable grasp of human behavior when he wisely determined which of two women was the mother of a disputed baby. As one may recall, Solomon declared that the child should be cut into two pieces in order to satisfy the claims of both women, whereupon the true mother expressed her willingness to give up the child rather than to see it killed. The act of giving up the baby, the king noted, was to be expected of the child's actual mother, and Solomon awarded the child to her. The king determined that truthful persons respond in ways that may be useful in distinguishing them from untruthful people.

A similar story arises from early India (Dunn, 1750). A wealthy man had two wives, one who bore him a son, and another, more fair and attractive, who was barren. The man had come to favor the second wife for her beauty at the expense of the one who had given him an heir. The first wife was driven to extreme measures in an attempt to garner her husband's affection, and concocted a radical plan. She began by making a dramatic show of affection on her son before all of the neighbors, telling them that this boy is her only comfort inasmuch as her husband has denied her any affection. Having convinced all of her love for her child, one night she killed the boy and placed it beside the second wife as she lay sleeping. The following morning she "discovered" the child dead next to the favored wife, and initiated boisterous histrionics that brought in the neighborhood. All who witness the scene are convinced of the guilt of the second wife, for they could not conceive of a loving mother killing her own child.

The case was brought before their Mariadiramen, wise king and judge, who listened to the testimony of both women and was unable to decide. Dunn (1750) tells what Mariadiramen said next:

Let the woman who is innocent, and who pretends that her rival is culpable, take a turn thro' the assembly in the posture which he should shew her. This posture was such as did not become a modest woman. Upon this the mother of the child said, In order to convince you that my rival is culpable I not only consent to take one turn before this assembly, in the manner you have ordered, but also a hundred, if requir'd. As for me, said the second, tho' innocent, yet I ought to be condemn'd to the most cruel death, if I did what is now requir'd of me. The first wife wanted to make a reply, but the judge ordering silence, declared that she was guilty, and her antagonist innocent; for, added he, a woman, who at the prospect of certain death will not do an indecent action, could never have committed so great a crime; on the contrary, a woman, who having lost all sense of modesty, without trouble commits the most indecent actions, sufficiently declares that she is capable of perpetrating the blackest crimes. The first wife, confounded to see herself thus discover'd, was forc'd publickly to acknowledge her crime. (p. 112).

Another behaviorally based approach was purportedly practiced in ancient Asia. According to Schafer (2008) "…around 500 b.c.e., priests in India tested people accused of thievery by placing them in darkened tents with donkeys whose tails were coated in soot. The priests would tell the suspected thieves to tug the animals' tails because the donkeys would bray when touched by thieves. Suspects who left the tents with their hands unsoiled by soot, and therefore presumed to have feared following the priests' instructions, were considered guilty." A virtually identical version is provided by Evans (2004). Keeler (1933) similarly claimed this practice was by Hindus in India, but he said that it took place in recent times. Keeler's story has been retold by many polygraph writers since. However, none of the accounts cite original sources, and the later references may be relying on polygraph articles that can be traced to Keeler's original 1933 paper. For this reason the story may be apocryphal.

There is an account reported by Shurreef (1832), however, which had many of the same elements of the donkey tail test, including taking place in India. A "thief-catcher" (person with magical abilities) would place in the center of a room a hand-mill, a device which had an upper and a lower grinding stone. The upper stone was suspended over the lower stone at a distance of one or two fingers by way of an inconspicuous arrangement. Between the two stones he rubbed a substance called asafetida, which had a strong unpleasant smell. About the room, on the floor and around the grinding stones were figures and objects of religious significance. The thief-catcher sends each suspect into the room alone with this admonition: "Behold, by the power of my science the stone is suspended. Whoever is the thief, his hand will be caught between the stones, and it will be no easy matter for him to extricate it. Nay, the chances are, the upper stone will fall and crush his hand to atoms." As each of the suspects exits the room, the thief-catcher smells his hands and then sends the person to a different room. Once a person presents himself to the thief-catcher without the aroma of asafetida on his hands, he is offered the opportunity to confess and return the stolen object (pp. 390–391).

Finally, practice among the native peoples of the Hawaiian Islands prior to the mid-1800s was based on the manifestation of hand tremors during a special ritual. According to Ellis (1842), it was called the "wai haruru" (shaking water) and began with a native priest offering a prayer over a water-filled wooden dish. Accused individuals were then singly required to place both hands over the bowl, fingers spread, while the priest concentrated on the water's surface. According to tradition, the water trembles when the guilty party holds his hands over it. Ellis suspected that fear of detection would compel the hands of the guilty party to shake, imparting the quivering to the bowl and water, thereby reveal his deception to the priest.

OBSERVATIONS OF PHYSIOLOGY

One physician, Erasistratus, in the second century BC made use of the pulse to uncover hidden information (Plutarch, cited in Trovillo, 1939). Erasistratus, who had earned a wide reputation for his lectures on the brain, had been called by Nicator, a general of Alexander the Great, to diagnose Nicator's son Antiochus. Antiochus had been suffering from an unknown disease. In the course of examining Antiochus, Erasistratus had occasion to feel the young man's pulse. He then began discussing, among other things, the new and beautiful young wife just taken by Nicator. Antiochus' pulse began to intensify during the discussion of his new step-mother, Stratonice. The surging pulse supported Erasistratus's suspicion that the youth was deeply enamored with the woman, and that his physical distress was the result of her marriage to Antiochus' father. Stratonice was later given to Antiochus by his father, and Antiochus reportedly rallied to a full recovery.

The following is a similar tale from the eleventh century by an Islamic writer, as translated by Browne (1921). Again, changes in pulse were used to detect the source of mysterious illness that had befallen the son of a prominent person. Interestingly, in this account the technique is a foreshadowing of the twentieth century polygraph method called the Searching Peak of Tension.

> *So they sought out Abú Alí[2] and brought him to the patient, whom he beheld to be a youth of comely countenance, whereon the hair had scarcely begun to shew itself, and of symmetrical proportions, but now laid low. He sat down, felt his pulse, asked to see his urine, inspected it, and said, "I want a man who knows all the houses and districts of Gurgan." So they brought one, saying, "Here you are"; and Abú Alí placed his hand on the patient's pulse, and bade the other mention the names of the different districts of Gurgan. So the man began, and continued to name the districts until he reached one at the mention of which the patient's pulse gave a strange flutter. Then Abú Alí said, "Now give the streets in this quarter." The man gave them, until he arrived at the name of a street whereat that strange flutter recurred. Then Abú Alí said, "We need someone who knows all the houses in this street." They brought such an one, who proceeded to give out the houses till he reached a house at the mention of which the patient's pulse gave the same flutter. "Now," said Abú Alí, "I want someone who knows the names of all the households and can repeat them." They brought such an one, and he began to repeat them until he reached a name at the mention of which that same flutter was apparent. Then said Abú Alí, "It is finished." Thereupon he turned to the confidential advisers of Qabus, and said, "This lad is in love with such-and-such a girl, so-and-so by name, in such-and-such a house, in such-and-such street, in such-and-such a quarter: union with that girl is his remedy, and the sight of her is his cure." The patient, who was listening, and heard all that Abú Alí said, hid his face in shame beneath the bed-clothes. When they made enquiries, it was even as Abú Alí had said.*

In a more salacious tale, Macrobius, a fifth century Roman writer, relates the narrative of a knight who comes to believe his wife has fallen in love with another man (Swan, 1905). He confronted his wife, but she remained firm in her denials. Unconvinced, the knight sought the aid of a "cunning clerk" who set about to test the woman. The knight invited the clerk to dinner so that he can observe his wife and determine her faithfulness. At the conclusion of dinner the clerk engaged the woman in conversation on several topics. Then he casually took the woman's hand so that he could press his finger against her pulse and nonchalantly began to talk about the man whom the knight suspected was the real owner of his wife's heart. According to Macrobius "her pulse immediately quickened to a surprising degree, and acquired a feverish heat." When the clerk then discussed the husband, her pulse slowed once more and the heat dissipated. From this, the clerk surmised that the woman no longer loved the knight, and that the knight's suspicions regarding the true lover were correct.

---

[2] Famous eleventh century Islamic physician, philosopher, prolific writer and author of *The Canon of Medicine*, a highly influential book on medical treatment and diagnosis. His full name was Abū Alī al-usayn ibn Abd Allāh ibn Sīnā, but was Latinized to "Avicenna" in most Western texts, and shortened to Abú Alí in this translation by Browne (1921).

MODERN DEVELOPMENTS
INSTRUMENTATION

The use of a mechanical apparatus in the application of deception tests had to wait until the nineteenth century. Multiple physiological recordings for deception tests went through an evolutionary process whereby single parameters were employed first, and later added together to bring about the device used today.

All forms of physiological recording depend on tracing the data on a medium at an even pace over time. Consequently, all of the earliest polygraphs used a mechanism that moved the medium at a reliable and prescribed speed. The first of these was the "kymographion," a clockwork mechanism for recording data at a uniform speed (Figure 1.1), and was the basis for the electric kymograph used on analog polygraphs until the advent of computer polygraphs in the 1980s.[3] A similar method was concurrently devised by Marey (1863) and used in medical research until at least 1900 (Figure 1.2).

Ludwig's final design allowed different recording speeds, horizontal or vertical orientation of the drum, and either clockwise or counterclockwise rotation of the drum.

CARDIOVASCULAR MEASURES

The first phenomenon to find application in deception tests was the change in relative blood volume which accompanies certain emotional states. The Italian criminologist Cesare Lombroso (Lombroso Ferrero, 1911) had observed in the 1880s, along with other researchers, that deception was often detectable by such physiological responses as blushing, perspiring, and changes in respiration. Lombroso used two types of devices in an attempt to detect the act of lying, the hydrosphygmograph and the volumetric glove (Figure 1.3). Changes in pressure were brought about by variations in blood volume in the subject's hand, an imprecise but serviceable method of

---

[3] Readers might note that the distinction between a kymographion (wave writing) and a polygraph (many writings) is ambiguous. Both recorded multiple channels of physiological data on a moving writing surface. Kymographions were used extensively in medical and psychological research labs for much of the nineteenth century. For example, the research of Angelo Mosso, taken up later, used a kymographion to record respiration and a cardiovascular measure in his research on the physiology of fear in the 1880s. In his survey of experimental devices MacDonald (1899) states that "[t]he term polygraph is in general a French name for an instrument used for a purpose similar to that of the kymographion or kymograph." Both terms, and devices, were used contemporaneously, and the kymographion is referenced in research well into the 1920s (Lagercrantz, 1927). Polygraph pioneer John Larson occasionally used "polygraph" in his publications as early as 1927, however in his book titled *Lying and Its Detection* (1932) he makes scant reference to polygraph, and none to the kymographion. In Leonarde Keeler's 1925 US Patent application he used neither of these terms, though he referred to the "kymograph" as the mechanism for moving chart paper. Neither did Keeler use either term in his first paper on lie detection (Keeler, 1930a). However, later that year Keeler (1930b) introduces the word "Polygraph" in his published account of a series of tests he conducted on police officers. By this time references to kymographion had all but disappeared from the scientific literature.

Modern developments

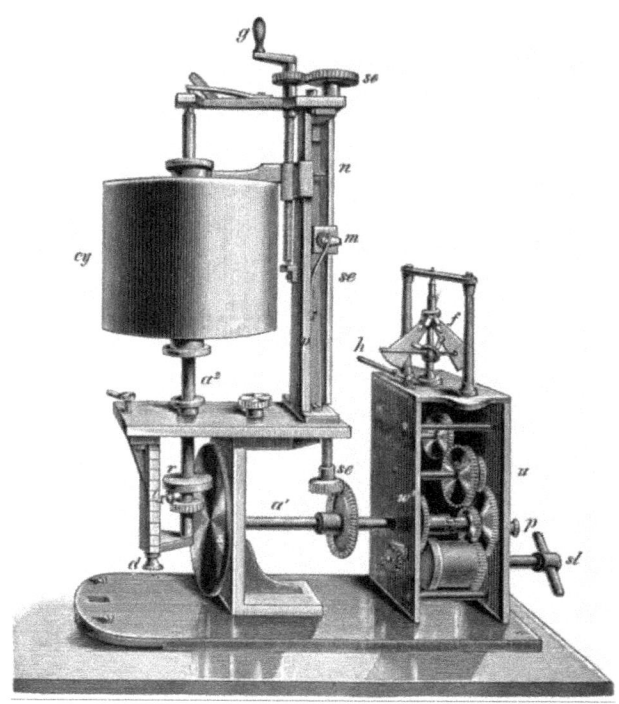

FIGURE 1.1

A later version of the Ludwig kymographion, developed by Carl Ludwig beginning in 1840s.

Frank (1911)

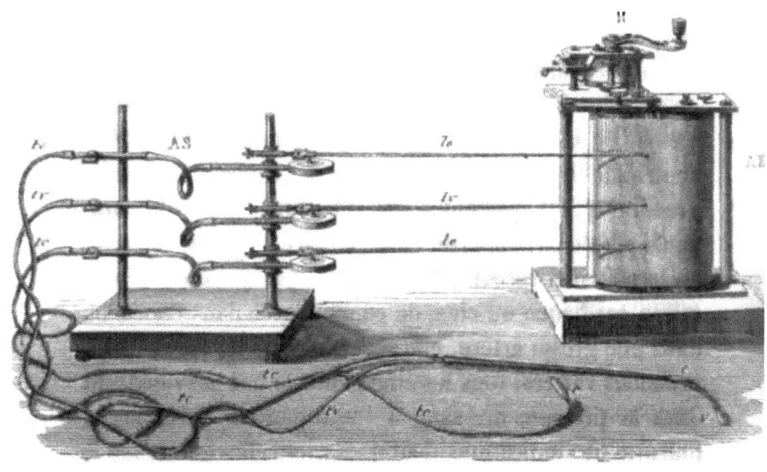

FIGURE 1.2

Marey multichannel recorder for cardiovascular data.

Marey (1863)

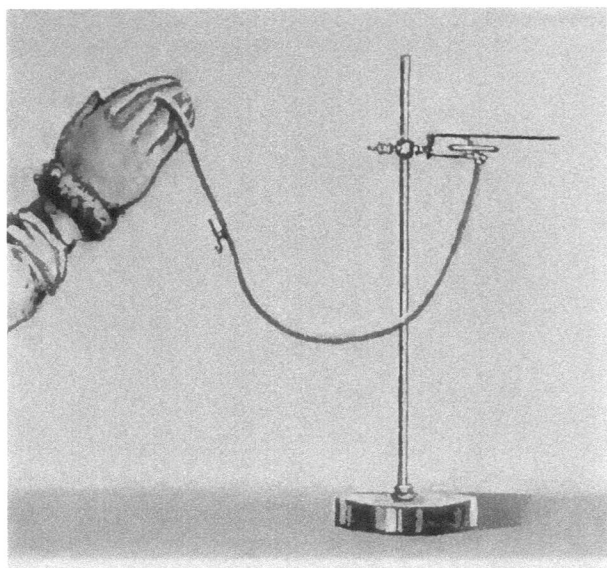

FIGURE 1.3

Volumetric glove used by Lombroso in his studies on deception detection in the 1880s.

Lombroso Ferrero (1911)

detecting relative blood pressure changes and a forerunner of one of the measures used in modern polygraphs. Lombroso reported success in testing actual criminal suspects, though the method did not enjoy widespread use.

A student of Lombroso, Angelo Mosso (1886) built upon the work of his mentor and demonstrated an interest in respiratory and cardiovascular responses to fear. In the course of his research, he devised a mechanism he called the "scientific cradle." It was a platform placed on a fulcrum on which a subject would lie. Counterweights could be adjusted until the platform was in perfect balance (see Figure 1.4). Using a kymographion, changes in the balance of the platform were recorded on the rotating smoked drum. With it Mosso was able to detect changes that occurred when he experimentally induced fear in his subjects.

Mosso also experimented with the plethysmograph, and used one of his own design before 1900 (MacDonald, 1899). A more generally available plethysmograph, called the Franck plethysmograph, was manufactured by Verdin in Paris (Figure 1.5).

Psychologist William Marston took a special interest in deception tests and developed one of his own while working at the Harvard Laboratory under the famed Professor Hugo Munsterberg. Using a standard blood pressure cuff, Marston used pressure changes for detecting deception. By 1915 he was applying his technique to criminal suspects (Marston, 1921). The method involved four phases: quiet period, free narrative period where the examinee tells his/her own story uninterrupted, cross examination by the tester in a friendly approach, and a final quiet period. Marston

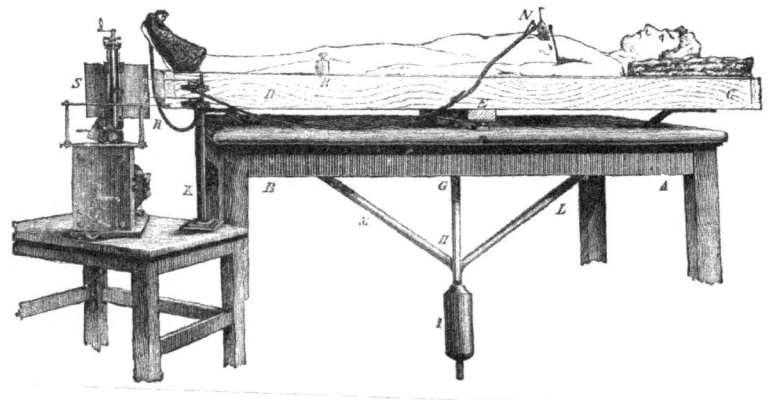

FIGURE 1.4

Mosso's (1886) "berceau scientifique" or scientific cradle. Mosso used this device in his studies of fear. Note the kymographion on the left and a Marey pneumograph (Figure 1.6) on the subject's chest. The counterweight is depicted to the side of the subject's left knee.

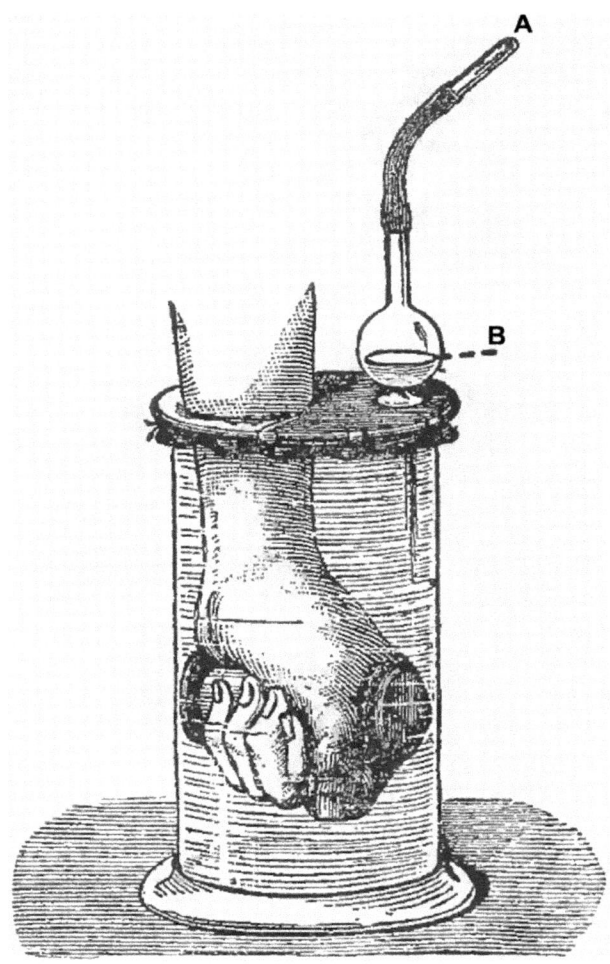

FIGURE 1.5

Franck plethysmograph manufactured by Verdin.

MacDonald (1899)

took a blood pressure measurement intermittently during the four periods, and plotted the readings over time, along with notations as to which of the four periods they were taken. Trends in the plotted data across the four periods were interpreted as indicating truthfulness and deception. It was called the discontinuous blood pressure method.

In his book, *The Lie Detector Test* (1938), Marston reported a series of cases where he had successfully used his blood pressure method to solve crimes. Much of the text contains sensational claims of accuracy for the method, ranging from 95% to 100% and no inconclusive outcomes, but there was no independent research reported, nor was any to be found in the psychology literature. While on active military duty Marston taught his method to the US Army (Marston, 1921) and wrote that his students had instant success, producing an average accuracy rate of 74.3% on their first try. The then-Lieutenant Marston was called upon to use his amazing technique to resolve a number of espionage cases during World War I, and Marston likewise reported them as successes (Abrams and Ansley, 1980). Marston offered his services to help resolve the guilt or innocence of Bruno Hauptmann, the man convicted and executed for kidnapping the baby of famed aviator Charles Lindbergh, though, as Marston details in his book, political forces ultimately prevented his involvement in the case.[4]

BREATHING

The movement of the chest that accompanies ventilation was investigated first by medical scientists who devised their own instrumentation. One of the earliest among them was Étienne-Jules Marey, a French physiologist in the 1800s. His was a device that used levers and tambours, and was held in place with a strip of silk (Figure 1.6). The device, though serviceable, was replaced by a newer design (Figure 1.7) that was similar to the one found on most modern polygraphs. It had a metal spring encased in rubber tubing, connected to a small rubber hose leading to the recording device. It was held in place around the torso with a small chain. Originally dubbed the Fitz pneumograph (Fitz, 1896), it was also called the Harvard or the Sumner pneumograph (Whitney, 1911).

The first published report of the use of pneumographic recording for the purpose of deception detection was by Benussi (1914). Benussi used changes in the time for inhalation divided by the time for exhalation (*I/E* ratio) to diagnose deceptive statements from truthful ones. This idea had reportedly been suggested 8 years earlier by German psychologist Gustav Störring (Levitt, 1955). Benussi's work with *I/E* ratios were applied more widely to various emotions by Antoinette Feleky (1916), who confirmed that changes in ratios corresponded with emotional responses. Benussi's seminal work with deception was later extended by Burtt (1918, 1921).

---

[4] Marston is also noted for his creation of the comic strip character Wonder Woman in 1941 under the pseudonym Charles Moulton. Working with illustrator Harry G. Peter, Marston wrote the story scripts until his death in 1947. The comic strip was immensely popular during World War II, and is well known in popular culture even today (Alder, 2007).

Modern developments

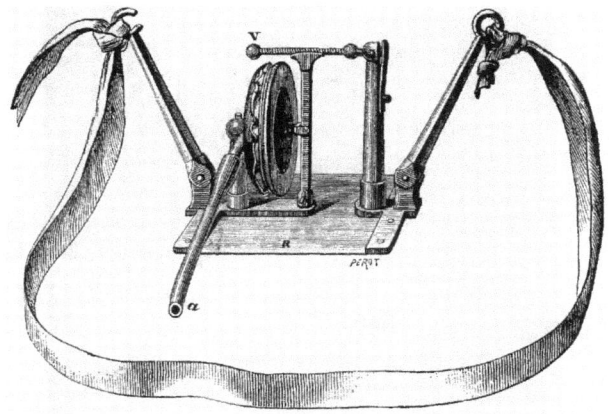

FIGURE 1.6

Marey's pneumograph sensor from the late 1800s.

Marey (1876)

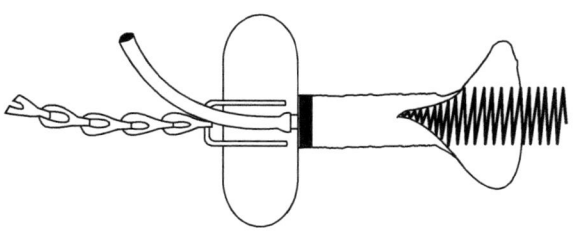

FIGURE 1.7

Fitz pneumograph sensor.

Fitz (1896)

ELECTRODERMAL

Electrodermal activity (EDA), previously known as the psychogalvanic reflex and the galvanic skin response, has been shown to be associated with emotions since the late 1800s (Féré, 1888). The connection between Luigi Galvani (1737–1798) with historical terms for EDA is an accident of history, as Galvani's most cited work focused on understanding the relationship between electricity and muscular contractions. Neither Galvani nor his students turned their attention to conductance changes of the skin. Nevertheless, the field of electrophysiology traces its roots to Galvani's discoveries.

The first recorded suggestion that it may have application to the field of lie detection was made by Dr. Georg Sticker (1897) in his article later translated into English by Binswanger for Carl Jung's book *Studies in Word Association* (1919). Indeed, it would seem that Sticker had anticipated the Concealed Information Test (CIT), one of the modern methods in polygraphy, when he wrote:

> *In a word—which will be listened to by many without any reaction—whoever takes the meaning of something to heart will react with a strong galvanic skin phenomenon. Whoever is from any cause emotionally roused on looking at a picture will react with a definite increase of the current whilst whoever is unmoved by the picture, in whom it rouses no memory, will have no skin excitation.*
>
> **Sticker, quoted by Binswanger (1919)**

Binswanger also cited the work of Otto Veraguth (1909)[5] who used the electrodermal response in his work with word associations. Veraguth's apparatus was the Deprez-d'Arsonval "deadbeat reflecting galvanometer" (Figure 1.8). Veraguth observed that salient words evoked larger phasic electrodermal responses than did neutral words. He also was the first to make note of the effect of habituation in the electrodermal data, wherein the first neutral words were evoking larger responses than subsequent neutral words. Veraguth did not investigate the use of the electrodermal

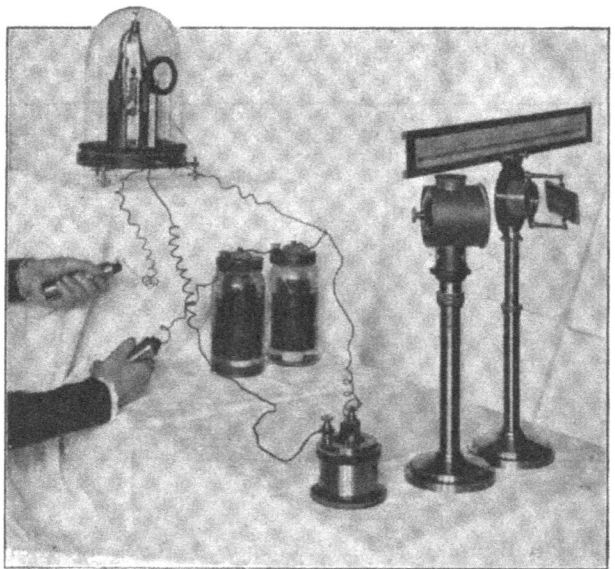

FIGURE 1.8

The electrodermal apparatus used by Veraguth (1909).

---

[5] A typographical error in Binswanger's chapter mistakenly identified Otto Veraguth as "S. Veraguth," an error that is often repeated in writings about polygraph history.

response for the purpose of deception detection, though his breakthrough discoveries did find direct bearing on psychophysiological principles that were foundational to polygraphy.

Carl Jung (1919) took to using EDA as an indicator of emotional complexes along with his word-association tests. However, the EDA was slow to be adapted to polygraph applications largely due to problems in devising a method of producing a permanent recording, and the difficulty in the interpretation of the recordings once they were available. It was not a channel recorded with either the Larson apparatus or the initial versions of the Keeler or Lee polygraphs. Marston (1938) reportedly tested the potential of EDA in deception tests for the Army in 1917 in support of the war effort. His writings show that he was unimpressed because "the instrument registers nearly every emotion experienced during the testimony of the subject, and so renders it nearly impossible to distinguish those emotions caused by deception" (Marston, 1921).

As the technology improved, the application of the electrodermal channel in criminal tests found an enthusiastic advocate in the Reverend Walter Summers (1936, 1939). Summers reported a success rate of more than 98% using his "Pathometer," an electrodermal recorder, though the vast majority of his tests with the device were on students in a laboratory setting. His method entailed constructing a series of test questions and then recording electrodermal response amplitudes during the presentation of the questions. In his 1939 article he referred to relevant questions as "significant questions" and irrelevant questions were "nonsignificant questions."

Summers used his device and technique on about 50 criminal suspects and he claimed tremendous success, though his criterion for verification of some of them would not stand up to current standards of proof. Unfortunately Father Summers died prematurely in the late 1930s, and interest in his work waned.

FIRST PRECEDENT IN LAW

The most famous case Marston conducted, and perhaps the most significant one involving any kind of lie detection method, was that of James Alphonso Frye. Stern and Krapohl (2003) expanded upon a rather sympathetic portrayal of events Marston reported (1938) in which Marston concluded he was correct in calling Frye truthful. The evidence, however, made quite a different case.

It began with the murder of Dr. Robert Brown, a well-respected physician in Washington DC, on November 27th, 1920. Brown was struck by two bullets shot during a robbery, one of them into Brown's head, and he died instantly. A suspect matching Frye's description was seen running from the scene and was not immediately apprehended.

Frye was no stranger to law enforcement. During the time of the shooting of Dr. Brown, the Washington DC police were already looking for Frye for a different robbery, and simultaneously he was being sought by the US Secret Service for a Treasury check fraud. When the police captured Frye, they notified the Secret

Service. Comparison of samples found that the handwriting on the Treasury check matched Frye's, and he ultimately confessed to a Secret Service agent to forging the signature.

After Frye's confession to forgery, a Washington DC police inspector told the Secret Service agent that a source had identified Frye for the murder of Dr. Brown. The agent returned to questioning Frye and told him that he would let the forgery case pass if Frye would talk about the murder of Dr. Brown and the other robbery of which they suspected him. Frye acknowledged the robbery but denied the murder. He was incarcerated and questioned over the course of a few more days, and finally admitted to killing Dr. Brown and provided details about the crime. However, he later recanted his confession. Nonetheless, a witness to the crime had positively identified Frye.

Frye's court-appointed attorneys approached Marston to conduct his lie detection method on Frye, not to exculpate him, but to get him to abandon his claim of innocence in hopes of a better defense against the death penalty. After the test Marston declared Frye truthful to his denials of killing Dr. Brown. The surprised attorneys' next move was to qualify Dr. Marston an expert so the lie detection results could be introduced at trial. The proffer of the Marston test was witnessed by the jury though the testimony was excluded. Frye was convicted of second degree murder on July 20, 1922. Marston contended that the maneuver in front of the jury, even without Marston's actual testimony, had saved Frye from a conviction of first degree murder and the death penalty.

Frye's attorneys filed appeals, most of them based on what they considered a trial court error in excluding Dr. Marston's deception test. They were not successful, and the case was ultimately taken up to the DC District Court. On December 21, 1923, the DC District Court rendered what became known as the Frye Decision (or General Acceptance Standard), denying Frye's appeal and setting a standard for the admissibility of scientific evidence that would remain well into the 1990s. Frye served out the rest of his prison sentence in Lorton, Virginia, and was released on parole in 1939. He died in 1953, and owing to his military service in World War I, was interred in Arlington National Cemetery.

Based on an erroneous understanding of the Frye case, some writers have characterized it as being about the polygraph. Marston is frequently cited as a polygraph pioneer, but this is inaccurate. Marston's deception testing method was quite different from polygraphy. Though he used a cardiovascular measure in the detection of deception, neither Marston's instrumentation, testing protocol, or method of analysis bear resemblance to polygraphy at any stage of its historical development. It would be more accurate to regard Marston as the developer of an approach competing with the polygraph, a method which like many others was ultimately abandoned. Marston, who for a time was "the best-known psychologist in America" (Alder, 2007), did not contribute meaningfully to the field of polygraphy. Nonetheless, Marston can genuinely be credited with helping capture the public imagination in instrumental lie detection, and paving the way for popular interest in this field.

THE ADVENT OF MULTIPLE RECORDINGS

The use of several psychophysiological indices for deception detection was suggested by the famous Harvard psychologist Hugo Munsterberg (1908), including those that would become the polygraph.[6] The real-world use of multiple simultaneous channels of physiological data in deception testing was reported for the first time by Larson (1921). Under the guidance and support of August Vollmer, then-Chief of Police in Berkeley, California, Larson constructed an instrument that simultaneously recorded on a smoked drum chart the respiration wave forms and a second tracing for relative blood pressure and pulse. The recording of respiration patterns was accomplished with a bellows pneumograph, the cardiograph employed an Erlanger sphygmograph, and time was also annotated to allow Larson to engage in response-time investigations. Larson used this device with a relevant-irrelevant test question sequence on actual criminal cases and reportedly solved several crimes.

Perhaps Larson's earliest and best-known case was reported in his seminal 1921 polygraph article titled *Modification of the Marston Deception Test*. In this article, Larson advocated for practices quite different from Marston's, very modern, such as continuous recording of multiple physiological channels, restricting examinee answers to yes and no, question spacing, and asking questions in a monotonic voice.

In the 1921 article Dr. Larson, then a police officer with the Berkeley Police Department, had set about to demonstrate the utility of his approach with the solving of a real crime. In a large hall in which 100 young women lived there had been a series of thefts. Hearsay given to the police investigator pointed to three or four possible suspects, all of whom lived in the building. Larson decided to use his "apparatus" (not yet given a name) to determine if he could find the thief. His testing procedure for that case involved 18 questions, and introductory instructions during which he recorded their physiological reactions.[7] He had decided to begin testing

---

[6] Two years later a fictional story appeared by Balmer and MacHarg (1910) called *The Man Higher Up*. The story's hero, a detective who was also a psychologist, prevailed upon a research professor to bring a laboratory device to the office of a corporate president who was suspected of a conspiracy of murder and smuggling. The device used a Marey pneumograph and a plethysmograph to record bodily changes on a smoked drum. With the device the hero was able to demonstrate that the suspect recognized objects only the criminal would have associated with the crimes. Physiological tracings printed in the article appeared authentic, suggesting they may have been taken from genuine recordings.

[7] Larson (1921) writes "… a control question, or one not concerning the subject under investigation, and yet calculated to stimulate various emotions, was alternated with one pertinent to the investigation." It is not clear whether Larson's use of "control question" could be similar to the "control question" introduced by Reid in the 1940s because Larson did not annotate which questions in the list they were. Larson had questions such as: How much is 30×40?; Did you at any time lie to shield yourself or others?; and During the past few nights do you remember having dreamed when you might have talked in your sleep? However, Larson's approach involved comparing the charts of nervous innocent examinees against the suspect's charts so that he could control for the influences of anxiety, anger, indignation or other emotions unrelated to deception when he interpreted the charts. In contrast, Reid and those who followed used examinees as their own controls, that is, he compared the various chart reactions among the test questions for each examinee by him- or herself.

the women in groups of 12, and the first group included the prime suspects. One of the women in this first group showed violent reactivity when asked the relevant questions, and the test was stopped when the woman "blew up." She jumped to her feet, walked over to the chart, there was a short confrontation, and she left angry. However, a few days later she confessed to the thefts. The promise of Larson's method became obvious.

The second polygraph constructed by the Berkeley Police group was by Captain Clarence D. Lee, the Chief of Detectives, in the 1920s (Bancroft Library, 1983). His innovations included a sprocket drive for movement of chart paper instead of Larson's smoked drum method, and an improved means of converting blood pressure signals into a reliable tracing. Lee marketed his device at least until the 1950s. In addition to instrumentation, Lee was interested in refining polygraph techniques to overcome what he saw as shortcomings in the prevailing methods. Lee was an early and persistent advocate of the Peak of Tension (POT) approach to polygraphy over the then-reigning Relevant Irrelevant (RI) technique (Lee, 1937).

While with the Berkeley Police Department, Keeler built upon the designs of Larson and Lee, and in 1925 he submitted a patent application for his device (see Figure 1.9 for images from that application). Leonarde Keeler is sometimes given credit for adding the EDA channel to the recording of respiration and relative blood pressure as early 1949 (Reid and Inbau, 1977). However, Trovillo (1939) reported that a colleague of Keeler, Charles Wilson, developed a polygraph that simultaneously recorded the three channels and had put the instrument into service in 1936. Keeler's polygraph was portable, ultimately had all of the current channels, and contained an inking system. It included a sprocket drive similar to that used earlier by Lee, but his kymograph had a differential gear train with three settings.[8] Keeler's instrument became the standard in the field and remained so for many years. The "Keeler Polygraph," as it was called, was designed to be reliable, rugged, and portable. By the 1970s, though, other manufacturers came to command the polygraph instrument market by offering more convenience of operation and attractive designs, and the Keeler Polygraph eventually went out of production.

MODERN INSTRUMENTATION

Since Keeler's instrument came into being the polygraph field has used virtually the same physiological channels, and little has changed in sensors between 1940 and today. The recording of pulse and relative blood pressure uses a blood pressure cuff

---

[8] Norman Ansley, longtime and respected Editor of the publications of the American Polygraph Association and an amateur historian, observed that the principal reason for having three different gears available was because in Keeler's time the electrical system across the US was not standardized. Some geographic areas used 30 Hz alternating current, while others used 60 Hz, and a minority used other frequencies. The changeable gears compensated for the different frequencies of the power so to allow a standard paper movement of 6 in. (15.24 cm) per minute.

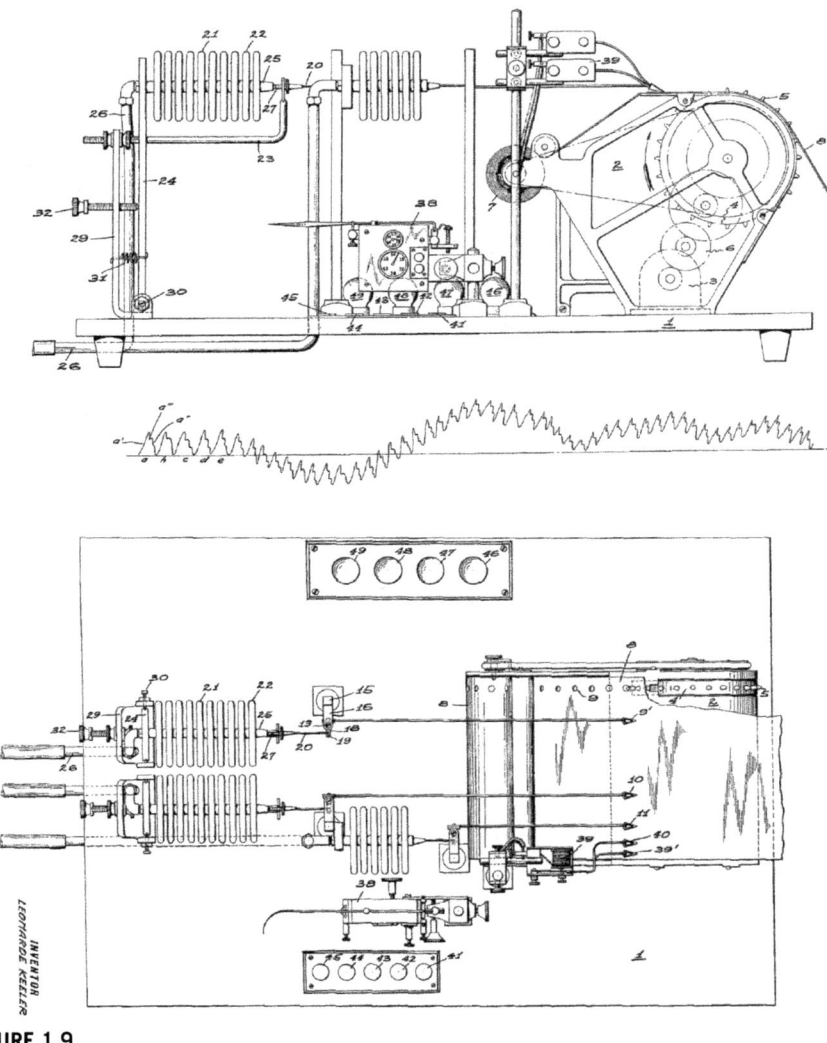

FIGURE 1.9

Diagrams from Keeler's approved US patent application which he submitted in 1925.

placed on the arm of the examinee. Respiration is typically captured with expandable rubber tubes placed about the abdomen and chest. Detection of EDA in the early days used large sensors placed on both hands, but modern instruments can record the same phenomena using metal plates on the examinees' fingers or adhesive pads on the palms.

The most visible difference between early and modern instruments is that the latter are computerized whereas older polygraphs were pen-and-ink recorders. Today's instruments are more likely to include two additional data channels that were rarely seen on older polygraphs. One of them is the movement sensor channel. Though some movement-sensitive sensors were proposed as early as the 1940s for polygraphs (Reid, 1945), websites advocating the use of covert movements as a countermeasure brought a resurgence of interest. The second data channel more often found on current instruments is the photoplethysmograph (abbreviated "PPG" by the scientific community). The PPG channel displays the pulse and changes in pulse amplitude at the sensor site, usually on the tip of a finger or thumb.

EVOLUTION OF TECHNIQUES

In the formative years of the new field of polygraphy, pioneers not only experimented with instrumentation but also with testing protocols. For example, in his experiments on respiration and deception, Benussi had his subjects give free narratives as their verbal responses. Similarly, Marston (1938) relied on long guided statements from his examinees. Larson (1932), however, was one of the first to advocate for the use of simple *yes* and *no* answers to direct questions. It was his view that long vocalizations, even those lacking in emotional content, can produce "disturbances in the polygraph record."

Larson's (1932) description of testing procedures did not reveal much in the way of standardization in test question formulation beyond a preference for the yes-or-no variety. Though often characterized as a RI procedure, it was markedly dissimilar to conventional RI methods that would come to be commonly used, and some of his test questions appeared to be neither relevant nor irrelevant (e.g., Do you object to this test? Do you gamble?). His examples of field cases showed a range of test questions from 10 to more than 30, and with the exception of not placing relevant questions in the first few positions, there was no consistent pattern in question sequencing.

Leonarde Keeler was strongly influenced by Larson, with whom he shared a working relationship at the Berkeley Police Department in the early 1920s when Keeler (b. 1903) was yet a very young man. Keeler had two primary approaches. The first was the RI test, which he learned from Larson, but came to devise his own methods later. The second is the POT (Keeler, 1938) test. The first reference Keeler made to the POT was in the early 1930s (Keeler, 1931) though not by name. According to Lee (1937), Keeler also experimented with a form of what would later be called the Yes-No Test (Golden, 1969), but there is no reference to this by Keeler himself.

Perhaps a most significant innovation in polygraph technique was the advent of the probable-lie comparison question (Reid, 1947) which Reid initially called the "comparative response" question and later the "control question." When using these questions, polygraph decisions were not based simply on the presence or absence of reactivity to relevant questions that was the mainstay for the RI technique, but rather decisions were based on the *relative* responsivity occurring to the relevant questions against benchmark responses to another category of questions.⁹ This approach allowed polygraph examiners to gauge the relative salience, and thereby possible deceptiveness to the relevant questions, for each examinee. This within-examinee method of analysis overcame the problem examiners faced trying to judge the meaningfulness of responses to relevant questions, or the lack of responses.

It should be noted that the idea of comparing responses to relevant questions to those of other potentially evocative questions appeared prior to Reid's time. One historical example is when Lombroso (1895) used a hydrosphygmograph (Figure 1.3) to test a criminal regarding two different thefts, and after comparing the reactions to one of the theft questions to the reactions of the other, he concluded that the suspect was guilty to only one of the crimes.

During an interview conducted by Dr. Gordon Barland and Norman Ansley (cited in Waller, 2001), William Marston's former assistant, Olive Richard, revealed that Dr. Marston had used "hot questions" in some of their examinations of suspects. The details she provided about these "hot questions" had much in common with Reid's "comparative response questions." Marston never published anything about these kinds of questions for fear that guilty suspects would learn of them.

About the same time that Marston employed his "hot questions," Summers (1939) was using something he called "emotional standards," questions that are in some ways like today's comparison questions. Here is how he described them, his testing method, and his approach to interpretation of the data:

The emotional standards are selected after careful analysis of the suspect's life history and after the examination of his psychogalvanic reactions to a preliminary series of questions. When chosen properly, the emotional standards tend to evoke within the individual rather intense psychogalvanic reactions due to surprise, anger, shame, or anxiety over situations which he would ordinarily prefer to

---

⁹ In an account by Robert Peters (2013), who knew John Reid personally, Reid had often told the story of how the idea of his probable-lie question originated. As the story goes, at that time in the 1940s Reid was a polygraph examiner with the Chicago Crime Laboratory conducting a polygraph test on a young man regarding a burglary. The technique in that era was the relevant-irrelevant test. After conducting the test Reid was unable to make a decision about the case because the polygraph data did not point in any particular direction. Reid opted to take a break and let the examinee go to the restroom, and then decided he would also go. In the restroom the examinee continued their discussion, denying the burglary, and pointedly telling Reid that he had never even stolen anything in his whole life. He suggested Reid add that question to the list and conduct another test inasmuch as it would show him to be a totally honest man and could not have been involved in the burglary. Reid decided to give it a try, and when they returned to the testing room he administered a new test that included the question "Have you ever stolen anything in your life?" Now the test showed a reduced reactivity to the relevant question, but a large reaction to the comparison question. Based on the test, Reid called the examinee truthful, which was verified by the capture of the actual burglar some days later. Thereafter Reid reviewed and used very broad probable-lie comparison questions with other examinees, and found what research later supported: truthful examinees tend to react greatest to the probable-lie questions and deceptive examinees react to relevant questions. A variety of comparison questions have since appeared (e.g., exclusionary, directed-lie, positive control) though none have yet been found to produce better accuracy than John Reid's original approach.

> *conceal. In the examination of suspects an emotional standard precedes each significant question. For purposes of interpretation we contrast and compare the reactions to the significant questions with the reactions to the emotional standards. If the deflections to the critical (significant) questions are consistently greater than the deflections to the emotional standards, the individual is consciously trying to deceive the examiner. If, on the other hand, the deflections to the critical questions are not consistently greater than those to the emotional standards, the individual is truthfully expressing his state of mind. This is the essential criterion of interpretation.*

Another type of comparison question, called the directed lie (DL), was developed by field examiners with the US Army Military Intelligence Group (Menges, 2004). It proved useful when examinees underwent routine screening polygraph testing several times, over the course of which probable lies appeared to lose their effectiveness. The DL was used in the field by the Army before 1970, though validation research was not undertaken until the 1980s (Barland, 1981). The DL is now used extensively by many US government polygraph screening programs.

Beginning in 1960, Cleve Backster changed polygraphy dramatically with a string of new concepts and innovations. He introduced the idea of a fixed order of test questions, called a *format*. Though other polygraph approaches had general guidelines for question sequences, Backster's technique had the most rigid, and therefore the most standardized, rules for polygraph testing. Called Backster's Zone Comparison Technique (ZCT) it became a framework for subsequent techniques such as the Federal ZCT, Matte Quadra-Track ZCT, the Integrated ZCT, and the Utah Probable-Lie Test.

Second, Backster devised a numerical scoring system that took advantage of the fixed question order. It was the 7-position scoring system, and like the Backster ZCT, it was to be the basis for several later systems.

The combination of question sequence and well-defined scoring system allowed all examiners similarly trained to come to the same decision on a set of charts. Previous to that time the polygraph field suffered from poor inter-examiner agreement. Indeed, some examiners as recently as the 1950s contended that only the testing examiner, who had access to all of the case information and had interacted with the examinee, could properly interpret the polygraph charts from that case. A more extreme view shared by some members of the polygraph community was that it was unethical to attempt to interpret the polygraph charts of another examiner. Backster strived to resolve these disputes by developing a common system. His system not only improved inter-examiner agreement but also set the stage for the later development of quality control review, where independent examiners far removed from the conduct of the examination could evaluate the polygraph charts and render reliable decisions.

In an age before there was much in the way of polygraph research, Backster intuited many things right. For example, his ZCT places a comparison question immediately before each relevant question, an important juxtaposition that would not be confirmed until more than 40 years later. Backster pushed for reviewing test questions with examinees before testing, and for more emphasis on the electrodermal channel, both which would later be considered best practices. Backster was a lifelong advocate for standardization of polygraph examinations, and though not all of his concepts would ultimately prevail, he was one of the most influential pioneers in modern polygraphy.

One last testing technique also deserves attention. In 1959 Dr. David Lykken published a method he called the Guilty Knowledge Test (GKT, now called the CIT). The CIT is a recognition test, as is the POT, but these two methods have distinct differences. In the CIT the key (or critical item) is placed in the question sequence at random, excluding the first position, while the POT users strive to place the key in the middle of the sequence. The CIT has a scoring system which it uses to assign rank order values to phasic responses, whereas the POT uses a global approach to chart interpretation. The CIT scoring system brings objectivity to the analysis of the charts, permits greater inter-examiner agreement for decisions, and the total CIT score allows the calculation of a false positive error. Lykken conducted only two studies on the CIT, but others have used the CIT paradigm to produce more than 100 published articles, far more than on any other approach to lie detection.

EVOLUTION OF ANALYTIC METHODS

In terms of the interpretation of polygraph charts, first efforts were based on scientific observation. John Larson (1926, 1932) assessed the physiological patterns recorded during criminal testing and the recording of patients of mental institutions to develop a general classification of the data. His method was largely impressionistic, for he offered no objective method. Field practitioners of that era were also using global analysis of the polygraph data to make veracity decisions. Those methods were very primitive, subject to individual experiences, and certainly limited the accuracy of polygraph testing. Judgment of diagnostic features varied among examiners, and the lack of standardization in testing protocols left the field in disarray. Though manual scoring of polygraph data would one day improve decision making, it would not come for several years, after Larson and many other pioneers had left the field. Even in more recent times a minority of examiners still adhere to global evaluation of chart data, a legacy that persists despite advances in the field.

Chart scoring is, in its essence, simple accounting. By applying a tabulation system that captures the frequency and intensity of reactions, it is possible to determine on which questions reactivity tends to occur. The first published attempt at tracking the frequency and intensity of reactions was by Winter (1936). In his system, he marked X's to denote the presence of reactions, and a separate notation for significance, for respiratory and cardiovascular reactions. Winter's system was experimental, and there is no published record of replication by anyone. It was an interesting approach, however, that had it been further pursued it might have speeded the movement of the field toward standardization.

The second scoring system to emerge was by Lykken (1959) for his GKT (later the CIT). His was a rank order system, and applied only to the electrodermal channel. Lykken's system had two principal advantages. First, it was objective. Response magnitudes were measured, and the relative size would determine the score. Second, the total score could be used to calculate the likelihood the examinee recognized details of the crime only known to the perpetrator. In combination this provided a potentially powerful tool for law enforcement, and a basis for courtroom admissibility. The GKT went largely unrecognized by the polygraph community, however.

A few years after Lykken's work, Cleve Backster (1963a,b) announced the development of 7-position scoring for polygraph charts. Backster had been working toward a method in which veracity decisions were based exclusively on interpretation of the chart data, and urged abandonment of then-prevailing approaches that incorporated case facts, interrogation tricks, and behavior analysis in the decision process. Though his system had not been based on published research, it did afford for the first time a uniform approach to chart interpretation that could improve inter-rater agreement among polygraph examiners. Backster's system was adopted by the US government shortly thereafter, and by most of the polygraph field by the 1970s.

Rank order scoring emerged again in the 1970s, first with Japanese researchers with the electrodermal channel (Suzuki et al., 1973, 1974), followed later by Howard Timm who used a rank order scheme with respiration responses (Timm, 1982). In 1987 two rank order systems were proposed that could be applied to three of the polygraph channels (Gordon and Cochetti, 1987; Honts and Driscoll, 1987). Rank order scoring did not become as widely accepted as 7-position scoring, though there are advocates who teach and use it.

The foremost empirical evaluation of polygraph scoring appeared in the publication from Kircher and Raskin (1988). In their paper, Kircher et al. identified which features were valid predictors, and how much each contributed to diagnostic accuracy. These features are discussed in detail in the chapter Analysis of Polygraph Data.

An important part of the Kircher et al. approach was a metric for analyzing respiration tracings, always considered the most resistant to objective assessment. The metric was respiration line length (RLL), which first appeared in a paper by Timm (1982) and for which he credits his mentor Dr. Frank Horvath for the suggestion. RLL later became the standard concept in scoring of probable-lie deception tests.

Computer algorithms for chart interpretation were envisioned well before computers became ubiquitous (Kubis, 1962). In the 1990s, research, development, testing, and evaluation of algorithms began in earnest at several sites (Adachi and Suzuki, 1992; DoD Polygraph Institute, 1991; Olsen et al., 1991), and several systems have since been validated. Algorithm use varies across the field, from complete reliance to complete avoidance, with both extremes vulnerable to different types of error. In the main, modern algorithms make correct decisions more often than does the average human scorer when assessing the same cases. Humans still retain an advantage when judging whether the data are suitable for analysis. Research remains to be conducted to determine the relative accuracy of the use of human and algorithmic methods in combination versus the use of either method alone.

FINAL COMMENT

As Trovillo (1939) and many writers have observed, there was no inventor of the "lie detector." Polygraphy has many forbearers and represents the confluence of many ideas and inventions. It is part instrumentation, part technique, part data analysis, part art, and part science. It is possible to trace its roots back over centuries. However, it is commonly heard from the lay public: When did the polygraph begin? To such a straightforward question often comes a complicated answer about medical devices and nineteenth century psychological research and the emergence of forensic science, a reply that can be at once excessive yet incomplete.

There may exist a point in time where polygraph emerged as a separate endeavor, the joining of ideas and technology that formed something new and distinct from what had come before. If there were such a point, it would be the publication of Larson's (1921) paper *Modifications of the Marston deception test*. It was a brief report, fewer than 4300 words, but in it Larson shows he had captured the best that science had to offer up to the time, added his field experience in criminal work, and combined them to give the world something unique, a true departure toward a new field. In addition, he offered a successful case study that demonstrated the usefulness of his methods. This paper would mark a turning point for lie detection, away from a single physiological measure during an examinee's marginally structured narrative and toward a more structured protocol with multiple physiological recordings during the presentation of questions requiring a simple answer: In other words, to turn a marginally structured procedure into a test. And, in doing so, it would mark the beginning of polygraphy.

REFERENCES

Abrams, S., Ansley, N., 1980. The Polygraph Profession. American Polygraph Association, Chattanooga, TN.

Adachi, K., Suzuki, A., 1992. A computer-based system for objective diagnosis in polygraph test. Rep. Nat. Res. Inst. Pol. Sci. 45 (4), 1–7.

Alder, K., 2007. The Lie Detectors: A History of an American Obsession. Free Press, New York.

Backster, C., 1963a. Standardized Polygraph Notepack and Technique Guide: Backster Zone Comparison Technique. Cleve Backster, New York.

Backster, C., 1963b. Do the charts speak for themselves? New standards in polygraph chart interpretation. Law and Order 11 (6), 67–68.

Balmer, E., MacHarg, W., 1910. The man higher up. The Achievements of Luther Trant. Small, Maynard & Co, Boston.

Bancroft Library, Regional Oral History Office, 1983. August Vollmer: Pioneer in Police Professionalism: Oral History Transcript and Related Material, 1972–1983. Regents of the University of California. Downloaded on June 19, 2013 at http://archive.org/stream/augustvollmer02vollrich#page/n9/mode/2up.

Barland, G.H., 1981. A validation and Reliability Study of Counterintelligence Screening Test. Report to the Security Support Battalion. 902nd Military Intelligence Group, Fort George G. Meade, MD.

Benussi, V., 1914. The respiratory symptoms of lying. Archiv fuer Psychologie 31, 244–273 (in German. English translation published in Polygraph 4(1): 52–76).

Binswanger, L., 1919. On the psychogalvanic phenomenon in association experiments. In: Jung, C.G. (Ed.), Studies in Word Association. Moffat, Yard & Co, New York, Translated by M.D. Elder.

Browne, E.G., 1921. Revised Translation of the Chahár Maqála (Four Discourses) of Nizámí-I-Arúdí Samarqand. Cambridge University Press, London.

Burtt, H.E., 1918. A pneumograph for inspiration-expiration ratios. Psychol. Bull. 15 (10), 325–328.

Burtt, H.E., 1921. The inspiration-expiration ratio during truth and falsehood. J. Exp. Psychol. 4 (1), 1–23.

DoD Polygraph Institute, 1991. Computer Assisted Polygraph System Final Evaluation Report. Ft. McClellan, AL.

Dubois, J.A., 1817. Description of the Character, Manners, and Customs of the People of India. Longman, Hurst, Rees, Orme, and Brown, London.

Dunn, J., 1750. A Collection of Curious Observations on the Manners, Customs, Usages, Different Languages, Government, Mythology, Chronology, Ancient and Modern Geography, Ceremonies, Religion, Mechanics, Astronomy, Medicine, Physics, Natural History, Commerce, Arts, and Sciences, of the Several Nations of Asia, Africa, and America. Vol. I. Translated from French, first printed in Paris in 1749. London.

Ellis, W., 1842. Polynesian Researches, During a Residence of Nearly Eight Years in the Society and Sandwich Islands. H. Fisher, Son, & P. Jackson, London.

Evans, C., 2004. Murder Two: The Second Casebook of Forensic Detection. John Wiley & Sons, Hoboken, NJ.

Feleky, A., 1916. The influence of emotions on respiration. J. Exp. Psychol. 1 (3), 218–241.

Féré, C., 1888. Note sur des modifications de la résistance électrique sous l'influence des excitations sensorialles et des emotions (Note on changes in electric resistance under the effect of sensory stimulation and emotion.). Comptes rendues de Societé de Biologie, Séance, In French.

Fitz, G.W., 1896. A study of types of respiratory movements. J. Exp. Med. 1 (4), 1–16.

Frank, O., 1911. Kymographien, schreibhebel, registrierspiegel, principiens der registrierrung. In: Tigerstedt, R. (Ed.), Handbuch der Physiologischen Methodic. Verlag von S. Herzel, Liepzig, German.

Golden, R.I., 1969. The Yes-No technique in polygraph testing. In: Paper presented at the American Polygraph Association Seminar, Houston, TX.

Gordon, N.J., Cochetti, P.M., 1987. The horizontal scoring system. Polygraph 16 (2), 116–125.

Honts, C.R., Driscoll, L.N., 1987. An evaluation of the reliability and validity of rank order and standard numerical scoring of polygraph charts. Polygraph 16 (4), 241–257.

Jung, C.G., 1919. Studies in Word Association. Moffat, Yard Co, New York, Translated by M.D. Elder.

Keeler, L., 1930a. A method for detecting deception. Am. J. Pol. Sci. 1 (1), 38–51.

Keeler, L., 1930b. The canary murder case (use of the deception test to determine guilt). Am. J. Pol. Sci. 1 (4), 381–386.

Keeler, L., 1931. Lie detector applications. In: IACP Proceedings, pp. 184.

Keeler, L., 1933. Scientific methods of crime detection with a demonstration of the polygraph. Kansas Bar Ass. J. 12, 22–31, Reprinted in Polygraph 23(2): 152–161.

Keeler, L., 1938. The detection of deception. Outline of Scientific Criminal Investigation. Edward Brothers, Ann Arbor, MI.

References

Kha'n, A.I., 1806. Trial by ordeal among the Hindus. In: Asiatick Researches, or Transactions of the Society Instituted in Bengal for Inquiring into the History and Antiquities, the Arts, Sciences, and Literature of Asia. T. Maiden, London, pp. 389–401.

Kircher, J.C., Raskin, D.C., 1988. Human versus computerized evaluations of polygraph data in a laboratory setting. J. Appl. Psychol. 73 (2), 291–302.

Kubis, J.F., 1962. Studies in lie detection: computer feasibility considerations. Report prepared for the Rome Air Development Center, US Air Force Systems Command. AF 30(602)-2270.

Lagercrantz, E., 1927. On Gestalt formation in dialects of the Lappish language. Z. Psychol. 104, 201–223 (in German).

Larson, J.A., 1921. Modifications of the Marston deception test. J. Am. Inst. Crim. Law Criminol. 12, 390–399.

Larson, J.A., 1926. Classification of polygraphic records in the evaluation of emotional reactions. Welfare Mag. (November), 71–89.

Larson, J.A., 1932. Lying and Its Detection. Patterson Smith, Montclair, NJ.

Lea, H.C., 1892. Superstition and Force, fourth ed. Lea Bros, Philadelphia.

Lee, C.D., 1937. Letter to J. Edgar Hoover, Director of the Federal Bureau of Investigation.

Levitt, E.E., 1955. Scientific evaluation of the "lie detector. Iowa Law Rev. 40, 440–458.

Lombroso, C., 1895. L'Homme Criminel. Ancienne Librairie Germer Bailliere et Cie. Paris.

Lombroso Ferrero, G., 1911. Criminal Man According to the Classification of Cesare Lombroso. The Knickerbocker Press, New York.

Lykken, D.T., 1959. The GSR in the detection of guilt. J. Appl. Psychol. 43 (6), 385–388.

MacDonald, A., 1899. Psycho-physical and Anthropometrical Instruments of Precision in the Laboratory of the Bureau of Education. Chapter V, Experimental Study with Children. Government Printing Office, Washington, D.C.

Marey, E.J., 1863. Physiologie Médicale de la Circulation du Sang. E. Thunot et cie, Paris, In French.

Marey, E.J., 1876. Physiologie Expérimentale. Libraire de L'Académie de Médecine, Paris, In French.

Marston, W.M., 1921. Psychological possibilities in deception tests. J. Am. Inst. Crim. Law Criminol. 11 (4), 551–570.

Marston, W.M., 1938. The Lie Detector Test. Smith, New York.

Matthews, J., 1791. A Voyage to the River Sierra-Leone, on the Coast of Africa. B. White & Son, London.

Menges, P.M., 2004. Directed lie comparison questions in polygraph examinations: history and methodology. Polygraph 33 (3), 131–132.

Mosso, A., 1886. La Peur: Étude Psycho-Physiologique (Fear: A Psychophysiological Study). Ancienne Librairie Germer Bailliere et Co, Paris (in French).

Munsterberg, H., 1908. On the Witness Stand. The McClure Co, New York.

Olsen, D.E., Ansley, N., Feldberg, I.E., Harris, J.C., Cristion, J.A., 1991. Recent developments in polygraph technology. Johns Hopkins APL Tech. Dig. 12 (4), 347–357.

Peters, R., 2013. Origin of the probable-lie comparison question (Historical Anecdote). APA Mag. 46 (2), 48–49.

Reid, J.E., 1945. Simulated blood pressure responses in lie detector tests and a method for their detection. Am. J. Pol. Sci. 36, 201–214.

Reid, J.E., 1947. A revised questioning technique in lie detection tests. J. Crim. Law Criminol. 37 (6), 542–547.

Reid, J.E., Inbau, F.E., 1977. Truth and Deception: The Polygraph (Lie Detector) Technique, second ed. Williams & Wilkins Co, Baltimore, MD.

Schafer, E.D., 2008. Ancient science and forensics. In: Embar-Seddon, A., Pass, A.D. (Eds.), Forensic Science, vols. 1–3. Salem Press, Inc, Hackensack, NJ.

Shurreef, J., 1832. Qanoon-e-Islam, or the Customs of the Moosulmans of India. Parbury, Allen, & Co, London, Translated by G.A. Herklots.

Stern, B.A., Krapohl, D.J., 2003. The infamous James Alphonso Frye. Polygraph 32 (3), 188–199.

Sticker, G., 1897. Ueber Versuche einer objectiven Darstellung van Sensibilitätsstörungen. Wiener klin. Rundschau, 30/31 (in German).

Summers, W.G., 1936. A recording psychogalvanometer. Bull. Am. Ass. Jesuit Scient. East. States Div. 14 (2), 50–56.

Summers, W.G., 1939. Science can get the confession. Fordham Law Rev. 8, 334–354.

Suzuki, A., Watanabe, S., Ohnishi, K., Matsumo, K., Arasuna, M., 1973. The objective analysis of GSR in the detection of deception: An analysis of GSR amplitudes in terms of rank scores. Rep. Nat. Res. Inst. Pol. Sci. 26 (4), 237–245.

Suzuki, A., Ohnishi, K., Matsumo, K., Arasuna, M., 1974. Amplitude rank score analysis of GSR in the detection of deception: Detection rates under various examination conditions. Rep. Nat. Res. Inst. Pol. Sci. 27 (3), 142–148.

Swan, C.S., 1905. Gesta Romanorum. George Bell & Sons, London.

Timm, H.W., 1982. Analyzing deception from respiration patterns. J. Police Sci. Adm. 10 (1), 47–51.

Trovillo, P.V., 1939. A history of lie detection. J. Crim. Law Criminol. 29 (6), 848–881.

Veraguth, O., 1909. Das Psychogalvanische Reflexphänomen. Von S. Karger, Berlin (in German).

Waller, J.F., 2001. A concise history of the comparison question. Polygraph 30 (3), 192–195.

Whitney, W.D., 1911. Century Dictionary & Cyclopedia. The Century Co, New York.

Winter, J.E., 1936. Comparison of the cardio-pneumo-psychograph and association methods in the detection of lying in cases of theft among college students. J. Appl. Psychol. 20 (2), 243–248.

CHAPTER 2

Anatomy and physiology for polygraph examiners

Joel M. Reicherter

Traditionally, most human anatomy and physiology experts recognize that the human organism is composed of 11 systems. However, some debate by the experts may argue a different number of systems. The knowledge gain in human body function, over time, has introduced diverse opinions of human body organization. For instance, the greater understanding of immunology has encouraged some authorities to consider the functional contribution of this discipline as a separate system, the "immune system," while other authorities consider it, traditionally, as a subdivision the circulatory system. For the mission and purpose of this chapter, that debate will be left to other authorities. The focus of this chapter will be limited to the anatomy and physiology of selected systems that best address the psychophysiological detection of deception (PDD).

BACKGROUND

It is well known in the behavioral sciences, such as psychophysiology and psychology, that stimuli such as auditory, vision, olfactory (smell), and skin sensation (touch) can stimulate the brain cognitively and emotionally of environmental changes. After integrating the environmental stimuli, the brain alerts and coordinates the visceral body systems to respond appropriately. Depending on the brain's assessment of stimuli, it will coordinate a physiological strategy response among the body organ systems. If the stimulus is perceived as threatening or hostile, the brain will alert the body's systems most linked to preservation responses. Often, these body responses are described by both the scientific and lay community, as the "fight or flight" response. Scientists in these behavioral disciplines have observed and researched that the nervous system, integumentary (skin) system, cardiovascular system, and respiratory system are significantly more responsive to threatening stimuli than other systems.

PDD methodology has capitalized on these observable physiological systemic responses and developed somewhat esoteric examination formats to assess the probability of a subject responding truthfully or deceptively. These polygraph examination designs are described in detail in Chapters 6-8.

Technically, the nervous, integumentary, cardiovascular, and respiratory systems can be monitored and evaluated in a relatively uncomplicated manner with transducers attached to the surface of the body. Transducers are devices that convert one energy signal into another. The basic understanding of the structural and functional design of these systems and their integrative roles is essential for the polygraph examiner.

The popular physiological reaction "fight or flight" mentioned earlier is a catchy rhyme phrase easy to remember. However, the polygraph examination setting is most unusual with respect to the body position which must be maintained during the question presentation. Namely, the subject is directed to sit and not move. This directive is counter to the more natural response of physical action experienced during a natural world "fight or flight" response. These physiological dichotomies will be addressed periodically in this chapter.

ORGANIZATION

From the smallest to the largest, the body is composed of atoms and molecules organized into cells. Cells of different types but similar in origin are organized into tissues which perform more complex functions than what a single cell can perform. Several different tissues are organized together to perform more complex functions, which is referred to as an organ. Different organs are organized together to perform even more complex functions than a single organ can perform, which is referred to as a system. Multiple systems are then organized to perform more complex tasks than a single system can perform. Ultimately, all of the systems working in harmony become the organism, AKA the Human Being (Figure 2.1).

As mentioned earlier, traditionally, the human body is considered to have 11 systems: integumentary, skeletal, muscular, nervous, endocrine, cardiovascular, lymphatic, respiratory, digestive, urinary, and reproduction. When these organ systems are integrated to perform holistic harmony for optimal body function, the body is often described as being in a state of wellness. These integrative physiological processes of the organ systems that can maintain the state of wellness are commonly described as being in a state of homeostasis.

For the body to perform its functions, like a well-organized factory, there is a division of labor in the body's organization. Enzymes and hormones are the directors and regulators of chemical reactions that take place in cells and throughout the body systems. For these regulators to perform their jobs, a complex internal environment must be maintained. For example, body temperature must be maintained within narrow limits. Most of the heat in the body is generated by skeletal muscle activity. But if this activity becomes excessive, such as in running or other physical activity, the body temperature could rise so high it would stop the chemical reactions needed by the body systems to maintain life. To prevent the temperature from going to unsupportable levels, sweat glands in the skin will increase their activity resulting in water evaporation and thereby a cooling process. If environmental temperature

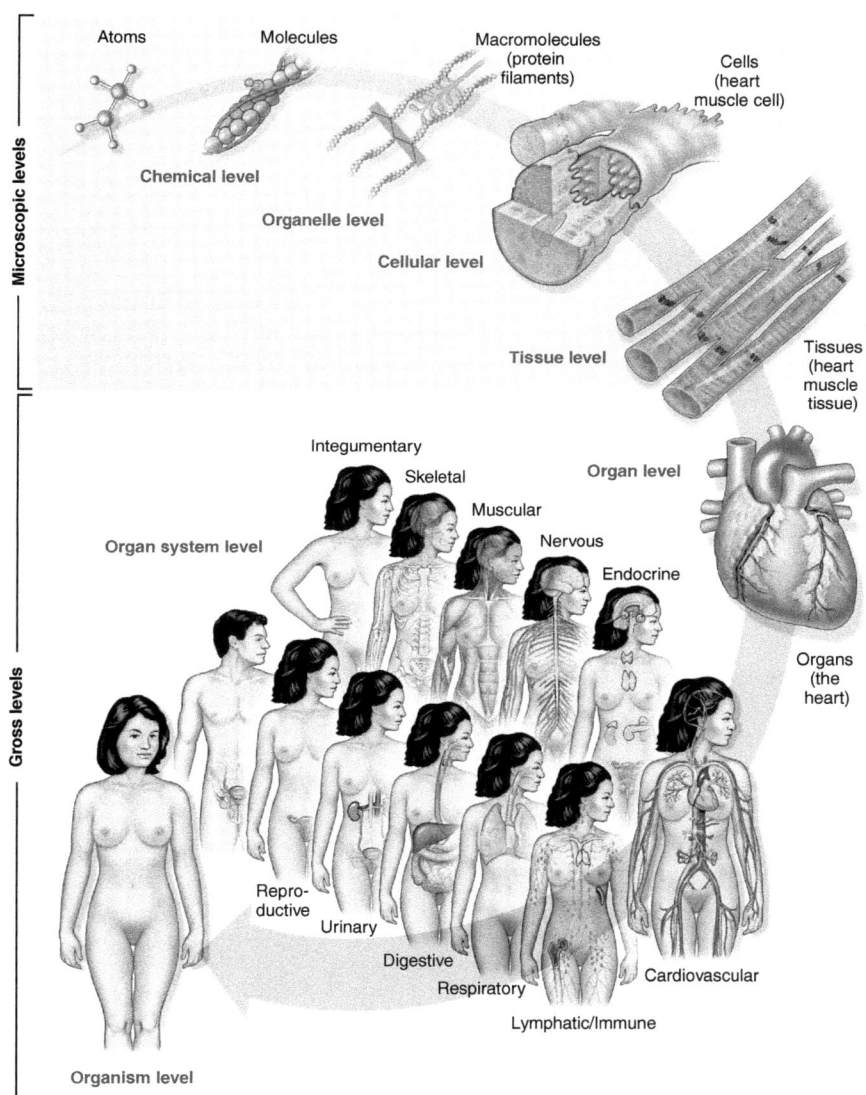

FIGURE 2.1

Levels of organization.

From Patton et al. (2012).

goes too low, the muscles will begin to shiver to raise the temperature. These heat-generating and heat-losing mechanisms continue non-stop to maintain a state of wellness concerning body temperature.

These homeostatic processes of opposing extreme changes in the internal environment are typically described as negative feedback. Thousands of other checks and balances of body activities are continuously ongoing, which may be reviewed in many physiology and medical texts. Occasionally, the body may be infected with a microorganism which can interfere with these homeostatic balances which we describe as being sick. Sometimes we take prescribed medicines to help us get back to a healthy homeostatic state of equilibrium, a state of wellness.

INTEGUMENTARY SYSTEM

The integumentary system is commonly referred to as the skin. Anatomically, the skin provides the physical end border of our being and is in direct contact with the environment. The skin provides the first line of defense against infection by sealing and protecting the underlying organ systems from invasion of pathogenic organisms.

Some authorities describe the skin as a complex membrane composed of a highly vascular (blood vessels) dermis covered by multiple layers of cells known as the epidermis (Figure 2.2). The portion of the epidermis next to the dermis which has access to blood supplying nutrients goes through rapid cell replication, pushing the cells up and away from the dermis and blood supply. Because the epidermis is avascular,

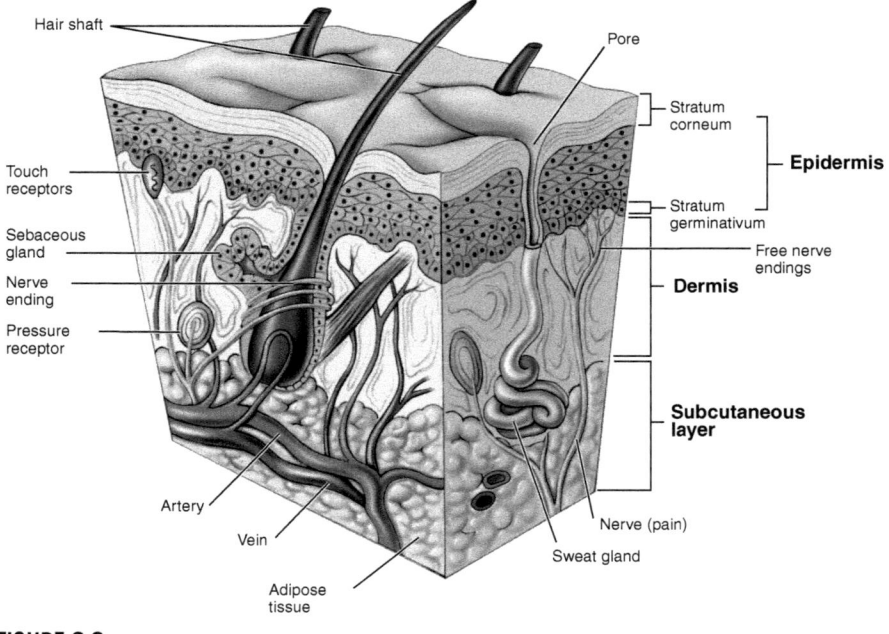

FIGURE 2.2

Cross section of human skin.

From Herlihy (2014).

the cells begin to die. The outermost layer of the epidermis is the corneum which is continuously flaking off inasmuch as it contains the oldest dead cells that have been pushed up and away from the blood supply of the dermis several weeks ago.

The skin's complex design varies in different parts of the body. In addition to protecting the other systems from infection and dehydration, it contains highly organized receptors discriminately distributed throughout the body surface dedicated to signaling the central nervous system (CNS) of changing environmental conditions such as temperature or the compression of a brick falling on you. When the brain and/or spinal cord integrates the signals (nerve impulses) received from the skin, it will send signals to the appropriate organ systems for response.

One of the most significant coordinating efforts for the brain is to organize the activation of selective sweat glands which will assist the body to adapt to the environmental stimulus. As mentioned earlier, maintenance of body temperature is most important in maintaining an internal homeostatic environment so the body organs can function in an orchestrated way. If temperature is increasing due to the contraction of muscles in sporting activities or in life-threatening reactions, many sweat glands must be activated to increase water evaporation which will prevent the temperature from increasing to levels unsupportable for living functions.

It must be noted that sweat glands on the palms of the hand and soles of the feet are designed to increase grasping effectiveness needed during times of arousal whether in sporting activities or defensive activities. Sweat glands on the hands and most of the body are classified as eccrine or merocrine type. However, sweat glands under the arms and in the genital areas are classified as apocrine sweat glands that secret body fluids containing unique body chemicals which generate characteristic odors which become our signature. These odors are easily recognized by family dogs and other animals. Interestingly, these glands do not become active until puberty which can lead to sexual attraction to the opposite sex. In more primitive times, these glandular secretions were often advance signals that strangers, either friend or foe were nearby. Furthermore, these glandular secretions become the host diet for many bacteria which can create even more odoriferous signals. More details of the eccrine and apocrine gland activity can be reviewed in published physiology texts.

Eccrine sweat gland activity on the palmer surface of the hand and fingers contributes very significant signal value in the PDD assessment. As mentioned above, when a subject is aroused, an increase in grasping capacity is warranted. When the brain perceives such a circumstance, it will signal the sweat glands of the hand to increase secretion to better achieve the grasping demand. The neurophysiological map of how the brain directs the activity of sweat gland function is reasonably well understood and will be discussed briefly in the Nervous System section.

When the eccrine sweat glands secrete sweat it contains salt (NaCl), which enhances the secretion of water and the consequent evaporation cooling process. Salt is known in the physiological and medical disciplines as an electrolyte because NaCl, in a watery environment such as the body, separates into two particles called sodium and chloride ions.

For many decades, behavioral scientists have come to a widely held understanding that cognitive and emotional activity in the brain will increase sweat gland activity to enhance the grasping capacity of the hand anticipating some form of combat. The increase in sweat gland activity is assessed by monitoring electrolyte production. This is achieved by placing two surface electrodes on the skin and conducting a minute electric current between them. If the production of the salt electrolytes increases, the current passing between the electrodes will increase. This increase in conductivity between two electrodes placed on the palmer surface of the hand observed in neurophysiology research has been accepted and researched further by the PDD scientific community.

The fundamental science underlying the recording of skin conductance or its reciprocal, skin resistance, is described as Ohm's Law, often written in the equation $I = V/R$. "I" equals current, "V" equals voltage or power (force), and "R" equals resistance. As a simple model, if you envision rolling a ball on a ground surface of wood, sand, or ice. These surfaces would represent R in the equation. V would be the force applied to the ball, and I would be the speed of the ball. Clearly, the ball would roll fastest on the ice and slowest on the sand because of the lower resistance of ice compared to sand to the force applied to the ball.

In skin conductance, if more sweat containing the salt electrolytes is produced at any given time, the current (I) between two electrodes will increase because the resistance is reduced. This reaction is observed as electrodermal activity (EDA). If the amplitude of the recording increases, it is the result of more sweat gland activity which reduced the resistance between the electrodes on the skin surface permitting an increase in current. The measurement of resistance can be calculated also but it is a more complicated measure. The original work on electrical resistance was done by the eighteenth century Italian researcher Luigi Galvani. Most modern psychophysiologists prefer to assess conductance rather than resistance activity because it is a more direct and simple measure of sweat gland activity.

NERVOUS SYSTEM

The nervous system, structurally and functionally, is composed of CNS and a peripheral nervous system (PNS). The CNS contains the brain and spinal cord and the PNS is composed of nerves in a somatic division and an autonomic division. The somatic division makes up about 95% of the nerves in the PNS, and are segregated into sensory and motor components. The remaining 5% of the PNS is the autonomic division. The autonomic division is further subdivided into sympathetic and parasympathetic divisions. The autonomic division is of particular interest to researchers and practitioners of PDD (Figure 2.3).

Based on structure and function, there are several categories of nerve cells that can be described. For practitioners of PDD, most of the attention will be focused on the neuron with a little attention given to the support cells in the system.

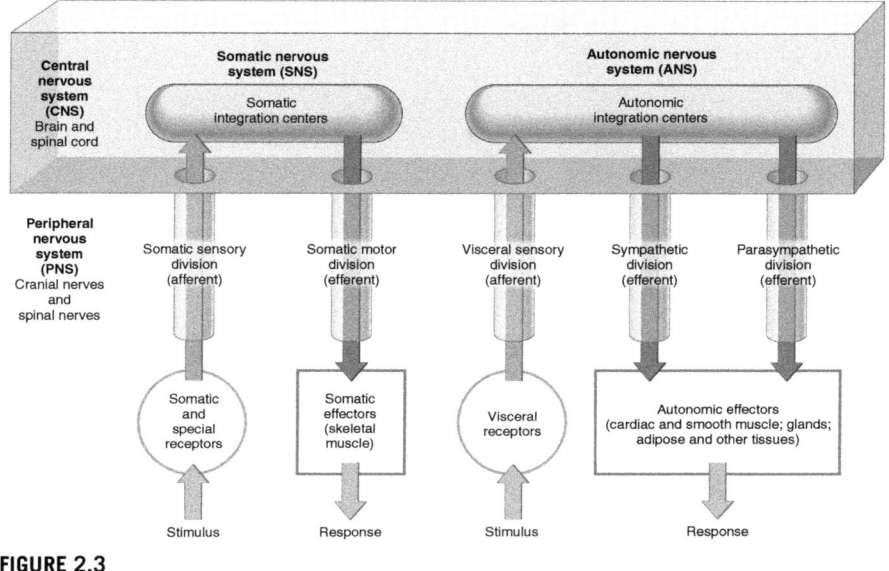

FIGURE 2.3

Organization of the nervous system.

From Patton et al. (2012).

Neurons can be divided into a variety of structural and functional groups. Sensory neurons convey stimuli from the body's peripheral organ systems to the brain in an impulse like pattern described in the scientific literature as action potentials. After the dedicated brain area receives the signal of sensory action potentials from the body area that generated the stimulus, it coordinates a cognitive and emotional understanding of the signal through many millions of association neurons. From this coordinated activity, motor neurons convey action potentials to a variety of body organ systems that best coordinate an appropriate response.

To provide a concise explanation of these systems, only a brief description of the neurophysiological concepts will be addressed. Readers interested in the physiological underpinnings of PDD are encouraged to review widely published texts in the pertinent subject areas to become familiar with the cellular physiology underlying the systems.

Most neurons are classified or named by their structural or functional roles. Overall, the portion of the neuron representing the nucleus and other cellular structures is often referred to as the cell body. The cell body will have from one to hundreds of projections extending from it depending on the neuron classification, somewhat like fingers extending from the hand. These extensions are referred to as dendrites. They receive action potential signals from other neurons. In complex ways, these signals are conveyed to another part of the cell body where the axon begins and may extend very long distances, such as through the length of your leg or arm. Other axons may be microscopic. The axon is the specific portion of the neuron that generates

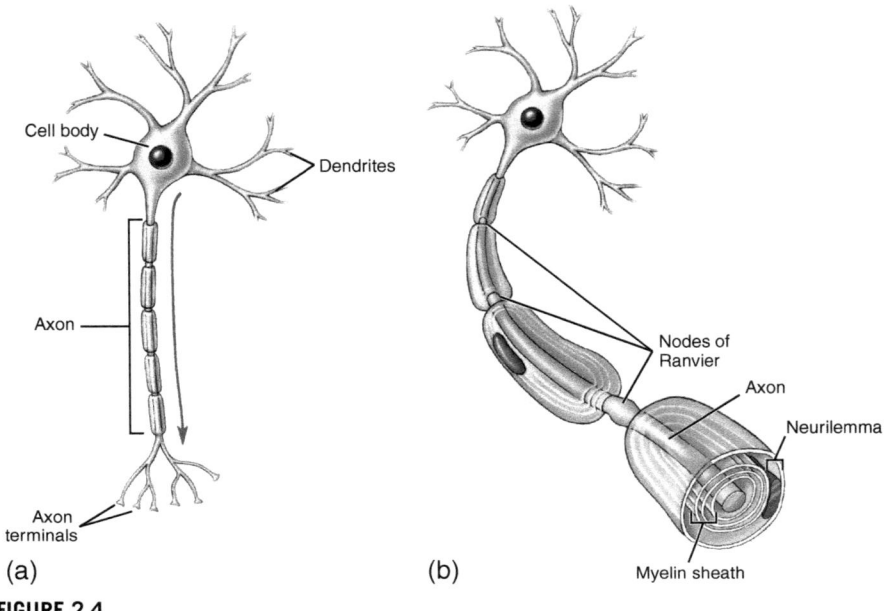

FIGURE 2.4

Structure of a neuron. (a) Dendrites, cell body, axon, and axon terminals. (b) Structure surrounding the axon, showing the myelin sheath, the nodes of Ranvier, and the neurilemma.

From Herlihy (2014).

and conducts the nerve impulse (action potential). Many axons, but not all, contain specialized wrappings of support cells known as Schwann cells. These cells produce a special substance called myelin which provides very rapid conduction of the nerve impulse (Figure 2.4).

At the end of the axon-specialized branches develop like branches of a tree and produce many different types of molecules called neurotransmitters. These neurotransmitters are released at a microscopic connection known as the synapse. The neuron that releases the neurotransmitter is described as the presynaptic neuron and the one that receives the neurotransmitter is the postsynaptic neuron. By conveying the neurotransmitter, the nerve impulse (action potential) is recreated from one neuron to another. As a model concept, the synapse releasing the neurotransmitter from one neuron to another would be like one person handing money to another. In simple terms this is how a society of people communicates, by exchanging money from one person to another. The nervous system's society of neurons works on the same concept.

Overall, concerning nervous system function as it relates to PDD application, it may be more helpful to have a global understanding of its organization than a detailed understanding of the function at the molecular level. Other publications will describe in detail the molecular and chemical functions in the nervous system for those readers who have an interest.

Brain: The brain has been studied and researched for many years by many scientists from numerous scientific disciplines. Although much has been learned about brain function, much mystery still remains concerning how it performs its tasks. We will only review some of its most basic understandings in this chapter.

Anatomically, the brain can be viewed as being composed of three main areas, a cerebrum, cerebellum, and brain stem (Figure 2.5). The cerebrum is the largest section, composed of two hemispheres, typically described as the left and right. The surface of the brain is referred to as the cortex and often described as gray matter because of its appearance. The cortex is only about 1/4 in. (6.5 mm) thick but contains billions of neurons which are able to communicate with each other through synapses. Interestingly, from the diagrams, you will notice that the cortex is convoluted and involuted many times. Furthermore, the two hemispheres are further segregated into lobe sections described as frontal, parietal, occipital, and temporal.

Although there is extensive integration of function among the neurons in each lobe, the dominance of many functions has been located in specific areas. For instance, much of our cognitive understanding of our circumstance has been identified

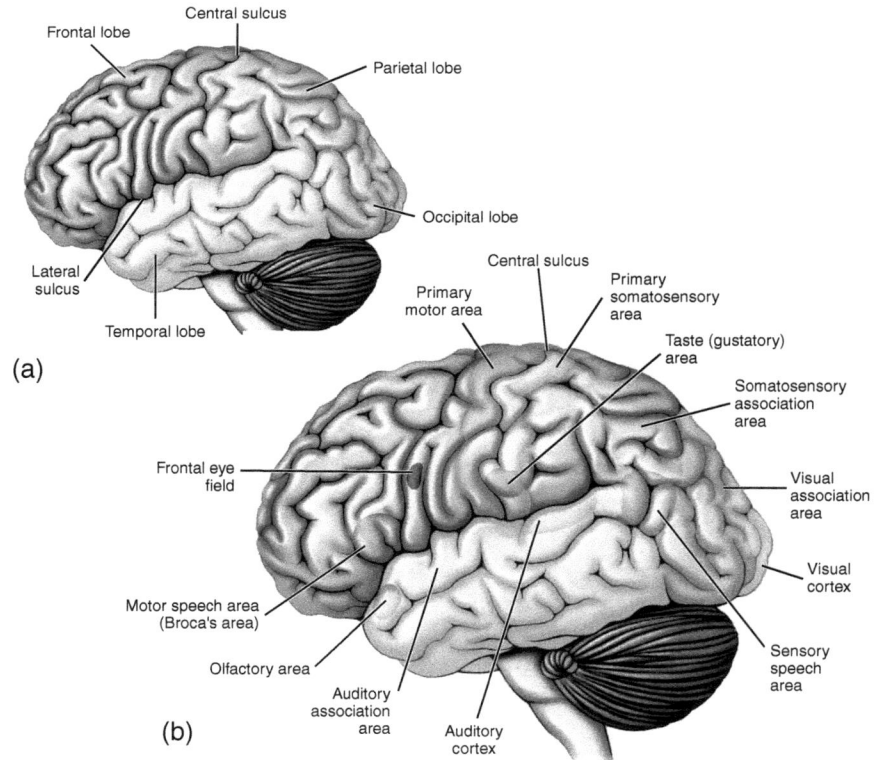

FIGURE 2.5

Structure of the brain.

From Herlihy (2014).

to neuron activities in the "frontal cortex." Visual stimulation has been shown to be dominated in the occipital lobe while auditory stimulation is found in the temporal lobe. Sensory evaluation of the environment generated by skin contact is evaluated in the parietal lobe. Motor function of body parts is regulated by activity in the posterior (back) portion of the frontal lobe coordinated by the cerebellum section of the brain located in the back of the cerebrum, just above the back of the neck.

Interestingly, neuroscientists have observed that right and left hemispheres can contribute different components of our cognitive skills and behavioral expression. For instance, the right hemisphere is often described as non-verbal, dominating our ability to navigate, create music, and art, understand architecture and other non-verbal skills. The left hemisphere dominates our ability to convert thoughts and ideas into a language, writing, speaking, and mathematic skills. The two hemispheres, however, are able to integrate (talk to each other) through a structure known as the corpus callosum which can provide a more complete understanding of issues (Figure 2.6).

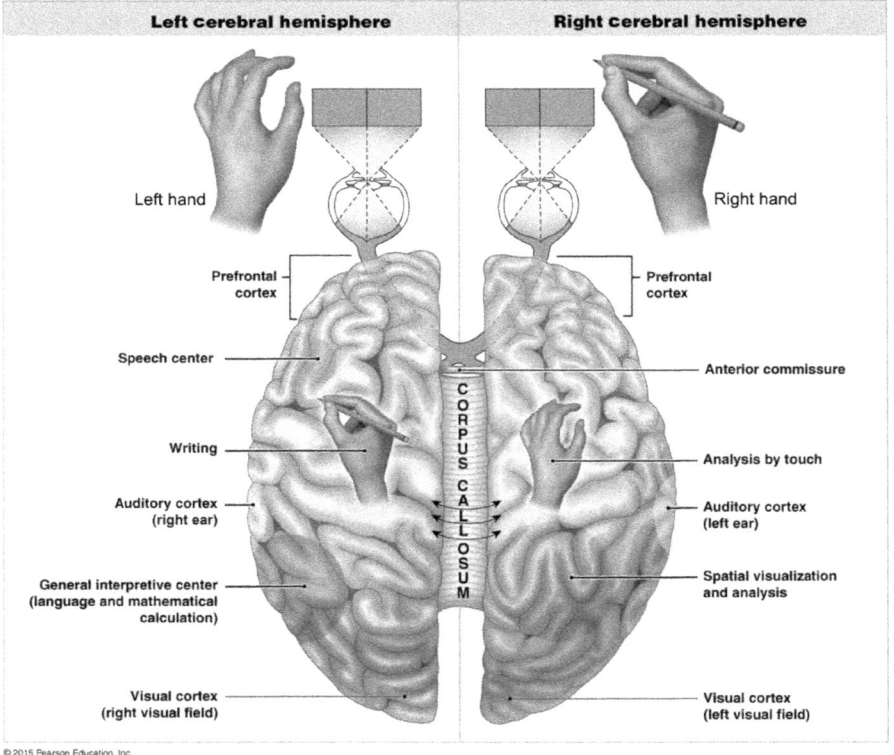

FIGURE 2.6

Hemispherical differentiation.

From Martini et al. (2014).

In addition to the cognitive mapping of brain sections, neuroscience has mapped out areas of the brain that dominate our emotional expression such as fear, sense of wellbeing, and experiences of pleasure, retrieval of memory, and many expressions of motivation. Collectively, these functional areas are described as the limbic system.

Our collective personality is a complex mixture of our cognitive and emotional skills and expression. The environmental stimuli the brain needs to activate its ability to evaluate it and construct the appropriate response is conveyed by neurons packaged in groupings located in the PNS.

The nerves in the PNS have been cataloged by neuroscientists into 12 pairs of cranial nerves, which originate in the brain and allow direct communication between the brain and certain selected body areas. These nerves have specific names and are numbered from 1 to 12. Some cranial nerves have only sensory axons, such as the optic nerve which conveys vision, olfactory—smell, and vestibulocochlear—balance and sound stimuli to the brain. Other cranial nerves have only motor axons. The oculomotor nerve, for example, moves the eyes in certain directions. Some cranial nerves are mixed because they contain both sensory and motor axons. The cranial nerve known as the vagus nerve (#10) is of particular importance in PDD because of its involvement with body organ function related to polygraph science. More about that nerve later.

Spinal Cord: The spinal cord is the main conduit to provide sensory information from most of the body organ systems to the brain and return motor stimulation to the organs for appropriate response. The peripheral mode of communication is by conducting action potentials in the axons of neurons which are cabled together in groupings identified as nerves. These nerves originate in the spinal cord between the vertebrae. The vertebrae are named after their location such as cervical, thoracic, lumbar, sacrum followed by a number to identify their specific location such as C1, C2, T1, T2, etc. (Figure 2.7). The spinal nerves are identified following the same location. Spinal nerves typically branch many times when they communicate with body organs, often adopting the name of its location or destination or origin (Figure 2.8).

There are 31 pairs of spinal nerves that contain both sensory and motor neurons and are therefore described as mixed nerves. About 95% of the neurons in nerves are described as somatic neurons, which communicate to the brain and spinal cord about muscle organs, joints, and skin. About 5% of the motor neurons are part of the autonomic nervous system (ANS). The ANS has a very significant role in PDD science and will be described shortly.

The spinal cord has two distinct areas known as gray matter and white matter. The gray matter is in the center of the spinal cord and shaped somewhat like the letter H or butterfly. This is the area where neurons synapse with each other to integrate many complex neural pathways. Surrounding the gray matter is the white matter. White matter is composed of bundles of axons dedicated to conveying sensory action potentials to the brain for evaluation and are grouped together with subdivisions as ascending (sensory) tracts. The brain then sends action potentials through descending (motor) tracts in the white matter to various levels of the spinal cord to communicate to the spinal nerves which regulate specific body organs.

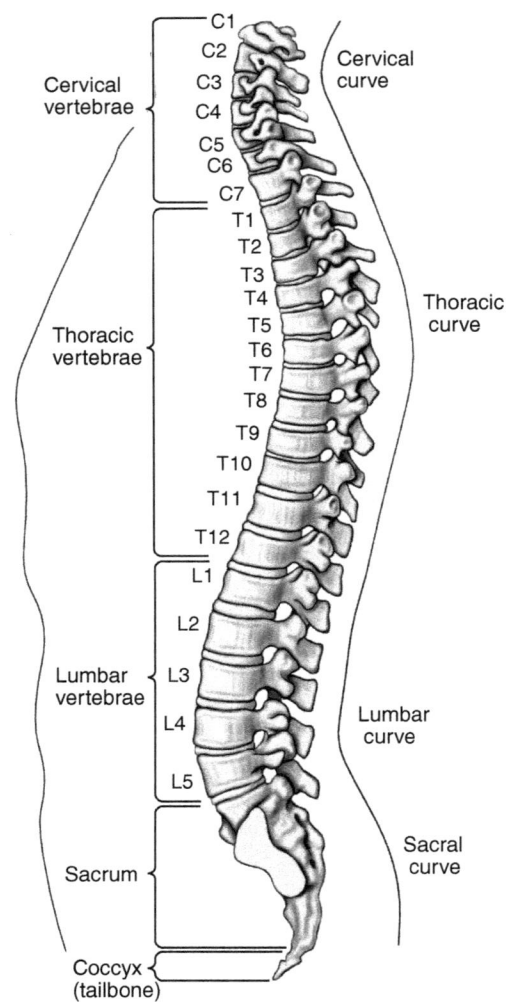

FIGURE 2.7

Vertebral column.

From Herlihy (2014).

ANS: The ANS has two subdivisions known as the sympathetic division and the parasympathetic division. The sympathetic division regulates specific organs during times of stress or perceived danger. The "fight or flight" expression often reflects the activity of the sympathetic division. During times of rest and repose, the parasympathetic division dominates the activity of these organs (Figure 2.9).

As mentioned previously, neurons communicate with each other at synapses through the release of neurotransmitters. Based on the type of neurotransmitter, the

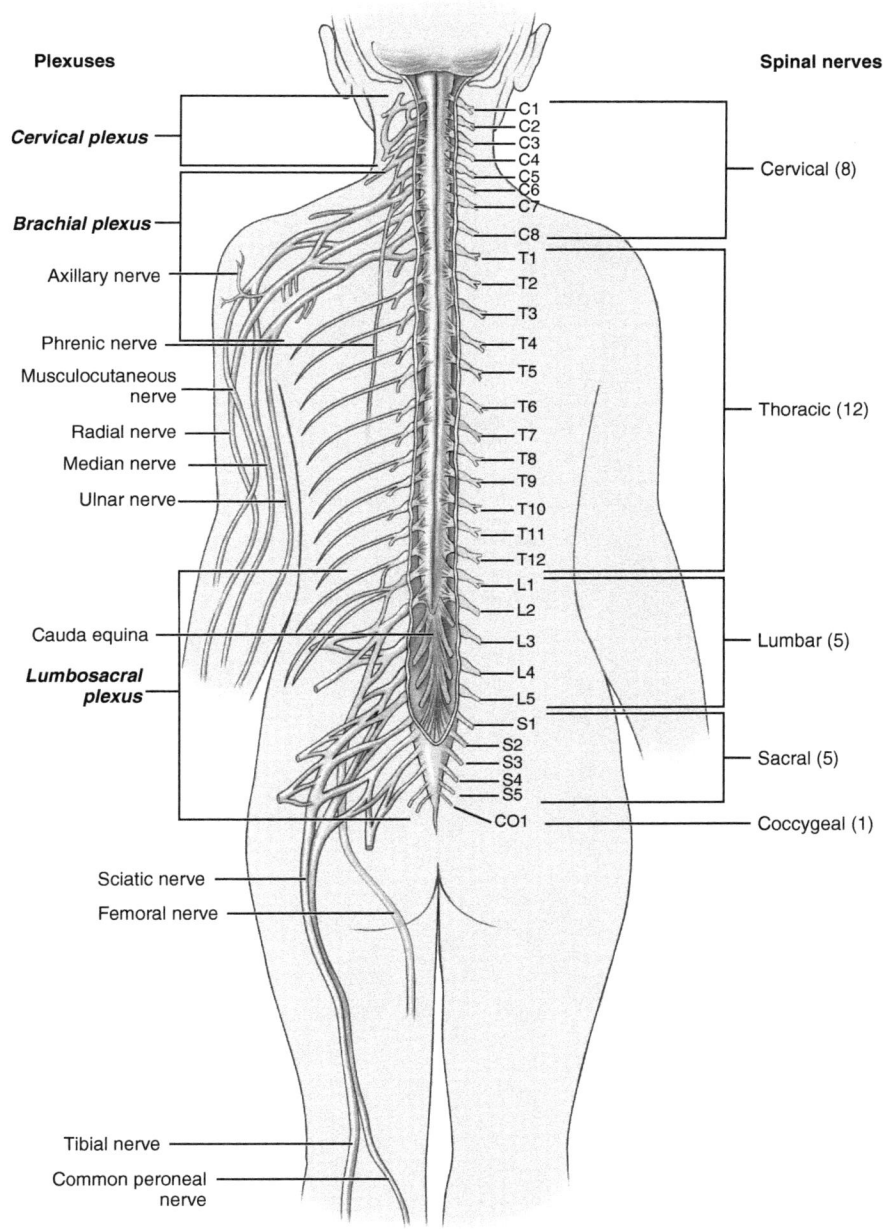

FIGURE 2.8

Spinal nerves and plexuses.

From Herlihy (2014).

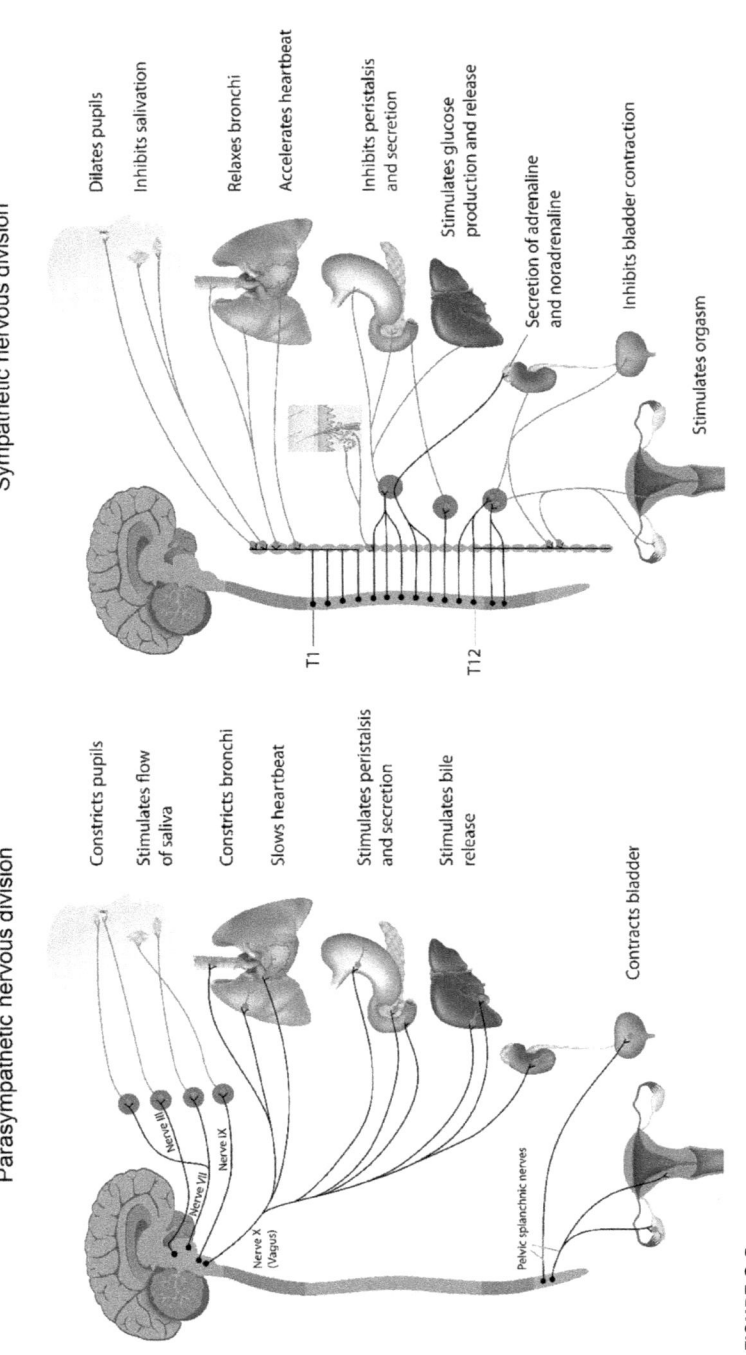

FIGURE 2.9

Structural organization of the autonomic nervous system.

subdivisions of the ANS are further subdivided. Medical and pharmaceutical sciences have studied the nature of these neurotransmitters and have developed many drugs that can enhance or inhibit the action of these agents. As a consequence, the activity of the targeted organ or system can be affected. Many practitioners in medicine prescribe specific pharmaceuticals to enhance or depress the function of these organ systems for the benefit of the patient. Unfortunately, many of these pharmaceuticals and similar drugs have entered the illicit market where individuals can consume these drug agents unregulated and alter physiological functions which can result in undesirable behavioral changes. Translated to the PDD setting, many pharmaceutical agents both prescribed and unprescribed can have an influence on body reactions which raise both medical and psychophysiological concerns affecting the PDD setting. Further details in this subject can be reviewed in other medical or physiological publications.

Sympathetic Division: The sympathetic division exits the spinal cord through T1 through L2. Most of the axons in this division leave the spinal nerves to enter into the sympathetic chain ganglia (Figure 2.10) where many of them synapse with neurons

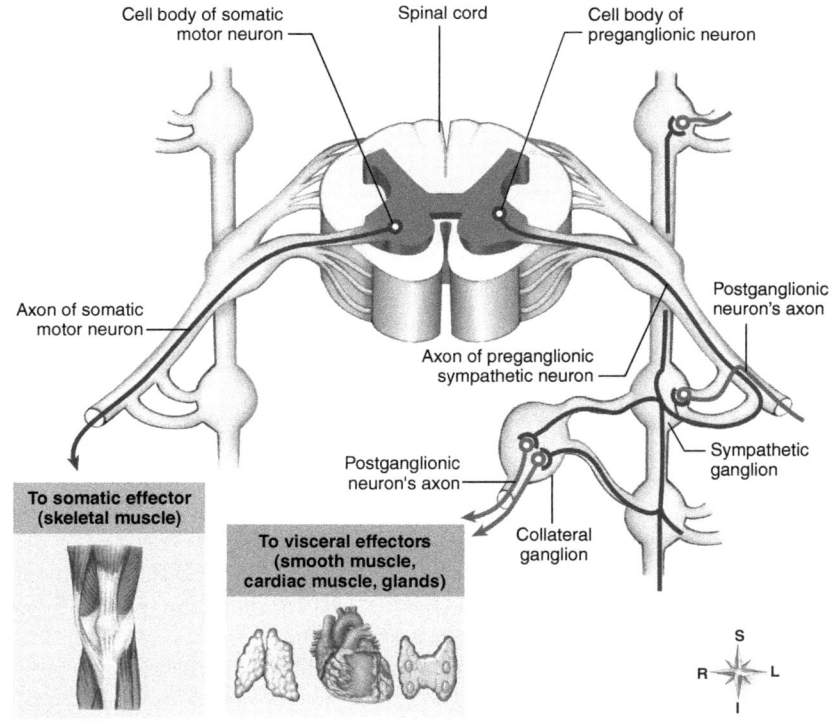

FIGURE 2.10

Autonomic conduction pathways.

From Patton et al. (2012).

going to specific organ destinations (Figure 2.9). In PDD the pathway to the heart, lungs, and sweat glands are most important.

As mentioned earlier, neurotransmitters allow neurons to communicate with each other. Furthermore, neurons regulate the activity of a specific organ by the release of neurotransmitters also. At the heart, the sympathetic division by way of the cardiac nerve releases the neurotransmitter norepinephrine (noradrenaline) which makes the heart beat faster and raises blood pressure when specialized receptors accept the neurotransmitter. Norepinephrine also causes the airway to dilate allowing air to enter the lungs more easily. Both these effects help the body to meet stressful situations. It is common medical practice to prescribe drugs which will inhibit the action of norepinephrine for the purpose of lowering blood pressure in patients with hypertension (high blood pressure). Many organs contain receptors to receive the neurotransmitters named with Greek letters such as alpha or beta. Readers may have heard of beta blockers prescribed to patients with high blood pressure. If the norepinephrine is not conveyed to the heart because of the blocker, the heart rate will slow down and blood pressure will be reduced.

An interesting exception to sympathetic release of epinephrine in these organs during times of stress is the release of the neurotransmitter acetylcholine at the sweat glands. The sympathetic release of acetylcholine during stress allows the glands to relax and release more sweat, helping the body dissipate the anticipated increase in heat produced during perceived danger.

Parasympathetic Division: The parasympathetic division is composed of cranial nerves III, VII, IX, X, and nerves originating in the sacral region of the spinal cord. These nerves go directly to the target organs innervated by the sympathetic nerves resulting in a dual innervation of the organs. One main exception is the sweat glands where there is no innervation of the parasympathetic division. As mentioned the parasympathetic division dominates these organ system functions during times of rest and repose. It is important to note that acetylcholine is the primary neurotransmitter that dominates during these restful times.

In PDD science the vagus nerve, cranial nerve X, is the primary nerve of concern. As Figure 2.11 shows, the vagus nerve has numerous branches going to many organs in the chest and abdomen. The role of the vagus nerve branches to the heart is to reduce the heart rate during times of rest and thus reduce blood pressure. There are many pharmaceutical drugs prescribed that stimulate the effect of acetylcholine and beta blockers to inhibit the effect of norepinephrine to achieve this goal.

As one might imagine, prescribed pharmaceuticals, some foods and beverages as well as illicit drugs can have profound effects on cardiac function, some with significant health benefits and others with detrimental effects. These factors are always a concern to the PDD examiner. How the brain interacts with the nervous system components can have considerable influence on circulatory and respiratory physiology which we are about to explore.

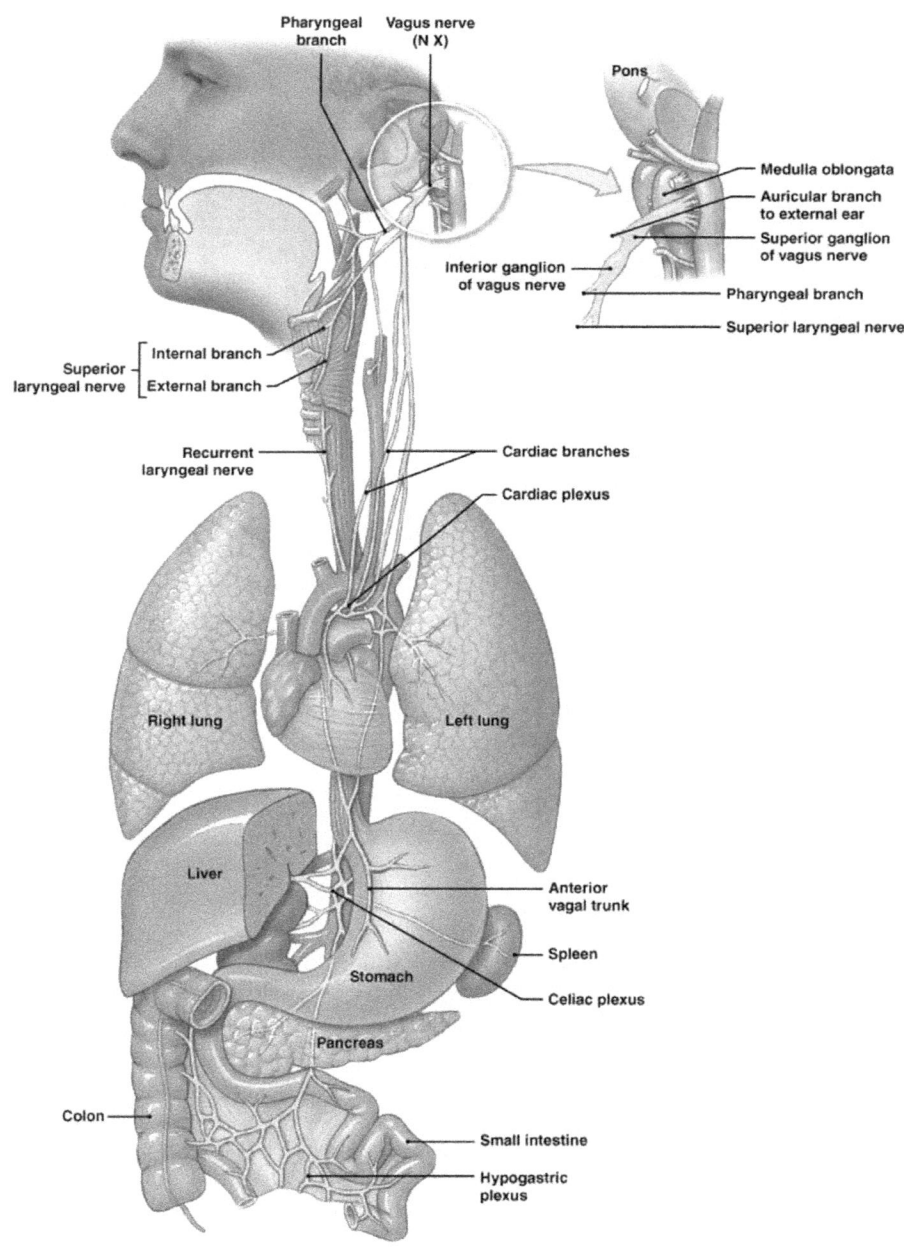

FIGURE 2.11

Vagus nerve.

From Martini et al. (2014).

CARDIOVASCULAR SYSTEM

The cardiovascular system (circulatory system) is dedicated to the distribution of nutrients and oxygen to all the cells of the body that compose the organ systems and transport metabolic cellular waste products primarily to the liver, kidneys, and lungs for removal to the outside. To achieve these functions, the circulatory system is composed of a pump (heart) and a vascular tubular network of vessels called arteries, capillaries, and veins. The vehicle of transport within the vascular system is a liquid blood tissue specially designed to load and unload nutrients, oxygen, and metabolic waste products.

Blood: The blood is a liquid tissue composed of 45% formed elements and 55% liquid plasma. An average size person has about 5 liters of blood. Of the formed elements about 99.9% is composed of red blood cells (RBCs) and 0.1% are white blood cells (WBCs) and platelets. The most important role of the RBC is to deliver oxygen to the body cells. RBCs are able to perform this role because they contain hemoglobin which is also the reason why blood is red in color. WBCs are involved in immune reaction of various types and platelets which initiate blood coagulation reactions in the event blood vessels are damaged.

The liquid plasma is composed of about 92% water and a host of complex molecular components. The plasma serves the role of delivering nutrients, hormones, enzymes and an assortment of life dependent substances to the cells of the organ systems and removal of metabolic wastes from cell physiology. Since blood physiology is not a direct concern in PDD, it won't be discussed further here but students are encouraged to learn more about this subject by reviewing appropriate publications.

Heart: The human heart is a four-chambered organ divided into two right chambers and two left chambers. The upper right chamber, described as the right atrium is designed to receive blood from the body organs during the return phase of a continuously circulating flow. Below the right atrium, the blood flows into a pumping chamber, the right ventricle. From the right ventricle, the blood is pumped to the lungs to pick up oxygen while liberating carbon dioxide that was picked up from the metabolism of cells. After the blood has passed through the lungs, it is high in oxygen and returns to the left atrium then on to the left ventricle to be pumped throughout the other body organ systems (Figure 2.12).

Blood returning to the right side from the body organs enters the right atrium through two large veins, the superior vena cava and inferior vena cava. The superior vena cava drains blood from the head, shoulders, and arms. The inferior vena cava drains blood from the legs, abdomen, and chest. The right ventricle pumps the blood to the lungs through the pulmonary trunk which divides into left and right arteries branching many times similar to tree branching. Returning blood to the left atrium from the lungs, thousands of veins eventually form two right and two left pulmonary veins. After the blood passes from the left atrium into the left ventricle, it is pumped into the aorta which branches many times, again like a tree, leading to the distribution of the oxygenated blood to all the body organ systems.

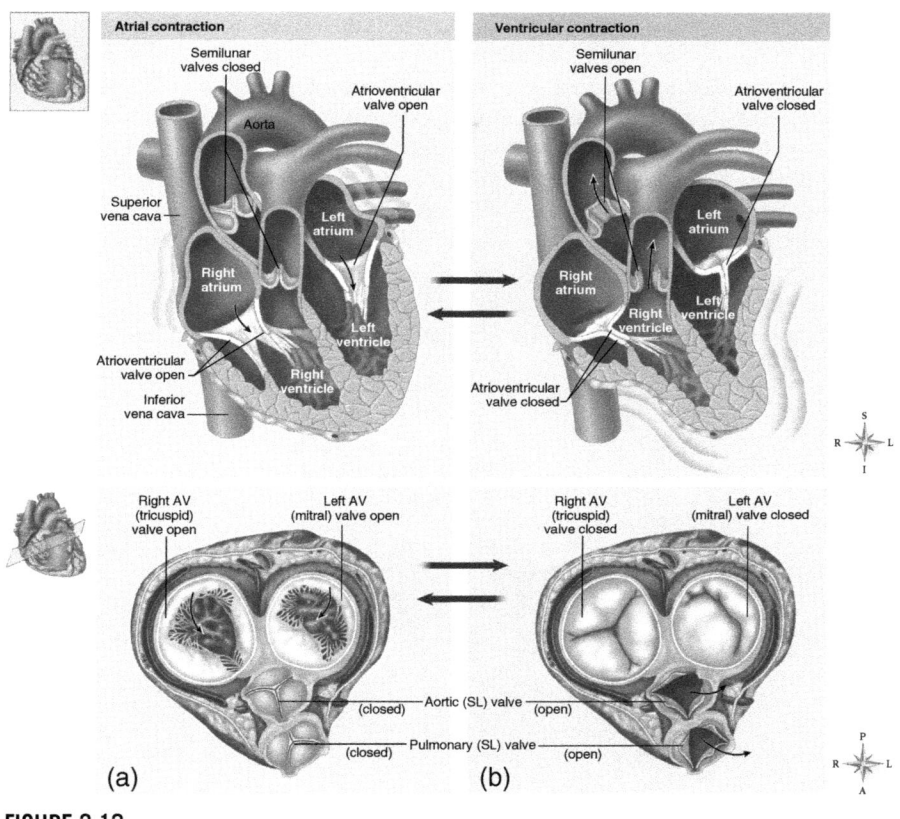

FIGURE 2.12

Chambers and valves of the heart.

From Patton et al. (2012).

During the cycling of the heart's pumping chambers, the action of contraction phases followed by relaxation phases (heart beats), require specialized valves to prevent the back flow of blood during the relaxation phases of the cardiac cycle. These valves are located between the atria and ventricles and between the ventricles and the pulmonary artery leading to the lungs and the aorta leading to the body organs. Between the right atrium and ventricle are the tricuspid valves; between the left atrium and ventricle are the bicuspid valves. Between the ventricles and pulmonary and aortic vessels are the semilunar valves (refer to Figure 2.12).

Heart Conductive System: The cardiac cycle of contraction results in blood being pumped from the heart to the lungs and the other body organ systems followed by relaxation which results in new blood being pulled back from the systems and lungs into the heart. This cardiac cycle is regulated by an intrinsic coordinating system within the heart and extrinsic control of the cardiac cycle by the sympathetic and parasympathetic nervous system with endocrine system influence.

The intrinsic system begins with a unique neuromuscular structure known as the sinoatrial (SA) node or pacemaker located between the superior vena cava and right atrium which sends specialized stimulus signals to both right and left atria causing them to contract. While this stimulus is occurring, another neuromuscular node, the atrioventricular (AV) node located in the muscular septum which separates the two ventricles, is being stimulated. From this node a signal is generated down the septum through the bundle branches then up through ventricles by way of Purkinje fibers causing them to contract and pump blood (Figure 2.13). This intrinsic conductive system can be easily monitored by an EKG. The intrinsic conductive activities can be increased by the sympathetic nervous system or decreased by the parasympathetic nervous system (Figure 2.14). When the brain perceives an environmental

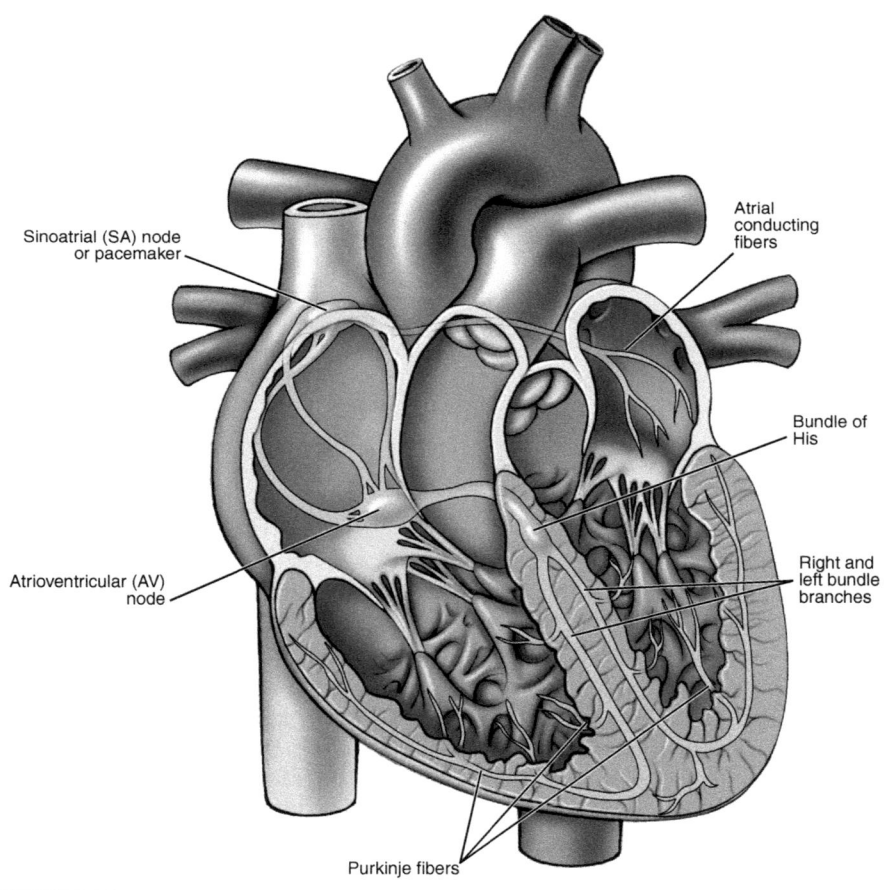

FIGURE 2.13

Conducting system of the heart.

From Herlihy (2014).

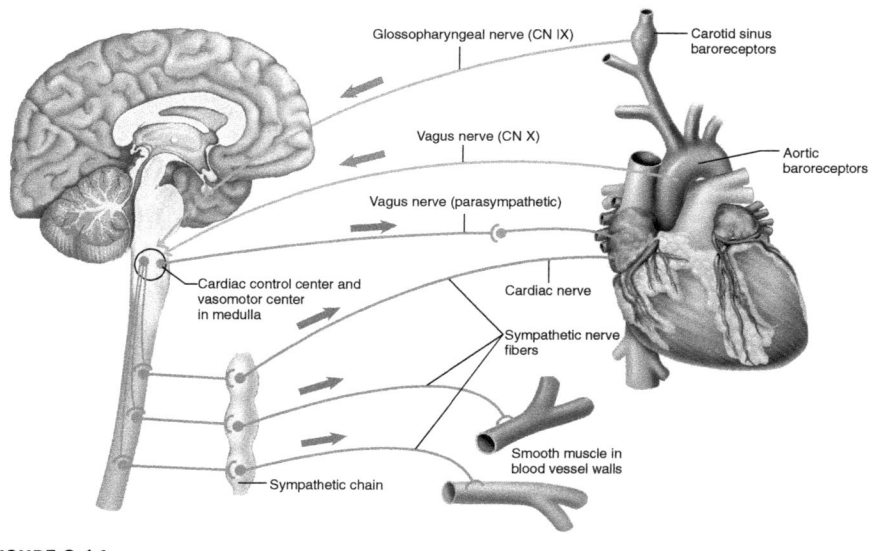

FIGURE 2.14

Influences on cardiac output.

From Patton et al. (2012).

circumstance as threatening, both cognitively and emotionally, the sympathetic division, by way of the cardiac nerve, will be aroused to increase the cardiac cycles and blood pressure which will deliver more blood to the muscles for the "fight or flight" response. If the environmental situation is benign, the parasympathetic division, by way of the vagus nerve, will reduce the cardiac cycles and blood pressure to accommodate a more relaxed state. Remember the main neurotransmitter released by the cardiac nerve in the heart is norepinephrine and the main neurotransmitter in the parasympathetic division is acetylcholine.

In PDD, a rather interesting paradox is in the mix of the sympathetic/parasympathetic management of cardiovascular dynamics. Typically, in the "fight or flight" response to environmental threat, the increase in cardiovascular response is to deliver more oxygen and nutrients needed caused by the increase in muscular activity. In the polygraph setting, the subject is directed not to move, which negates the muscle demand for more oxygen and nutrients. Consequently, heart rate and breathing cycles may slow down rather than increase when the questions with greater jeopardy are presented. Respiratory dynamics in the polygraph setting will be addressed later.

Blood Vessels and Circulation: Blood pumped from the left ventricle enters muscular tubes called arteries which branch like a tree thousands of times before reaching organ tissue destinations. Upon reaching the organs, the arteries have branched into microscopic arterioles and finally into capillaries. Through the vessel walls of the capillaries nutrients, hormones, enzymes, and oxygen are delivered to the cells in exchange for metabolic waste products and carbon dioxide. Fluids collected from

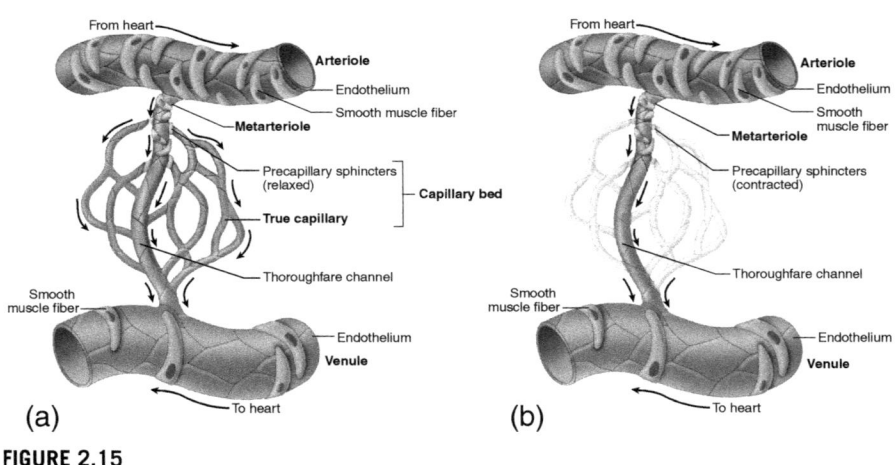

FIGURE 2.15

Microcirculation.

From Patton et al. (2012).

the tissues enter capillaries, which become venules, which join other venules, and eventually veins (Figure 2.15).

Special micro sphincter muscle cells regulate the flow into organ tissues. When body organs are less active during a particular time, the sphincter muscle cells constrict, causing a restriction of blood flow to that tissue. This restriction of blood flow to the less active tissues will make more blood available for the more active tissues. For instance, during exercise blood flow will increase to active muscles and less to the digestive system. During dinner and for several hours afterward blood flow increases to the digestive system while blood flow decreases to the muscular system often making a person less interested in exercise.

As the arteries branch, vessels are named reflective of nearby anatomical structures or locations much like highways change names along their course (Figure 2.16). As the aorta leaves the left ventricle, it arches distinctly before descending to lower body systems. At the top of the arch, three prominent arteries arise, the brachiocephalic trunk, left common carotid, and the left subclavian. These vessels branch many times as they course through the head and arms. The descending aorta also branches many times to deliver blood to the body organs below the heart.

Please note the brachial artery. This artery is the most frequently accessed artery by the medical community to monitor blood pressure dynamics created by heart cardiac cycles. When the left ventricle contracts, it pushes the blood through the arterial system. This push of blood creates a pressure in blood vessels referred to as the systolic pressure. When the ventricle is in the relaxation phase of the cardiac cycle, the pressure falls to the diastolic pressure.

The oscillating pressure changes of the cardiac cycles can be monitored by placing an air bladder, the sphygmomanometer (blood pressure cuff) around the arm where the brachial artery is located (Figure 2.17). Pumping air into the bladder will

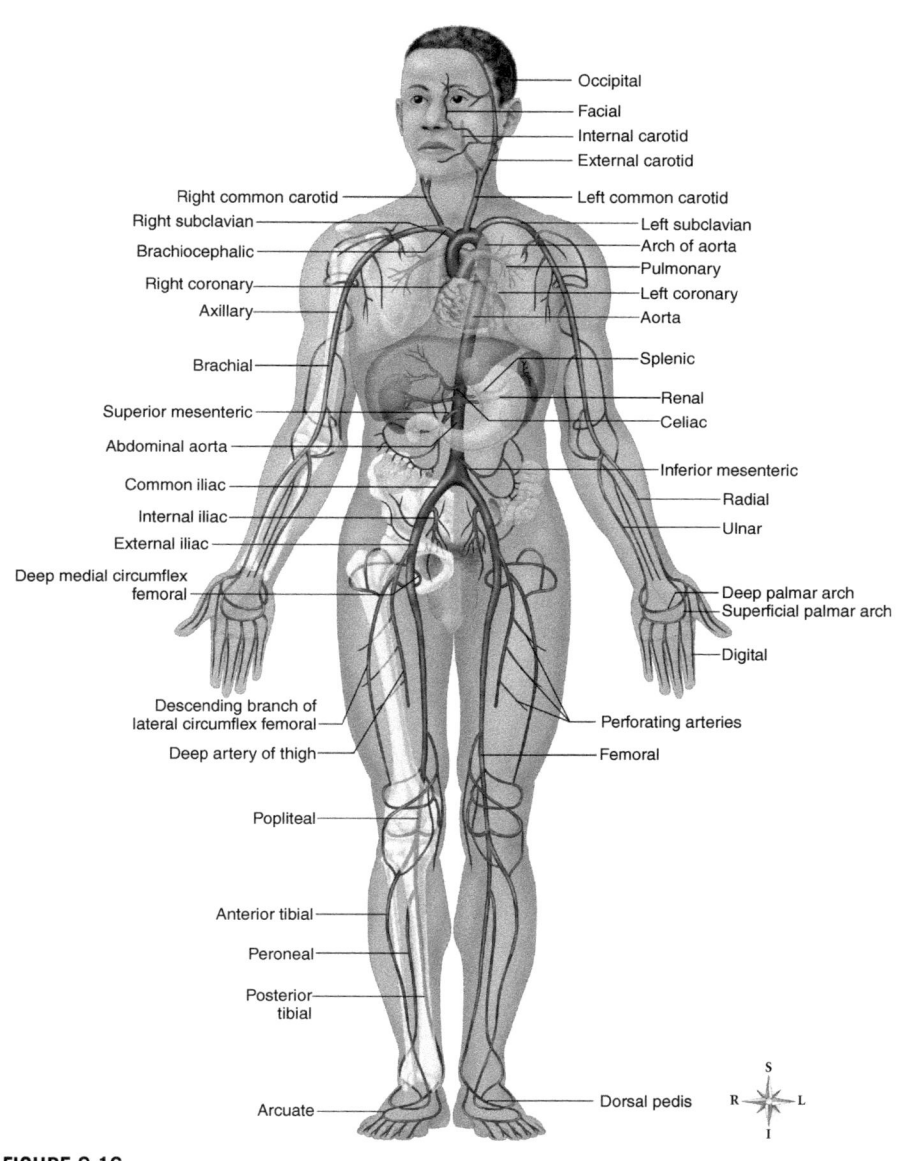

FIGURE 2.16

Principal arteries of the body.

From Patton et al. (2012).

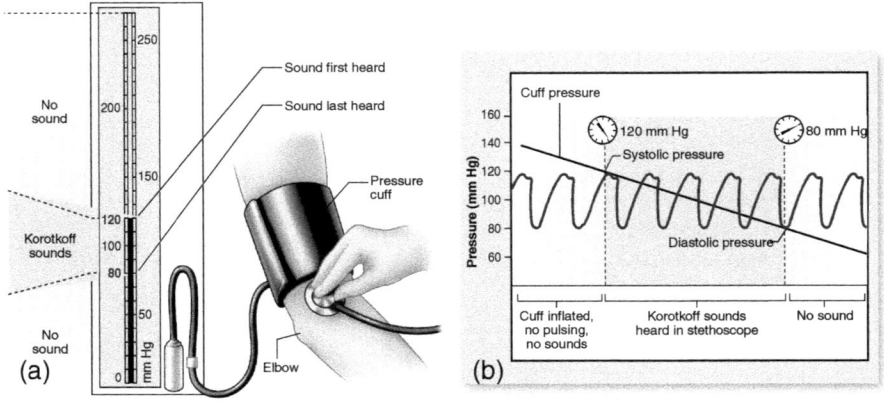

FIGURE 2.17

Sphygmomanomter.

From Patton et al. (2012).

collapse the artery against the humerus (bone in the arm). When the air in the bladder is slowly released, changes in characteristic sounds of systolic and diastolic blood pressure phases of the cardiac cycle can be detected with a stethoscope and be observed on a gage measured in metric units. One typically common systolic/diastolic blood pressure ratio may be 120/80 mm Hg (mercury). In PDD, the air pressure in the blood pressure cuff is typically set to 60 mm Hg which is below diastolic pressure for most people. With amplification from the polygraph instrumentation, changes in cardiac cycles and consequent blood pressure dynamics related to PDD assessment can still be achieved.

It should be noted that the cardiovascular design is a closed system much like a plumbing system of water supply to a home is a closed system. Therefore, pressure dynamics can be taken from other sites such as the ankle if unusual circumstances require. Since veins are conduits of blood return from the organ systems they do not have to bear the systolic/diastolic pressure changes typical of arteries. Consequently, they have reduced muscle in their structure with many of them located near the skin surface or between muscles which help return the blood to the heart.

Because many important veins are located between muscles, during exercise or laborious work, contracting muscles greatly assist the heart by squeezing on the veins to help return the blood back to the heart. The expression "muscular pump" is often used to describe this activity. Veins near the surface of the skin promote reduced resistance to blood flow and also encourage blood flow return to the heart.

The extended time application of the blood pressure cuff during one chart presentation of questions can cause a partial collapse of the thin-walled superficial veins resulting in a damming effect of blood flow return. The hemodynamic effect of this prolonged use of the cardio cuff during a PDD setting is not well understood.

Polygraph examiners are encouraged to use adequate recovery times between chart recording or even changing arms when using the cardio cuff.

RESPIRATORY SYSTEM

The respiratory system is designed to extrapolate oxygen from the air and return carbon dioxide from metabolic cellular function. The blood being the conveyer of these gases, the relationship between the respiratory and cardiovascular systems is intimate. Since the respiratory system, by necessity, is directly in communication with the environment and consequently potentially vulnerable to pathological contaminates, the airway between the lungs and the environment is specially adapted to prevent airborne infections.

The respiratory airway between the nose and the lungs is referred to as the conducting zone or dead air space. This pathway contains specialized cells which secrete mucous and collectively remove most of the air pollutants before they reach the lungs. This respiratory pathway also moistens and warms the air to better disperse oxygen into the blood (Figure 2.18).

The oral cavity as the entry portion of the digestive system and the nasal passageway as the entry portion of the respiratory share a common pathway, the pharynx

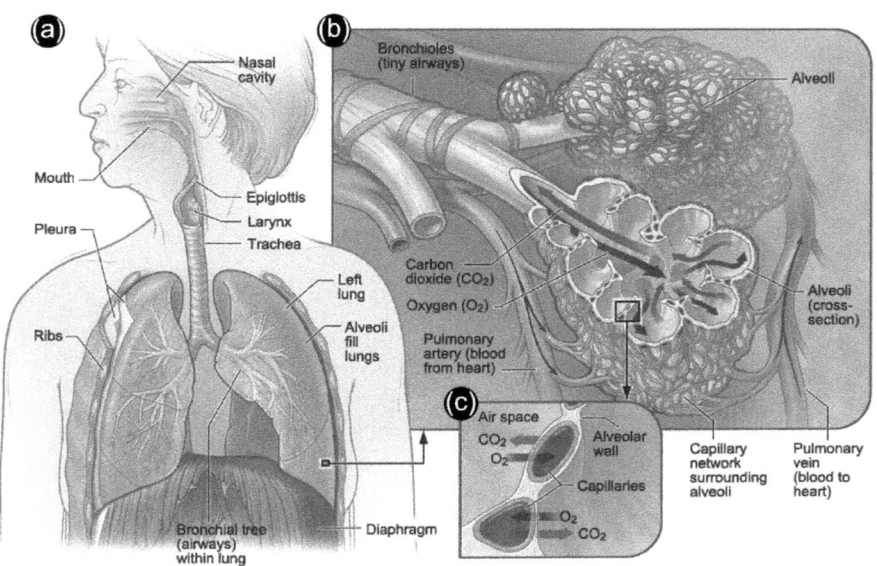

FIGURE 2.18

(a) Location of the respiratory structures in the body. (b) An enlarged view of the airways, alveoli (air sacs), and capillaries (tiny blood vessels). (c) A close-up view of gas exchange between the capillaries and alveoli. CO_2 is carbon dioxide, and O_2 is oxygen.

From National Heart, Lung, and Blood Institute, National Institutes of Health (2015).

(throat). As a consequence, one cannot swallow and breathe at the same time but rather alternately. Food and drink pass through the pharynx to enter the esophagus toward the stomach. Air passes through the nasal passageway to the pharynx to enter the larynx (voice box) passing through the trachea to a left and right bronchus which continue to branch thousands of times to terminate in a left and right lung. Note that food or drink cannot normally enter the airway through the larynx because a cartilaginous epiglottis flap seals it off during swallowing. The larynx contains specially designed vocal cords that can vibrate in a variety of ways when air is exhaled resulting in speech and voice sounds (Figure 2.19).

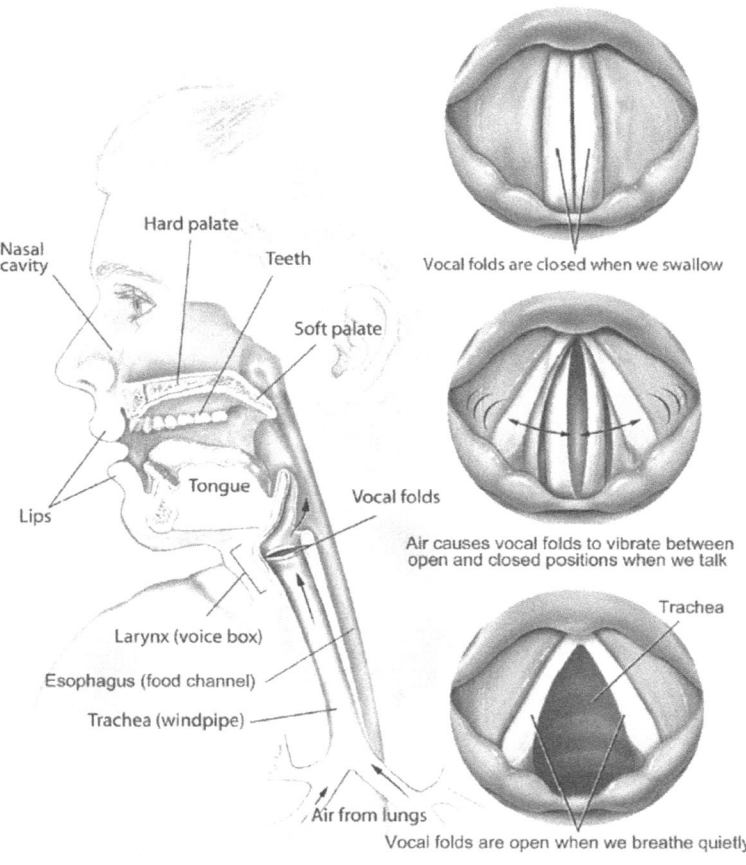

FIGURE 2.19

Larynx and structures for sound production.

From Department of Health and Human Services, National Institutes of Health, National Institute on Deafness and Other Communication Disorders (2015).

The lungs are segregated into sections called lobes. The right lung has three lobes and the left lung has two lobes and is slightly smaller than the right lung because it has to accommodate the heart which is slightly positioned toward the left. Each lung is composed of millions of microscopic air sacs known as alveoli, each of which is surrounded by capillaries (refer to Figure 2.18). When blood flows into alveoli pumped by the right ventricle through the pulmonary arteries it contains high levels of carbon dioxide produced by cellular metabolic waste, and releases it in exchange for oxygen. Blood now rich in oxygen flows into pulmonary veins back to the left atrium, into the left ventricle to be pumped throughout the body.

Between the lungs and the walls of the chest (thoracic) cavity is a doubled layered membrane that maintains a negative pressure (suction) to keep the lungs inflated. Readers may have heard of a collapsed lung (pneumothorax). This condition may occur if an injury occurs which disrupts the negative pressure between the lung and chest causing the lung to pull away from the chest. Fortunately, each lung is independently separated so the conditions which cause the pneumothorax of one lung don't affect the other lung.

Air flow into and out of the lungs follows the gas laws of physics known as Boyle's Law. Namely, if the volume of a gas increases, the pressure decreases, and vice versa. Gases will flow from the higher pressure area to the lower pressure area. Breathing dynamics is a function of this law (Figure 2.20).

The primary muscles responsible for enlarging the chest cavity and lung volume, reducing the pressure allowing air to flow into the lungs (inspiration), are the diaphragm and external intercostal muscles (muscles between the ribs). When these muscles relax, the chest cavity and lungs return to their smaller resting state which increases the pressure allowing the air to flow out of the lungs to the surrounding environment (exhalation). In a typical resting state, the average person will repeat this cycling 14-16 times per minute. This breathing resting cycling rate is termed eupnea or quiet breathing. Although the inhalation phase requires active contracting muscle action, the exhalation phase is passive, only requiring the muscles to relax. During exercise, however, the breathing cycles increase (hyperpnea) which is assisted by the action of internal intercostal muscles and other muscles which actively engage the exhalation phase of breathing.

The mechanism of the breathing cycles is regulated by the somatic division of the nervous system. Although all breathing cycle characteristics are done without conscious control, they can modify when we speak loudly, whisper, or sing. By regulating the intensity and management of the diaphragm and other muscles, we can effectively communicate to one another through the generation of the voice and even convey emotional expression with voice intonation.

The diaphragm is innervated by a pair of phrenic nerves which originate from neurons exiting the spinal cord from C3, C4, and C5. These nerves receive stimulation from breathing regulatory centers in the brain stem which, in turn, receive stimulation from the cognitive and emotional brain centers. The external intercostal and other breathing muscles receive innervation signals from the intercostal spinal nerves which receive signals from the brain stem and other brain areas (Figure 2.21).

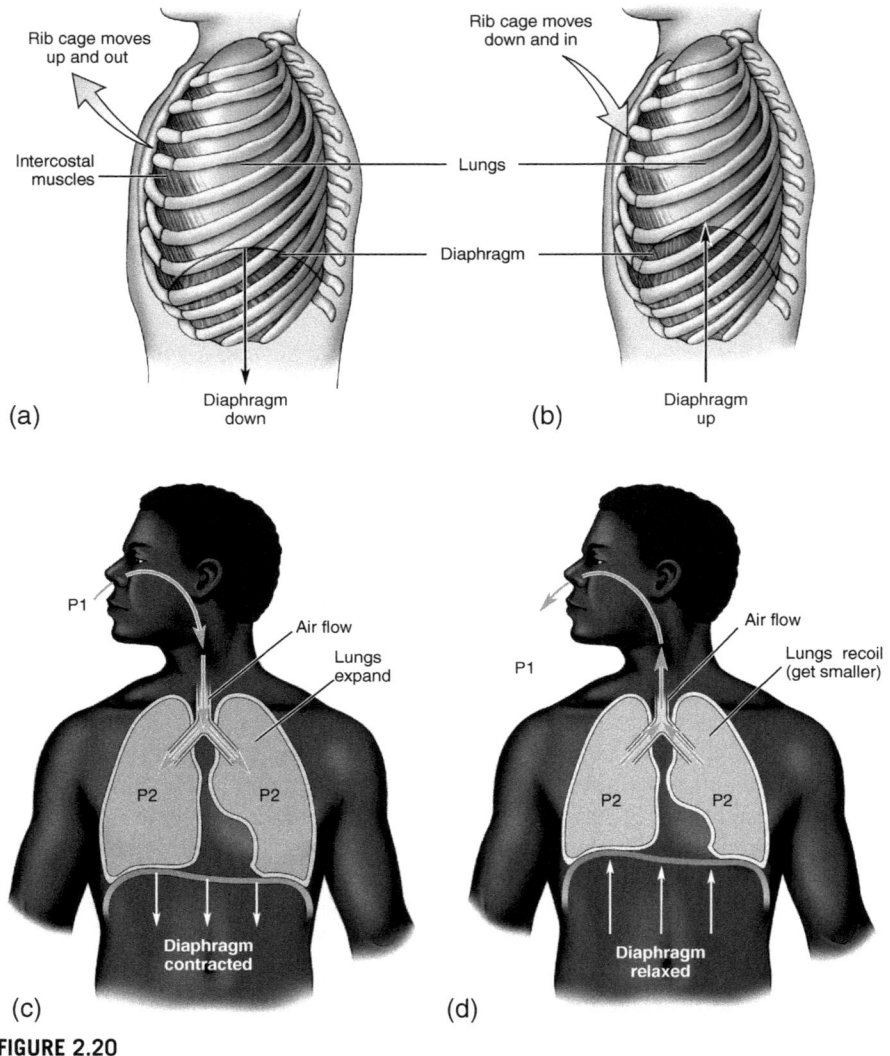

FIGURE 2.20

Dynamics of inhalation and exhalation. As the chest volume expands (a and c), air moves into the lungs. As the chest volume decreases (b and d), air moves out of the lungs.

From Herlihy (2014).

Based on various organ system activity, blood oxygen and carbon dioxide levels are changing continuously, sometimes dramatically. These chemical changes signal the brain stem areas which can alter breathing cycles to maintain or restore normal homeostatic gas levels in the blood (Figure 2.22).

Importantly, breathing cycles in the PDD setting can appear somewhat unusual when considering the "fight or flight" concept when the body is addressing

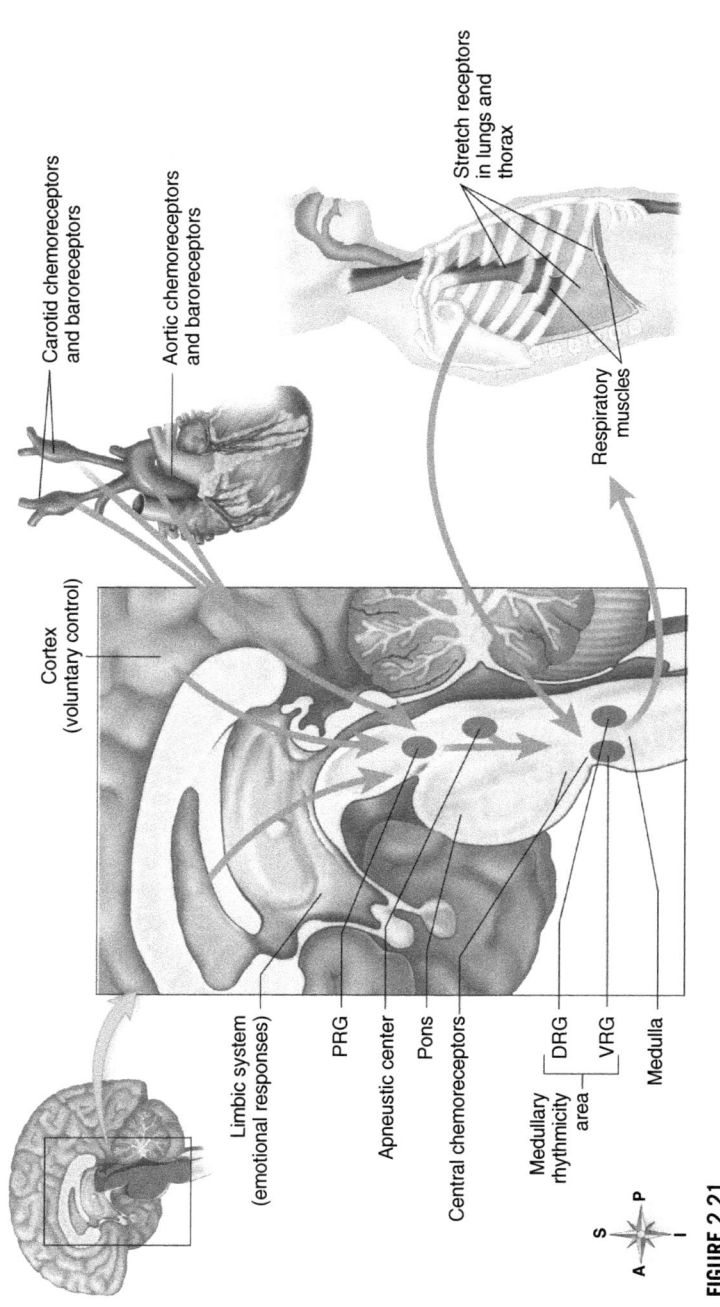

FIGURE 2.21

Regulation of breathing.

From Patton et al. (2012).

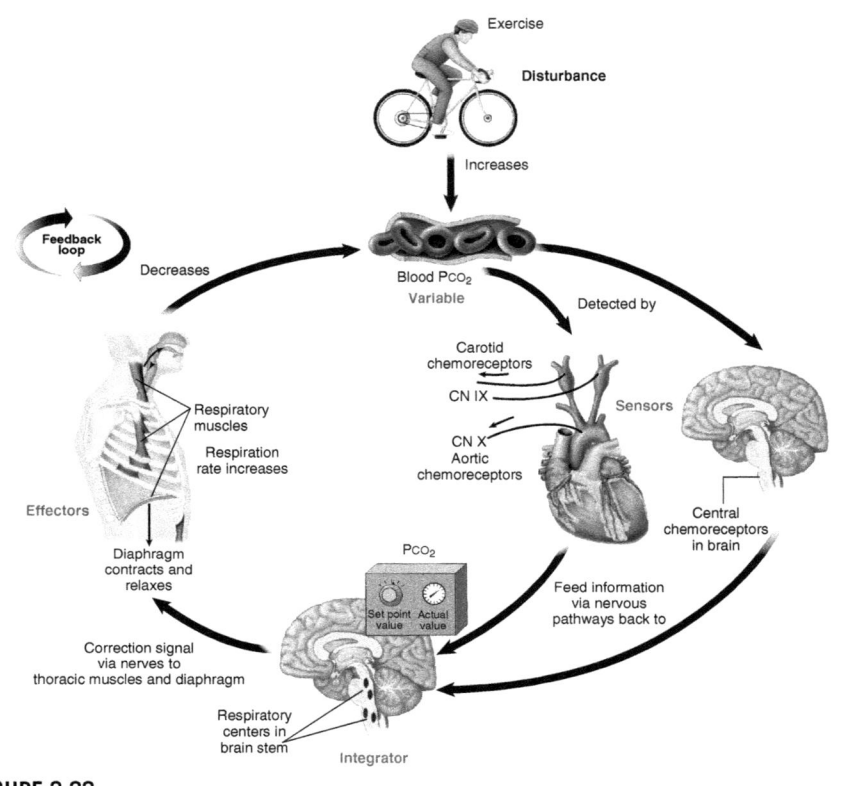

FIGURE 2.22

Feedback control of respiration.

From Patton et al. (2012).

a threatening situation. In the typical defensive body reaction to a stressful circumstance, breathing (ventilation) dynamics would dramatically increase to get more oxygen and nutrients to muscles and remove potentially toxic levels of carbon dioxide. Initially, these reactions begin with cognitive and emotional perception of the circumstance followed by blood chemistry changes brought about by vigorously contracting muscles. During the PDD examination, the examinee is instructed not to move. This lack of muscle contraction will not generate the typical change in blood chemistry, found in the physically active fight or flight response.

If an individual perceives the jeopardy of a situation, whether physical or otherwise, the sympathetic division will alter air and blood flow to the organ systems to address the matter. Concerning the respiratory system, the sympathetic pathway will release the neurotransmitter, norepinephrine to the muscles which dilate the diameter of the airway resulting in less resistance with a consequent increase in air flow to the lungs. Since muscle physiology in the arms and legs are not increasing as they would be in the physical fight or flight response, the respiratory system will get adequate air flow with fewer breathing cycles and less inhalation muscular dynamics.

The consequence of this sympathetic response in the PDD setting is a reduction in breathing cycles and a reduction in the intensity of inhalation in the breathing cycles. Reduced amplitude recordings of the breathing cycle can be observed when the subject perceives the question with greater jeopardy compared to other questions. The waveforms (tracings) recorded during these episodic breathing patterns become important signal values for the polygraph examiner.

In the blood vessel section, the expression "muscle pump" was described as assisting the circulatory system return of the blood to the heart by squeezing venous blood vessels located between muscles. In addition to the muscle pump, there is the "respiratory pump." The largest blood vessel in the body mentioned in the heart section is the inferior vena cava, located in the abdominal and thoracic (chest) cavity. It drains blood from all body organs and systems below the heart and returns it to the right atrium and right ventricle.

During the inspiration phase of breathing, when the diaphragm contracts downward it increases pressure in the abdominal cavity which compresses on the abdominal section of the inferior vena cava. Simultaneously, the chest cavity is expanding, reducing the pressure on the thoracic inferior vena cava. One might easily envision the compression in the lower section while releasing pressure in the upper section would generate pump like action, the respiratory pump. Furthermore, it may be easily visualized that the blood return to the heart will increase as breathing dynamics increase, such what would occur during exercise. Within limits, the heart will expand to accommodate the increase in blood return and pump more forcefully in the next cardiac cycle, which will raise blood pressure.

Typically, during an evening of sleep, blood pressure is relatively low. Upon waking, there will be a need to raise blood pressure to accommodate the vertical position and begin the day's activities. In preparation for the increase in physical activity a person may begin yawning and stretching which will activate the respiratory and muscular pumps, raising blood pressure. It is common for an individual to begin yawning and stretching after extended periods of immobility when the blood pressure falls in anticipation of resting or sleeping. When circumstances negate the lying down position, an increase in yawning dynamics and muscle stretching will help raise the blood pressure and keep the body alert.

In closing, the immobility of the polygraph subject, particularly if the examination is offered late in the day when fatigue is likely to set in, may generate occasional "deep breaths." These deep breaths, a somewhat minor yawn, will likely launch a reflective rise in blood pressure and an increase in EDA. The outcomes generated by the deep breath would, in effect, create a recording artifact. Furthermore, the intentional application of using the respiratory system to alter the other physiological recordings may be incorporated when the examinee is attempting countermeasures to defeat the polygraph data recordings.

CONCLUSION

The somewhat brief and contracted explanation of human anatomy and physiology in this chapter may be viewed by some students of PDD with academic life science backgrounds as rather an incomplete explanation and superficial in the subject matter. Other PDD students from the non-life science backgrounds may find this chapter presentation a bit overwhelming. Many students enter the PDD profession mid-career, coming from diverse academic disciplines, and it is a writer's challenge to present the subject material in a manner that is both informative and engaging for those arriving with different levels of previous experience. The focus of this chapter is to provide a common understanding of psychophysiological principles at the core of polygraph testing. The reader is encouraged to pursue more advanced studies which will bring about a deeper appreciation of this unique field.

ABOUT THE AUTHOR

Professor Emeritus, SUNY, Farmingdale: Discipline—Anatomy & Physiology, Membership: Human Anatomy and Physiology Society; Scientific Detection of Deception 1981-1982: American Polygraph Association, 1985; Adjunct Instructor National Center for Credibility Assessment (NCCA) 1997-present; Former Adjunct Instructor at three APA polygraph schools; Adjunct Instructor: Suffolk County Community College, 1980-present; Private polygraph practice, New York. Website: www.universitypolygraph.com; email contact: univpoly1@aol.com.

REFERENCES

Department of Health and Human Services, National Institutes of Health, National Institute on Deafness and Other Communication Disorders, 2015. Available at: http://www.nidcd.nih.gov/health/voice/pages/vocalparal.aspx.

Herlihy, B., 2014. The Human Body in Health and Illness, fifth ed. Saunders, St. Louis, MO.

Martini, F.H., Nath, J.L., Bartholomew, E.F., 2014. Fundamentals of Anatomy and Physiology, tenth ed. Pearson, San Francisco, CA.

National Heart, Lung, and Blood Institute; National Institutes of Health; U.S. Department of Health and Human Services, 2015. Available at: http://www.nhlbi.nih.gov/health/health-topics/topics/hlw/system.

Patton, K.T., Thibodeau, G.A., Douglas, M.M., 2012. Anatomy and Physiology. Mosby, St. Louis, MO.

CHAPTER 3

Test question construction

> *"That,"* said Don Quixote, *"is not and ought not to be called deception which aims at virtuous ends."*
> **Miguel de Cervantes Saavedra in *Don Quixote***

For polygraph examiners to extract meaning from an examinee's physiological reactions, attention must be given to the questions that elicit those reactions. Test question construction (TQC) is an essential skill for polygraph examiners, and the *sine qua non* for effective polygraph testing. TQC is neither entirely art nor science, though there are established scientific principles and collective experiences to draw upon for the development of guidelines. It is instructive to begin with a review of some scientific principles to understand the framework from which these guidelines come.

In the most general terms, cognitively generated physiological responding can be evoked by the novelty, intensity, or salience of the stimulus. In the context of polygraph testing, the stimuli are test questions.[1] The role of the examiner is to devise and present test questions that minimize differences in novelty and intensity among the questions. Salience, as will be taken up in a moment, may be more nuanced.

Examiners attempt to control for novelty by thoroughly discussing all of the test topics during the pretest interview. In this way, questions will be familiar to the examinee when testing begins. Every question is reviewed using exactly the same words as will be used in the testing phase. Therefore, the examinee will not perceive that something new has been added during testing. Asking an unreviewed question during the test phase will evoke a reaction, but that reaction would only demonstrate the examinee was capable of reacting, nothing more. The response would be of limited value for assessing deception to that question, or as a gauge against which to evaluate responses to other relevant questions inasmuch as it had been driven by a process different from that arising from the salience of the question.

---

[1] It might be important to address early the common misconception that physiological reactions are driven by the examinee's verbal lie. The act of lying may augment a physiological reaction in some cases, but the reaction is initially triggered by the test question. One obvious indicator of this fact is that the reactions typically begin before the examinee has answered. Also, examiners who include the Silent Answer Test in their examinations can attest that examinees respond to the same test questions irrespective of whether the examinees answer verbally. Finally, examiners can test the idea for themselves by conducting a Peak of Tension or Concealed Information Test on a willing volunteer, and have him answer "yes" to all questions. These tests will still work despite the fact that the examinee has verbally "lied" to all items except the key.

The second factor, the intensity of questions, can also be controlled during testing. Examiners use the same intensity of voice when presenting test questions while the examinee's physiology is recorded. Changing volume for one question, or category of question, can result in reactions generated by how the question is presented.

The third source for responses to a stimulus, salience (AKA signal value, personal significance), should emerge to the degree possible only from deceptiveness to the test question. A working definition for deception in a polygraph setting is that a person's statements about an event are not in accord with the memories of the event the person holds. If true, relevant questions should separate the truthful and deceptive examinees because, in properly devised questions, deceptive examinees will have memories associated with the question they are overtly denying, while innocent examinees will not. Both truthful and deceptive examinees should find comparison questions personally significant because they are likely to evoke memories they are withholding.

Salience can take the form of a gradient, as opposed to being all-or-none, in which different questions can have different degrees of salience.[2] Examinees who are deceptive to more than one question will not typically have equally strong physiological responses to all of them, but rather will have degrees of responsiveness that correspond with the differential salience engendered by the individual test questions.

The wrong kind of salience can be attached to test questions if the examiner is not careful. For example, evocative or taboo words are salient to nearly every examinee, as is the examinee's name, but not for the reason that allows inferences of deception. There is an entire field of study dedicated to determining the emotional content of words, which has not surprisingly found some words generate affective responses more than others (Bradley and Lang, 1999). Some of the differences are subtle and are not likely to induce physiological changes, while others are more powerful. Examiners should avoid using emotionally charged words in test questions whenever possible. In a murder investigation, as an illustration, examiners should not use verbs such as *slaughter*, *murder*, or *massacre*. These words may generate physiological responding among some examinees irrespective of truthfulness. The problem could be further compounded if the comparison questions use gentler terms like *hurt*, *hit*, or *strike*, which would be intrinsically less powerful than the more evocative verbs in the relevant questions. The results of the examination in which there are severe violations of this principle could be tipped in one or the other direction

---

[2] Older polygraph literature uses a concept called Psychological Set (PS) to explain why innocent and guilty examinees react to comparison and relevant questions, respectively. Briefly, PS posits that examinees respond because of fear of detection, and that they react to the strongest threat to their interests and not to others. The purported "fear of detection" rationale for polygraph reactions is challenged by the use of directed lies in polygraph testing, where there is no fear, and to the laboratory research showing differential physiological responding even in the absence of fear. The all-or-none effect predicted by PS, that guilty examinees do not react to comparison questions nor truthful examinees to relevant questions, is contrary to the experience of field examiners. These facts call for a reconsideration of the PS theory. The replacement theory would have to accommodate the effects missed by PS (see Chapter 9).

simply because of differences in emotional intensity of the words. Having words of comparable emotional force among the relevant and comparison questions, and none of them evocative in themselves (e.g., taboo words), reduces one source of reacting not associated with deception.

There are real world circumstances that make for exceptions to the rule regarding avoidance of taboo words. Testing of sex offenders can be one of those exceptions. It is not uncommon for these examinees to use crude or even obscene expressions for body parts and sexual activities. If these are the terms the examinee offers, and there is a common understanding between the examiner and examinee as to what they mean, the use of vulgar terms in test questions would be a better option than using medical or sophisticated words for which the examinee is unfamiliar. However, it is prudent to provide a justification in the technical notes and report of the examination when choosing to use taboo words in the relevant questions. As a more general rule, test questions should consider the culture, intelligence, vocabulary, and education of the examinee.

There is a second consideration regarding salience, and that is in the testing of potential victims of violent offenses. Recall that relevant questions should evoke a memory of the event in question. For the victim of a traumatic event such as rape or wartime actions that are central to the relevant issue, behaviorally descriptive questions about the event can summon recollections that may generate physiological responding even among truthtellers, for obvious reasons. Conducting polygraph testing under these conditions will require an adjustment to standard procedures using methods covered in Chapter 11.

The so-called "fear of detection" model has been offered to explain the reactions of guilty examinees during deception, though the model is certainly incomplete. It does appear to explain some degree of the profile of reactions if not the *per se* existence of reactions. Fear may interplay with salience in field conditions, generating stronger emotional reactions than occur in lab studies. This relationship might be better understood with the following example.

Suppose in a laboratory study participants who were assigned to the guilty condition would be directed to steal a ladder from a building on campus. Enactment of this pretended crime might have some level of engagement for the "thief" by virtual of its approximation to an actual offense. Now let's suppose under field conditions a ladder was stolen from campus which caused a worker to fall and become permanently disabled. An investigation finds a potential suspect for polygraph testing, who, as it turns out, did steal the ladder. Under both field and lab conditions the behavior of the "guilty" person might be the same (stealing a ladder), but because the potential consequences were greater in the field than in the laboratory, reactions to the test questions could be different. This was precisely the finding of Pollina et al. (2004). Though decision accuracy between laboratory and field cases in the Pollina study were not significantly different from each other (consistent with prediction that salience is the underlying phenomenon), there were larger reactions in field cases among physiological channels most closely associated with emotional responding.

If it is correct that salience is a central component to test question construction, it follows that better test questions should use clear descriptors of the behavior of interest. This is because examinee's more easily link vivid descriptors to their memories of the behavior. In this regard, relevant test questions should be sufficiently specific as to trigger a recollection from a guilty examinee, evoking an image of having done the behavior. This degree of particularity in question construction should remove ambiguity from the mind of truthful examinee. As an exaggerated example, consider which of the two relevant questions below is more likely to prompt a guilty examinee's memory of a crime involving identity theft.

1. Did you violate Public Law 108-275 on July 16th?
2. Did you use John Smith's identification information to transfer money from his First Savings and Loan account last week?

While both of these questions might address the same crime, Question 2 better represents how the examinee would recall what he had done. It also affords an innocent examinee certainty that he does not have a memory for this crime. For this reason, it would be the better approach.

With this general understanding regarding the psychological underpinnings of question construction, we move on to guidelines for developing test questions.

IRRELEVANT QUESTIONS

The irrelevant question is intended for several purposes. The important among them are: to establish stability, to facilitate recovery from a reaction or artifact, and to identify certain countermeasure strategies (Ansley, 1998). An overarching principle of the irrelevant question is that it must not evoke an emotional reaction. As such, irrelevant questions should be neutral, known to be true and unrelated to the relevant or comparison question issues.

Irrelevant questions can be answered *yes* or *no*. One method of ensuring that the examinee is paying attention during testing is to construct irrelevant questions for which the answer is the opposite of that to relevant and comparison questions, or even alternating irrelevant questions that have *yes* and *no* answers. When examinees answer irrelevant questions incorrectly, it may be a sign that they are not paying attention, or are trying to manipulate the examination. Some examiners use time-barred irrelevant questions.

EXAMPLES OF IRRELEVANT QUESTIONS

Is today Tuesday?
Are we in Virginia now?
Are you more than 18 years old?
Do you have a driver's license?
As an adult have you always been a US citizen?
Did you learn to drive before the age of 18?

RELEVANT QUESTIONS

In the most general terms, there are two types of relevant questions: primary and secondary. While all techniques use primary relevant questions, the inclusion of secondary relevant questions will depend on the testing technique. There are some general rules that apply to both types. In addition to describing the behavior, relevant questions should:

Be concise.

Example: On or about May 4th did you fire the bullet that ultimately led to the death of John Jones?
Better: Did you shoot John Jones?
Example: Did you participate in any way in the theft of that Vacheron Constantin Les Cabinotiers watch from the XYZ Jewelry store on Saginaw Street the week of November 7th?
Better: Did you steal that missing gold watch?

Be clearly understandable to the examinee.

Example: Did your actions result in critical O_2 deprivation to Mary Smith?
Better: Did you drown Mary Smith?
Example: Did you ignite a petroleum-based volatile substance near the rear egress of Toy Barn on Saturday?
Better: Did you start that fire at Toy Barn on Saturday?

Not be presumptive of guilt.

Example: After you stole that money, did you conceal it somewhere?
Better: Do you know where any of that stolen money is now?
Example: After you smashed the front window, did you take any electronics from the ABC Stereo Store?
Better: Did you steal any electronics from the ABC Stereo Store?

Not test for intentions, state of mind, or ask for an opinion.

Example: Did you intend to steal that jewelry?
Better: Did you steal that jewelry?
Example: Did you stab Fred Roberts because you were afraid of him?
Better: Did you stab Fred Roberts?

Avoid legalisms.

Example: Did you violate US Federal antibribery laws last year?
Better: Did you accept an unreported cash payment from the XYZ company?
Example: Have you ever committed espionage?
Better: Have you ever given classified information to anyone without a security clearance?

Not test for more than one issue per relevant question.

Example: Have you ever committed robbery, assault, or threaten physical harm to anyone?
Better: Have you ever committed a violent offense against anyone?
Example: Did you shoot that man and take his wallet?
Better: Did you shoot that man?

Directly address central details rather than tertiary facts.

Example: Did you cover JonBenét Ramsey with a blanket last Christmas?
Better: Did you choke JonBenét Ramsey with a cord?
Example: Did you cut the screen window of the Smart house the night of June 4th?
Better: Did you forcefully take Elizabeth Smart from her home last week?

In addition, during the discussion of relevant questions examiners should avoid revealing information that might be useful later for Peak of Tension or Concealed Information Tests. There is some benefit when such information is available to the examiner that he or she begins with a recognition test before moving on to deception testing.

One possible pitfall examiners should avoid is the blind acceptance of relevant questions recommended by advocates of the examinee, including the examinee's family members, legal counsel, representatives, or the examinee himself. These questions can potentially be crafted in such a way that the examinee can answer truthfully, though still be culpable for the crime. Relevant questions should be constructed from the perspective of an independent investigator, and never from that of an interested party. Examiners should generally be careful with questions proffered by any individual not trained in question construction, including the examiner's superiors, inasmuch as these questions may not always be suited to valid testing.

Examiners can also improve their multiple-issue examinations by giving attention to the uniqueness of the beginning of each relevant test question. This is because examinees normally recognize the question after the examiner has spoken the first few words. If all of the relevant questions begin with the same phrase (e.g., "Are you withholding any information about . . .) the examinee will not know the content of the question until the end of it. If the examinee intends to lie to one of the test questions, this method can evoke an anticipatory response which can complicate chart interpretation. Examiners are encouraged, therefore, to work toward developing relevant questions that do not share beginning phrases.

PRIMARY RELEVANT QUESTIONS

Primary relevant questions specifically address the underlying reason the examination is taking place. Essentially, they are the "did you do it" questions. They target the action or behavior that is the reason for the polygraph examination, and as described earlier, they should describe the event in terms that directly link a guilty person's mental image with the test question.

There are some cases in which investigators may not have full confidence in case details. This is often the case in robberies, where there may be motivation by the victim to exaggerate the loss. When missing money is the primary relevant area, the phrase "any of" should be included to address the possibility that the guilty person many not have taken all of the money reported stolen. Similarly, when more than one item has been stolen, vandalized, or destroyed, "any of" is also appropriate.

> Did you steal any of that missing money from the First Bank and Trust?
> Did you start any of those wildfires in Yellowstone Park last July?
> Did you strike any of those mailboxes on Maple Avenue last week?

During the development of relevant questions during the pretest interview, sometimes examinees will make admissions that require the questions be modified before testing. Suppose during a pretest interview a 38-year-old job applicant acknowledged stealing a car for 4 hours when he was 17 years old, a felony, but given the age of the applicant and the number of years since the crime, it may not disqualify the applicant. A test question about serious criminal activity could be amended to read "Other than what you told me, have you ever committed a serious crime?" The qualifying phrase is always placed at the beginning of the question when presenting relevant questions. Here are more examples:

> Other than what you told me, have you been out of the state without notifying your probation officer?
> Excluding those three times, since your probation began have you driven after drinking alcohol?
> Besides what we discussed, have you removed any classified materials without permission?

The relevant questions used with suspects are phrased to be answered "no", with very rare exception. Tests of victims and witnesses, however, often use relevant question that can be answered "yes". For example:

> Did you purchase marijuana from John Smith?
> Did you see Joe Jones shoot at that man?
> Last Wednesday did that man hold a knife against your body?
> Did Jane Doe tell you she intended to poison John Doe?

Some examiners, accustomed to testing suspects, may try to force-fit that approach to testing witnesses and victims, that is, compose test questions for a "no" answer. They may phrase their test questions such as: Did you lie about being robbed last week; or, Is your police report about your car being stolen false? Unless the examinee experienced emotional trauma during the event, it is better to test about the event directly than to test about what they said about the event. For this reason, "yes" answered relevant questions are appropriate.

SECONDARY RELEVANT QUESTIONS

Secondary relevant questions focus on ancillary aspects that tie the guilty examinee to the crime, such as helping, planning, concealing, or providing any type of support for a crime. They should describe the activity, and the linkage between the activity and the crime should be obvious:

> Did you handle any of those weapons after they were stolen?
> Did you help someone steal any of that missing cash?
> Were you present when Fred Johnson was stabbed?
> Do you know where the stolen gold is right now?
> Did you cut that woman's clothing?
> Did you plan with John Wilkes Booth to kill the President?

PROBABLE-LIE COMPARISON QUESTIONS

Probable-lie comparison (PLC) questions have been included in most polygraph techniques since the 1950s. They are useful to determine whether the examinee is capable of responding, and as a gauge against which to compare reactions elicited by relevant questions. Like relevant questions, PLC questions should evoke memories, or at least a sense that there may be memories, regarding past behaviors of significance but not specific to the relevant questions. Examiners should be able to convey a rationale for including these questions in the test.

Comparison questions that are too weak or too strong can affect the numerical scores, and consequently the ability to arrive at a definitive and accurate decision. Comparison questions operate on what might be called the "Goldilocks Principle[3]," because they must not be "too hot" nor "too cold," but "just right." They must be carefully chosen and introduced to each examinee to achieve high accuracy. Shortcuts in PLC development and execution may lead to decrements in accuracy.

General rules for all PLCs are that they should:
Not be confused with the relevant topic.

Crime: Burglary of a department store
Example: Have you ever stolen anything from a department store?
Better: Have you ever stolen anything?

Be a probable lie.

Crime: Vandalism by spray painting a car
Example: Did you ever hit anyone's house with a brick?
Better: Have you ever damaged anything out of anger?

---

[3] For those unfamiliar with this children's fictional bedtime story, Goldilocks is a child character who enters the home of a family of bears who had departed for a walk in the forest. In part of the story Goldilocks tries the bowls of porridge of the father, mother and baby bear, and finds their porridge too hot, too cold, and just right, respectively.

Be meaningful to the examinee.

Crime: Counterfeiting currency
Example: Did you ever fall asleep in class?
Better: Did you ever place false information on a government form?

There is also a firm guideline regarding the selection of verbs used in PLCs that correspond with the relevant questions. The list below shows the recommended matches between PLCs and relevant questions:

Relevant Question Topic	PLC Topics
Assault/Murder	Harm/Hurt/Injure
Bomb Threat/Bombing	Harm/Hurt/Injure
Child Abuse (Physical)	Harm/Hurt/Injure
Child Abuse (Sexual)	Adult Sexual Activities
Confirmatory Testing	Betray Trust/Cheat/Lie
Destruction/Vandalism	Damage/Destroy
Drug Possession	Possession of nondrug illegal items
Drug Use	Lying (except about drug use)
Forgery	Cheat/Falsification
Robbery/Theft	Deceive/Cheat/Steal/Trick
Sexual Assault	Sex/Lie about Sexual Activities[a]
Threats of Harm	Harm/Hurt/Injure/Threaten

[a]Sex offenders often have extensive histories of sexual crimes. Care must be taken when using a comparison question about sex with these examinees inasmuch as they may be more salient than the relevant questions for even guilty examinees. Many examiners eschew these kinds of comparison questions entirely for that reason, using questions about lying instead.

A common practice, indeed a policy for some organizations, is to devise comparison questions that require a "no" answer. Empirical evidence supporting this preference is lacking. Nonetheless, there is no reason to believe that the requirement would diminish accuracy. When tests use relevant questions that call for a "yes" answer (e.g., confirmation testing), examiners have the discretion to use "yes" answer PLCs.

There are two schools of thought about which PLC questions are better: the broad ones that implicitly encompass the relevant issue, and those that use phrases that explicitly exclude the relevant issue. Some schools teach that PLCs must be separated from the relevant question by time, place, or category. The other side teaches that PLCs must be as broad as possible, and contend that placing exclusions on the PLCs works against making these PLCs effective. Both types are covered here, so that examiners may choose those that fit their methods. The available evidence indicates that explicit separators between relevant and comparison questions are not necessary so long as the PLC is broad. Those who use exclusionary PLCs may wish to continue with their preferences, as much of the supporting research on the Comparison Question Test rests on these types of PLCs. However, so long as the PLCs are not explicitly relevant, current evidence indicates nonexclusionary PLCs can be at least equally effective.

EXCLUSIONARY PHRASES

The rationale for exclusionary PLCs is to ensure that the probable-lie comparison question does not accidentally become a relevant question. In the following section some exclusionary phrases examiners might use with their comparison questions if they prefer this approach are given. These phrases must be selected according to the relevant issue, case facts, and history of the examinee. Examiners should also be mindful that the final wording of the comparison question must be a probable lie, and using too restrictive of language will reduce the probability. Also, if using exclusionary phrases with PLCs, the same phrase should not be used for all PLCs. Finally, examiners should be sensitive to the prospect that examinees planning to engage in countermeasures try to identify comparison questions by looking for exclusionary phrases. Examiners can improve their chances of a successful examination by disguising the comparison questions, or at least avoiding the tendency to use stock phrases that sound similar or obvious. The exclusionary phrases below are usually placed at the beginning of the PLC, but some examiners use them at the end of the question.

> During your 20s,
> Before this year,
> While in high school,
> Before coming into the military,
> When you were in the military,
> Between the ages of 18 and 25,
> Before moving to this area,
> When you were in college,
> Prior to the year,
> At your last job,
> When you lived in,
> As a child/teen,
> As a soldier,
> Not related to this incident,

EXAMPLES OF PLCs

Because of differences among examinees and circumstances, no list of comparison questions could cover every possibility. The lists found here include the more common questions that might be useful in most polygraph examinations. Polygraph examiners must tailor their questions to the facts of the case and the characteristics of the examinee. While examiners may find the suggested questions to be very useful, the questions were designed as potential areas for an examiner to explore when designing the final comparison question. Exclusionary phrases can be added for those examiners or programs that require them.

Physical attacks (e.g., homicides, assaults, robberies, etc.)

> Have you ever wanted to hurt someone badly?
> Have you ever threatened anyone with physical harm?

Have you ever thought about hurting another person?
Have you ever hurt anyone (close to you)?
Have you ever harmed anyone out of revenge?
Have you ever harmed anyone out of spite?
Have you ever harmed anyone out of anger?
Have you ever lost your temper and struck anyone?
Have you ever done anything to get even with someone?
Have you ever hurt a living creature out of meanness?
Have you ever lied about hurting another person?
Have you ever had a desire to hurt someone?
Have you ever hurt someone deliberately but claim it was accidental?
Have you ever done something malicious to someone you were angry with?
Has anyone ever seen you damaging something in a state of anger?
Were there any occasions when you would have hurt someone badly if the circumstances would have allowed it?
Have you ever wished someone would die or be seriously injured?
Have you ever done anything that would hurt another person?
Is there anyone who would say that you deliberately hurt them?
Has your temper ever caused you to hurt someone?

Sex Crimes

Have you ever done anything sexually unusual?
Have you ever lied about your sexual activities?
Have you ever fantasized about having sex with an underage girl?
Have you ever touched someone sexually without permission?
Have you ever done anything sexually you are ashamed of?
Have you ever touched yourself sexually in a public place?
Have you ever used pornography (excessively) for sexual purposes?
Have you ever wanted to have sex with someone under the age of 18?
Have you ever tried to view anyone's private parts without her permission?
Have you ever tried to have sex with anyone after she said "no?"
Have you ever taken part in an unusual sex act?
Have you ever done anything sexually unusual that no one knows about?
Have you ever done anything sexually that you would not want anyone to know about?
Have you ever done anything sexually that you would lie about if asked?
Have you ever thought about touching a young girl's private parts?
Have you ever done anything during a sex act that would be considered excessive?
Have you ever been sexually excited by something not normal?
Have you ever thought out a plan on how you could have sex with an underage girl?
Have you ever seen (tried to see) the private parts of a girl or woman without her knowledge?
Have you ever done anything sexual that could bring shame to your loved ones?

Damage to Property (e.g. vandalism, sabotage, arson, etc.)

Have you ever damaged anything?
Have you ever (deliberately/intentionally) broken the property of someone else?
Have you ever (deliberately/intentionally) broken something without taking responsibility for the damage?
Have you ever caused any damage to someone else's belongings?
Has your temper ever brought you to breaking anything?
Have you ever damaged someone's personal property out of revenge?
Have you ever (deliberately/intentionally) broken something that was not yours?
Have you ever thought about damaging someone's property for any reason?
Have you ever destroyed any object that was not your own?
Have you ever been tempted to break something out of anger to get even with someone?
Have you ever lied about damaging someone's property?
Have you ever damaged any schoolbooks or property in the school you attended?
Have you ever done anything malicious to someone's belongings?
Have you ever been present when someone damaged or destroyed someone else's property, and you hid this information?
Was there anyone whose property was broken due to your actions or neglect?
Have you ever damaged anyone's belongings and not gotten caught?
Have you ever been tempted to break the belongings of someone else just for fun?
Have you ever marred or defaced anyone's property?
Have you ever damaged any public property?
Have you ever reduced the value of anyone's personal property by a malicious act?

Stealing

Have you ever stolen anything?
Have you ever cheated anyone?
Have you ever obtained anything dishonestly?
Have you ever stolen anything from a store?
Have you ever stolen anything from an employer?
Have you ever stolen anything from a friend?
Have you ever cheated a friend?
Have you ever been tempted to steal something you wanted badly?
Have you ever cheated on your taxes?
Have you ever stolen anything worth more than $_____?
Have you ever left a job with property belonging to your employer?
Have you ever cheated anyone out of anything?
Have you ever lied about stealing anything?
Have you ever padded your expense account?
Have you ever stolen something that you would not want your family to find out about?
Have you ever been caught stealing anything?

Have you ever stolen anything on impulse?
Have you ever taken someone's property that you really didn't need?
Have you ever dishonestly taken someone else's belongings?
Have you ever taken property to your home that was stolen from somewhere?

Lying (e.g., false police report, perjury, etc.)

Have you ever lied to cover up something?
Have you ever lied for personal gain?
Have you ever knowingly falsified tax information?
Have you ever lied to a person in a position of authority?
Have you ever lied about someone else?
Have you ever lied to get someone into trouble?
Have you ever lied to make yourself look better?
Have you ever lied to someone who trusted you?
Have you ever spread lies about someone?
Have you ever lied behind someone's back?
Have you ever shifted responsibility for your error to someone else?
Have you ever lied to an employer?
Have you ever done anything that would dishonor your family if it were known?
Have you ever blamed someone else for your mistake?
Have you ever gossiped?
Have you ever done anything unethical?
Have you ever misrepresented the truth for your personal benefit?
Have you ever betrayed a trust?
Have you ever done anything that would cause others to question your honesty?
Have you ever lied about something important?

Victims of Sexual Offenses

Did you ever lie about something important?
Have you ever lied to make yourself look more important?
Have you ever gossiped about a friend or coworker?
Have you ever told a lie to someone who trusted you?
Have you ever lied to someone in a position of authority?
Have you ever lied to cover up a mistake or accident?
Have you ever lied to advance your own interests at the expense of someone else?
Did you ever say something hurtful about another person because you were angry?

DIRECTED LIE COMPARISON QUESTIONS

The directed lie approach was a solution used by field examiners to overcome the problem of habituation to comparison questions for examinees who were tested repeatedly over short periods of time, initially used by US Army examiners during the Vietnam War (Menges, 2004). They are now commonly used in the first phase of screening examinations, such as the Test for Espionage and Sabotage and some forms of the Air Force Modified General Question Test including the Law Enforcement Preemployment Test. Their use in specific-issue testing is less well developed empirically.

The directed lie comparison (DLC) question method has a number of advantages over PLCs. They entail no manipulation of the examinee, are easier to implement and standardize, and can help avoid resistance from examinees. When properly used they are more resistant to habituation over multiple examinations. They also garner fewer complaints from examinees, an important consideration for large screening programs.

General rules for all DLCs are that they should:

Not be confused with the relevant screening topics.
Involve minor transgressions most people commit.
Not embarrass the examinee.
Not be "set" as are PLCs.
Encompass the examinee's entire life.

Introduction of DLCs is fairly straightforward. Examinees are informed that there will be two kinds of questions on the test: those to which they must answer truthfully (previously discussed and reviewed), and others where the examinee will be directed to lie. The examiner should explain that the latter type of question is to confirm that the examinee is capable of responding throughout the test. Then the DLCs are reviewed individually. The examinee must acknowledge that he has committed the minor transgression, but the examiner must ensure the examinee does not say what he had done. The examinee must then be told to answer "no" to the question despite knowing he has done the thing in the question. The examiner should read the question once again and have the examinee answer to ensure he understands the instructions to answer "no". Further reinforcement of the significance of the DLC is unnecessary in most cases, and excessive emphasis brings with it more chance of error.

EXAMPLES OF DLCs

Did you ever borrow anything and forget to return it?
Did you ever lie to make yourself look more important?
Did you ever brag about yourself to impress others?
Did you ever say anything in anger that you later regretted?
Did you ever say anything about someone that wasn't true?
Did you ever exaggerate your accomplishments?
Did you ever do anything that you knew would make a friend mad at you?
Did you ever cheat at a game?
Did you ever intentionally lie to a close friend?
Did you ever violate a state traffic (or hunting, construction, etc.) law?
Did you ever lie to a supervisor about anything?
Did you ever commit a minor traffic violation?

Did you ever say anything negative about another person behind his back?
Did you ever take any employer office supplies for your personal use?
Did you ever lose your temper?

OTHER COMMON QUESTIONS

Some techniques have unique technical questions. They include the sacrifice relevant and the symptomatic (sometimes called "outside issue") question. These questions have specific wording.

SACRIFICE RELEVANT QUESTION

This question originated with Cleve Backster in the early 1960s. It was intended to introduce the relevant topic with a question that was not used for interpretation or scoring. It was "sacrificed" for the purpose of orienting the examinee to the issue of the examination. Though subsequent research specific to this type of question is minimal and equivocal, the sacrifice relevant question has been included in techniques that have undergone replicated studies and validation. It is found in all forms of the Zone Comparison Test, all versions of the Air Force Modified General Question Test, the Test for Espionage and Sabotage, and others.

Sacrifice Relevant questions are generally designed to be answered "yes", and appear early in the test question sequence, most often in the second position. Phrasing is something similar to:

Regarding the (relevant topic), do you intend to answer each question truthfully?

In the case of a burglary, for instance, the question might be:

Regarding the break-in of 1234 Maple Street last week, do you intend to answer each question truthfully?

A comparable approach has been used in screening examinations, where there are two or more relevant topics tested. To accommodate this fact, the sacrifice relevant question might be broader to address the general areas of the examination. For example:

Concerning national security issues, do you intended to answer each question truthfully?
Concerning the information about your application process, do you intend to answer each question truthfully?
Regarding the security questions we discussed, do you intended to answer each question truthfully?

SYMPTOMATIC QUESTIONS

This was also a Backster concept from the 1960s. It is predicated on the assumption that when examinees fail to react to any question on the examination, it may be because of an overwhelming concern about something outside of the scope of the test. Backster hypothesized that a strong distraction could diminish reactivity to relevant and comparison questions that is essential for making decisions. Research on the symptomatic question has been sparse and unsupportive, though the question continues to be widely used by practitioners. Symptomatic questions have been incorporated into many versions of the Zone Comparison Test, including the Backster, Federal, Matte, Integrated, and others. They are not used in any non-Zone techniques. Symptomatic questions are not scored, but in the initial conception the combination of reactivity to symptomatic questions and flat responsiveness on other questions would signal that an outside issue was affecting the examination. In such cases examiners were expected to reassure the examinee there were no other test issues, and return to testing. In the field, however, this practice has fallen into disuse for most examiners.

Here are a few commonly phrased symptomatic questions:

Do you believe I will not ask you any unreviewed questions?
Do you believe I will only ask you the questions we reviewed?
Is there something else you are afraid I will ask you a question about?

INTRODUCTORY QUESTION

The Utah Probable Lie Test uses a question that has some similarities in appearance to the symptomatic question. It is placed in the first position of the test question sequence. It is not used for any technical purpose. Called the "Introductory Question," it is phrased as:

Do you understand I will only ask you questions we have reviewed?

LESS COMMON QUESTIONS

Some polygraph techniques include test questions that are unique or not frequently used. As such, they are discussed here only briefly so that examiners may recognize them if they review the work of examiners who use them.

COUNTERMEASURE QUESTION

In the earlier years of polygraph testing examiners would use the Countermeasure Question, anticipating reactions when an examinee intended to manipulate the physiological data in some way (e.g., use of drugs, covert muscle movements, etc.) There are isolated anecdotal reports of success with the Countermeasure Question, but research under controlled conditions has not been supportive. As a method to detect countermeasures, this question has been largely abandoned by most examiners. A standard Countermeasure Question might be:

Have you done anything to beat this test?
Did you deliberately do anything to try and beat this test?
Regarding drugs, are you holding back information about any drugs or medication you have taken during the last 12 hours?

GUILT COMPLEX QUESTION

This question was introduced by the late John Reid (1947) in the same seminal article that he first described the probable-lie approach to polygraphy. One can do no better than Reid's original description:

> *The "guilt complex" question is based upon an entirely fictitious crime of the same type as the actual crime under investigation, but one which is made to appear very realistic to the subject. For instance, if the subject is being examined regarding an actual murder at 222 Superior Street on December 1, 1945, he may also be asked, as a "guilt complex" question about an entirely fictitious killing on March 17, 1945, at 1121 State Street, an address familiar to the examiner and at which he definitely knows no murder was committed....The purpose of the "guilt complex" or fictitious crime question is to determine if the subject, although innocent, is unduly apprehensive because of the fact that he is suspected and interrogated about the crime under investigation. A reaction to the fictitious crime question which is greater than or about the same as that to the actual crime question would be indicative of truthtelling and innocence respecting the real offense. (p. 545)*

Today the Guilt Complex Question is little used, and there is no published research about it. The concept appears reasonable, and the question may be a good choice in rare cases.

HOPE/FEAR QUESTIONS

In 1978 James Matte extended Backster's hypothesis regarding the outside issue question and added two additional questions. One addressed the concern of the truthful examinee that the examination will result in a false positive error (calling the truthful examinee deceptive) and the other the hope of a guilty examinee that the examiner will make an error by calling him truthful. The questions were placed together in the question sequence as follows:

Are you afraid an error will be made on this test?
Are you hopeful an error will be made on this test?

The pretest interview of the Matte method was augmented with careful instructions about the meaning, and implications, of these test questions. They were scored just as if they were a pairing of relevant/PLC questions, with the first of the pair considered a comparison question. There were also intricate scoring rules that accompany the technique.

Matte's own field research and that of other advocates have found accuracy of the Matte method approaching or meeting perfection. Others have pointed to potential methodological flaws in the research that could have inflated the accuracy estimates beyond those of other more closely grouped Zone-type techniques. The Hope/Fear Questions are not used with any other technique.

OVERALL TRUTH

Users of the Relevant-Irrelevant Screening Test sometimes add what is called an Overall Truth question. The purpose is to verify that an examinee is capable of responding. They are ordinarily placed early or late in the test question sequence, and not used for interpretation of the physiological data. Most often, they are designed to be answered "no."

> Do you intend to lie to any question on this test?
> Did you lie to any question on this test?

POSITIVE CONTROL

First proposed by Golden (1969) as the "Yes-No Technique", the Positive Control Technique was advocated by others using a testing approach with only relevant and irrelevant questions. Each question was asked twice in a row. The examinee was instructed to answer the first presentation with a lie, and the second time truthfully. In most cases, examinees would answer "yes" the first time, and "no" on the second. The Positive Control Technique enjoyed some followers in the 1970s and 1980s (Gordon, 1982; Howland, 1978; Reali, 1978) but interest in this method has waned.

CONCLUSION

What readers of this chapter may have garnered is that test question construction requires a degree of training and experience to become proficient, and can be far more nuanced than generally appreciated by those outside of the profession. Examiners who follow the principles of good test question construction are more likely to produce valid results, have a reduction in inconclusive outcomes, and provide more value to their clients, agencies, and departments. While acknowledging the need to tailor questions to the circumstances, examiners should also recognize that significant departures from the recommended guidelines may be easier, faster, and make some customers happy (e.g., entertainment industry, high-volume clients), but they incur increases in the risk of error. Examiners who adhere to best practices in question construction and their other professional duties will represent themselves, and the profession, far better.

REFERENCES

Ansley, N., 1998. The irrelevant question: a descriptive review. Polygraph 27 (4), 276–283.
Bradley, M.M., Lang, P.J., 1999. Affective Norms for English Words (ANEW): Stimuli, Instruction Manual, and Affective Ratings (Tech. Report C-1). University of Florida Center for Research in Psychophysiology, Gainesville, FL.
Golden, R.I., 1969. The yes-no technique in polygraph testing. In: Paper Presented at the American Polygraph Association Annual Seminar, Houston, TX.

References

Gordon, N.J., 1982. The positive control concept and technique. Polygraph 11 (4), 330–342.

Howland, D.P., 1978. An application of the positive control concept of polygraph examinations. Polygraph 7 (4), 286–294.

Matte, J.A., 1978. Polygraph quadri-zone comparison technique. Polygraph 9 (4), 266–280.

Menges, P.M., 2004. Directed lie comparison questions in polygraph examinations: History and methodology. Polygraph 33 (3), 131–142.

Pollina, D., Dollins, A.B., Senter, S.M., Krapohl, D.J., Ryan, A.H., 2004. A comparison of polygraph data obtained from individuals involved in mock crimes and actual criminal investigations. J. Appl. Psychol. 89 (6), 1099–1105.

Reali, S.F., 1978. Reali's positive control technique. Polygraph 7 (4), 281–285.

Reid, J.E., 1947. A revised questioning technique in lie-detection tests. J. Crim. L. Criminol. 37, 542–557.

CHAPTER 4

Data collection

> *"Dr. Reiland,"* Trant went on more somberly, *"you have taught me the use of the cardiograph, by which the effect upon the heart of every act and passion can be read as a physician reads the pulse chart of his patient; the pneumograph, which traces the minutest meaning of the breathing; the galvanometer, that wonderful instrument which, though a man hold every feature and muscle passionless as death, will betray him through the sweat glands in the palms of his hands."*
>
> From ***The Achievements of Luther Trant*** (Balmer and MacHarg, 1910)

Interpretable polygraph data is not just essential to the polygraph decision process; it is one of the key characteristics that distinguishes the professional examiner. Exceptional interview skills, perfect test questions, expensive instrumentation, or sophisticated algorithms cannot compensate for haste or shortcuts in data collection. Investment in best-recording practices is repaid by a reduction of inconclusive results, reduction in rejections by quality control reviewers, and reduction in criticism in court. And if these reasons were not already sufficient, there is a very practical reason for giving attention to these steps: it will actually make the job of the examiner easier. Care here will give the examiner more confidence in the test results, and ultimately resolve more cases.

There are four distinct steps in polygraph data collection: preparing the examinee, placing the sensors, setting the display, and if necessary, troubleshooting. Because by now most polygraph examiners have made the transition to computer polygraphs, this section has been directed toward digital systems. With the exception of setting the display, the following steps apply to all types of polygraphs.

EXPLAINING SENSORS TO THE EXAMINEE

There is value in letting the examinee know what the sensors do and what the examinee may experience during testing, especially if it is his first polygraph examination. The explanations need not be in agonizing detail. Indeed, examinees are not normally prepared for deep technical discussions in the early portion of an exam, and providing too much information is not helpful. However, letting the examinee know what to expect in general terms will reduce general anxiety, and promote more stable data. It is important to touch on the fact that the testing process will not hurt the examinee, and to reinforce the message that he needs to follow instructions if the examination is to be successful.

Below are some simple scripts for explaining each of the sensors, which should be altered to meet individual style preferences. The order in which the examiner chooses to explain the sensors is optional. The order here is arbitrary, but it does correspond with the suggested sequence of sensor placement on the body. Some examiners pick the sensors up in their hands as they discuss them for illustration purposes, and to emphasize that they are safe.

GENERAL INTRODUCTION

In the course of today's examination, I will give you several tests. This is a standard procedure, and you should not read anything into having the test repeated a few different times. The tests will all have the same questions, which we will review first. During the testing I will turn on each of these sensors and begin to record physiological activity in your body. In a moment I'm going to place the polygraph sensors on you, but before I do I'd like to explain what they do.

PNEUMOGRAPHS

I have here on the desk two sensors. One of them will be placed around you just below your heart, and the other just above your heart. You will barely notice them during the test. They are sensitive to movements in the upper half of your body, all kinds of movements including changes in posture, muscle movements, and breathing.[1]

ELECTRODERMAL

For these next two sensors I'll be placing sensor pads on the palm of your hand. They will pick up minute changes in perspiration on the surface of your skin. I'm not too concerned if your hands are a little wet right now; most peoples' are. If your hands suddenly get dryer or wetter, these sensors are designed to detect it. During the test I will be recording the level of perspiration on your hands at each given moment.

Or:

For these next two sensors I'll be placing these plates on your fingertips. They will pick up minute changes in perspiration on the surface of your skin. I'm not too concerned if your hands are a little wet right now; most peoples' are. If your hands suddenly get dryer or wetter, these sensors are designed to detect it. During the test I will be recording the level of perspiration on your hands at each given moment.

---

[1] There is tentative evidence that mentioning breathing during the pretest interview can draw excessive attention to it for some examinees, and prompt very controlled respiration. For this reason examiners may choose to exclude references to breathing.

PHOTOPLETHYSMOGRAPH

I'll also be placing this sensor on the same hand. The clip will go over the end of one of your fingers. If you look closely you can see a small red light inside. This light is designed to detect blood flow in your hand during the test. It will not cause any discomfort, but like all of the sensors, it is very sensitive to movements, so you'll have to make sure you do not move your hand during the tests.

CARDIOVASCULAR

This is a standard blood pressure cuff, which I will place on your upper arm. It might look familiar since it's just like the one your doctor uses. At the beginning of each of today's tests I will place a little bit of air in the cuff, and it will stay that way for a few minutes. The pressure is less than a third of what your doctor uses to test your blood pressure, but nonetheless a few people say they feel a little tingling in their arm. If this happens to you, don't worry. The tests are kept very short, only about four minutes, and the air is let out immediately after each test.

MOTION SENSOR

Finally, there is a sensor placed on the seat of your chair. It will tell me of any movement in the lower half of your body: your feet, calves, and upper legs. Sometimes people accidentally move during testing in a way that might affect the things we record on the polygraph, and this sensor will alert me if this happens.

SENSOR PLACEMENT
PNEUMOGRAPH SENSORS

Respect for the examinee's sense of body modesty is of the utmost importance during the placement of the pneumograph sensors, especially when the examinees are women. Examiners should take deliberate care to demonstrate professionalism. Talking casually about the process as the sensors are placed can often reassure the examinee in a way that silence may not.

Begin by standing to the side of the examinee, and asking him to place his hands together over his head. It is sometimes helpful to demonstrate the position. With the pneumograph sensor[2] in one hand, reach around the lower torso of the examinee, and grasp the end of the sensor with the other hand. Pull the sensor around the examinee, with the sensor centered over the sternum, and attach the ends of the connector, either beaded chain or cloth strap. Repeat this step with the upper pneumograph sensor, centering it on the upper chest with the beaded chain or cloth strap coming at about the bottom of the arm pits. Ask the examinee to lower his arms again. The distension

---

[2] Some instruments require that the pneumograph system be vented or open before placing the sensors on the examinee, and securely closed before testing.

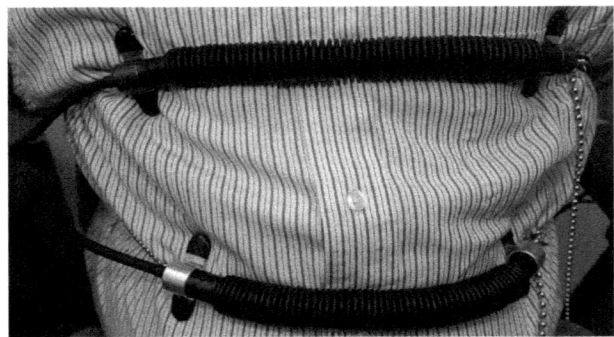

FIGURE 4.1

Proper placement of the pneumograph sensors.

Photos courtesy of the Lafayette Instrument Company.

of both sensors should be about an inch, and the anti-roll bars firmly against the torso. The sensors should not be so loose as to slide from their positioning, but not so tight as to cause discomfort or loss of signal. Hoses cannot be crimped, nor allowed to be on the floor space where they can create a tripping hazard. See Figure 4.1 for proper placement of the pneumograph sensors.

ELECTRODERMAL SENSORS

First, a general comment about electrodermal recording: it is important that there be a good connection between the dermis and the sensor. If the examinee has unusually thick skin (e.g., bricklayers) or injured skin (those that work with harsh chemicals), you may have to place your sensors on the back of the hand rather than the palmer surface. In exceptional circumstances (e.g., the examinee has no hands), adequate recordings can be achieved with sensors placed on the inside of the foot, between the ankle and the large joint for the big toe (Edelberg, 1967). As a truly last choice, sides of the forehead are also a possible location for adhesive pad sensors.

It is a standard practice to place the electrodermal sensors on the hand opposite the side where the cardiograph cuff was positioned. This is because blood in the arm is partially occluded during testing, and in some situations may generally dampen electrodermal activity in the hand overall.

There are two important technical issues to keep in mind with the placement of EDA sensors: the coupling between the sensor and the skin, and the number of sweat glands between the sensors. In an ideal situation there is a perfect melding of the sensor with the skin, and the greatest concentration of sweat glands between the sensors. If there is any change in amount of surface area of the sensor in contact with the skin, there will be a change in the tracing that is unrelated to EDA. Also remember that the EDA sensors do not detect changes in EDA *under* the sensors; they detect changes *between* the sensors.

If using the adhesive pads for recording electrodermal activity (recommended), remember that the gel may take a few minutes to permeate the skin and establish a good coupling. Some examiners place the pads on the examinee before any of the other sensors to allow a little extra time for the coupling to complete. One sensor should be placed on the palm at the base of the thumb, and the second on the other side of the base of the hand or base of the little finger (see Figure 4.2). Once you have placed the sensors, they can be snapped to the connector wire at any time. If you intend to conduct an acquaintance test as the first chart, and the examinee will need his hand free to write, you need not snap on the connector wire until just before testing.

If the metal plates are used, they should be placed at the end segment of two nonconsecutive fingers (see Figure 4.3). Placing the sensors apart minimizes the risk of them coming in contact with one another and causing a spike in the tracing. Ensure the skin is clean and dry. The examinee may have to wash his hands if they are dirty or sweaty. It can also help to clean the fingers with an alcohol swab, ensuring the alcohol does not come in contact with open cuts that might cause pain. Wrap the Velcro® straps around the finger so that the sensors are snug against the skin. In terms of snugness, it should be about the same as when applying an adhesive bandage. If the sensor is too loose, it will slip and alter the surface contact with the skin. If it is too tight the examinee may feel his pulse in his fingers, or the fingers may show

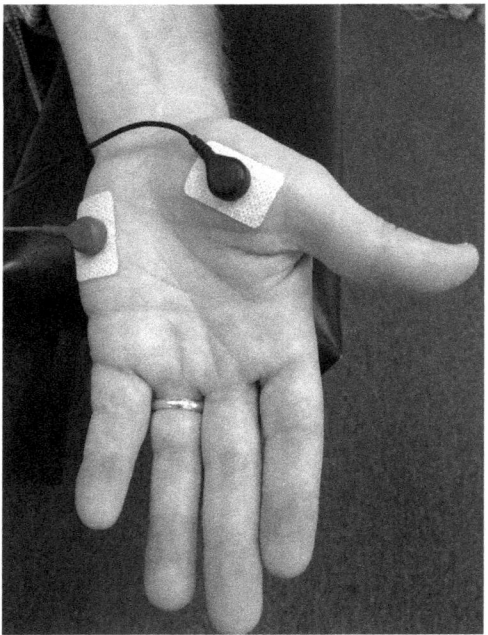

FIGURE 4.2

Proper placement of the adhesive pads for electrodermal recording.

Photo courtesy of Mr. Ben Blalock, Credibility Assessment Training Academy of Polygraph Science.

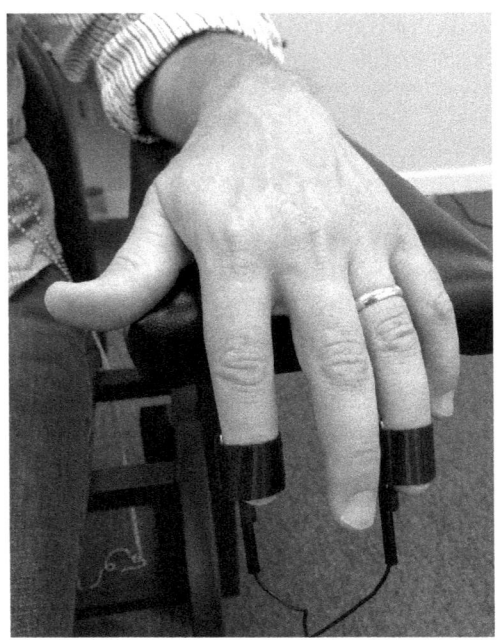

FIGURE 4.3

Proper placement of metal plates for electrodermal recording.

Photo courtesy of Limestone Technologies.

signs of blood flow restriction. For health reasons, the metal plates should be cleaned between examinees with alcohol or another type of antiseptic preparation.

PHOTOPLETHYSMOGRAPH SENSOR

The PPG sensor is placed on the same hand as the electrodermal sensors, at the end of one of the fingers. With the clip open, the finger is slid against the back of the holder, and the clip is released. It should fit snugly to minimize shifting. It may require adjustment to gain the best signal from the skin (Figure 4.4).

BLOOD PRESSURE CUFF

Ask the examinee to extend his left arm forward, palm up. Standing to the outside of the examinee's arm, wrap the cuff around the upper arm such that:

1. The cuff bladder is immediately over the brachial artery.
2. The cuff is not over thick clothing.
3. The cuff is snug, though not restrictive to blood flow.
4. The Velcro® adhesive surfaces are firmly attached to one another.
5. The cuff does not pinch the examinee when inflated.
6. The connector hose is unobstructed between the cuff and the sensor box.

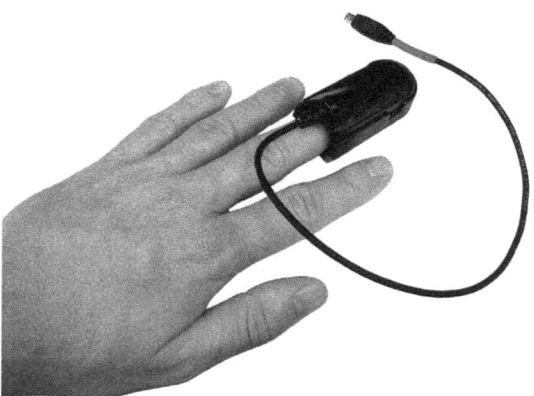

FIGURE 4.4

Proper placement of the photoplethysmograph sensor. It may be placed on any of the digits, wherever the best signal is obtained.

Photo courtesy of the Lafayette Instrument Company.

Return the examinee's arm back to the place it will be during testing. Ensure that the cuff is not in physical contact with the examinee's torso, as the act of breathing can apply pressure to the cuff and introduce undulations in the cardiovascular tracing. Also, the coupling of the cuff to the arm is impeded by thick clothing, so long-sleeved sweatshirts, sweaters, suit coats, or other thick garments should not be between the cuff and the examinee's arm (see Figure 4.5). During the process of placing the cuff, reinforce the message that the examinee will feel a little pressure during testing, but that this will be only for a few minutes, and there will be no air in the cuff otherwise.

Alternatively, the forearm and wrist can be used as sensor sites so long as the cuff fits the area. There are specialty cuffs available from the polygraph manufacturers.

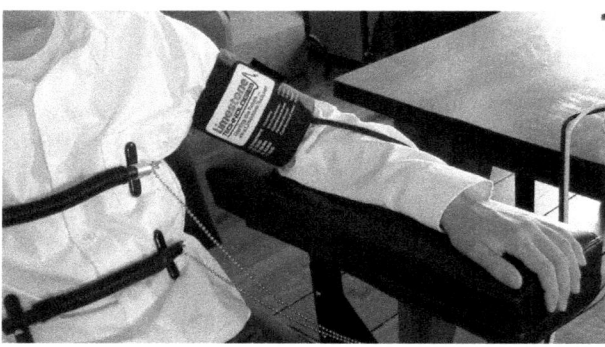

FIGURE 4.5

Proper placement of the blood pressure cuff.

Photo courtesy of Limestone Technologies.

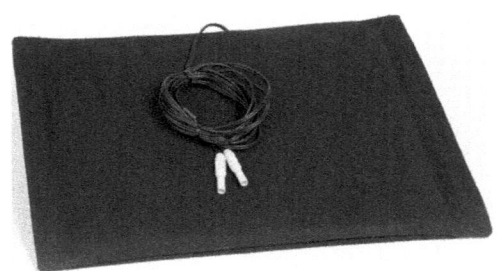

FIGURE 4.6

Photo of the piezo-electronic StingRay_SE seat sensor.

Photo courtesy of Limestone Technologies.

The bladder must be placed over the main artery, and cuff pressure must be maintained at a higher level to boost the signal to the sensor box. It is important that there be a good coupling between the sensor and the arm. In exceptional circumstances (i.e., the examinee has injuries to his arms), it is acceptable to record at the calf of the leg, with exquisite attention to decorum and professionalism. Be especially careful of pantyhose and sheer stockings, as the Velcro® fasteners will quickly attach to them and will not easily detach without damaging the material.

MOTION SENSOR

Modern professional standards require examiners have, and use, a sensor designed to detect covert movements. Called a "motion sensor" here, others may know it as an "activity monitor." The most popular among them is the seat cushion (Figure 4.6), though there are other types. These sensors are typically based on air pressure or piezoic sensors, or both. To be effective the examinee must have the maximum contact with the sensor pad. Otherwise, there is a risk of not detecting certain examinee movements, and an attendant risk of misinterpreting physiological reactions in the tracings.

TRACING APPEARANCE
PNEUMOGRAPH

Turn up the gain until the pneumograph tracings average about three-quarters to one inch in height (1.9-2.5 cm). The number of chart divisions will depend on the screen size and the choice of polygraph-operating software, but typically it will be between one and a half and three chart divisions (see Figure 4.7).

Troubleshooting

If the tracings remain too small, even at maximum amplification, it could be a sign that:

1. The connector line is pinched.
2. The sensor or connector line has a leak in it.

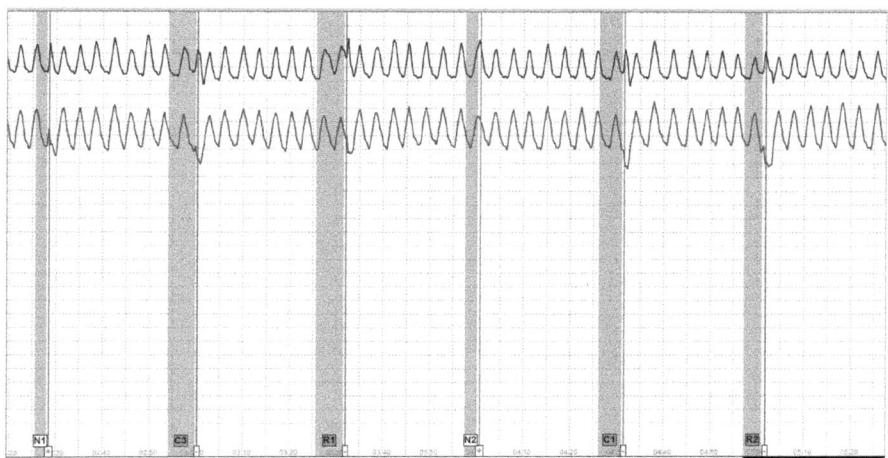

FIGURE 4.7

Tracing appearance for the pneumograph channel.

3. The connector line is not firmly seated in the sensor or the sensor box.
4. The sensor is improperly placed.
5. The sensor assembly is either too tight or too loose.
6. The pneumograph sensor was not vented, or remained open during data collection.

ELECTRODERMAL

Set the gain such that the reactions range from 1 to 10 chart divisions, or about 3 in. (7.5 cm) maximum. The examinee will probably produce an electrodermal response when the cuff is inflated, and this provides a general indication as to whether the gain setting is proper. If the largest reaction on the chart is less than 1 in. (2.5 cm) high, discriminating between reaction magnitudes will be difficult (see Figure 4.8).

Troubleshooting

If the electrodermal tracing is flat, it could be a sign that:

1. The sensors are not in good contact with the examinee.
2. The sensors have become disconnected from the snaps.
3. The connector wire is broken.
4. The connector wire is disconnected from the sensor box.
5. The examinee is not generating electrodermal activity. Test the system on yourself to determine whether the source of the problem is the examinee or the instrumentation. If it is the examinee, have him wash his hands in warm water. This should remove materials on the skin. Also, warm the examinee's hand by wrapping it in an insulating cloth or holding a warm bottle of water. Finally, see if good tracings can be acquired from sensors on the back of the examinee's hand.

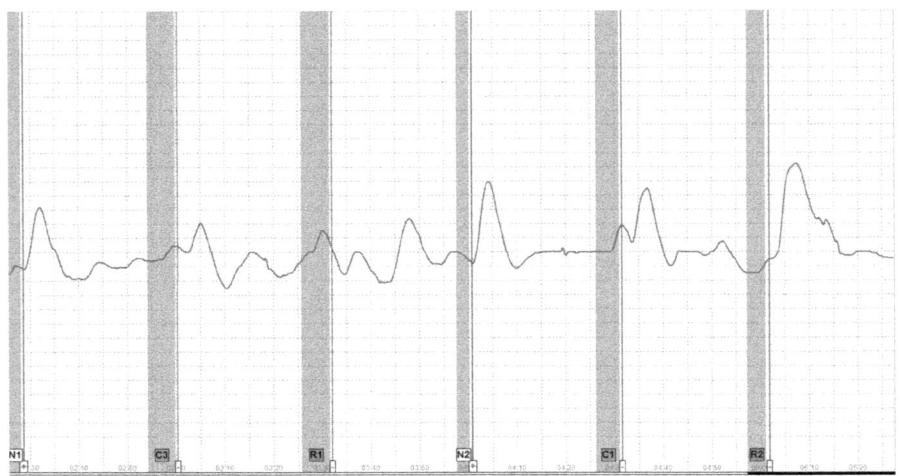

FIGURE 4.8
Tracing appearance for the electrodermal channel.

If the tracing is moving up and down very quickly, it may be that:

1. The examinee is touching the sensors together.
2. The examinee is pressing the sensors down and then releasing them.
3. There is an instrument problem.

PHOTOPLETHYSMOGRAPH

Adjust the gain so that the tracing amplitude is about three-quarters of an inch (1.9 cm). It should become narrower during a reaction, such as when the examinee notices the cuff being inflated. See Figure 4.9 for as an example of proper amplitude.

If the tracing appears unstable or nonresponsive, it is an indication that the sensor should be adjusted. This can involve moving it forward or back on the fingertip or even placing it on another finger. Spikes in the data can be due to skipped heart beats (if always in the downward direction) or examinee movements (in either direction).

MOTION SENSOR

The gain on the motion sensor should be sufficient to pick up the convert movements the examiner needs to see. Because it is unknown whether the examinee will try to tighten those muscles during the test, it is not possible to establish a gain setting *a priori*. The best setting for the motion sensor is where it picks up some activity, such as that associated with breathing. If the tracing is sensitive enough to detect the subtle bodily shifts associated with breathing, it is probably sensitive enough to detect muscular movement in the lower part of the body. See Figure 4.10 as an example.

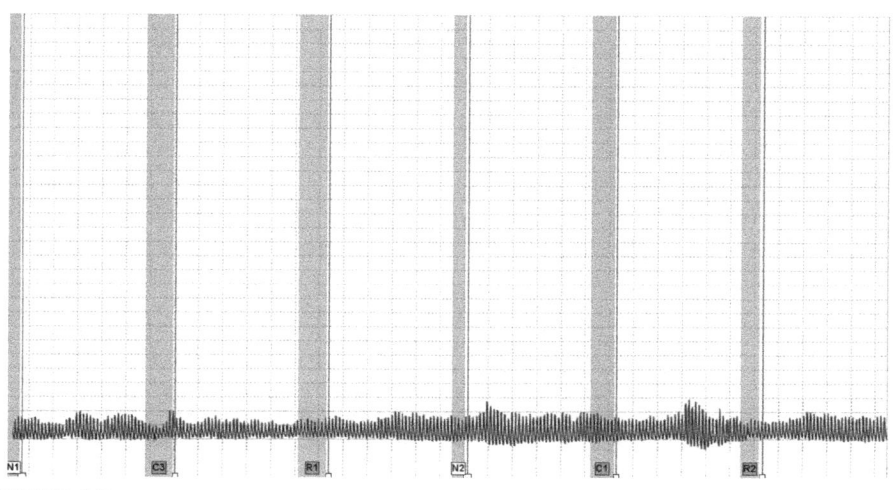

FIGURE 4.9

Tracing appearance for the PPG channel.

CARDIOVASCULAR[3]

Because the air pressure in the cuff is the most likely source of any discomfort that might arise for the examinee during testing, the cardiovascular tracing is adjusted last. The right amount of cuff pressure during testing is about 60-70 mm Hg. If the pressure is too low, it will not produce the coupling with the arm necessary to obtain a good signal: Too high, it will cause the blood to pool in the arm and cause discoloration and discomfort. We recommend inflating the cuff to about 90 mm Hg, and then massaging[4] until it stabilizes at the proper level of 60-70 mm Hg. It may be necessary to inflate and massage a second or even third time to achieve stability in the tracing.

The correct gain setting for the cardiovascular channel will produce a tracing amplitude of about three-quarters of an inch (1.9 cm). The number of chart divisions will depend on the screen size and operating software, but typically it will be about two chart divisions (see Figure 4.11).

If the tracing is unstable, it could indicate poor coupling with the arm. The cuff may need to be rewrapped to form a better fit. Some stability may also come with a little higher cuff pressure, or elevating or straightening the arm. If these remedies are

---

[3] The use of the finger cuff was introduced to the polygraph profession in the mid-2000s. The research for this cardiovascular measure in polygraphy is scarce, but the little available evidence suggests that it does not contain as much diagnostic information as the traditional blood pressure cuff. The finger cuff is not widely used, and the evidence to support it is in short supply. The Cardio Activity Monitor (CAM), available since the 1980s, also suffers these dual challenges. Consequently, neither of these cardiovascular alternatives are addressed in this chapter. Interested readers should contact instrument manufacturers for more information.

[4] Some schools teach examiners to refrain from touching the examinee as much as possible. Examiners can successively inflate and deflate the cuff to the recommended pressure without the massage if they prefer.

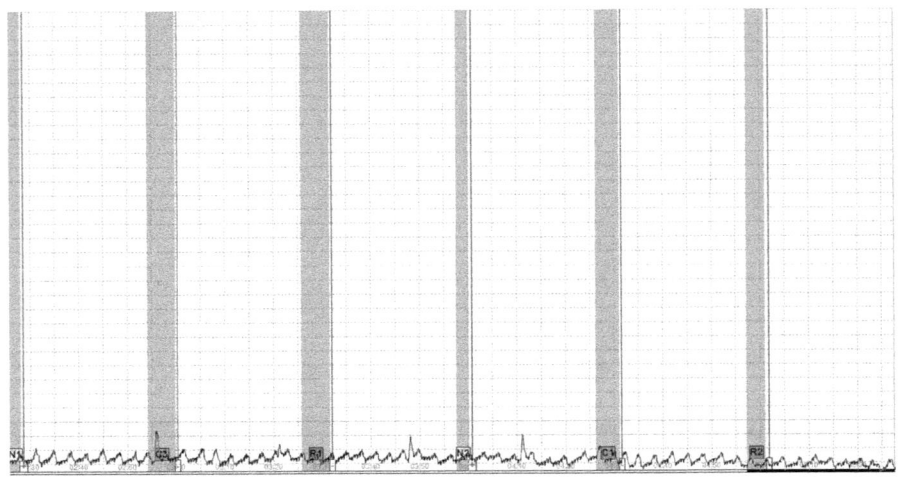

FIGURE 4.10

Tracing appearance for the motion sensor.

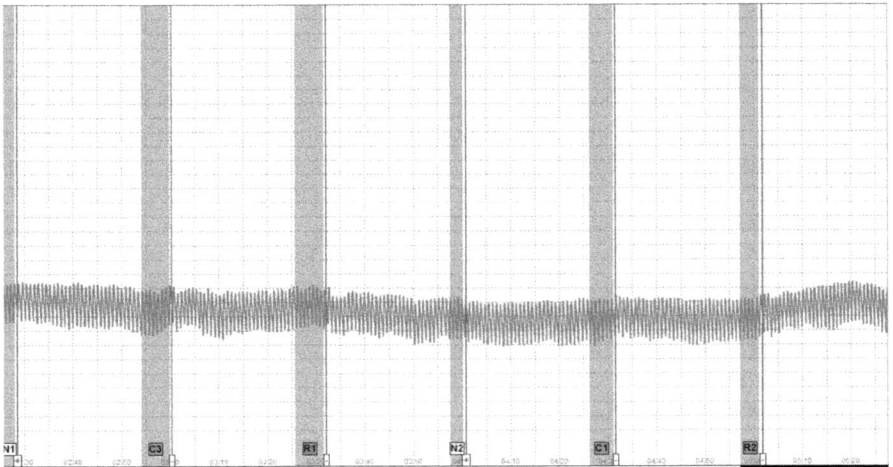

FIGURE 4.11

Tracing appearance for the cardiovascular channel.

not effective, the cuff may also be placed on the forearm, where the pressure can be increased to about 80 mm Hg without much discomfort. This option comes at a cost, however, because the dampening of the instability also entails a dampening of the blood pressure amplitudes important for chart interpretation. Examiners should also be mindful of pinching of the connector hose. This may reduce the signal significantly. A rapid falling in the tracing points to a leak in one of several possible sites: at the connection to the sensor box, hole in the tubing, leak in the pump bulb assembly, or a breach in the bladder.

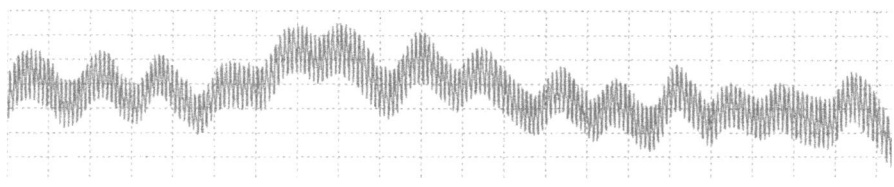

FIGURE 4.12

Undulations in the cardiovascular channel.

If the cardiograph tracing has regular undulations in it, such as in Figure 4.12, it can mean:

1. The cuff has come in contact with the torso and is picking up pressure from the chest against the cuff. Put some distance between the cuff and the torso.
2. The examinee is exaggerating his breathing, causing compensatory changes in the cardiovascular system. So long as the examinee exaggerates his breathing the pattern will continue.
3. This is a normal pattern for this examinee, and caused by fatigue, medication, age, or cardiovascular disease. Typically the undulations correspond with the breathing but are delayed about 2-3 s behind the breathing. While a good night's rest will fix the problem in some cases, they are often without a remedy.

APPEARANCE OF THE CHART

With all the tracings set correctly, the polygraph chart should appear orderly, centered, and clean. The use of different colors for each channel helps to track their excursions even when they run over another channel of data. Figure 4.13 shows a chart segment with all of the channels properly positioned, centered, and with the correct gains.

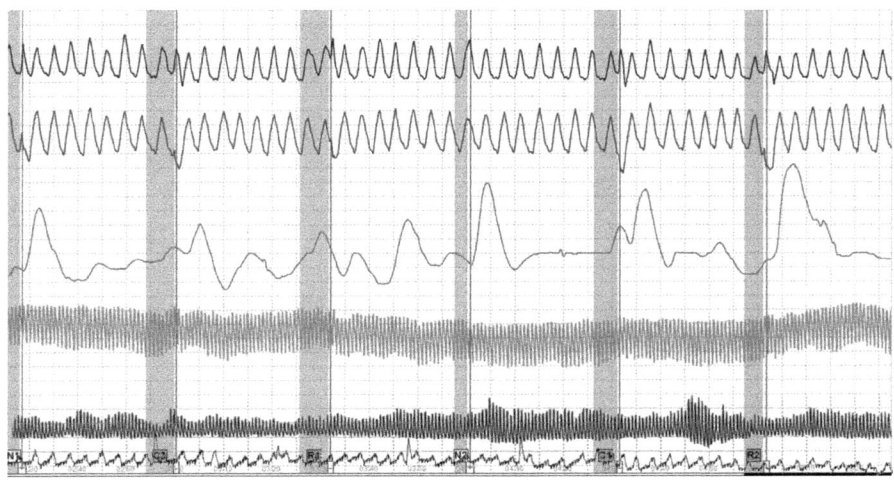

FIGURE 4.13

All polygraph tracings in their proper positions and proportions.

FINAL COMMENT

There may be instances in which, despite the greatest of care, the examiner will not be able to collect stable and interpretable data. Fortunately, this is rare. In those instances, there should be evidence that the examiner took every step possible to correct the problems, and if the data continue to be unstable, to simply do the most professional job possible.

REFERENCE

Edelberg, R., 1967. Electrical properties of skin. In: Brown, C.C. (Ed.), Methods in Psychophysiology. Williams & Wilkins, Baltimore, MD.

RECOMMENDED READINGS

Geddes, L.A., 2005. What does the photoplethysmograph indicate? Polygraph 34 (3), 210–216.

Geddes, L.A., Newberg, D.C., 1977. Cuff pressure oscillations in the measurement of relative blood pressure. Polygraph 6 (2), 113–122.

Handler, M., Reicherter, J., Nelson, R., Fausett, C., 2009. A respiration primer for polygraph examiners. Polygraph 38 (2), 130–144.

Handler, M., Nelson, R., Krapohl, D., Horvath, F., 2010. An EDA primer for polygraph examiners. Polygraph 39 (2), 68–108.

CHAPTER 5

Analysis of polygraph data

The palest ink is better than the best memory.
Chinese Proverb

Of the many important ingredients of a valid polygraph examination, none has undergone more scientific investigation than chart interpretation. This research has provided a firm foundation for the information and recommendations that follow. Much credit is due to the researchers at the University of Utah for their substantial body of work in the area since the 1970s, to the National Center for Credibility Assessment (NCCA) scientists for their insightful research since the 1980s, and to the many other scientists who have uncovered important evaluation principles. This chapter on polygraph chart evaluation focuses on those practices that can be supported by scientific findings, and may depart in some important ways from the training some polygraph examiners have received in the past. Care has been taken to provide citations to the relevant scientific research.

There is very little discussion of the issue of countermeasures here. This is not an oversight, nor an attempt to minimize its importance. To the contrary, countermeasures pose a real threat to examiners who lack training and vigilance. Fortunately, there are effective methods that examiners can use to detect and deter countermeasures. Polygraph professionals are encouraged to attend any of the excellent educational offerings at state and national polygraph seminars.

Finally, there are other scoring systems beyond those given in this chapter. Most of the other systems are proprietary, taught only in individual polygraph schools, or are used by a small minority of examiners. The aim of this chapter is to cover validated methods in common practice, and there has been no attempt to catalog all variations of chart interpretation found across the field.

DEFINITIONS

Two terms central to physiological data analysis are *phasic* and *tonic*. Phasic responses are those that tend to be relatively rapid and of shorter duration. They are an index of arousal to a sudden stimulus. For example, if someone hears an unexpected loud noise, phasic responses could include pupillary dilation, an increase in skin conductivity, a sudden rise in blood pressure, vasomotor constriction at the extremities, and other responses indicating the body has automatically marshaled its resources to respond to a significant stimulus. Tonic activity, in contrast, tends to change at a slower rate and might be considered the background activity in polygraphy. By the way of example of tonic changes, if one adjusted the temperature in a room, skin conductivity would shift to respond to the new temperature over the course of minutes. There may also be changes in heart rate or respiration that follow the temperature changes. The time course of tonic changes would be relatively long. A phasic response could occur on top of these tonic changes in response to a presentation of a new abrupt stimulus.

The distinction between phasic and tonic is important in polygraphy. The tonic level will set the limit of the phasic response due to the law of initial values: a high tonic level will place the body nearer to its response ceiling so that any phasic response would be expected to be smaller than if the body were nearer the center of its tonic range. Because traditional chart scoring compares relative response sizes within the examinee rather than absolute response sizes across examinees, tonic levels should have minimal effect on decision accuracy. Because the time course of tonic changes is so long, it permits a meaningful comparison of phasic responses that occur close in time to one another. Phasic responses are used almost exclusively in the interpretation of polygraph charts. The sole exception is in the Peak of Tension (POT) test, where a change in tonic levels is often interpreted as indicating that the critical item, or key, has passed. For all other techniques the phasic arousals elicited by individual questions are used.

OTHER DEFINITIONS

Decision Rules: Criteria for decisions based on scoring data. Most often in polygraphy, they relate to the spot and cutoff scores.

Electrodermal Activity (EDA): Expression for changes to the electrical properties of the skin. The three most common types are skin conductance (SC), skin resistance (SR), and skin potential (SP). In conventional polygraph, SC and SR are most often used.

Electrodermal Response (EDR): Phasic response in the EDA.

Finger Pulse Amplitude (FPA): Measure of the pulse wave recorded at the finger with a photoplethysmograph (PPG).

Finger Pulse Line Length (FPLL): A linear measure of the PPG waveform over a specified period of time.

Respiration Line Length (RLL): A linear measure of the respiration waveform over a specified period of time.

PPG: In polygraphy, a device which uses red light and a light sensor to monitor relative blood volume at the finger or thumb.

Scoring Rules: Criteria for assigning numbers to physiological reactions.

Spot Score: Sum of scores for a single relevant question. Sometimes called subtotals.

HOW TO APPROACH CHART INTERPRETATION

Biological signals can be volatile, complicating the task of human evaluators of polygraph data. Effective chart analysis requires an attention to detail, a systematic approach, and an ability to distinguish phasic response patterns from artifacts or manipulations. Chart interpretation must begin with an assessment as to whether the charts are adequate for scoring. The assessment will consider the tonic activity, how labile (dynamic) the tracings are, whether there is an excess of artifacts, whether the data are manipulated by the examinee, and the appearance of sudden tonic changes during or between charts. This information is useful in weighing how much reliance to place on the data. It is the context upon which all analyses depend. Dramatic departures from normal responding should cause the evaluator to forego scoring altogether, to score more conservatively, or to ignore some portions of the data.

The scoring approach chosen here is both logical and simple. The most basic components are the tracing features, or the signature responses. Once those have been identified, the proper number assignment is discussed, followed by how those numbers are to be tabulated. Decision rules are covered last, and different decision rules shall be proposed for certain examination methods, and for different applications. These steps will lead to results that are both reliable and accurate.

FEATURES

The foundation of chart interpretation is the identification of those physiological features that are more diagnostic from those that are less so, or not at all. Polygraph students have historically been taught scoring systems that use all manner of tracing patterns, from the elegant to the exhaustive. Some polygraph examiners incorrectly believe that the more features one has on his features list, the greater will be the accuracy of his polygraph decisions. This perception is false as there is a limit for the number of reliable tracing features, after which the system becomes so cumbersome it begins to erode agreement among scorers. It may include features that may be diagnostic only for a subgroup or even a single individual, but are merely random events for most examinees. The preference of quantity over quality in some scoring systems has not served well either the examiners who hold these views nor the aim of accuracy. The features depicted hereafter are the only ones with a scientific foundation (see Bell et al., 1999; Kircher et al., 2005; Krapohl et al., 2003). There are other features that could be unique to certain cases, but do not generalize beyond those single individuals (e.g., persons who may hiccup or stutter when they lie). Idiosyncratic features have not been included for this reason.

As noted earlier, it is important to recognize that the relative magnitudes are more important than absolute sizes, and that absolute sizes are mediated by the gain setting on the amplifiers. Proper tracing amplitudes are essential and are covered in Chapter 4.

Diagnostic information is carried in the relative differences in amplitude between types of questions. These differences can be characterized as *noticeable*, *significant*, and *dramatic*. A noticeable difference is one that is clear, though perhaps just barely so. A significant difference is unmistakable. To be considered dramatic, there needs to be an enormous difference between the amplitudes. Discerning whether a difference is noticeable or significant or dramatic requires experience and proper training. The exemplars found in the next section are designed to help practitioners classify the responses according to this system, and they assume that the tracings are stable and free of manipulations. Where measurements aid in those decisions, recommendations are offered that are based upon the published research.

ELECTRODERMAL

Phasic EDA comes in three common forms: SR, SC, and SP. Tonic information is differentiated from phasic information by expressing the former as "level" (i.e., skin resistance level, SRL), while phasic is called "response" (i.e., skin conductance response, SCR). Both SR and SC information are detected by the introduction of minute amounts of electricity across the surface of the skin, and recording the changes in resistance or conductance over time. SP, a form not commonly used in polygraphy, relies on bioelectrical changes that are generated by the body itself. SR and SC are uniphasic, that is, a response can only occur in one direction, while SP is biphasic. SP may one day be included among the standard polygraph channels, but because it is generally not recorded outside of the research laboratory, the focus here will remain on SR and SC.

Of all of the physiological information in polygraph charts, perhaps none is as easy to analyze as the electrodermal channel. EDA is represented as a single line of data from which the primary feature, amplitude, can be easily seen and measured. By comparing the amplitude among questions, it is a relatively simple task to assign numbers to the differences in phasic responses. It is for this reason that inter-scorer agreement is highest for EDA.

In addition to amplitude, there are two secondary features found to have some diagnostic value: response complexity and response duration. Between these two, complexity appears to contain the lesser diagnostic value. Duration is a valuable source of information, but unfortunately it has been filtered out in some field instruments. Examiners should use polygraphs that retain the EDA duration information, and avoid using the self-centering option whenever possible when recording EDA.

It is also helpful to remember that the minimum latency of an EDR is one-half of a second (Kircher and Raskin, 1988). Responses that begin in a shorter time cannot be associated with the stimulus: they are caused by something other than the test question. Latencies are subject to individual differences and must be judged according to the average seen with each examinee. Unusually long latencies (>5 s) are not

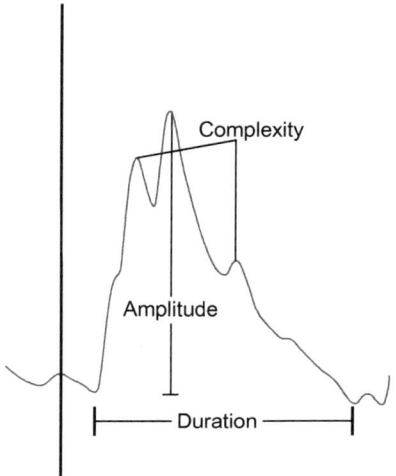

FIGURE 5.1

Diagnostic features in the electrodermal channel.

common, but may be normal for some individuals. There should be consistency within individuals. Very long latencies that occur only on comparison questions should be viewed with caution. Figure 5.1 identifies the three diagnostic features of the EDR.

EDR EXEMPLARS

In the following section are the exemplars of EDRs. They are identified as noticeable, significant, and dramatic. The EDA channel uses ratios of the response amplitudes for score assignment, and these ratios are taken up later.

AMPLITUDE

See Figures 5.2–5.4.

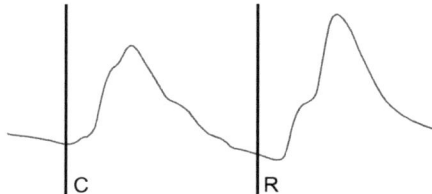

FIGURE 5.2

Noticeable EDR differences.

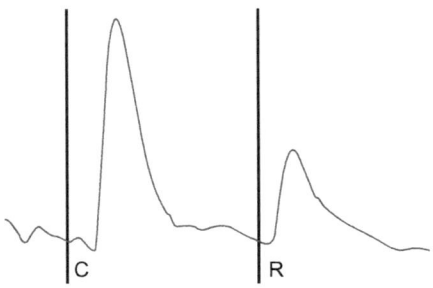

FIGURE 5.3

Significant EDR differences.

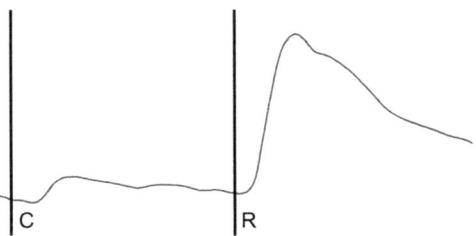

FIGURE 5.4

Dramatic EDR differences.

CARDIOVASCULAR

In the polygraph literature this tracing is sometimes referred to as relative "blood pressure" and at other times relative "blood volume." There is less than universal agreement regarding which is correct. For the present purposes, the former expression will be used though some may disagree. While it is likely that there is a blood volume change in the major muscles as blood is shunted to them from the extremities, the largest contributor of diagnostic information is believed to be the rise in systemic blood pressure.

There are two types of cardiovascular signals represented in this polygraph channel: pulse wave and blood pressure. Some diagnostic information has been found in pulse rate deceleration in the first few seconds after question onset (Dollins et al., 1998; Gödert et al., 2001; Podlesny and Kircher, 1999; Rovner, 1986; Verschuere et al., 2004); however, the effect is modest. Moreover, human scorers have difficulty detecting these subtle changes in the tracing, and this feature will not be further considered here. A pulse wave feature identified by Kircher et al. (2005) is the increase of the pulse amplitude over the course of the response window. However, the increase in blood pressure is the largest contributor toward decision accuracy. The modest but significant effect is also found in the duration of the blood pressure response (see Figure 5.5).

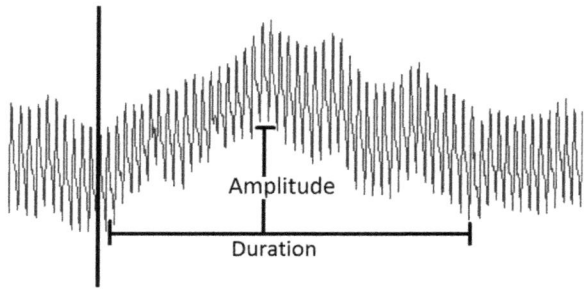

FIGURE 5.5

Diagnostic features in the cardiovascular channel.

CARDIOVASCULAR EXEMPLARS

Below are the exemplars of noticeable, significant, and dramatic blood pressure amplitude increases (Figures 5.6–5.8).

ARTIFACTS IN THE CARDIOVASCULAR CHANNEL

The cardiovascular channel may show irregular pulse patterns for some individuals. One of those patterns is associated with skipped heartbeats, called premature ventricular contractions (PVCs), and another is caused by movements. Recognizing

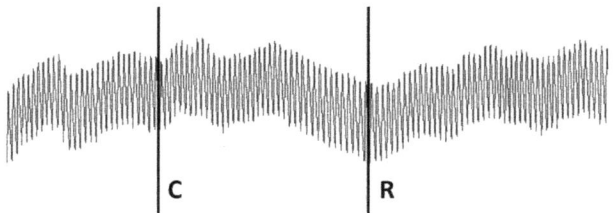

FIGURE 5.6

Noticeable blood pressure differences.

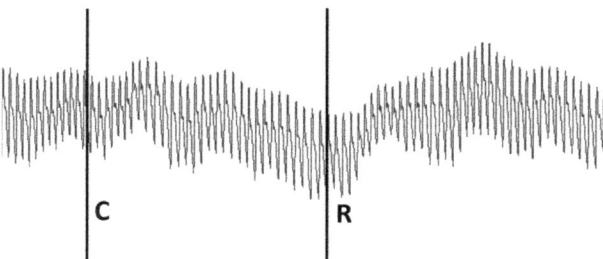

FIGURE 5.7

Significant blood pressure differences.

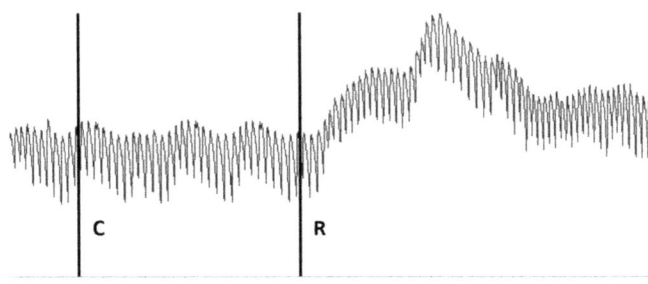

FIGURE 5.8

Dramatic blood pressure differences.

the difference is important. PVCs are involuntary and cannot be remedied by the examiner. Movements may signal a lack of cooperation by the examinee, or even an attempt to avoid detection of deception, and would require an examiner's attention.

PVCs can be distinguished from movements by the fact that PVCs always show a sudden drop in the tracing, and there appears to be a pulse missing in that segment of the tracing. Conversely, movements can cause a spike in either direction, and there is no indication that a pulse is missing from the waveform. Also, PVCs tend to show a compensatory rise in blood pressure after the sudden drop, but movements typically do not.

Below are the exemplars of PVCs and movements for comparison (Figures 5.9 and 5.10).

While movement patterns may reveal an examinee's strategy to defeat testing, neither movements nor PVCs can be the basis for decisions of deception or truthfulness. Neither event in the cardio channel is reliably associated with deception to the relevant issue(s).

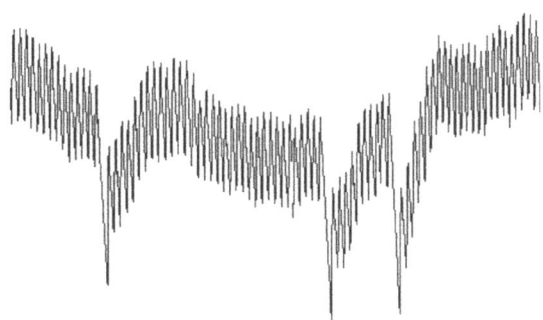

FIGURE 5.9

PVCs in the cardiovascular tracing.

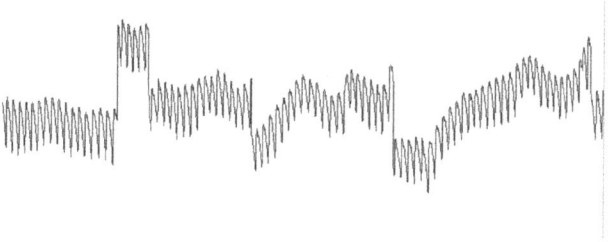

FIGURE 5.10

Movements in the cardiovascular tracing.

VASOMOTOR

During sympathetic nervous system arousal, blood is moved from the periphery. The reduction in blood at the fingers can be easily captured using a PPG, a sensor available on most modern polygraphs. It operates by sending a small amount of red light into the skin and recording the amount of light that returns. The pulse is recorded as the capillaries respond to the push of blood throughout the system at each heartbeat. As the capillaries constrict to move blood out of the extremities, there is less red light reflected back to the sensor. The net effect is a pulse wave tracing that loses amplitude when the sympathetic nervous system is activated. This response has been shown to provide diagnostic information for the detection of deception (Elaad and Ben-Shakhar, 2006; Kircher and Raskin, 1988) (see Figure 5.11).

PNEUMOGRAPH

The pneumograph is considered by many as the most challenging polygraph channel to interpret, and virtually all would agree that it is the most complex. This is because of the many factors that influence this tracing. For one, respiration can easily be altered by examinees. Indeed, most examinees attempting countermeasures try to influence this tracing first. The pneumograph channel is further affected by naturally occurring behaviors such as sniffles, coughs, sneezes, and swallowing. Also, examinees in extremely high states of tonic arousal can display unstable respiration patterns that can obscure the diagnostic information. Finally, respiration patterns are sometimes altered by the examinee's act of answering the examiner's questions

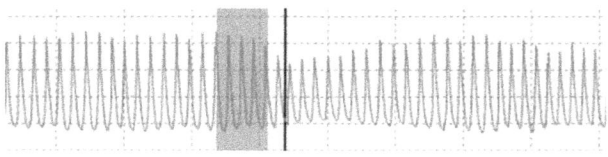

FIGURE 5.11

Vasomotor pulse wave constriction. Sometimes called finger pulse amplitude.

during testing. All of these influences can complicate the task of examiners to extract meaningful information from this channel.

The current state of the research has shown a relatively small handful of reliably diagnostic tracing features. The first is suppression. Suppression is characterized as a reduction in the amplitude of the respiration waveform. It can also include apnea, where respiration amplitude is suppressed entirely for a period of time. Suppressions can begin immediately, or progress over a small number of breaths. A second diagnostic feature is the slowing in rate of breathing, sometimes called bradypnea in the medical literature or an increase in cycle time in the polygraph validity literature. This slowing can be accompanied by a change in the inhalation/exhalation ratio, a feature first reported as a deception indicator by Benussi (1914). Suppression and slowing account for most of the diagnostic information in the pneumograph channel. A fourth feature, the rise in baseline, is also highly diagnostic when it occurs.

It is important to note that these features have been repeatedly shown to be diagnostic in probable-lie techniques and relevant/irrelevant (RI) techniques: they may not apply to directed-lie comparison question (DLC) techniques. Replicated research on the directed-lie technique has suggested there may not be as much useful information in the respiration channel (Horowitz et al., 1997; Kircher et al., 2001; but also see Honts and Handler, 2014). For this reason, examiners who use DLC methodology may wish to exercise conservatism when interpreting this channel.

The following are the exemplars of suppression, slowing of respiration rate, and baseline rise.

SUPPRESSION
See Figures 5.12–5.14.

SLOWING
See Figures 5.15–5.17.

BASELINE RISE
See Figures 5.18–5.20.

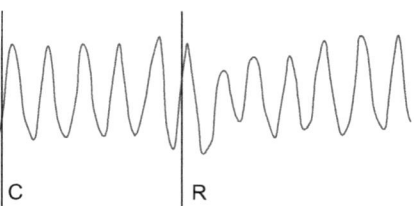

FIGURE 5.12

Noticeable difference.

Pneumograph 105

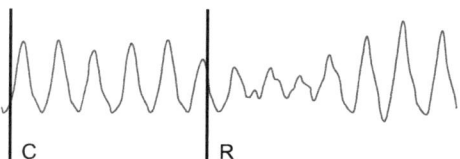

FIGURE 5.13

Significant difference.

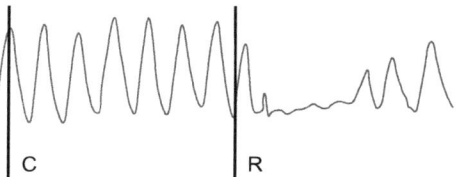

FIGURE 5.14

Dramatic difference.

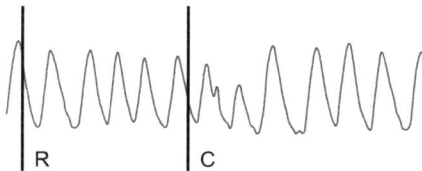

FIGURE 5.15

Noticeable difference.

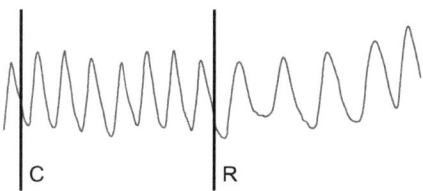

FIGURE 5.16

Significant difference.

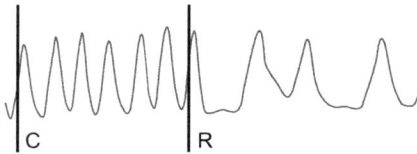

FIGURE 5.17

Dramatic difference.

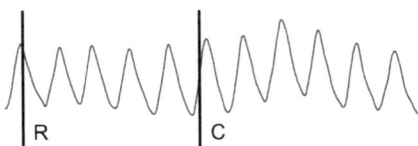

FIGURE 5.18

Noticeable difference.

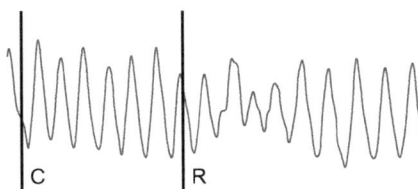

FIGURE 5.19

Significant difference.

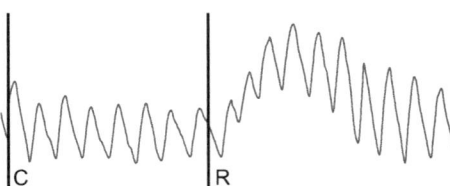

FIGURE 5.20

Dramatic difference.

MOVEMENT SENSOR

Most modern polygraphs are now equipped with movement sensors. They are used to reveal an examinee's muscular contractions that might be difficult to detect otherwise. Covert movements are recommended in some countermeasure articles and books as a strategy to defeat the polygraph. Figure 5.21 shows a tracing exemplar of a movement sensor taken from an examination of a carjacker who injured a woman and threatened her small child. He later confessed to the crime, and to using a countermeasure strategy he learned on the Internet.

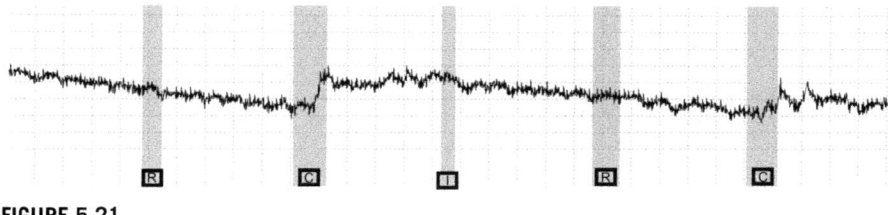

FIGURE 5.21

Tracing of a movement sensor that detected the attempted countermeasures of a carjacker.

SCORING SYSTEMS

Assignment of scores depends on the magnitude of the responses, the context in which those responses occur (labile or stable tonic levels), and to the magnitude of the response against which it is being compared. With regard to the latter factor, there are different schools of thought regarding which comparison question should be used for a given relevant question. Some believe that the stronger of two adjacent comparison questions should be used, and this is the method recommended here. Others argue that the stronger comparison question should be used unless there is a reaction to the relevant question: if this happens, the weaker of the comparison questions is used. A third approach is to use the comparison question that immediately precedes the relevant question on the chart. For this latter method there should also be a rotation of questions within the charts.

Here is a general comment about question rotation. It is not used in all techniques, though it can offer certain advantages. For one, it can compensate for order effects. It is generally accepted that within-chart habituation reduces the differential reactivity to questions later in the chart. In other words, there is more reactivity earlier in a chart than later in the chart, on average. The rotation of both relevant and comparison questions, in opposite directions, better distributes the available responsivity to all relevant questions than when the same sequence of questions is used for all charts. In this way, scores are less influenced by where in the sequence a test question is presented. Also, it is commonly recognized that different comparison questions do not evoke responses of the same magnitude. Some comparison questions induce large reactions, while others may trigger smaller ones or none at all. Therefore a relevant question that is scored against a stronger comparison question would have more positive scores than the same relevant question that would be scored against a less evocative comparison question. A systematic rotation of questions helps mitigate the effects of habituation and differences in strength of comparison questions.

After consideration for the valid tracing features listed earlier, we are now ready to move on to the evaluation of polygraph data. In the next section we take up five approaches to chart analysis: 7-position scoring, 3-position scoring, the Empirical Scoring System (ESS), rank order scoring, and global analysis. The 7-position,

3-position, and the ESS scoring are highly similar, and will be addressed first followed by rank order scoring. Global analysis is taken up last.

ABOUT 7-POSITION SCORING

The 7-position scoring system now found almost universally in the field was first proposed by Cleve Backster (1962). As the name suggests, 7-position scoring entails the use of seven scores to represent the relative reactivity of relevant questions. The values are −3, −2, −1, 0, +1, +2 and +3. By convention, negative values are assigned when the reaction to the relevant question is greater than corresponding reactions to the benchmark comparison question. Positive values are given when the reaction to the benchmark comparison question is greater than that of the relevant question. The term "benchmark" is used here to indicate that there are specific pairings of relevant and comparison questions that are used against one another for analysis. This is to avoid the erroneous conclusion that any relevant question can be gauged against any comparison question. Different schools teach different rules for question pairing. The recommended rule is to use the stronger of two adjacent comparison questions, and score channel-by-channel. This means, for example, that the pneumo can be scored against a stronger preceding comparison question and the EDA to a stronger following CQ, and so on. Examiners should use techniques that have comparison questions placed immediately before the relevant questions. Techniques that do not precede a relevant question with a comparison question appear to have a structural problem that can affect decision accuracy (Blackwell, 1998; Cullen and Bradley, 2004; Krapohl and Dutton, 2005).

For obvious reasons, artifacts in the data can preclude the assignment of scores if the artifacts are sufficiently distortive. Artifacted data are denoted in the score sheet with the symbol Ø. This notation distinguishes artifacted data from cases where a zero (0) is assigned when there were no significant differences between the reactions of two questions being compared. Examiners should pay attention to the patterns in distortions: low frequency and randomness may be not strategic whereas the appearance of targeted distortions could signal intent.

ABOUT 3-POSITION SCORING

The 3-position scoring system is an abbreviated form of the 7-position scale. In the 3-position scale, the only values used are −1, 0, and +1. When ±2 and ±3 scores would be assigned with the 7-position scale, those values would only be ±1 in 3-position scoring. Research suggests that for single-issue testing, 3-position scoring can have equivalent accuracy to the 7-position scoring scale if the decision rules are adjusted (Capps and Ansley, 1992; Harwell, 2000; Krapohl, 1998; Van Herk, 1990).

ABOUT THE ESS

The ESS first appeared in a paper in 2008 (Nelson et al., 2008) followed by others that explored its accuracy and reliability for several polygraph techniques (Blalock et al., 2009; Handler et al., 2010; Krapohl, 2010; Nelson, 2011; Nelson and Krapohl, 2011). As a scoring technique, it is among the most studied.

ESS is a 3-position scoring system. It is different from traditional 3-position scoring in the score assignment in the electrodermal channel, and the ESS decision rules, which will be taken up later. A thorough description for performing the ESS was written by Nelson et al. (2011) on which is based the ESS procedures found here.

SCORING RULES

Scoring is the manual assignment of numbers to polygraph data. Proper scoring entails clearly defined rules. These rules allow an examiner to execute the system in a highly reliable way, producing consistent results that agree with a second examiner using the same system. Validated rules permit higher decision accuracy, which will be the goal of this section.

The scoring systems of 7-position, 3-position, and ESS use most of the same scoring steps, and differ only in the numbers they assign and the cutoff scores for decision making. All use the same scoring features, as outlined earlier, as well as the rule regarding which comparison question against which to score. Another central concept they share is that of Response Windows, which refers to the time periods in which physiological data can be evaluated. Response Windows will determine how much confidence an examiner can have that a physiological response was triggered by a test question.

RESPONSE WINDOWS

Examinees tend to produce physiological responses that have a certain latency after the question presentation, and last for a certain period of time. A response that begins very late may not be associated with the test question. Some data channels require a minimum amount of time for the physiological system to respond, so a response that begins too early was not elicited by the test question. Therefore, there is a period of time in which a response begins that an examiner can have confidence that it was elicited by the test question. The expression that encompasses this concept is called the Response Onset Window (ROW). The ROW for each data channel will be addressed later in the respective sections.

As an overarching principle, examinees tend to have consistent response latencies. If longer response latencies are normal for a given examinee, the latencies should be consistently longer for all questions. Conversely, shorter latencies should also be uniform across the charts for examinees inclined toward this pattern. Inconsistent latencies, especially as those that are different for relevant versus comparison questions, are not typical and should be a warning flag to an examiner. It may also be helpful to remember that the physiological response is normally driven by the test question rather than when the examinee answers the question. For this reason, response latency is tied to question onset.

A second concept regarding chart interpretation is called the Evaluation Window (EW). The EW is the entire period that should be considered when assigning scores to responses, from beginning to end. It is different for each channel, and in some cases, different for each examinee. The EW will also be covered in the sections for each data channel.

SCORING THE PNEUMOGRAPH

The ROW for the pneumograph can be set at question onset, that is, at the examiner's first utterance of the test question and the ROW can extend up to one breath after the examinee's answer. This is the ROW in widest practice, and generally runs from 0 to 7 s. The ROW for ESS is taught to begin at question onset, and continue until 5 s after the examinee's answer or question offset. Responses that consistently begin within this window can be considered to have been prompted by the test question. Responses that begin after this window are less likely driven by the test question, and should be scored more conservatively, if at all. The EW for a response that begins within the normal ROW extends to the presentation of the next question.

When using RLL (discussed later in this section) as a guiding principle in scoring, there is a more sophisticated and individualized approach to setting the EW. First, the examiner determines which question, relevant or comparison, has the stronger response. The duration of that response then becomes the EW for both questions. Consider the following example. Suppose the relevant question has elicited an apnea beginning 2 s after question onset, and the apnea lasts 14 s. The response to the comparison question in this example is a noticeable suppression beginning 3 s after question onset, and lasts 7 s. The stronger response in this case is the apnea. It had a duration of 14 s. In this example, the EW for both questions would be 14 s and RLL would be applied for this period.[1] Called the idiographic approach, it tailors the scoring procedure to the individual rather than using population norms on individual cases. This method is widely practiced and scientifically reasonable but has not been subject to research.

In terms of everyday manual scoring, scores are assigned by subjectively gauging the relative intensity of response. Noticeable differences in responses between relevant and comparison questions warrant a numerical score of ±1 for 7-position, 3-position, and the ESS methods. For 7-position only, significant differences provide the bases for a score of ±2. Scores of ±3 are reserved for dramatic differences (see Table 5.1). For 3-position scoring and ESS, all noticeable differences or greater yield ±1 scores in the pneumograph.

---

[1] Because apneas can be intentionally produced by examinees, some courses of instruction, especially those that cover the ESS, teach students to ignore apneas except when they take place on relevant questions. This practice is derived from a principle known as Barland's Inequality wherein very strong reactions that are easy for an examinee to produce are only scored when they take place to relevant questions. Barland's Inequality, named for Dr. Gordon Barland who proposed it, is based on Dr. Barland's observations arising from a long study of polygraph countermeasures. Though not researched specifically, Barland's Inequality is somewhat consistent with other studies showing that, on average, liars react more strongly to relevant questions than truth tellers react to comparison questions. It is generally accepted that apneas are not commonplace in general, and authentic ones on comparison questions are even rarer.

Table 5.1 Assignment of pneumograph scores for 7-position, 3-position, and ESS approaches

Ratio	Score		
	7-Position	3-Position	ESS
Noticeable	±1	±1	±1
Significant	±2	±1	±1
Dramatic	±3	±1	±1

RLL: Manual scoring systems are based largely on visual assessments of the data. Quick and simple measurements of the EDA amplitude are standard practice in terms of chart divisions, but measuring the pneumograph is rarely done in routine examinations. When the highest level of precision is required, such as for evidentiary exams, examiners may choose to use to evaluate the pneumograph using a metric called respiration line length (RLL; Timm, 1982). RLL is merely a quantification of the tracing excursion. To understand the RLL concept, imagine that the respiration tracing is made of string. If the string were cut at question onset, cut again after 10 s, and the resulting section pulled straight, the string would have a length that could be measured with a ruler or similar device. This is the essence of RLL. Lab research suggests that 10 s of data after question onset is optimal (Kircher and Raskin, 1988), while other research has found RLL to be effective up to 15 s (Timm, 1982).

The tracing features that RLL captures are suppression (both short and longer progression), apnea (the strongest form of suppression), and respiratory slowing (or decrease in rate). Though baseline rises do not shorten RLL, these tracing features are almost always associated with respiratory suppression or slowing, which will reduce RLL. Baseline rises in which there is an increase in respiratory amplitude or speed are generally not physiologically based.

Phasic pneumograph responses reduce the excursion of the tracing, thereby reducing its overall line length for a given unit of time. Because the line lengths are both a function of tracing excursions and the gain settings on the polygraph, it is helpful to consider *ratios* of responses rather than absolute measurements. To calculate the ratios, take the line lengths of the relevant question and the comparison question for the 10 s after stimulus onset (or whatever standard period selected), and divide the longer line length by the shorter line length. This will produce a value of 1.0 or greater. For example, if the line length for the comparison question is 2.5 units, and the line length for the relevant question is 3.5 units, dividing the longer by the shorter will produce a value of 1.4 (3.5/2.5 = 1.4). The greater the ratio, the greater is the difference between these two questions. If the shorter line (stronger phasic response) came from the comparison question, the score would be in the positive direction, and if the shorter line were from the relevant question the score would be negative.

All computer polygraphs include software that automatically measures RLL, and does it with much greater precision and reliability than the older manual methods. Some also calculate ratios for the convenience of the examiner. The RLL-based scoring method has tentatively been shown to outperform seasoned human scorers using traditional methods in blind scoring (Krapohl and McManus, 1999). Because RLL relies entirely upon measurements, it is totally objective. In light of this objectivity, and performance relative to human scorers, it is a method that should be given careful consideration when conducting examinations that will be scrutinized by other examiners.

The question naturally arises as to what RLL ratios should be used to assign values in the 7-position scoring system. This is a difficult question to answer. The optimal ratios have been empirically demonstrated, but they are difficult to memorize and unwieldy to put into practice (Krapohl and McManus, 1999). It would be hard to recommend them for routine field use. For guidance only, we offer the following more convenient ratios for routine use: 1.25:1 for ±1, 1.50 for ±2, and 2.0 for ±3. For 3-position and ESS methods, a ratio of 1.25:1 is offered as a relatively conservative yet useful guide. These ratios presuppose that the tracings are stable, unmanipulated, and artifact-free.

SCORING THE ELECTRODERMAL CHANNEL

In 7-position and 3-position scoring, the ROW for the EDA is 0.5 s after question onset to the examinee's answer. In individual cases, the ROW may be extended beyond the examinee's answer, such as with examinees who are mentally very slow, affected by drugs or medication, or especially fatigued. In those unique cases, the response latencies will be similarly long for all questions, not just for certain questions. For ESS, the ROW begins at 0.5 s after question onset, with the end based upon the normal latency for the examinee. In no case, though, will an EDR commence earlier than 0.5 s after question onset because of limits of the nervous system. The EW for this channel ends at the presentation of the following question or item.

As stated previously, the primary diagnostic feature in the electrodermal channel is the amplitude of the phasic response. For physiological reasons, EDA amplitude is the most powerful feature found in polygraph tracings for most individuals. This feature alone accounts for about half of all of the diagnostic information available in polygraph charts. There is a small degree of additional information to be found in the duration and complexity of the EDA response; however, the emphasis remains with the amplitude. These amplitudes can be measured in chart divisions, inches, millimeters, or the raw values in ohms or microsiemens can be used if the examiner has access to those data.

The assignment of scores for 7-position scoring depends to some extent upon the ratio of EDA amplitudes between relevant and comparison questions. Ratios have been adapted by many schools from those proposed in the early 1960s by Cleve Backster, from whose method most scoring systems originated. The basis of Backster's ratios is not in the published record, though they appear to be reasonably effective and easy for examiners to use. They most likely represent a compromise between convenience and optimization, inasmuch as the optimal ratios uncovered in other research delivered more diagnostic power for the EDA, but were awkward for human scorers to employ.

Table 5.2 Ratios for score assignment for the electrodermal channel

Ratio	Score		
	7-Position	3-Position	ESS
Bigger is better	±1	±1	±2
2:1	±1	±1	±2
3:1	±2	±1	±2
4:1	±3	±1	±2

One major modification to Backster's ratios by the US government has been the adoption of the Bigger is Better Rule (BBR). Under this rule, a score of ±1 can be given even when the ratio is less than 2:1 when one reaction is noticeably larger than the one against which it is being scored. The BBR adds more diagnostic information than the standard Backster ratios and is also easy to use. For score assignments listed in Table 5.2, the BBR is used. As the table shows, the BBR is, in effect, the only one used in 3-position scoring and ESS. Note also that in ESS the EDA scores are always 0 or ±2.

SCORING THE CARDIOGRAPH

The ROW for the cardiograph data is from question onset to the examinee's answer in 7-position and 3-position scoring. The ROW for ESS has the same onset point, and ends based on the normal latency of the examinee. The EW continues to the next test question.

Most of the diagnostic information in the cardiograph channel comes from the baseline rise. Because the rise in the diastolic tips during sympathetic nervous system arousal captures both the baseline rise and the reduction of pulse amplitude, they are used as the preferred reference points for measurement. Duration information is used as a tie-breaker, except with ESS which uses only amplitude information (see Table 5.3).

Unlike the electrodermal channel, there is no generally accepted ratio scheme for assigning scores to the baseline rise. Most scoring systems rely on some version of the noticeable-significant-dramatic rating discussed earlier in this chapter,

Table 5.3 Assignment of cardiograph scores for 7-position, 3-position, and ESS approaches

Response	Score		
	7-Position	3-Position	ESS
Noticeable	±1	±1	±1
Significant	±2	±1	±1
Dramatic	±3	±1	±1

Table 5.4 Rule-of-thumb ratios for scoring cardiovascular amplitude responses

Ratio	Score		
	7-Position	3-Position	ESS
1.5:1	±1	±1	±1
2.0:1	±2	±1	±1
2.5:1	±3	±1	±1

though ratios have been proposed. Based on the rules of the Utah Scoring System (Bell et al., 1999), and the ratios that resulted from the development of the Objective Scoring System (OSS) (Krapohl and McManus, 1999), suggested ratios are found in Table 5.4. These ratios should be considered a heuristic rather than a strict rule. Scorers need to consider the stability of the tracing and whether changes in the baseline are driven by respiratory activity.

This is a good point to discuss the regular undulations sometimes seen in the cardiovascular channel that appear to be associated with the examinee's breathing. In the past, this was mistakenly but routinely called "vagus roll," but is more correctly labeled "respiratory blood pressure fluctuations," or RBPF (Handler and Reicherter, 2008). When the inhalations and exhalations track exactly with the changes in the cardiovascular data, and they occur simultaneously, the cause is likely that the blood pressure cuff is in direct contact with the torso. The torso can transfer mechanical pressure to the cuff during breathing which will appear as a regular slow wave in the tracing. If the result is an increase in the tracing baseline during a scoring window, it can complicate the analysis of the data. The solution is to reposition the arm or cuff so that the cuff no longer comes in contact with the torso.

There are individuals who display what appear to be RBPF, but for whom there is a delay in the cardiovascular response by about 2-3 s after the associated inhalation and exhalation. These changes are not caused by any contact between the cuff and the torso. They are driven by the body's imperfect striving for internal equilibrium that is kept slightly off-balance by inefficiencies in the cardiovascular regulatory system. Factors that give rise to these patterns include vascular disease, advanced age, fatigue, medication, and obesity. Sometimes they are caused by examinees who control or exaggerate their breathing, especially when it is altered to be very slow or very deep, as this behavior also interferes with the body's natural regulatory mechanisms (Figure 5.22). Controlled breathing can readily be identified by an examiner, who can take corrective action. Notwithstanding manipulated respiration, examiners may try to improve the quality of the recording by considering alternate sites for the blood pressure cuff, such as on the forearm, or in rare cases, the calf of the leg. Though the patterns cannot be avoided when they are generated physiologically, they can sometimes be attenuated when recording blood pressure further from the heart.

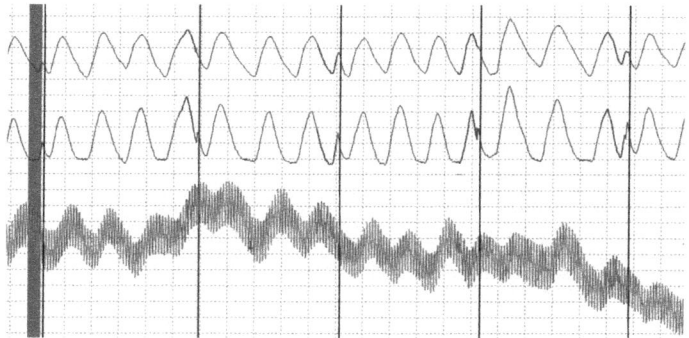

FIGURE 5.22

Chart wherein the examinee has exaggerated his breathing, creating corresponding undulations in the blood pressure tracing delayed by about 3 s (AKA respiratory blood pressure fluctuations). EDA, PPG, and motion sensor tracings removed.

SCORING THE PPG

The ROW for the PPG is from 2 to 8 s after question onset, and the EW extends to the presentation of the next test question.

Scoring of the PPG is fairly straightforward. Noticeable vasoconstriction warrants a score of ±1 for 7- and 3-position scoring. Note that the PPG data may influence the error probability estimates to a very small degree, though its contribution to normative distributions has not been investigated. Because the PPG offers additional diagnostic information, current look-up tables of error estimates may slightly overestimate error probabilities when PPG data have been added to scoring.

Scores of 0 and ±1 represent virtually all PPG scores. Though ±2 and ±3 scores are theoretically possible for 7-position scoring, research summarized by Bell et al. (1999) found that zeros are assigned about 70% of the time, and the remainder of the scores are ±1. Scores greater than ±1 had a zero frequency among the 450 samples they reported. These data do not suggest that greater scores are impossible, only extremely rare.

Researchers have reported a metric for PPG that uses line length of that tracing (Elaad and Ben-Shakhar, 2006). Called FPLL, it is a promising new approach to the analysis of PPG. The window of analysis is 4-15 s from question onset. Future research may suggest a scoring scheme using ratios such as those for RLL.

RANK ORDER SCORING

A less common method of chart interpretation comes in the form of rank ordering polygraph responses. Ranking of response magnitudes first appeared in Lykken's research on the Guilty Knowledge Test (now the Concealed Information Test, CIT) in 1959. In the 1970s, it was reported in Japanese research, again with the CIT. Two ranking systems for CQT formats were published in 1987: the Horizontal Scoring System by Gordon and Cochetti (1987), and the Rank Order Scoring System (ROSS) by Honts and Driscoll (1987). In the Honts et al. report, ranking of responses proved to be accurate, perhaps as accurate as the 7-position scoring system. A replication of the Honts and Driscoll study was published by Krapohl et al. (2001), who found equivalent accuracy between the 7-position scoring and rank ordering. Rank ordering is only appropriate for single-issue tests.

The Honts et al. ROSS is covered here. In ROSS, an examiner assigns numbers to reactions by channel. The scorable tracing features are RLL, EDR amplitude, blood pressure amplitude, and PPG constriction. Only relevant and comparison questions are ranked. The largest rank is equal to the number of questions being ranked. For example, suppose that an examiner is scoring three relevant and three comparison questions, for a total of six questions. In this case, the largest rank would be a "6." The scorer would assess the pneumograph and give a rank of 6 to the question with the strongest reaction. The second largest reaction would receive a 5 on the score sheet, and so on down to 1 for the smallest reaction. Artifacted responses receive the lowest ranks. In the case of a tie, the ranks would be averaged. For example, if there were two questions of the six questions being evaluated that had equal reaction intensity, they would each receive the average of ranks 6 and 5, or 5.5. Each channel is scored in this manner. Only one pneumograph score is used, however. At the end of scoring all charts, the ranks for the relevant questions are summed together, and the ranks of the comparison questions are summed together. The total score for the relevant questions is subtracted from the total score for the comparison questions, resulting in a final score for the case. Figure 5.23 lays scores over a chart to show how these ranks are assigned.

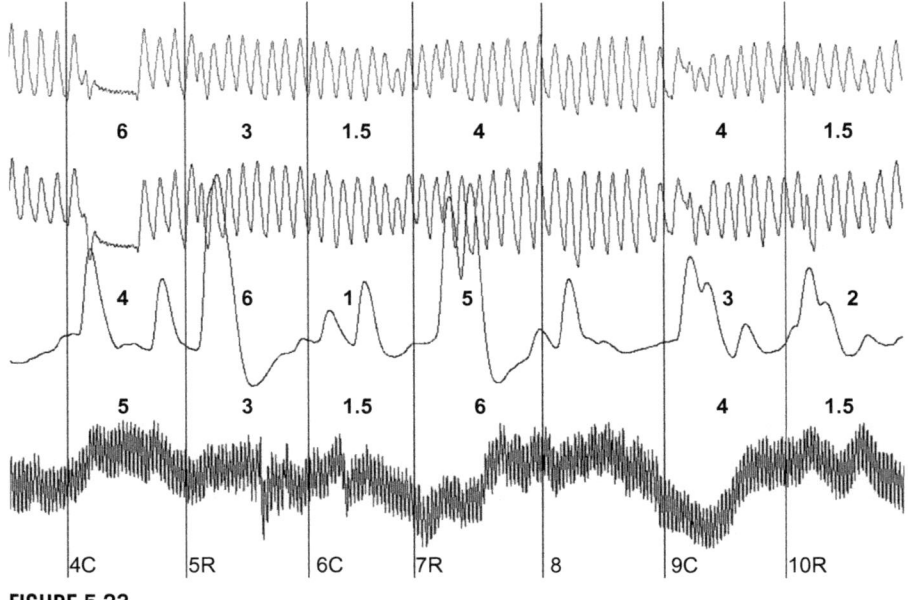

FIGURE 5.23

Rank order scoring system (Honts and Driscoll, 1987).

A related version of ROSS was proposed by Miritello (1999). It also ranked response intensities by channel, but converted the values to ratios. It was not intended for decision making, inasmuch as there were no decision rules. Rather, it afforded the examiner a means to compare reactivity among all of the questions on the test. It may be useful in screening examinations to help direct the examiner to where the examinee's concerns are. However, the method entails more mathematical computation than most examiners may wish to perform. ROSS is rarely used in the field. An abbreviated version in which only the top three reactions are ranked does have more field users. It is discussed in detail in the section "Global Analysis."

DECISION RULES

With decades of good research to call upon, the development of a body of scoring rules as outlined earlier is a straightforward matter. One's selection of which decision rules (cutoffs) to apply to the scores, however, depends upon a number of factors. For example, if all of the relevant questions covered a single act, it is a single-issue test, and will have certain decision rules that are appropriate for it. Other decision rules may apply to multiple-issue tests and multiple-facet tests (those that cover a single event but different elements of the event). There are also decision rules unique to techniques that have no scoring system, such as the RI screening test. Decision rules for recognition tests such as the POT and Concealed Information Tests are discussed in Chapter 8.

The single most important factor in selecting decision rules is the accuracy and inconclusive rate the user prefers. Decision rules can vary in the types of errors they make and the proportion of inconclusives they produce. Some decision rules are ideal for investigative examinations (Blackwell, 1998; Light, 1999) because they result in the best detection of liars. These are the rules that are most commonly used in the field. Nevertheless, investigative decision rules are not optimal for examinations conducted for evidentiary or paired-testing purposes (Marin, 2000, 2001) because of their poorer ability to detect truthfulness. Other methods, such as evidentiary decision rules, have a much better balance of accuracy and half the inconclusive rate (Krapohl, 2005; Krapohl and Cushman, 2006) with a small but measurable loss in detecting liars. Inasmuch as testimony on the polygraph is not frequently used in courtroom settings, evidentiary rules are rarely needed.

The following section will be organized according to these factors: single-issue and multiple-issue/facet, nonnumerical (global) systems, and investigative versus evidentiary applications. There are other approaches in the field that may be valid but have not been adequately researched, are proprietary, or are much less commonly used.

MULTIPLE-ISSUE AND MULTIPLE-FACET EXAMINATIONS

The multiple-issue/facet techniques used by most polygraph examiners are the Air Force Modified General Question Technique (AFMGQT) and the Law Enforcement Pre-Employment Test (LEPET). Though their names are different, they are two variations of a single methodology and will be jointly considered in this section.

7- AND 3-POSITION SCORING

For the AFMGQT and related techniques, a decision of Deception Indicated (DI) is made when the total score of any individual relevant question is −3 or lower. For a decision of No Deception Indicated (NDI), every individual relevant question must have a total score of +3 or higher. All others cases would be Inconclusive. Research has found these decision rules to produce very high detection of deception, but does not perform equally well with truthful cases (Blackwell, 1998; Krapohl and Norris, 2000; Podlesny and Truslow, 1993; Raskin et al., 1989; Senter, 2003). Nevertheless, they still play a significant part in criminal investigations if they are employed in a series of steps called the *successive-hurdles approach* (Meehl and Rosen, 1955).

When a form of the AFMGQT is used in the screening application, a spot score of −3 on any one of the relevant questions calls for a decision of Significant Responses (SR) to the test. For a decision of No Significant Responses (NSR), each relevant question must have a spot score of +3 or greater. All other results are No Opinion. It is not permitted to make a decision question-by-question, only by test. In multiple-issue testing, the use of SR and NSR results is appropriate, but DI and NDI can be used when the MGQT is employed in single-issue diagnostic testing. Moreover, it is recommended that SR results be followed by more interviewing and focused testing according to the successive-hurdles approach.

EMPIRICAL SCORING SYSTEM

Because with ESS the cutoffs are based on normative data, it is possible to estimate the likelihood of decision error with ESS. The proposed cutoffs here are recommended, though others may be more appropriate in some settings. Note that with MGQT formats the total score is not used in decision making. To find exact error estimates at different cutoffs, refer to the description found in Polygraph by Nelson et al. (2011).

For decisions of NSR, each spot score must be greater than 0. An SR decision results when any one of the spot scores is −3 or lower. All others are No Opinion. It is not permitted to make a decision question-by-question, but only by test.

Before going on, let us review the components of the successive-hurdles approach. It is nothing more than the deliberate use of multiple tests within a larger decision process. In polygraphy, it starts with a screening technique that is very good at detecting deception, even at the expense of a modest loss of ability to detect truthfulness. For the examinees who pass this initial screening test, the process is considered complete. For the subset of examinees who do not pass the initial screening phase, there are additional steps that come into play. Testing is not complete for these individuals, and the examinee should not be reported as deceptive based only on reactions in the initial screening phase: diagnostic decisions should never be based on screening results.

When an examinee has responded to one or more issues during the screening test, the examiner should solicit an explanation for the response from the examinee. Many times the examinee will volunteer new admissions or new details about admissions offered during the pretest interview. Some examinees will discuss past behaviors that troubled them that they associate with the relevant issues, but these behaviors are inconsequential to the agency or client. Other examinees may dig in their heels and deny having anything in their mind about the test questions.

The second stage of the successive-hurdles approach is the retesting of the examinee with a focus on the topic of interest. For the new test, the relevant questions should be modified to accommodate any new admissions. As a firm rule, it is recommended that no new testing takes place until the examinee has provided new information on which to base a test, or a plausible explanation for the reactions on the multi-issue phase. Retesting right after a screening test without the examiner having pursued more information is an ineffective methodology and may increase the likelihood of a decision error. It is a poor investment in time and effort.

More tightly focused questions are to be used in the second test. The narrower the focus is, the more confident a truthful examinee can be with his answers. Likewise, deceptive examinees will have less of an opportunity to rationalize when direct and focused questions are employed, and the examiner can have more confidence in what appears on the charts.

Some agencies or departments conduct the second stage of testing during the first session, while others delay it for another session. There is nothing lost in conducting the retest in the first session. The examinee may clear up his testing or may make admissions that exceed the acceptability threshold of the hiring agency, either of which will obviate the second session.

Many agencies also permit the examination to have more than two stages, moving to more focused testing with each step. The number of stages an agency should authorize is a function of resources. If the examiner's resources are tight, the examinee may be limited to the number of retests that can be accomplished in two sessions. For agencies with more resources, third and sometimes fourth sessions are permitted.

SINGLE-ISSUE EXAMINATIONS: INVESTIGATIVE

Many criminal examinations are focused on a single issue. For those tests, the Federal ZCT (FZCT), the "You Phase," and the Utah Probable-Lie Test (UPLT) are good choices. The UPLT has been researched with both probable and directed lies.

FEDERAL ZONE COMPARISON TECHNIQUE

Decision rules for the FZCT with both the 3- and 7-position scoring are: a total of −3 or lower for any question across three or more charts warrants a DI call, regardless of the scores of the other questions or the total of all questions. A DI call is also rendered when the total score is −6 or lower. For an NDI, the aggregate of scores for the entire exam must be +6 or greater, and the total for each relevant question must be +1 or greater. All other results would be Inconclusive or No Opinion. The FZCT protocol requires that, if the scores are not adequate for making a DI or NDI call after three charts, one or two more charts may be recorded. The scores from the additional charts are added to those of the

Table 5.5 Recommended cutoff scores for ESS for the Federal ZCT examinations for standard and conservative NDI decisions

	Stage 1: Grand total score	Stage 2: Spot score
NDI	+2	NA
NDI conservative	+5	NA
DI	−4	−7

first three for both spots and total, and the same three-chart decision rules are applied. If the results after five charts are Inconclusive or No Opinion, this becomes the final call.

Two-stage rules are used to make decisions with ESS when evaluating single-issue tests such as the Zone Comparison Test. The first stage considers only the grand total of scores. If a definite decision can result from the grand total, this is the decision that is reported. However, if the results would be Inconclusive, only then is the second stage brought into play. In the second stage, the spot scores are evaluated. If any of the spot scores falls below the specified cutoff, the call is DI. Otherwise, the final call is Inconclusive or No Opinion. If the second stage is executed, the results cannot be NDI.

The developers of ESS have offered two suggested sets of decision rules, based on the level of risk the user is prepared to accept. These cutoff scores were established by normative data so that error estimates could be calculated. As can be seen in Table 5.5, there are recommended cutoff scores for an NDI decision, and a different, more positive score for a conservative NDI result. The higher threshold for making an NDI decision allows users to avoid more false negatives, with the tradeoff of more inconclusive results for truthful examinees.

For decision rules of the Rank Order Scoring System, Honts and Driscoll (1987) systematically tried pairs of cutting scores symmetrical to zero, and determined that ±13 were optimal for three charts. Using a different method, and discarding symmetry, Krapohl et al. (2008) arrived at −1 and −13 as the cutoffs. In a separate study, Nelson and Handler (2013) tried several different sets of decision rules, all of which performed similarly. When relying only on the total score, they found −13 and +9 to be optimal. Because Rank Order Scoring is more time intensive, is not appropriate for screening and multiple-facet examinations, has little research, and affords no advantages over 3- and 7-position scoring or ESS, it is not a primary method for any but a small percentage of examiners.

"YOU PHASE"

For the "You Phase" with both the 3- and 7-position scoring, a spot score of −3 or lower or a total score of −4 or lower is DI. An NDI requires a positive in each spot and a total of +4 or greater. All other results would be Inconclusive.

As with the three-question Federal ZCT, the ESS offers two sets of decision rules that correspond with risk acceptance (see Table 5.6).

Table 5.6 Recommended cutoff scores for ESS for the "You Phase" ZCT examinations for standard and conservative NDI decisions

	Stage 1: Grand total score	Stage 2: Spot score
NDI	+2	NA
NDI conservative	+4	NA
DI	−4	−6

UTAH PROBABLE-LIE TEST

The UPLT uses only the total score rule for single-issue exams, that is, where the examinee must be either truthful to every question or deceptive to every question. In the UPLT if the grand total of all scores is −6 or lower, the call is DI; if the grand total of all scores is +6 or greater, the call is NDI. All others are Inconclusive. The testing protocol for the UPLT allows for the recording of up to five charts, but the same cutoff scores are used for both the three- and five-chart exams.

SINGLE-ISSUE EXAMINATIONS: EVIDENTIARY

For those examinations intended as court evidence, as well as paired-testing (Marin Protocol) examinations (Marin, 2000, 2001), it is essential that false positive and false negative rates are not strikingly different from one another. Western traditions of jurisprudence rest on an assumption of fairness, and while investigative decision rules are useful in the investigative process, their unbalanced accuracy limits their evidentiary value. One alternative approach is called Evidentiary Decision Rules.

Evidentiary Decision Rules were conceived specifically for evidentiary and Marin Protocol applications, with the goal of rendering balanced accuracies (Krapohl, 2005; Krapohl and Cushman, 2006). Evidentiary Decision Rules exploit two significant research findings: two-stage decision rules, and asymmetric cutoffs. Two-stage decision rules were originally proposed by Senter (2003), in which he found that inconclusive decisions could be dramatically reduced without reducing polygraph decision accuracy when inconclusive outcomes were subject to an additional step. A second discovery has been reported by several researchers that on average liars produce scores further below zero than the corresponding scores from truthful examinees are above zero (Franz, 1989; Krapohl and McManus, 1999; Krapohl et al., 2001; Raskin et al., 1989). In response to the asymmetry in responding, some scoring systems have turned to asymmetric cutoffs (e.g., Backster, Matte Scoring Systems). Evidentiary Decision Rules are also asymmetrical, and were established by the degree of asymmetry found during the development of the OSS (Krapohl and McManus, 1999). Evidentiary Decision Rules have only been assessed with the Federal ZCT.

The first step to the Evidentiary Decision Rules is to consider the total score from the entire examination. If the total score is −6 or lower, the result is DI. If the total score is +4 or greater, the result is NDI. For cases with a total score of −5 to +3, a second stage is invoked. For those instances, the spot scores are considered. If the total score of any single relevant question is −3 or lower, the decision is DI. All others are Inconclusive or No Opinion.

GLOBAL ANALYSIS

By and large, numerical analysis is the prevailing method of analyzing polygraph data. At least one technique does not have a validated scoring system: the RI screening technique (Correa and Adams, 1981; Krapohl and Rosales, 2014; Krapohl et al., 2005; Weir, 1974). This polygraph method is widely used, and decisions are based on a form of global analysis. The RI does not have comparison questions against which to gauge reactions to relevant questions, and so 7-position scoring is not appropriate despite it having been tried (Horowitz et al., 1997). Also, analysis used in the POT is not well suited for the RI because the standard protocol for the RI precludes the examinee knowing the question order, and some relevant questions are repeated in the same chart. These factors work against the expected anticipation-and-dissipation effect with the POT. Therefore, it was necessary to devise a special method for analyzing the RI data. That method is called *conspecnificance*.

Conspecnificance is a mnemonic used by examiners which stands for *cons*istency, *spec*ificity, and sig*nificance*. If a reaction consistently takes place specifically and consistently to one question that is significantly greater than reactions to other questions, it is said to have conspecnificance. This principle teaches examiners to ignore trivial and random reactions, but to attend to those that are seen repeatedly to the same question. It can aid the examiner in sorting out where the actual concern of the deceptive examinee is.

Rank Order Analysis (ROA; Miritello, 1999) is a helpful numerical approach for RI cases as a self-check, and it uses only scores from 3 down to 1. It is conducted for each polygraph channel. The largest reaction on a chart within a channel is given a score of 3, the second largest a 2, and the third largest a 1 (see Figure 5.24). The pneumograph channels are treated as though they were one channel. All of these ranks are summed so that each relevant question has a total score for all charts. When one of the relevant questions has a total that is much higher than the scores of the other relevant questions, it is a signal that this relevant question has received the most reactivity. The question as to what constitutes a score that is "much higher" than the rest is subject to interpretation. No published research is available to answer this question. A useful rule of thumb would be that a separation of five points should cause the examiner to reconsider a decision to call the examinee truthful to all issues. Because this is a rule of thumb, it should neither be used to base formal policy nor should clear reactions to relevant questions that do not attain the five-point separation be ignored. Rather, a commonsense approach should prevail regarding the place of ROA in the decision process. It should be noted that no numerical scoring system has yet been found that outperforms the original testing examiner using global analysis with the RI screening test (Krapohl et al., 2005).

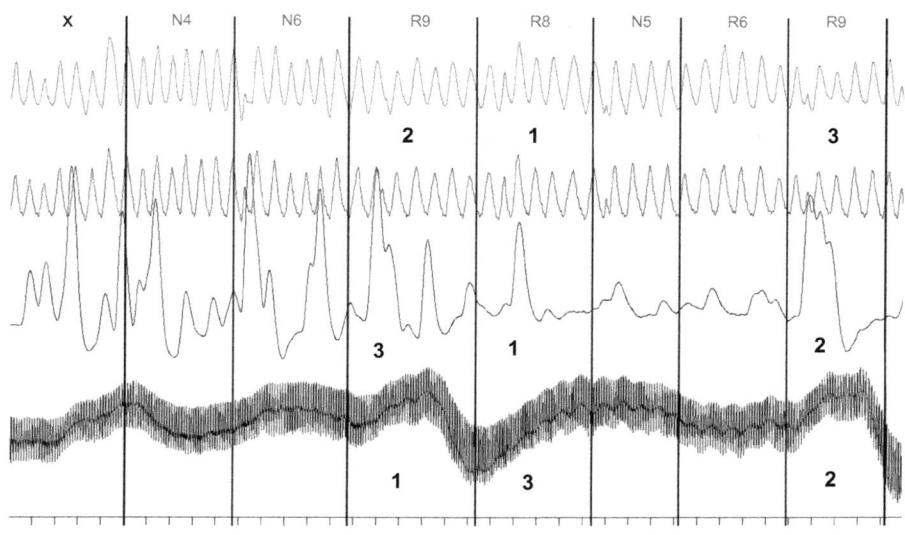

FIGURE 5.24
One RI chart showing rank order scoring of the top three strongest reactions.

PURPOSEFUL NON-COOPERATION

Polygraph decisions of DI, NDI, SR, NSR, and Inconclusive all assume the examinee has cooperated with the examination process. Many times, examinees will employ stratagems that manipulate the physiological data or interfere with testing (Jayne, 1981). If the examiner has sufficient evidence to conclude that the examinee has repeatedly failed to follow the examiner's instructions and warnings (using confirmation methods such as Yes Tests,[2] surreptitious physiological recording, movement sensors, visual observation, etc.), this may be the basis for a decision of Purposeful Non-cooperation (PNC). A PNC decision is not a veracity decision, but rather a statement regarding the examinee's compliance with the instructions necessary to conduct a valid examination. As such, it replaces veracity decisions when it is used. If the PNC decision is invoked, a generic description of the behavior is warranted in the final report.

REFERENCES

Backster, C., 1962. Technique tips and polygraph chart interpretation. Newsletter of the Academy for Scientific Interrogation, Sep-Oct.

Bell, B.G., Raskin, D.C., Honts, C.R., Kircher, J.C., 1999. The Utah numerical scoring system. Polygraph 28 (1), 1–9.

---

[2] See a description of the Yes Test in the chapter Advanced Topics.

Benussi, V., 1914. The respiratory symptoms of lying (Die atmungssymptome der lüge). Archiv fuer die Gesamte Psychologie 31, 244–273, English translation in 1975 in Polygraph 4 (1), 52–76.

Blackwell, N.J., 1998. PolyScore 3.3 and psychophysiological detection of deception examiner rates of accuracy when scoring examination from actual criminal investigations. Polygraph 28 (2), 149–175.

Blalock, B., Cushman, B., Nelson, R., 2009. A replication and validation study on an empirically based manual scoring system. Polygraph 38 (4), 281–288.

Capps, M.H., Ansley, N., 1992. Comparison of two scoring scales. Polygraph 21 (1), 39–43.

Correa, E.J., Adams, H.E., 1981. The validity of the pre-employment polygraph examination and the effects of motivation. Polygraph 10 (3), 143–155.

Cullen, M.C., Bradley, M.T., 2004. Positions of truthfully answered controls on control question tests with the polygraph. Can. J. Behav. Sci. 36 (3), 167–176.

Dollins, A.B., Cestaro, V.L., Pettit, D.J., 1998. Efficacy of repeated psychophysiological detection of deception testing. J. Forensic Sci. 43 (5), 1016–1023.

Elaad, E., Ben-Shakhar, G., 2006. Finger pulse waveform length in the detection of concealed information. Int. J. Psychophysiol. 61 (2), 226–234.

Franz, M.L., 1989. Technical report: relative contributions of physiological recordings to detect deception, Contract Number MDA 904-88-M-6612.

Gödert, H.W., Rill, H.G., Vossel, G., 2001. Psychophysiological differentiation of deception: the effects of electrodermal lability and mode of responding on skin conductance and heart rate. Int. J. Psychophysiol. 40, 61–75.

Gordon, N., Cochetti, P.M., 1987. The horizontal scoring system. Polygraph 16 (2), 116–125.

Handler, M., Reicherter, J.R., 2008. Respiratory blood pressure fluctuations observed during polygraph examinations. Polygraph 37 (4), 256–262.

Handler, M., Nelson, R., Goodson, W., Hicks, M., 2010. Empirical Scoring System: A cross-cultural replication and extension study of manual scoring and decision policies. Polygraph 39 (4), 200–215.

Harwell, E.M., 2000. A comparison of 3- and 7-position scoring scales with field examinations. Polygraph 29 (2), 195–197.

Honts, C.R., Driscoll, L.N., 1987. An evaluation of the reliability and validity of rank order and standard numerical scoring of polygraph charts. Polygraph 16 (4), 241–257.

Honts, C.R., Handler, M., 2014. Scoring respiration when using directed lie comparison questions. Polygraph 43 (4), 71–78.

Horowitz, S.W., Kircher, J.C., Honts, C.R., Raskin, D.C., 1997. The role of comparison questions in physiological detection of deception. Psychophysiology 34 (1), 108–115.

Jayne, B.C., 1981. Purposeful non-cooperation: a diagnostic opinion of deception. Polygraph 10 (3), 156–174.

Kircher, J.C., Raskin, D.C., 1988. Human versus computerized evaluations of polygraph data in a laboratory setting. J. Appl. Psychol. 73, 291–302.

Kircher, J.C., Packard, T., Bell, B.G., Bernhardt, P.C., 2001. Effects of prior demonstrations of polygraph accuracy on outcomes of probable-lie and directed-lie polygraph tests, DoDPI02-R-0002. DTIC AD Number A404128. University of Utah.

Kircher, J.C., Kristjansson, S.D., Gardner, M.K., 2005. Human and computer decision-making in the psychophysiological detection of deception. Final Report to the DoD Polygraph Institute, University of Utah, Salt Lake City, UT.

Krapohl, D.J., 1998. A comparison of 3- and 7-position scoring scales with laboratory data. Polygraph 27 (3), 210–218.

Krapohl, D.J., 2005. Polygraph decision rules for evidentiary and paired-testing (Marin Protocol) applications. Polygraph 34 (3), 184–192.

Krapohl, D., 2010. Short report: A test of the ESS with two-question field cases. Polygraph 39 (2), 124–126.

Krapohl, D.J., Cushman, B., 2006. Comparison of evidentiary and investigative decision rules: a replication. Polygraph 35 (1), 55–63.

Krapohl, D.J., Dutton, D.W., 2005. A comparison of response profiles for test formats used in the zone comparison and army modified general question techniques. Polygraph 34 (1), 1–10.

Krapohl, D.J., McManus, B., 1999. An objective method for manually scoring polygraph data. Polygraph 28 (3), 209–222.

Krapohl, D.J., Norris, W.F., 2000. An exploratory study of traditional and objective scoring systems with MGQT field cases. Polygraph 29 (2), 185–194.

Krapohl, D.J., Rosales, T., 2014. Decision accuracy for the Relevant-Irrelevant screening test: a partial replication. Polygraph 43 (1), 20–29.

Krapohl, D.J., Dutton, D.W., Ryan, A.H., 2001. The rank order scoring system: replication and extension with field data. Polygraph 30 (3), 172–181.

Krapohl, D.J., Stern, B.A., Bronkema, Y., 2003. Numerical scoring and wise decisions. Polygraph 32 (1), 2–14.

Krapohl, D.J., Senter, S.M., Stern, B.A., 2005. An exploration of methods for the analysis of multiple-issue relevant/irrelevant screening data. Polygraph 34 (1), 47–61.

Krapohl, D.J., Gordon, N., Lombardi, C., 2008. Accuracy demonstration of the Horizontal Scoring System using field cases conducted with the Federal Zone Comparison Technique. Polygraph 37 (4), 263–268.

Light, G.D., 1999. Numerical evaluation of the army zone comparison test. Polygraph 28 (1), 37–45.

Marin, J., 2000. He said/She said: polygraph evidence in court. Polygraph 29 (4), 299–304.

Marin, J., 2001. The ASTM exclusionary standard and the APA "litigation certificate" program. Polygraph 30 (4), 288–293.

Meehl, P.E., Rosen, A., 1955. Antecedent probability and the efficiency of psychometric signs, patterns, and cutting scores. Psychol. Bull. 52 (3), 194–216.

Miritello, K., 1999. Rank order analysis. Polygraph 28 (1), 74–76.

Nelson, R., 2011. Monte Carlo study of criterion validity for two-question Zone Comparison Tests with Empirical Scoring System, 7-position and 3-position scoring models. Polygraph 40 (3), 146–156.

Nelson, R., Handler, M., 2013. Extended analysis of a rank order scoring model and the multifacet hypothesis with the federal zone comparison technique. Polygraph 42 (2), 80–111.

Nelson, R., Krapohl, D., 2011. Criterion validity of the empirical scoring system with experienced examiners: comparison with 7-position evidentiary model using the federal zone comparison technique. Polygraph 40 (2), 79–85.

Nelson, R., Krapohl, D.J., Handler, M., 2008. Brute-force comparison: a Monte Carlo study of the objective scoring system version 3 (OSS-3) and human polygraph scorers. Polygraph 37 (3), 185–215.

Nelson, R., Handler, M., Shaw, P., Gougler, M., Blalock, B., Russell, C., Cushman, B., Oelrich, M., 2011. Using the empirical scoring system. Polygraph 40 (2), 67–78.

Podlesny, J.A., Kircher, J.C., 1999. The Finapres (volume clamp) recording method in psychophysiological detection of deception examinations. Foren. Sci. Commun. 1 (3), 1–18. Available at: http://www.fbi.gov/hq/lab/fsc/backissu/oct1999/index.htm.

Podlesny, J.A., Truslow, C.M., 1993. Validity of an expanded-issue (modified general question) polygraph technique in a simulated distributed-crime-roles context. J. Appl. Psychol. 78 (5), 788–797.

Raskin, D.C., Kircher, J.C., Honts, C.R., Horowitz, S.W., 1988. A study of the validity of polygraph examinations in criminal investigation. Final report, Grant # 87-IJ-CX-0040, National Institute of Justice, Washington, DC.

Rovner, L.I., 1986. The accuracy of physiological detection of deception for subjects with prior knowledge. Polygraph 15 (1), 1–39.

Senter, S.M., 2003. Modified general question test decision rule exploration. Polygraph 32 (4), 251–263.

Timm, H.W., 1982. Analyzing deception from respiration patterns. J. Police Sci. Adm. 10 (1), 47–51.

Van Herk, M., 1990. Numerical evaluation: Seven point scale +/−6 and possible alternatives: a discussion. Newslett. Can. Assoc. Police Polygraph. 7 (3), 28–47.

Verschuere, B., Crombez, G., De Clercq, A., Koster, E.H.W., 2004. Autonomic and behavior responding to concealed information: differentiating orienting and defensive responses. Psychophysiology 41 (3), 461–466.

Weir Jr., R.J., 1974. In defense of the relevant/irrelevant polygraph test. Polygraph 3 (2), 119–166.

CHAPTER 6

Polygraph screening

Like money, lies are of economic value only when they will pass current.
Hubert Howe Bancroft

Though the earliest application of polygraphy was in criminal investigations (Larson, 1921), its value in screening of private and public employees was soon proposed as a means of detecting and deterring undesirable activities among employees (Keeler, 1930). Shortly afterward began the screening of bank workers in Chicago to uncover thievery (O'Leary, 1934; Slawson, 1937), and with that the inchoate field of polygraph screening was established. It would not take long for the suggestion that the US government commence screening of government employees in sensitive positions to sniff out subversion (Bledsoe, 1941). During WWII the US government conducted a polygraph screening program of German prisoners of war for their use as a trusted security force in postwar Germany (Linehan, 1978), and afterward to support security of the US nuclear program (Linehan, 1990).

The use of the polygraph in screening grew rapidly for the next few decades, largely unregulated. Fueled by the potential of personal fortunes, polygraph screening experienced explosive growth, an expansion without the constraints that might be imposed by legislation, supporting research or a body of best practices. In the private sector, business pressures strongly influenced field practices, and to remain competitive in this environment, some polygraph examiners engaged in excesses that not only took advantage of examinees, but so departed from defensible practices that their test results were of no value. Government and law enforcement polygraph examiners were not entirely innocent of excess. Polygraph examiners from departments and agencies responded to demands from superiors who asked for test coverage that expanded, in scope and number, well beyond what polygraph techniques could actually deliver. By the late 1980s the US Congress passed the Employee Polygraph Protection Act (EPPA, Appendix A) which severely restricted polygraph testing in the private sector. Government agencies and law enforcement were exempt from the provisions of EPPA, though some in Congress were loath to carve out those exemptions due to scattered reports of examiner misbehavior in those settings, too.

In the decades since the enactment of EPPA there has been more research on polygraph testing and screening, which laid the foundation for the development of best practices in more recent years. Independent oversight and quality control (QC) processes that emerged in the 1990s also improved the polygraph product of those organizations that instituted them. The continued increase in government counterintelligence testing programs after the 1980s and the expanded use of the polygraph to manage sex offenders have benefited from a greater knowledge as to what constitutes good screening practices.

Currently there are three main areas in which screening is widely used: vetting of applicants, routine periodic testing of employees (almost exclusively among federal government agencies), and recurrent testing of criminal offenders to detect and deter illegal behaviors, or precursors to illegal behaviors. There is an immense overlap in methods among these three areas. Though examiners make subtle but important adjustments to the examination protocol in response to the examinee population (habitual criminals vs. young applicants), examiners generally use the same test and analysis techniques, changing only the test questions to meet the needs of the consumers of the polygraph product.

Polygraph screening is very difficult when done correctly. Unlike specific issue testing where the task is to determine whether the examinee was responsible for a clearly defined and known crime, the screening examiner's mission is to establish whether the examinee has done anything on a list of possible behaviors covering longer periods of time, and if so, when and how often the examinee did it. Given the sheer complexity arising from the range of individual differences among examinees, it is little wonder why screening research has garnered so little scientific attention. From the practitioner perspective, effective polygraph screening relies on their compliance with empirically derived practices. This chapter is drawn from the best work of researchers and from thought-leaders in this field with the aim of helping examiners deliver a useful and reliable product.

Polygraph screening will be defined here as the methodologies used to develop and verify information examinees provide on multiple relevant issues during a polygraph session. The phrase "develop and verify information" is important. Examiners must diligently pursue both aims: test results without information are as incomplete as information without confirmation. Readers will find suggestions for both later in this chapter.

A second benefit to polygraph screening is its demonstrated deterrence effect (Central Intelligence Agency, 1990; Grubin et al., 2004; National Research Council, 2003), at least as it regards traitors and sex offenders. The evidence suggests that these groups consider the prospect of their detection by routine polygraph testing in their decisions whether to commit their crimes. There has been no assessment of an effect on unqualified job applicants who might self-select out of applying for departments or agencies that use the polygraph, though it would not seem reasonable to limit a deterrence effect only to criminal populations. Nevertheless, in all these circumstances a desirable effect can only arise and continue when polygraph screening is effective and fair.

OVERVIEW

As with all worthwhile endeavors, conducting polygraph screening requires some thoughtful policies if it is to best deliver what it can. The following are some considerations that should be resolved prior to embarking on a standardized polygraph screening system.

SUCCESSIVE HURDLES

As in all polygraph examinations, there are three essential phases in polygraph screening: pretest, test, and data analysis. Depending on the organizational policy or client agreements, there may also be a posttest discussion or interview conducted by the examiner or others when polygraph results are unfavorable. What is unique about polygraph screening, however, is that new information elicited during the posttest may provide a basis for additional testing. In other words, polygraph examiners can employ focused testing to verify that the examinee is not withholding yet additional information elicited after a failed screening test. This process of testing, interviewing, more focused testing, and more interviewing is called "successive hurdles," or sometimes "successive screens." It allows polygraph screening examinations to boost decision accuracy by the stepwise use of more powerful polygraph techniques while simultaneously encouraging more candor from the examinee. Recall that the goal of screening is to develop and verify information. The successive-hurdles approach is designed to do just that.

Consider this brief example. An applicant is given a multiple-issue polygraph test covering past criminal activity, use of illegal drugs, and falsification of his application. He makes no admissions during the pretest interview. Suppose the applicant reacts significantly to the drug question. If the testing stops at this point, it is impossible to know the reason for the reaction, and it could be because of minor behaviors within the bounds of the hiring standards. Suppose, though, that in a posttest discussion the applicant acknowledges withholding the use of cocaine a single time 3 years previous to the examination, and this new information is not disqualifying for the agency. A new test can be developed, sometimes called a "breakdown" test (Weir, 1976), that focuses exclusively on the drug topic, with questions about the use of more types of illegal drugs, more recent use, and more frequent use. If the applicant does well to this breakdown testing, the examiner can have more confidence that the applicant has honestly disclosed his drug use. The applicant then can be placed back in the applicant pool. Failure on any question can give the examiner direction as to where to lead a new discussion on the topic, and a better likelihood of developing new information. Ultimately, the examiner would have to return to the remaining issues and retest them unless disqualifying information was volunteered by the applicant. These same processes can be applied to other settings, such as multiple-issue testing of convicted offenders in government-sponsored programs intended to deter and detect reoffending.

Managers of polygraph programs should pay attention to how the "successive-hurdles" approach is executed by their examiners. Weaker examiners can be tempted to move immediately from the screening phase to the breakdown without first undertaking a thorough discussion of the troublesome issue with the examinee. In other words, they do not try to resolve the issue through the development of additional information, but rather simply by more testing. This risks elevating the possibility of a false negative as examiners eventually "test the examinee out," that is, conducting tests until the examinee no longer responds when deceptive. Examiners should never initiate breakdown testing without a dedicated effort to determine through discussion with the examinee the cause of the reactions on the screening test.

The "successive-hurdles" method does come with a cost of additional effort and time from the examiner, and may lower examiner throughput. The benefits are that it can mitigate false positive screening results, produce more actionable information, and increase confidence in the final polygraph decision. It is the best practice.

TEST TOPICS

In most screening settings, the test issues have been predetermined by the client or agency. In others cases there is some flexibility, and in rare instances the examiner has full discretion what topics to include in the screening examination. Here are some general rules about screening test topics.

As a general rule, the fewer the number of test topics, and the narrower the focus of those questions, the more accurate the testing. Each additional test topic reduces test accuracy, if for no other reason that it gives one more opportunity for a false positive result. Similarly, test questions covering long periods of time can tax an examinee's memory, and in extreme cases deny the examinee certainty that he is answering truthfully. On the other end, narrowing questions too much may exclude examinee behaviors that are important to the agency or client. Therefore, test topics and their time periods should not extend beyond what is necessary and consider the limits of human memory. For example, if hiring officials do not disqualify candidates for drug use that occurred more than 5 years ago, there is no value in extending the test question beyond that period. Conversely, if lifetime drug experiences are important to hiring officials, such as when assessing the extent of an earlier addiction, the test question can be scoped to go back as far as necessary.

Another factor to take into account is complexity. Relevant test questions should be clear, unambiguous, concise, and not require subjective assessments. This is necessary to avoid physiological responses that have causes unrelated to deception.

> Good example: Have you ever accepted a bribe?
> Bad example: Have you violated your agency's policy as regards preferential treatment in exchange for reward, tangible or intangible?
> Good example: Has a previous employer ever counseled or disciplined you for verbal or physical abuse?
> Bad example: Have you ever used excessive force or offensive language in your official duties.

Though the polygraph is helpful to decision-makers in assessing the potential future behavior of an examinee, future behavior should not be used as relevant test questions. This approach introduces uncertainty to the relevant questions, a factor that should be vigorously avoided. No one can know with certainty what his behavior might be in as-yet unknown circumstances. Examinees facing such questions are left to speculate, which by definition would make for an inappropriate relevant question. The best predictor of future behavior is past behavior, which should be the focus of the polygraph (Handler et al., 2009). Relevant questions covering an examinee's potential actions have no basis in empirical research, and overextend the capabilities of polygraphy.

The base rate of behaviors covered by test topics is also something policy makers need to think about when choosing which to use, especially when large numbers of individuals will undergo the testing. Test questions that cover behaviors that are extremely rare or extremely common are not additive to the overall screening process. This takes a little mathematics to explain. The following is a little thought experiment which highlights the effect of extreme base rates.

Suppose an agency's primary concern is the leakage of classified information to the spy agencies of other countries. Non-polygraph leadership may logically prefer a polygraph test question something like "Have you ever committed espionage against the US?" It meets the definition of being clear, unambiguous, concise, and does not require a subjective assessment. The agency's hope is that this question will find the rare traitor in its ranks.

However, it is generally accepted that polygraph screening has imperfect accuracy. How imperfect will depend on adherence to best practices, the number and scope of the test questions, competency of the examiner, use of oversight, suitable examinees, and a variety of other conditions. Suppose for the present purposes that the polygraph program can detect 7 out of 10 liars, and 9 out of 10 truthtellers. This is not an unreasonable estimate with what is currently known about polygraph screening. Also suppose that the agency uses polygraph screening with its employees, and among them is one traitor for every 1000 loyal employees.[1]

When the agency conducts polygraph screening on its employees it will have some results of deception and some of truthfulness. Using the assumptions in the previous paragraph, it is likely to detect the one traitor. A 90% ability to detect truthfulness will produce about 900 correct decisions for the loyal employees, and 99 false decisions of deception for this group. Therefore, 99 out of the 100 decisions of deception are incorrect. If adverse actions are taken against those with failed polygraphs, it is easy to see that polygraph screening puts large numbers of innocent employees at risk. That risk may be reduced if the polygraph is only used much like a tripwire, to trigger other investigative processes to confirm or disconfirm the polygraph results: focused polygraph testing, more expanded background investigations, etc. However, the use of the polygraph as the sole basis for hiring or firing decisions can be reasonably challenged on low base rate topics because of the problem of false positives, a problem identified in the report of the National Research Council (2003).

Similarly, test issues with extraordinarily high base rates can produce very lopsided accuracies. Changing the traitor scenario mentioned earlier to one such as sex offender management, where deception is typically quite high when offenders initially enter the program, confidence in polygraph decisions of truthfulness is seriously eroded. Consequently, polygraph test questions with extreme base rates should be avoided. A more complete explanation about base rate and test topic selection is available in the classic paper by Honts and Schweinle (2009).

---

[1] The effect of base rates on the proportion of false negatives and false positives is explored in greater detail in Chapter 9.

Another essential factor affecting choices of test questions has to do with prediction, at least so far as applicant screening is concerned: the behaviors at the focus of the test question should be predictive of the candidate's future success on the job. A good example might be a candidate's history of criminal activity. Propensity toward crime tends to be relatively stable in most individuals, and so serious criminal conduct in the past is a fairly good index of future problems. It would make for a defensible polygraph screening topic. At the other extreme is legal sexual behavior that some might consider immoral. At one time homosexuality and infidelity were routinely covered in polygraph screening among some US government agencies and police departments with only the most tangential linkage to job performance. There are many other examples where the predictive value of polygraph test topics is equally tenuous.

Somewhere in the middle of this continuum is the use of illegal drugs, especially marijuana. Experimentation with marijuana among applicants of a certain age is the rule rather than the exception. In some jurisdictions casual marijuana use is even legal, and in many others there is a lax enforcement policy. The dividing line on what is "experimentation" and what constitutes a level of use that predicts a risk to a candidate's future job performance is difficult to discern, and could depend on circumstances. For fairness and standardization an organization must have clear selection guidelines in place. Those guidelines will affect the type of polygraph test question used with applicants regarding drug use.

Another factor of which to be mindful is the disproportionate effect some questions could have on minority groups. Polygraph questions should be sexually and racially neutral, though not every agency is equally sensitive to this concern. A good example taken from a state police applicant screening program, before the program was threatened by litigation, was the question "Have you ever witnessed a crime you did not report?" It is easy to see this topic could have different outcomes depending on where one lived: Applicants from disadvantaged neighborhoods are more likely to have an increased exposure to crimes while also being at some personal risk if they were to report them.

To summarize, when polygraph screening is used to predict future behavior, the test topics must be valid predictors. This must be done with relevant questions that test past behavior of a type associated with proscribed future behavior. Asking many questions simply cover all possibilities is not as efficient, nor effective, as restricting the coverage to only those areas that are associated with behavior that agencies or clients need to know for better decision making. Questions should be fair for all candidates. For nearly all applications, three to six topics are sufficient when examinees are afforded only one polygraph session.

ADJUDICATIONS

In larger organizations there is great value in the use of a centralized and independent body to make selection and firing decisions except in cases of clear criminal conduct. One advantage is the reduction in preferential treatment by managers in these decisions. Another is confidentiality. During background investigations, and especially during polygraph examinations, adverse information arises about a candidate that might be embarrassing but not disqualifying. Maintaining this information in restricted channels serves the interest of the employee and can reduce to a degree the fear of self-disclosure during polygraph examinations. It also removes a potential opportunity for misuse if placed in the hands of a bad manager.

RECORDING

Electronic recording of the polygraph session is an option for polygraph programs and individual examiners. These recordings can protect those examiners and examinees who behave responsibly, while providing an indisputable record of those who do not. Modern technology makes recording and storing a trivial matter, both audio and video. An additional benefit of recording is that exceptional cases with educational value can be provided to newer examiners for learning purposes.

SURVEYS

For applicant and employee screening it is very useful to monitor examinee attitudes about the examination process. Offering each examinee an anonymous survey form is one method for managers to verify that their examiner staff is treating examinees professionally. Moreover, if examinees tend to report favorably their polygraph experiences, the survey results are useful in countering erroneous characterizations of polygraphy. The surveys need not be long, but should cover the examinee's attitude regarding the professional treatment, fairness, and respect afforded by the polygraph examiner.

SIGNIFICANT CASE TRACKING

Experienced examiners know to maintain a record of their best cases. This practice has a couple of benefits. For the examiner working in a larger polygraph screening program, it provides a useful reference when it comes time for management's annual review of the examiner's performance. For polygraph programs it provides a very impactful record of the importance of polygraph in the hiring, reinvestigative, or offender management process. While statistical tracking may also be important, senior leadership are heavily influenced by representative cases where the polygraph was the only tool that delivered essential information. Fortunately, in well-managed programs these cases are commonplace.

RESULTS

Finally, a word about the use of polygraph test results. As a rule, polygraph results regarding truthfulness or deception should not be the sole basis for decisions for or against an examinee who has taken a screening test. There are many undesirable second-order effects when the polygraph has unilateral power over an examinee's employment fate. Among them is the overreliance on the polygraph while neglecting other processes that could improve decision making, as well as the potential for costly litigation. Certainly polygraph screening adds unique value to the decision-making process, perhaps more than any other single contributor, but it is not infallible. If other processes are available, information and results coming from them should be given weight in the overall decision that is commensurate with their validity and significance. Admissions made during a polygraph screening examination might be included among them.

There will always be some examinees who may attempt to "game" their polygraph examinations. Those examinees are best handled organizationally the same as those who are detected trying to cheat on or defeat any of the other processes the examinee is subject to (e.g., psychological interviews, application forms, intelligence tests, fitness tests, drug tests).

GENERAL SUGGESTIONS FOR PRETEST INTERVIEWS

The pretest interview of the screening test is somewhat similar to those of a specific issue exam. Where the pretest interview is different is in how it incorporates specially developed procedures to elicit more information from the examinee. When examinees volunteer more during the discussion of the question topics, it allows the examiner to craft better screening questions, which in turn helps truthful examinees do well during the testing phase of the examination.[2] It can also lead to significant admissions from the examinee that are invaluable to an agency or client. For these reason, a carefully executed pretest interview is a wise investment.

One of the major innovations to the polygraph screening examination was introduced by Dan Weatherman (2011) and is called Interview Route Maps (IRM). It is based on a large body of cognitive and learning research which shows that attention and comprehension can be improved when information is visually represented according to their memory relationships. Weatherman adapted the research to the polygraph screening process where there can be greater ambiguity about the scope and definition of the relevant topic areas.

IRMs in the polygraph screening context have a number of advantages. They can serve to jog the examinee's memory, solidify the examinees understanding of what the topic encompasses and what it excludes, and it can prompt more interaction

---

[2] The examiner should not stop an examinee from talking during the dialog covering the relevant topics, even if the examinee volunteers tangential information that, at first, appears to be out of scope of the relevant questions. Sometimes these harmless admissions lead to reportable information, though it might not be obvious at first. Other times the examinee wants to get a concern off his chest so that it does not become an issue during testing. The examiner should pursue the information to its logical conclusion, then inform the examinee whether the information is in or out of the scope of the test questions. The only exception might be if the examinee is volunteering highly personal information that is well outside of the intent of the relevant questions. In those circumstances the examiner should exercise sensitivity and tact in discouraging such disclosures.

between examinee and examiner. Two essential components of the IRM approach are that the examinee must come to understand his responsibility for providing all information on the topics discussed if he wants to pass the examination, and the other is that the examiner must ensure the interview is very interactive. Field evidence suggests that proper use of the IRMs can prompt significantly more self-disclosure from the examinee during the pretest interview, and perhaps relatedly, reduce the rate of inconclusive results.

The IRMs are introduced after all of the other pretest steps have been completed, but before the reviewing of the test questions. They are discussed singly, with one for each test question. The interview is nonconfrontational and uses open-ended questions about each of the areas on the IRM. The examiner points to each area on the IRM as the interview progresses so that the examinee is aware of the topic just as it is to be discussed.

IRMs can be displayed on flipcharts, computer screens, or sketched on a sheet of paper by the examiner on the spot. IRMs have a central idea or topic, usually placed in the center of the IRM, that corresponds with a relevant topic area, with the elements of that topic area radiating outward (see Figure 6.1). The examiner points

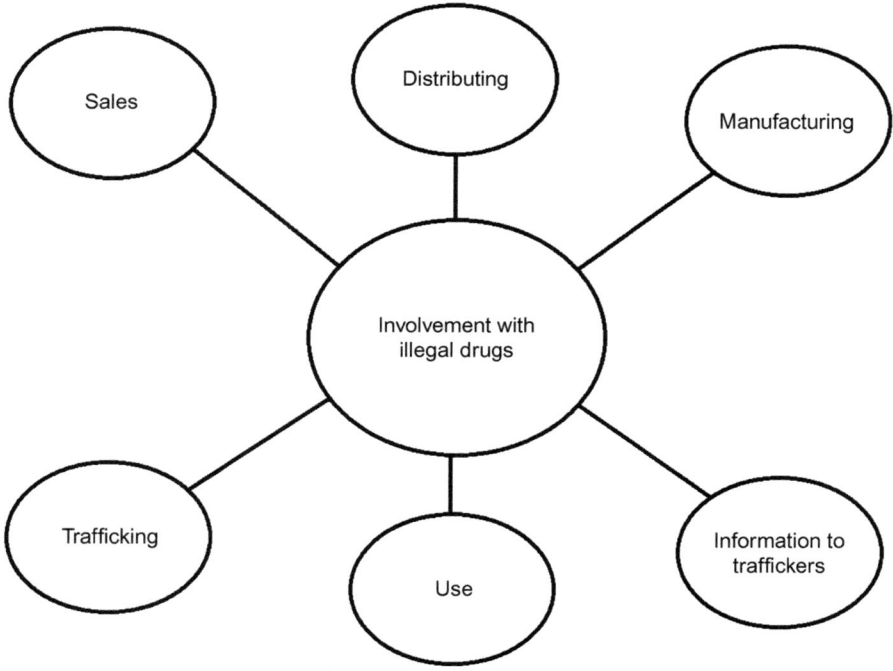

FIGURE 6.1

Possible Interview Route Map (IRM) for the pretest discussion of involvement with illegal drugs. The center portion encapsulates the topic as it will be covered in the polygraph test question.

to each element, in turn, and engages in an exchange with the examinee in order to elicit examinee concerns and relevant information. At the end of the discussion the examiner explains to the examinee that each of the elements is part of the polygraph test question on that topic.

The information shared by the examinee during the IRM discussion is vital. With it the examiner can gauge whether the examinee understands the scope of the relevant question, is trying to rationalize a behavior, or whether the wording of the test question must be adjusted to accommodate an examinee who is trying to be truthful. There is one IRM for each relevant topic on the examination, and the results of the discussion with the examinee will determine the final wording of the polygraph test question. In addition to helping the examiner communicate the scope and boundaries of the relevant topics, the use of IRMs can ensure standardized testing for all examinees by the examiner, as well as identical coverage for all examinees when there are multiple examiners. IRMs can be used in any screening context, and potentially in complex criminal cases. Currently they are not commonly used to discuss comparison questions, though there are no technical reasons IRMs could not be used for them as well. They may prove useful in Directed Lie tests to help maintain the salience of the comparison questions.

DIRECTED-LIE SCREENING TEST

The directed-lie screening test (DLST) is patterned after a polygraph screening method called the test for espionage and sabotage (TES) which, unlike many polygraph screening methods, is a technique that was validated before being implemented in the field (Reed, 1994; Research Division Staff, 1995a,b; Handler et al., 2008). It was designed to overcome problems encountered in large polygraph screening programs with the overuse of probable-lie comparison questions, and to introduce a greater degree of standardization into the screening processes. Its greatest innovation was the inclusion of the directed-lie question, until then a little-known approach used as early as the late 1960s by US Army polygraph examiners in Vietnam (Menges, 2004).

The DLST is a screening technique, with all of the strengths and limitations inherent to screening tools. It is highly standardized and flexible, and useful in many applications. In contrast to the more popular probable-lie comparison question techniques, as a directed-lie method the DLST is less intrusive, more easily standardized, and entails no manipulation. It can accommodate up to two relevant questions per series, and perhaps as many as three series in a polygraph session.

It is not a diagnostic test, however. It is best used as the first step in a successive-hurdles approach where reactions to relevant questions are followed by more interviewing as well as more testing with narrower relevant questions on a single topic. The DLST also requires training, combined with practical exercises, to become competent. Finally, there is suggestive evidence that the pneumograph does not provide as much information with directed lies as it does with other polygraph methods (Horowitz et al., 1997; Kircher et al., 2001).

DLST PRETEST INTERVIEW

Most of the DLST pretest interview is similar to that conducted for other techniques. The examiner should make introductory remarks to place the examinee at ease, and to explain the examination process. Some of the routine and repetitive parts of the pretest interview can be turned over to automation, using voice files presented by computer. Pretest areas most amenable to automation are the explanation of rights, overview of the testing process, explanation of the relevant physiology, instructions for cooperation, and introduction of the DLCs. Automation allows each examinee to be given the exact same instructions, making the process more standardized and fair (see Blalock, 2009, for a suggested script).

After gathering biographic and health details, many examiner's move to the acquaintance test, also called a demonstration test. Previous research has shown that the acquaintance test boosts the accuracy of the subsequent tests. As a practical matter, it affords the examinee the opportunity to become acquainted with the testing process, which will reduce the general tension of truthful examinees. It also allows the examiner to establish the proper gain settings, ensure the sensors are properly placed, and to see anomalies prior to initiating the screening tests. Finally, some examiners contend that a properly conducted demonstration test tends to prompt more frankness from examinees.

Following the acquaintance test the examiner will begin to discuss the relevant topics using the IRMs. The examiner should use open-ended questions and encourage the examinee to discuss anything about the relevant topic, irrespective of whether it falls within the scope of reporting. Encouraging candor allows the examiner to devise relevant questions that exclude the examinee's past behaviors that are not of interest to hiring officials, to have available information that could be used for probable-lie comparison questions in subsequent testing (if necessary), and to avoid reactions to test questions due to the examinee's minor concerns that could have been addressed during the interview phase. Also, examinees who have committed major offenses often test the waters by first disclosing minor indiscretions, and if the examiner continues to pursue information on the topic in a low-key nonjudgmental manner, examinees are often more willing to share information of interest to hiring officials.

INTRODUCTION OF THE DIRECTED LIES

One difference between the directed-lie and probable-lie approaches is in the manner in which these questions are introduced to the examinee. Recall that for the probable-lie approach the examiner prefers that the examinee be deceptive, or at least uncertain about his complete truthfulness, to the comparison questions. In contrast, with DLCs there is an agreement struck between the examinee and examiner that the examinee will give a "no" answer to a question that both of them know to be untrue. Regardless of whether the examinee knows the purpose of the DLCs, they can still function well.

DLCs are not just any question that the examinee will deny but are designed to be personally relevant (see Horowitz et al., 1997). For example, the question "Is today

Tuesday?" would be a poor choice for a DLC, whereas the question "Have you violated a minor traffic law?" would function better. Other good choices might include:

- Have you ever later regretted something you'd said to someone?
- In your life have you cheated in any contest, game, or competition?
- Have you ever been dishonest with a coworker?
- Have you ever spread false information about another person?
- Have you ever exaggerated about yourself to impress someone?
- Have you ever lied to a past employer?
- Have you ever intentionally done something to make someone mad?
- Do you ever lose your temper?
- Have you ever lied to a friend about something significant?

In introducing the DLCs to the examinee, let him know that they will be the only questions he will have permission to lie to, and like the acquaintance test, he will react to the questions regardless of how small the lie. Select two DLCs for each test and introduce each of them something like this:

> The next couple of questions I'm going to ask you will be a little different. First I will ask you about having lied to a past employer. You have, haven't you, even if it was about something small? Can you remember a time, maybe a couple times, when you did this? Good. Now, when I ask you on the test whether you've lied to your employer, I want you to answer "no". You will know that this answer is not true when you say it. Let's practice it: Have you ever lied to a past employer? (Examinee answers "no"). Excellent. Don't forget to say "no" during the test. If you make a mistake it will be okay, but we will have to start all over. (For a complete script, see Blalock, 2009).

Use a variation on this script for each DLC, and ideally one should use two different DLCs for each test. In some schools of thought the earlier DLCs can be used in subsequent test series, but others believe that examiners should use a different DLC for each test. Evidence for a preference for either approach is lacking.

DLST TEST PHASE

The DLST is a one-chart test. It has exactly two relevant questions, two DLCs, a sacrifice relevant question, and two neutral questions. For every additional pair of relevant questions a new DLST is conducted. The question pacing is at every 20-30 s. Here is the question sequence:

N1	Neutral question	
N2	Neutral question	
SR	Sacrifice Relevant question	
1C1	First presentation of DLC #1	
1R1	First presentation of Relevant question #1	
1R2	First presentation of Relevant question #2	
1C2	First presentation of DLC #2	

2R1	Second presentation of Relevant question #1
2R2	Second presentation of Relevant question #2
2C1	Second presentation of DLC #1
3R1	Third presentation of Relevant question #1
3R1	Third presentation of Relevant question #2
2C2	Second presentation of DLC #2

There must be three presentations of each of the relevant questions that are free of artifact to satisfy the scoring protocol. Relevant questions are not rotated in the DLCT. In those cases where artifacts have occurred, it is permissible to repeat the questions a fourth time, or to conduct a separate chart with the following sequence:

N1	Neutral question
N2	Neutral question
SR	Sacrifice Relevant question
3C1	Third presentation of DLC #1
4R1	Fourth presentation of Relevant question #1
4R2	Fourth presentation of Relevant question #2
3C2	Third presentation of DLC #2

Like routine portions of the pretest, the presentation of the test questions can be automated, and there are practical reasons for doing so. It ensures that the proper question labels are assigned, the examiner does not misspeak, stutter, hesitate, or talk louder on some questions, and it allows the examiner to watch the examinee instead of the question sheet during testing. It permits quality assurance programs to approve of the question presentations in advance, and the automated voice ensures that question onset with the voice matches precisely with the annotation on the chart. There can be no examinee claims of unequal treatment, and it lets the examiner's voice rest for a few minutes, not an unattractive feature. Most computerized polygraphs have this function.

DLST SCORING

The DLST uses either 7-position scoring or the Empirical Scoring System (ESS). Each relevant question can be scored channel-by-channel to the stronger of the two closest DLCs. For example, 1R1 could be scored against either 1C1 or 1C2. The scoring features are the same as those used in probable-lie tests, except with regard to the pneumograph. Some research has found the pneumograph loses much of its diagnostic value with the DLC questions. Therefore, if examiners choose to score the pneumograph at the DLCs, they should do so with caution.

All scores are added to create spot scores (subtotal for each relevant question) and a grand total score (sum of all spot scores).

DLST DECISION RULES

The decision rules for the DLST using either 7-position scoring or ESS are outlined in Table 6.1. If the scores do not meet the requirements for either a significant responses (SR) or no significant responses (NSR), the results are Inconclusive.

Table 6.1 Decision rules for the DLST with ESS and 7-position scoring

		Spot score	Conditional	Total score
Decision	No Significant Responses	+1 or more	and	+4 or more
	Significant Responses	−3 or lower	or	−4 or lower

Unlike other techniques, if the results are Inconclusive after the one-chart DLST, the test can immediately be given a second time. It is recommended that the examiner reviews both the relevant questions and the DLC instructions with the examinee before attempting to repeat the same DLST.

There is a second approach for reducing inconclusives that is reported less often. In the original TES studies, when the decision rules in Table 6.1 did not result in a definitive decision, the examiner could score the first portion of the charts a second time, but exclude 1C1 in the rescoring. Then the same decision rules were applied with the new scores. The effect of this procedure was to reduce inconclusives without affecting decision accuracy. The value of the method is that it often averted the need to rerun the test. Because the first DLC often evokes a tremendous orienting response, some examiners never score against it. Unpublished research supports this approach.

As with all screening techniques, results are reported for the entire test. That is, decisions are not made by individual question, but on the examination. As an example, if an examinee were NSR on the first relevant question in a series, but SR on the second, they are report as SR for the exam. Split calls, where different decisions are made for each test question, are explicitly prohibited. As a matter of practice, however, when examinees are returned for additional testing the examiner would begin with the SR series. If the examinee were cleared in this second session, he would be called NSR for the examination.

NEXT STEPS

If the examinee favorably resolves all of the relevant questions and the examiner renders a decision of NSR, the examination can be concluded.

During the debriefing at the end of the NSR exam, an examiner can explain that there is a QC process, and that in a small number of cases the QC recommends a retest. The examiner should ask whether the examinee would participate in a retest if requested. The examiner should then review the examinee's admissions to ensure they are accurate. Even if the session had not been electronically recorded, it is best that this final review is captured on tape along with the examinee's acknowledgment that the information is accurate. The examiner then closes with an expression of appreciation for cooperation, leaving him with a positive impression of his polygraph experience.

If the DLST resulted in a decision of SR or Inconclusive, it is the best practice to interview the examinee further, and expend every effort to uncover information that could be responsible for the reactivity on the charts. This is more than a cursory step. The goal is to secure information that could be used in a new test, using a technique such as the Air Force Modified General Question Technique (AFMGQT). This new test should not be undertaken until it is reasonably certain that the examinee has volunteered the information that caused the problems in the DLST, which typically is not completed quickly. Examiners need to keep the discussion moving until the examinee provides a realistic explanation for the reaction to the test question(s). Information that is not reportable can be used as the basis for probable-lie comparison questions, whereas reportable information will require modifications of the relevant questions to exclude that which the examinee now says. This additional test can be conducted in the same session.

If the examinee continues to react significantly to the relevant questions in the second test, the policy of the agency should prevail. Some agencies will ask the examinee to return for a second session to resolve the outstanding relevant topics. Other agencies will discontinue testing, and evaluate the candidate against others also competing for the same position. They may consider the polygraph results in that evaluation, but as stated earlier, it is usually unwise to use the polygraph results alone when making hiring decisions except in extraordinary situations.

AIR FORCE MODIFIED GENERAL QUESTION TECHNIQUE

The AFMGQT is a flexible technique for conducting multiple-issue and multiple-facet polygraph testing such as applicant screening, aperiodic employee testing, and offender management. It can accommodate two, three, or four relevant questions. The AFMGQT is also suitable for single-issue criminal investigative examinations.

The AFMGQT is an improvement over the older Army version of the Modified General Question Technique (MGQT). The MGQT has been found to have excellent sensitivity to deception but does not detect truthfulness at a rate greater than chance (see Krapohl, 2006). The MGQT is a derivative of the Reid Technique in structure, whereas the AFMGQT is most similar to the Zone approach.

The use of DLCs with the AFMGQT is an optional approach, and though gaining popularity in field practice, they are less frequently found. If the examiner opts for DLCs, these questions should be introduced in the same way they are in the DLST as covered previously.

A very specific form of the AFMGQT is the Law Enforcement Pre-employment Technique (LEPET). What distinguishes the LEPET from other forms of the AFMGQT is a minor variation in question sequence, and the use of standardized relevant questions. The LEPET has two phases, a counterintelligence phase (not used by law enforcement) and a suitability phase. Except where specified, references to the AFMGQT hereafter will also apply to the LEPET.

AFMGQT PRETEST

The standard screening pretest interview is conducted, beginning with the gathering of demographic information and that necessary to make a determination as to whether the examinee is a good candidate for polygraph testing.

The session next moves to the acquaintance test. Following the acquaintance test the examiner introduces the relevant topics using open-ended questions. Information volunteered by the examinee can be used to modify the relevant questions, and non-reportable information can be held in reserve for the development of probable-lie questions. As for all screening methods, examiners should place value on gathering as much information from the examinee on the relevant issues as can be professionally done using elicitation methods. The information will aid in question development, thereby helping the cooperative examinee pass the exam. The information will also assist the consumer of the polygraph report in making better decisions.

The LEPET form of the AFMGQT uses specific relevant questions, though there is no reason to believe that other appropriate test questions could not be used instead. The standard relevant questions are:

Phase I[3]

R4 Have you had any unauthorized foreign contacts?
R6 Have you intentionally mishandled any classified information?
R8 Have you ever been involved in terrorist or subversive activity?

Phase II

R24 Have you ever committed any serious crime?
R26 Are you intentionally withholding any information about your involvement with illegal drugs?
R28 Have you intentionally falsified or omitted any information on your application forms?

The AFMGQT, including the LEPET version, can be used with directed or probable-lie comparison questions. The introduction of the directed-lie questions is identical to the manner in which they are reviewed during the DLST. If the examiner chooses to use probable-lie comparison questions, the rules for development and introduction are the same as used in specific-issue testing. However, in screening the probable-lie questions do not need to be time-barred. They need only be probable lies that are broad in scope, of lesser import than the relevant issues, and do not overlap the relevant questions. An example taken from the Federal Examiner Handbook (2006) is "Have you ever done anything academically dishonest?"

AFMGQT TEST PHASE

There are versions of the AFMGQT to handle two, three, and four relevant questions, and each of these versions has two variations in question sequence (see Tables 6.2–6.5 for formats). If more than four relevant issues are needed in order to cover all of the

---
[3] This phase is rarely included in non-federal screening examinations.

Table 6.2 AFMGQT with two relevant questions

Position	Variation 1	Variation 2
1	Irrelevant	Irrelevant
2	Sacrifice Relevant	Sacrifice Relevant
3	Comparison 1	Comparison 1
4	Relevant 1	Relevant 1
5	Comparison 2	Relevant 2
6	Relevant 2	Comparison 2
7	Comparison 3	

Table 6.3 AFMGQT version with three relevant questions

Position	Variation 1	Variation 2
1	Irrelevant	Irrelevant
2	Sacrifice Relevant	Sacrifice Relevant
3	Comparison 1	Comparison 1
4	Relevant 1	Relevant 1
5	Comparison 2	Relevant 2
6	Relevant 2	Comparison 2
7	Comparison 3	Relevant 3
8	Relevant 3	Comparison 3

Table 6.4 AFMGQT version with four relevant questions

Position	Variation 1	Variation 2
1	Irrelevant	Irrelevant
2	Sacrifice Relevant	Sacrifice Relevant
3	Comparison 1	Comparison 1
4	Relevant 1	Relevant 1
5	Comparison 2	Relevant 2
6	Relevant 2	Comparison 2
7	Comparison 3	Relevant 3
8	Relevant 3	Relevant 4
9	Comparison 4	Comparison 3
10	Relevant 4	

Table 6.5 Law Enforcement Pre-Employment Test

Position	
1	Irrelevant 1
2	Sacrifice Relevant
3	Comparison 1
4	Relevant 1
5	Comparison 2
6	Relevant 2
7	Comparison 3
8	Relevant 3
9	Comparison 4

topic areas, it is recommended that more than one series be conducted, with the relevant topics grouped logically. For example, in sex offender management the first series could address compliance with probationary restrictions and the second series could cover compliance with treatment conditions. Typically, the more serious topics are covered in the first series. It is also helpful to note that there is no version of the AFMGQT for just one relevant question, so it is beneficial to balance the number of relevant questions across the different series to avoid leaving one relevant topic to be tested alone.

In all AFMGQT versions the relevant and comparison questions can be rotated systematically. Rotation allows each relevant question to be scored against a different comparison question, and it mitigates to some extent the effect of habituation that might occur to a relevant question when it is posed only at the end of the test. It is also good practice to include additional irrelevant questions during the pretest interview in case they are needed during testing. On the first chart of the LEPET, it is standard practice to insert a second reviewed irrelevant question somewhere in the middle of the question sequence at the discretion of the examiner. It is optional whether to use it in subsequent charts.

Each of these versions requires a minimum of three charts. Four or even five may be collected to resolve Inconclusive results. Once the results are definitive; however, testing should stop. The AFMGQT is commonly used as a second step in the successive-hurdles model.

Tables 6.2–6.5 show the positions of each of the test questions in the initial series. To help keep track of the types of questions in the format while rotating them, letters can be used to designate the category of question. Using Variation 1 of the two-question AFMGQT in Table 6.2 as an example, the sacrifice relevant question could be labeled SR2, the first comparison question C3, the first relevant R4, and so on. In doing so, other examiners can more easily evaluate the charts recorded by the testing examiner.

AFMGQT SCORING

The AFMGQT can be scored with the 3- or 7-position scoring systems and ESS. If a relevant question is bracketed by comparison questions, it is scored channel by channel against the stronger of the two comparison questions. For Version 2 of the AFMGQT, where there are two adjacent relevant questions, either of them can be scored against the comparison questions that immediately bracket the relevant question pairs. If a relevant question is not bracketed by comparison questions, it is scored against the comparison question immediately preceding it. There also exist automated algorithms that can be used to guide polygraph decisions, though their validity in screening examinations has not been as well established.

AFMGQT DECISION RULES

With Federal scoring rules, when the examinee has achieved a spot score of −3 or lower, the decision for the multiple-issue test is SR. For a decision of NSR, every spot score must be +3 or greater. The total score is not considered. All else is Inconclusive. ESS decision rules can be based on tolerance for risk, and a complete explanation for selecting ESS decision rules is found in a how-to article by Nelson et al. (2011). The default ESS decision rules are: Any spot score of −3 or lower results in an SR decision, and an NSR decision requires a +1 spot score for every relevant question. All else would be Inconclusive.

The general rule of the AFMGQT is when an examinee is found SR or Inconclusive to one question, he is considered SR or Inconclusive to the test. Split decisions within a series are not permitted. For example, in a series where the 7-position spot scores for three relevant questions are +9, −3, +7, the test would be called SR even though the total score would be quite high. One could not make a call of NSR to the first and third relevant questions despite the scores because split calls are not permitted. To make different decisions for each question, they must be individually tested with single-issue tests. If the examinee fails one of the single-issue examinations, it is appropriate to make a DI call. This is the "successive-hurdles" methodology, and is described in greater detail by Krapohl and Stern (2003).

RELEVANT/IRRELEVANT SCREENING TEST

The Relevant/Irrelevant (RI) screening test has many variations, and there may not be any generally agreed upon approach to the RI. Outlined here is a version first reported by Weir (1974, 1975), who described the method he used as a federal polygraph examiner. Also included are updated details from research reports for or by the US Government (Kircher et al., 2006; Krapohl and Rosales, 2014; Krapohl, 2005; Weaver and Garwood, 1985), and from US Government presentations (Dutton, 2005; Manley, 2010).

The RI is a versatile method for polygraph screening, and one more resistant to examinee manipulation than others. It is also a good method for testing other polygraph examiners. It has only two established shortcomings. One is that there is no scoring system, and consequently it must be interpreted globally. Second is that its validity is the weakest among the researched polygraph screening techniques. Nevertheless, in the hands of the competent and experienced examiner, it can be used selectively in cases where comparison question techniques may not function well.

Some of the reasons for using the RI include concerns that the examinee might try to manipulate the physiological data, periodic and frequent testing of an examinee (e.g., informants), testing of polygraph examiners, and an examinee is reluctant to answer any but relevant and irrelevant questions.

RI PRETEST

The RI screening pretest interview is performed similarly to other screening techniques. Following the gathering of demographic information the examiner conducts an acquaintance test. The examiner then introduces the relevant topics using open-ended questions. The examiner encourages the examinee to fully disclose information, concerns, and details regarding every relevant question so as to allow the development of good relevant questions. However, because the RI screening test does not use probable- or directed-lie comparison questions, any sensitive and non-reportable information volunteered by the examinee should be held for the post-screening phase of the examination, if necessary. It may be helpful in posttest interviewing, or for areas for comparison questions if subsequent testing is required, to use a comparison question technique.

There are three types of questions with the RI screening test: relevant, irrelevant, and overall truth. Relevant questions cover the topics for which the examination is conducted, and are labeled R1, R2, up to R5. Irrelevant questions should be straightforward, emotionally neutral, unrelated to the relevant topics, and known to be true by both the examiner and examinee. They are labeled I1, I2, etc. An alternative is the use of letters, for example, A, B, C, etc.

Overall truth questions are helpful to gauge an examinee's response capability. For example, if an examinee does not respond to these kinds of questions, the examinee may not be able to respond to relevant questions even if deceptive to them. However, overall truth questions do not play the role of traditional comparison questions, that is, the magnitude of the response to the overall truth questions is not compared to those of the relevant questions. It is simply important that examinees continue to respond to the overall truth questions. A lack of responsivity may indicate fatigue, inattention, or other problems.

Overall truth questions are labeled T1, T2, etc. They normally occupy a position near the front of the test, though not the first position, and sometimes at the end of the test. If an examinee has shown the capability to respond to relevant questions over the course of testing, a final overall truth question is not necessary. Examples of overall truth might include.

T1 Do you intend to answer truthfully to each of the questions on this test?
T2 Do you plan to lie to any of the questions on this test?
T3 Did you lie to any question on this test?
T4 Have you answered truthfully each question on this test?

RI TEST PHASE

Among polygraph techniques, the rules for question order for the RI screening test are the most flexible. There is no fixed order, only rules that govern how the examiner sets the order in a given case. The rules are

Table 6.6 Possible question sequence for the RI screening test

| Chart 1 | I1, T1, R3, R1, R2, I2, I1, R4, R2, R1 |
| Chart 2 | I2, I1, R4, R3, I1, R1, R3, R2, I2, R4, T2 (optional) |

- The test always begins with an irrelevant question.
- The second position can be occupied by an irrelevant question, or by an overall truth question.
- There should be pattern avoidance, that is, the examinee should not be able to predict which question will be presented next in a series.
- Questions are repeated within a test. Examinees are made aware of this fact during the pretest interview. The first repeated questions should be an irrelevant question, and no question is repeated back-to-back.
- No more than three relevant questions may be asked in a row before an irrelevant question is presented.
- Each relevant question must be presented at least three times for a decision to be rendered. If a movement or other artifact interferes with the data, a question can be given additional times.
- There should be no more than 12 question presentations on a chart with the RI.

Table 6.6 shows a possible test sequence for two charts (adapted from Kircher et al., 2006).

RI SCORING RULES

The RI does not have a scoring system, but relies on global evaluation of the data. This method is taken up in the chapter Analysis of Polygraph Data, and is only summarized here. When reactions consistently accompany a specific question in a significant manner, it is an indication that the examinee has concerns, and is possibly deceptive, to that question. The term *conspecnificance* is a mnemonic for the three conditions that signify that a reaction warrants an examiner's attention: consistency, specificity, and significance (Weir, 1976).

RI DECISION RULES

No screening test is a stand-alone method but serves only as the first step in a successive-hurdles approach. If conspecficance takes place, the examiner must explore that topic area with the examinee, discussing it until a plausible explanation for the reaction is offered by the examinee. The new information is then used to develop a breakdown test using a technique with better accuracy (e.g., AFMGQT) to determine whether the examinee is withholding additional information on that topic. The remaining issues from the screening test continue to be unresolved until they are tested again, this time without the topic to which the examinee responded to earlier.

Decisions of deception and truthfulness to different test questions in the same test should never take place.

SCREENING EXAMINATION REPORTS

Polygraph screening reports should include information necessary for identification of the examinee, details of the examination, the relevant questions, admissions to relevant questions, and the polygraph results. The examiner should only make recommendations and offer opinions he is qualified to make. For example, if the examinee presents unusual behavior that might suggest psychological or emotional problems, the examiner would be proper in describing those behaviors but only offer a psychological opinion if he is qualified to do so.

The examiner should avoid reporting admissions volunteered by the examinee regarding comparison questions unless relevant. Examinee confidentiality must be respected as regards disclosures during the test, and made available solely to designated individuals. Separately, examiners should discourage decision makers from acting solely on polygraph results without additional supporting information except when the cost of error is so substantial that such decisions can reasonably be justified.

Because polygraph screening methods are not as powerful as specific-issue testing, it is not appropriate to issue diagnostic decisions of deception indicated (DI) or no deception indicated (NDI) based on a multiple-issue screening test. Results of SR and NSR are more precise and better represent the polygraph data. There has also been a trend toward including test scores and algorithm results at the end of reports when they are used as a basis for providing the consumer with error estimates of the results. This trend applies most generally when the consumer is someone trained to understand the meaning of these statistics. These probability statements are recognizable to others who rely on testing, such as practitioners in psychological assessment and medicine. Now that normative data have been developed in polygraphy, error estimates have been calculated for most screening tests. Additional information on polygraph reports can be found in Chapter 11.

REFERENCES

Blalock, B., 2009. Capitalizing on technology to increase standardization and reliability in a polygraph examination. Polygraph 38 (2), 154–166.

Bledsoe, A.H., 1941. The lie detector and national defense. Police Peace Officer's J. Calif. 12, 44.

Central Intelligence Agency, 1990. Project SLAMMER Interim Report. Memorandum for the Members of the DCI Security Forum.

Dutton, D.W., 2005. Relevant-irrelevant screening test. In: Presentation at the Ohio Association of Polygraph Examiners, Columbus, OH.

Grubin, D., Madsen, L., Parsons, S., Sosnowski, D., Warberg, B., 2004. A prospective study of the impact of polygraphy on high-risk behaviors in adult sex offenders. Sexual Abuse 16 (3), 209–222.

Handler, M., Nelson, R., Blalock, B., 2008. A focused polygraph technique for PCSOT and law enforcement screening programs. Polygraph 37 (2), 100–111.

Handler, M., Honts, C.R., Krapohl, D.J., Nelson, R., Griffin, S., 2009. Integration of pre-employment polygraph screening into the police selection process. J. Pol. Crim. Psychol. 24 (2), 69–86.

Honts, C.R., Schweinle, W., 2009. Information gain of psychophysiological detection of deception in forensic and screening settings. Appl. Psychophysiol. Biofeedback 34, 161–172.

Horowitz, S.W., Kircher, J.C., Honts, C.R., Raskin, D.C., 1997. The role of comparison questions in physiological detection of deception. Psychophysiology 34 (1), 108–115.

Keeler, L., 1930. A method for detecting deception. Am. J. Pol. Sci. 1, 38–51.

Kircher, J.C., Packard, T., Bell, B.G., Bernhardt, P.C., 2001. Effects of prior demonstrations of polygraph accuracy on outcomes of probable-lie and directed-lie polygraph tests. University of Utah. Report to the DoD Polygraph Institute, DTIC AD Number A404128.

Kircher, J.C., Woltz, D., Bell, B., Bernhardt, P.C., 2006. Effects of audiovisual presentations of test questions during Relevant/Irrelevant polygraph examinations and new measures. Polygraph 35 (1), 25–54.

Krapohl, D.J., 2005. An exploration of methods for the analysis of multiple-issue relevant/irrelevant screening data. Polygraph 34 (1), 47–61.

Krapohl, D.J., 2006. Validated polygraph techniques. Polygraph 35 (3), 149–155.

Krapohl, D.J., Rosales, M.T., 2014. Decision accuracy for the relevant-irrelevant screening test: a partial replication. Polygraph 42 (1), 20–29.

Krapohl, D.J., Stern, B.A., 2003. Principles of multiple-issue polygraph screening a model for applicant, post-conviction offender, and counterintelligence testing. Polygraph 32 (4), 201–210.

Larson, J.A., 1921. Modification of the Marston deception test. J. Crim. Law Criminol. 12 (3), 390–399.

Linehan, J.G., 1978. An aspect of World War II use of the polygraph. Polygraph 7 (3), 233–239.

Linehan, J.G., 1990. The Oak Ridge polygraph program, 1946–1953. Polygraph 19 (1), 131–138.

Manley, D., 2010. Relevant-irrelevant screening test for law enforcement. In: Presentation to the South Carolina Association of Polygraph Examiners, Columbia, SC.

Menges, P., 2004. Directed lie comparison questions in polygraph examinations: history and methodology. Polygraph 33 (3), 131–142.

National Research Council, 2003. The Polygraph and Lie Detection. Committee to Review the Scientific Evidence on the Polygraph. Division of Behavioral and Social Sciences and Education. The National Academies Press, Washington, DC.

Nelson, R., Handler, M., Shaw, P., Gougler, M., Blalock, B., Russell, C., Cushman, B., Oelrich, M., 2011. Using the empirical scoring system. Polygraph 40 (2), 67–78.

O'Leary, N., 1934. A criminologist to the rescue. Literary Dig. 118 (14), 22.

Reed, S., 1994. A new psychophysiological detection of deception examination for security screening. Psychophysiology 31 (Suppl. 1), S80, Abstract.

Research Division Staff, 1995a. A comparison of psychophysiological detection of deception accuracy rates obtained using the counterintelligence scope polygraph and the test for espionage and sabotage question formats. Department of Defense Polygraph Institute, Fort McClellan, AL, DoDPI94-R-0008. DTIC AD Number A319333.

Research Division Staff, 1995b. Psychophysiological detection of deception accuracy rates obtained using the test for espionage and sabotage. Department of Defense Polygraph Institute, Fort McClellan, AL, DODPI94-R-0009. DTIC AD Number A330774.

Slawson, H.H., 1937. When science polices business. Nations Bus. 25, 54–60.

Weatherman, D., 2011. Interview route maps. In: Presentation at the Annual Seminar of the American Polygraph Association, Austin, TX.

Weaver, R.S., Garwood, M., 1985. Comparison of Relevant/Irrelevant and Modified General Question Technique structures in a split counterintelligence-suitability phase polygraph examination. Polygraph 14 (2), 97–107.

Weir, R.J., 1974. In defense of the relevant/irrelevant polygraph test. Polygraph 3 (2), 119–166.

Weir, R.J., 1976. Some principles of question selection and sequencing for relevant-irrelevant testing. Polygraph 5 (3), 207–222.

CHAPTER 7

Specific-issue testing techniques

Hateful to me as are the gates of Hell,
Is he who, hiding one thing in his heart,
Utters another.
Homer, Iliad.

Modern polygraphy is rooted in the law enforcement quest to use technology as an aid in criminal investigations. The earliest reported "lie detection" cases were in the investigation of criminal offenses. Though the polygraph can be found in many nonpolice applications, it is the testing of the accused that remains its core. Nearly all state police agencies and large city departments have polygraph examiners on staff whose principal function is to test suspects. The majority of the membership in national polygraph professional associations comes from the law enforcement sector. In view of this, it should be no surprise that the foundation of the education of new polygraph examiners rests on specific-issue testing techniques.

Discussed here will be three principal methods of specific-issue testing: the Federal Zone Comparison Technique (FZCT) (two variations), the Utah Probable Lie Test (UPLT), and the Air Force Modified General Question Technique (AFMGQT) (six variations). Beyond criminal investigations, the AFMGQT can also be used in polygraph screening, and rules that apply to it in that application are found in Chapter 6.

There are other approaches to specific-issue criminal testing. One is recognition testing, such as the Concealed Information Test, the rules for which are given in Chapter 8. There are also several proprietary approaches to deception testing, including the Integrated Zone Comparison Technique, Backster Zone Comparison Technique, the Marcy Technique, the Matte Quadri-Track Zone Comparison Technique, the Reid Technique, the Arther Technique, the Keeler Relevant/Irrelevant Technique, almost all of them named for their developer and taught at one time at a specific polygraph school. There are a few reasons we have selected three particular specific-issue testing methods for this chapter and none of the proprietary techniques. First, in some cases the polygraph schools teach one of the proprietary methods exclusively, and we wish to respect their intellectual property interests. Others of these polygraph techniques are linked to schools that no longer exist, and the practitioners of those methods have substantially declined or no longer practice. Finally, the three methods included in this chapter are currently employed by the overwhelming majority of field examiners, and collectively have the most supporting research. As such they are the best choices for a text on specific-issue polygraph techniques. Readers interested in alternate approaches will find articles in the technical journals published by the professional associations.

There are three steps in common among the FZCT, the UPLT, and the AFMGQT. They are case preparation, pretest interview, and the Acquaintance Test, variously known as a demonstration, stimulation, or numbers test. Before covering the three techniques in particular, here are generalizable descriptions of the three processes they all share.

CASE PREPARATION

When preparing to conduct a criminal examination, examiners should carefully examine the case file, giving special attention to the selection of the test issue. First, it has to be testable: it must be an overt act (i.e., Did you shoot that man?), not a mental state (i.e., Were you afraid when you shot at that man?) or about motives (Did you shoot that man out of revenge?), or about beliefs (Did you believe you would only wound that man?). The test issue must be unambiguous with no room for rationalization. It must also be an issue for which there are perceived consequences for the guilty person if detected.

When testing a suspect, the first test should always cover the most serious aspect of the crime. For example, if the investigation reveals that the victim was raped, robbed, and murdered, the examination would always start with the murder. The test issue also should focus on the crime, not on a secondary detail or the suspect's written denial.

An exception to the recommendation against testing an examinee's written statement may be with the self-reported victim or witness of a violent crime. These cases sometimes call for special care (see Chapter 11). The reason for considering testing the veracity of written statements is due to how the polygraph works. First, it is important to remember what the polygraph records: physiological responses in which the magnitude indicates relative salience. The polygraph is used to identify areas of greatest salience. Witnesses and victims of a traumatic crime can often have a physiological response when the crime is recalled because traumatic events are always salient. Test questions that cause a potentially traumatized examinee to relive the event are generally ill-advised. For this reason, the examinee could be tested about the accuracy of his or her own brief written statement about the event. Truthful examinees are less inclined to react to this question because it brings to mind the writing of a document, while lying examinees can be made to understand that they can be prosecuted for the crime of false reporting if the information in the document was fabricated. Not all confirmatory examinations are about traumatic crimes, of course. For those types of investigations (i.e., reporting one's car stolen and vandalism of personal property), it would be appropriate to test on the examinee's claims directly.

The testing suite should be prepared prior to bringing the examinee into it. All forms and documents necessary for the conduct of the exam need to be in place, and filled out as much as possible. Turn off, silence, or remove telephones. Temperature and lighting must be properly set. Confirm that the examination will not be interrupted by outside noises or third parties. The testing suite should be tidy and visitor ready: no gym bags, food containers, stacks of books, or newspapers. Put away distractions such as family pictures, awards for significant cases, political or religious items, or things that would remind the examinee of the consequences of crime. The examiner should ask himself: What would be someone's first impression upon entering the testing room?

Current professional standards also include the recording of the polygraph session, preferably with video. Though polygraph examinations should always be recorded, it is especially important for criminal examinations. It is good practice to verify the equipment is functioning prior to the session.

The examiner should also prepare himself or herself for the exam. Good grooming and professional attire are essential. Care should be taken to avoid any aromas or smells that can distract from the examinee's focus during testing, or receptiveness to the examiner. Certain scents such as colognes and perfumes can also trigger migraines or allergic reactions in some individuals. Finally, the examiner must also be mentally prepared for the possibility that the session may require an interrogation to resolve the issue and to have a plan in place.

PRETEST INTERVIEW

The initial phase of the examination process is the pretest interview. It serves several purposes: preparing the examinee for testing, gathering information to help assess the examinee for any apparent indications of unsuitability for testing, developing and reviewing of proper test questions, etc. The standard approach to the pretest interview can be broken down into seven steps. It begins with the introduction, followed by an overview of the process, signing of consent/rights form, gathering biographic information, explaining the polygraph, discussing the test issue, and introducing the test questions.

THE INTRODUCTION

It is in the first moments of their meeting that the examinee formulates his impression of the examiner, and it is therefore at this point the examiner begins the process of rapport building and management of the session. The examinee should always be met in a friendly yet professional manner. If the examiner is a law enforcement officer, there is an obligation for the examiner to identify himself. By policy, it may also be necessary to show a badge or credentials.

After initial courtesies, the examiner asks whether he can call the examinee by his first name. The examiner inquires as to what the examinee's understanding is regarding the purpose of the examination, affirming the answer if it is correct or correcting it if it is incorrect or off-target. The examiner also points out any recording equipment, microphones, cameras, or observation mirrors in the room.

Unless the examinee's identity has been verified earlier, the examiner would next request a valid form of picture identification from the examinee. The examinee's documented name is compared to the consent/rights advisement forms. Any uncertainty regarding the identity of the examinee must be resolved before continuing with the session.

OVERVIEW OF THE PROCESS

The majority of examinees will not have experienced polygraph testing before, and could harbor distorted images portrayed in television, books, Internet, or well-meaning friends. Most examinees will be visibly nervous and anxious. A polygraph test is, after all, a significant event for many. Part of an examiner's job is to inform the examinee of the entire examination process. This overview typically does little to reassure the guilty, but goes a long way in securing the confidence and cooperation of the innocent, and therefore a worthwhile investment.

An effective overview will include an explanation of the testing process in layman's language. It helps to make it engaging and somewhat interactive, and not scripted. The examinee should recognize from the overview that the process is thorough, fair, and standardized using the best instrumentation and examination protocol available.

CONSENT FORM, RIGHTS ADVISEMENT

In criminal testing all examinees are given a rights advisement. Departments and agencies develop standard advisements based on policy as well as state and federal law and judicial rulings. It is a best practice for the examinee to read the advisement form aloud before signing it, allowing the recording equipment to capture it in case it is needed during trial. Then attention is turned to the consent form. The examinee can also read this form aloud. Once signatures are on the consent form, the examination shifts to gathering of information.

GATHERING BIOGRAPHIC INFORMATION

This phase of the pretest interview is essential for assessing the suitability of the examinee for testing, his level of education and intelligence, and for the development of appropriate test questions. In settings where examiners also conduct posttest interrogations, information in this phase can be brought to bear in development of themes and strategies should the examinee be found deceptive during testing. Finally, background information can be very helpful for devising salient comparison questions for the individual examinee.

Evaluating examinees to gauge their suitability for testing can be fairly straightforward in some circumstances, but very complicated in others. As an overarching principle, an examinee should not undergo polygraph testing if it is reasonably likely the testing process could negatively affect the examinee's health, or that the examinee's physical or mental condition is such that a definitive polygraph result is not expected. Examples of the former might include examinees with at-risk pregnancies, those with heart conditions triggered by stress, or those with injuries that could be aggravated by the polygraph sensors. A partial list of physical and mental conditions that could preclude testing might include extreme fatigue, intoxication, functional maturity less than age 12, psychosis not controlled my medication, mental retardation (e.g., IQ score<55), excessive anxiety, and compulsive movement disorders, among others. When in doubt about suitability for polygraph testing, examiners may avail themselves of the relevant medical practitioner for guidance.

The exchange with the examinee regarding his biographic information is also important for shaping test questions. The examiner should attend to the examinee's vocabulary and word choices so that the test questions will communicate the examiner's intent in the language the examinee understands.[1] This issue is covered in more detail in Chapter 3.

Some topic areas should be scrupulously avoided during the gathering of background information. Topics such as religious and political beliefs and affiliations pose a distraction to the examination process, and inquiring about them in the polygraph setting may also be illegal in some jurisdictions. Similarly, the examinee's opinion regarding race and sexual matters should not be discussed, unless they relate to relevant areas to be tested.

EXPLAINING THE POLYGRAPH

Some examiners explain the polygraph during the overview of the process rather than after the gathering of biographic information, an insignificant variation of the pretest interview. The aim of the explanation is to reduce the examinee's general nervous apprehension about the instrument. The explanation to the examinee should be brief, and placed in terms familiar to the examinee. There are several ways to approach this task, and a sample dialog is offered in Chapter 4.

DISCUSSION OF TEST ISSUES

At the completion of the earlier steps it is time to introduce the relevant topic of the examination. This is done in a nonaccusatory way, allowing the examinee to give a full narrative of his version of the event. The examiner does not interrupt the examinee, except when necessary for the purposes of clarity or detail. The examiner does not challenge the examinee about inconsistency in the examinee's account, but does record it in his notes in case it is needed later.

Some polygraph examiners may develop the test questions during or shortly after the discussion of the test issues. Other examiners may step out of the testing suite to write up the questions alone or with the assistance of a colleague who has monitored

---

[1] Even in a predominantly English-speaking country like the United States there are regional differences in the meaning of certain words. Examiners should not assume that they and the examinee have a common understanding of terms. For example, an examinee from portions the South may relate that he is "feeling pretty puny today." An examiner from a different part of the country may interpret this to mean the examinee feels small or unimportant whereas a Southerner would recognize that the examinee is saying he does not feel physically well. When it comes to the construction of test questions, differences in word meaning must be accommodated to ensure the examinee is answering the question the examiner intends.

the session. Either way, after the questions are composed, the examiner moves to the next step: introducing the test questions to the examinee.

QUESTION INTRODUCTION

The examinee should be informed that the test questions are based upon his statements during the interview, and that they will now be reviewed with him using the exact wording that he will hear during the testing phase. The examinee should also be told that he must be able to answer each one with a *yes* or *no*, and if either of these answers does not fit the test question, he should bring it to the attention of the examiner. Finally, the examiner should say that the order of the questions will be different from the order given during the test, that there will be several tests with the questions, and that the order may change every time.

The order that the examiner reviews the test questions is

Sacrifice relevant question.
Relevant questions.
Comparison questions.
Irrelevant questions.
Symptomatic question(s) (Federal Zone) or introductory question (Utah techniques).

The prudent examiner should also review additional irrelevant questions in case they are needed during testing. They can be useful if necessary to allow responses to return to baseline after an artifact or an especially strong physiological response.

ACQUAINTANCE TEST

For the FZCT and AFMGQT, the Acquaintance Test is given just after the question review. When using the Utah method, it is given before the question review. The Acquaintance Test, combined with effective feedback to the examinee, can improve polygraph decision accuracy (Bradley and Janisse, 1981; Kircher et al., 2002; but also see Elaad and Kleiner, 1986).

The most popular Acquaintance Test is the "known numbers" type. Briefly, the examinee is asked to select a number between 3 and 8, excluding 3 and 8, and to write the number on a slip of paper. The paper is then placed in a location where the examinee can clearly see the number he wrote. The examinee is told that there will be a test on that number in which you will read the numbers 1-9, and that he should answer *no* to each number, including the one he wrote on the paper. The test is then run as a one-chart Peak of Tension test (see Chapter 8).

FEDERAL ZONE COMPARISON TECHNIQUE

Long regarded by examiners as a mainstay to criminal testing, the FZCT (formerly known as the Army Zone Comparison Technique) is arguably the most popular single-issue specific-issue testing technique in use. The FZCT is a method taught by the US government polygraph school from the mid-1960s to today. It is a variation of the Backster Technique, which was initially introduced to the government school by way of government examiners who attended the Backster school. In the intervening years the government modified the Backster method substantially by establishing its own rules regarding question sequencing, scoring procedures, decision rules, and chart minima. Some of the Backster terminology was adopted and retained for decades (e.g., "Zone," "anti-climax dampening," and "super-dampening"), though more recently there has been a marked shift toward mainstream scientific vocabulary and principles (e.g., differential responsivity, habituation, and salience).

There are two versions of the FZCT. The shorter of them contains two primary relevant questions, and it is called the "You Phase" test. The second type also has two primary relevant questions, but it has a third relevant question that covers evidence-connecting topics. Below are the six types of questions used in the FZCT:

1. The *primary relevant questions* focus entirely on a single act, though they are phrased slightly different from one another. A typical primary relevant question could be: Did you shoot Theodore Roosevelt on October 14th? An alternate version might be: On October 14th did you shoot Theodore Roosevelt in front of the Hotel Gilpatrick? Both versions of the FZCT use this type of question.
2. *Secondary relevant questions* can cover knowledge or evidence-connecting details. For example: Do you know who shot Theodore Roosevelt? Or: Did you help the person who shot Theodore Roosevelt? Or: Did you handle the gun used to shoot Theodore Roosevelt? Only the three-question FZCT uses this type of question.
3. *Probable-lie comparison (PLC) questions* with the FZCT have historically always been exclusionary, that is, they have explicitly excluded the relevant topic by the use of time, place, or category bars. Both versions of the FZCT use this type of question. Though the preponderance of the evidence suggests that broad inclusive comparison questions may produce better accuracy (see Amsel, 1999; Horvath, 1988; Horvath and Palmatier, 2009; Podlesny and Raskin, 1978) examiners wanting to stay close to the researched methods for the FZCT, or for whom their quality control requires them, exclusionary PLC questions should be used.
4. Because examinees may be expected to react to the first mention of the relevant issue during testing, the *sacrifice relevant question* has been added to introduce the topic with a question that is not used during chart interpretation. It is "sacrificed" to ensure responding to scoreable test questions is not contaminated by an orienting response. It is typically phrased: Regarding the shooting of Theodore Roosevelt, do you intend to answer truthfully? Both versions of the FZCT use this type of question.
5. The *symptomatic question*, like the sacrifice relevant question, was taken directly from the Backster Technique. Its intended purpose is to determine whether the examinee is distracted by an outside concern that ultimately dampens responsiveness to the relevant and comparison questions. Both versions of the FZCT use two of this type of question. Though central to all ZCT methods, evidence that the symptomatic question functions as intended is

equivocal (Capps et al., 1993; Honts et al., 2004; Krapohl and Ryan, 2001). The two symptomatic questions used in the FZCT are: Do you believe I will only ask you the questions we reviewed? and Is there something else you are afraid I will ask you a question about?

6. *Irrelevant questions* are neutral in character, and about which both the examiner and examinee know the truthful answer. They are typically crafted to be answered *yes*. An irrelevant question might be something like: Is today Wednesday?

Once the examinee acknowledges that he understands the test questions, and that he can answer them completely truthfully with a *yes* or *no* answer, testing can commence.

FZCT TEST PHASE[2]

Both the two-question (You Phase) and the three-question versions of the FZCT require a minimum of three charts. A fourth chart is conducted if the first three FZCT charts result in an Inconclusive, and a fifth chart if it remained Inconclusive after four charts. No more than five charts can be conducted.

Table 7.1 shows the question sequences for both versions of the FZCT. The comparison questions may be rotated from chart to chart so long as it is done systematically. All other questions remain in the same position in the sequence, except that

Table 7.1 The two-question (You Phase) and three-question versions of the FZCT

Position	Two question	Three question
1	Irrelevant	Irrelevant
2	Sacrifice relevant	Sacrifice relevant
3	Symptomatic 1	Symptomatic 1
4	Comparison 1	Comparison 1
5	Relevant 1 (primary)	Relevant 1 (primary)
6	Comparison 2	Comparison 2
7	Relevant 2 (primary)	Relevant 2 (primary)
8	Comparison 3	Symptomatic 2
9	Symptomatic 2	Comparison 3
10		Relevant 3 (secondary)

---

[2] This portion of the examination may be called the "in-test" elsewhere. "In-test" is not used here owing to its perception as polygraph jargon. Moreover, if one follows the logic of using "in-test" to represent the test, other parts of the examinations might similarly be called "pre-in-test," "post-in-test," and "in-test data analysis." When referring to one continuous presentation of questions, we will refer to it as a "test." "Testing" will be the period in which physiological data are collected, and "examination" will encompass all phases of the technique protocol.

irrelevant questions can be inserted to bring the tracings back to normal after an artifact or an exceptionally long-lasting phasic response.

FZCT SCORING RULES

Interpretation of the charts relies on the tracing features listed in Chapter 5 (also see Bell et al., 1999). The chart data can be scored channel by channel using the 3-position, 7-position, or empirical scoring systems (ESS). Each relevant question is scored against the comparison question with the stronger reaction, except when the relevant question is not bracketed by comparison questions. In that case, the relevant question is scored against the immediately preceding comparison question.

Scores are totaled both by relevant question and for the entire test. The total score for a relevant question is often called a "spot score" (or sub-total score) and the sum of scores for the entire test is called the "grand total." Both are considered in the decision rules.

FZCT DECISION RULES

Once all of the scoring has been completed and the spot scores and grand totals are calculated, decision rules are applied to the scores. As with most validated techniques, three charts are collected. At this point the examiner scores them. If the results would be Inconclusive, a fourth chart is collected and scored. If, when the scores from the four charts are added together, the results would still be Inconclusive, a fifth and final chart is collected. No more than five charts are permitted. Unlike some other ZCTs, the FZCT does not have escalating cutoffs as the number of charts is increased.

When using the You Phase version of the FZCT, if the spot score is −3 or lower, *or* the total score for the test is −4 or lower, the decision would be Deception Indicated (DI). For a decision of No Deception Indicated (NDI) each spot score must be greater than 0 *and* the grand total must be +4 or greater. All else is Inconclusive. These rules apply to the 3-position, 7-position, and ESS methods.

When using the 3-question version of the FZCT, if the spot score is −3 or lower, *or* the total score for the test is −6 or lower, the decision would be DI. For a decision of NDI each spot score must be greater than 0 *and* the grand total must by +6 or greater. All else is Inconclusive.

ESS allows selection of cutoff scores based on risk tolerance. For balanced accuracy (equal proportion of false positives and negatives), ESS uses two-stage rules, also called Senter Rules. In the first stage, only grand total scores are considered. A total of +2 would be NDI, and a total of −4 would be DI. If the results would be Inconclusive, the examiner would move to the second stage. In the second stage, a sub-total or "spot score" of −7 or lower would call for a decision of DI in the 3-question FZCT and a "spot-score" of -6 or lower would be DI in the 2-question FZCT. The results would be Inconclusive otherwise. Other decision rules are found in Chapter 5.

UTAH PROBABLE LIE TEST

No Comparison Question Technique has been subject to more peer-reviewed publications than has the UPLT, an approach developed by Dr. David C. Raskin and his colleagues[3] at the University of Utah starting in the 1970s. In sharp contrast to the developers of polygraph techniques up to that time, the Utah group enjoyed a command of the relevant foundational scientific areas: psychophysiology, decision theory, and psychometrics. Also noteworthy is that Dr. Raskin did not start out as a polygraph examiner, but as a well-established psychophysiologist. For his polygraph education he attended the Backster School of Lie Detection with the intention of learning more about the field, but Dr. Raskin found the course content was not scientifically satisfying. Raskin returned to the University of Utah to test some of the concepts he had learned, and so began what would become the longest running series of scientific studies in polygraphy anywhere up to that time. The body of published works on the polygraph from Raskin, his students, and his students' students is voluminous. No single group has contributed more to the field.

UPLT TEST PHASE

There are five types of questions in the single-issue UPLT: sacrifice relevant, relevant, PLC,[4] irrelevant, and introductory. They are reviewed with the examinee in that order.

1. The *sacrifice relevant question* is generally phrased similar to: Regarding whether you did X, to you intend to answer all of my questions truthfully?
2. The *relevant questions* focus entirely on a single act, though they are phrased differently. A typical relevant question could be: Did you do X last October 19th?
3. *PLC questions* with the UPLT have historically been exclusionary, that is, they have explicitly excluded the relevant topic by the use of time, place, or category bars. Testimony by Honts (1996) suggests this precaution may not be necessary.
4. *Irrelevant questions* are questions that are neutral in character, and about which both the examiner and examinee know the truthful answer. They are typically crafted to be answered *yes*, but they need not be. An irrelevant question might be something like: Is today Wednesday?
5. The *introductory question* in the UPLT is derived from the Backster outside-issue question. Its purpose in the UPLT is merely to occupy the first position where an orienting response is expected, and serves no diagnostic value. The introductory question would typically be phrased as: Do you understand I will only ask you the questions we discussed?

Once the examinee acknowledges that he understands the test questions, and that he can answer them completely truthfully with a *yes* or *no* answer, physiological

---

[3] Drs. Gordon Barland, John Podlesny, Lou Rovner, Ronald Craig, Charles Honts, Robert Hodes, John Kircher, and Steve Horowitz.
[4] The UPLT can also be conducted using directed-lie comparison (DLC) questions in place of PLC questions. Research studies looking at the DLC in mixed-issue screening have been encouraging. For specific-issue testing, however, the body of DLC research is substantially less than that of the PLC, making the DLC somewhat more controversial. It is not further discussed here.

Table 7.2 Three-question format of the UPLT for the single-issue and multiple-facet for the first chart. The relevant and comparison questions should be systematically rotated in each successive chart

Position	Single-issue	Multiple-facet
1	Introductory	Introductory
2	Sacrifice relevant	Sacrifice relevant
3	Irrelevant 1	Irrelevant 1
4	Comparison 1	Comparison 1
5	Relevant 1 (primary)	Relevant 1 (primary)
6	Irrelevant 2	Irrelevant 2
7	Comparison 2	Comparison 2
8	Relevant 2 (primary)	Relevant 2 (primary or secondary)
9	Irrelevant 3	Irrelevant 3
10	Comparison 3	Comparison 3
11	Relevant 3 (primary)	Relevant 3 (primary or secondary)

Table 7.3 Question order for the four-question UPLT

Position	Multiple-facet
1	Introductory
2	Sacrifice relevant
3	Irrelevant 1
4	Comparison 1
5	Relevant 1 (primary)
6	Relevant 2 (secondary)
7	Comparison 2
8	Relevant 3 (secondary)
9	Relevant 4 (secondary)
10	Comparison 3

recording can commence. There are two formats for the UPLT: the three-question and the four-question (Tables 7.2–7.3). The three-question version can be employed for single-issue or multiple-facet testing, whereas the four-question version is used only for multiple-facet testing. Decision rules are different for the single-issue approach, which are discussed later.

Question rotation is also a part of the UPLT. In much of the research the comparison and irrelevant questions were rotated to allow each comparison question to be adjacent to each relevant question, assuring that the effectiveness of good comparison questions would be shared equally across the relevant questions. It also provided a level of uncertainty to the examinee regarding which question would come next.

Finally, keeping the relevant questions in the same position each time made summing scores in the score sheet for each relevant question easier. Other research has found that there is within-chart habituation, meaning that reactivity at the end of a test is significantly less than it is at the beginning of the test. Consequently, keeping the relevant questions in the same order may not be the best approach.

The four-question UPLT is one option for multiple-facet exams. Table 7.3 shows the question order for the first chart. The relevant and comparison questions should be systematically rotated from chart to chart.

Question pacing is from 25 to 35 s. For both the three-question and four-question, UPLT, examiners are advised to add irrelevant questions into the sequence if it becomes necessary to return a long-lasting phasic response back to baseline, or when the stability of the tracings are temporarily disrupted by movements, coughs, or other artifacts.

One unique aspect of the UPLT is that the protocol calls for discussions of the test questions between the tests. This is done in a low-key and nonchallenging way, inquiring whether anything came to the examinee's mind on the relevant and then the comparison questions. The purpose is to dishabituate the examinee to the questions as the testing progresses, and to refresh memories associated with the questions that can improve reactivity in subsequent tests. There should not be emphasis for any one question nor to any one category of question. If there are admissions to a comparison question, it is modified to accommodate the new information, reviewed with the examinee, and used in subsequent tests. Changes to any question should be accompanied by a change to the question label (i.e., C2 to C2a), as well as documenting the reason for the change in the technical notes.

UPLT SCORING

Interpretation of the charts relies on the tracing features listed in Chapter 5. The charts are scored channel by channel using the 7-position scoring system.[5] In the three-question version of the UPLT, each relevant question is scored against the immediately preceding comparison question, unless the tracing of that comparison question is unusable due to artifacts or loss of signal. In that case the relevant question is scored against the nearest comparison question.

In the four-question version of the UPLT, each relevant question is scored against the stronger of the two nearest comparison questions. For example, in Table 7.3 on chart 1 both Relevants 1 and 2 could be scored against either Comparisons 1 or 2.

UPLT DECISION RULES

Once all of the scoring has been completed, decision rules are applied to those scores. The selection of rules will depend on the scope of the relevant questions.

---

[5] There is every reason to believe ESS should perform as well with the three-question Utah single-issue technique as it does for the FZCT, however there exists less supporting research.

If the examinee must be either truthful or untruthful to every relevant question, such as in a single-issue exam, the total score is used. If the examinee could be truthful to some relevant questions and untruthful to some relevant questions (multiple-facet and multiple-issue), only the totals of the individual questions are considered.

Another unique aspect of the UPLT is the number of charts that are recorded. As with most validated techniques, three charts are collected. At this point the examiner scores them. If the results would be Inconclusive, two more charts are collected, and all of the charts are scored together. The same cutoff scores are used regardless of the number of charts.

Single-Issue
Only the total score is used in the decision rules of the single-issue UPLT. If the total score is −6 or lower, the results are DI. When the total score is +6 or greater, the results are NDI. Scores between −5 and +5, inclusive, are deemed Inconclusive.

Multiple-Facet
If all of the total scores for each relevant question are in the same direction (0s excluded), the total score is used. Those cutoffs are ±6. If the total scores for each relevant question are on opposite sides of 0, decisions are made by individual question. A −3 or lower for a relevant question results in a DI for that question, while +3 for a question would call for a decision of NDI for that question. All others would be Inconclusive. Note that the accuracy of these tests is substantially lower than where examinees had been either completely truthful or completely untruthful to all questions.

Mixed-Issue
The UPLT is not generally used for screening, but it is as suited to that application as any other. In screening examinations only the total scores of individual questions (spot scores) are used for decision making. Because they are screening examinations, it is assumed that adverse results to any question will be followed up with more interviewing and focused testing on that topic(s) to which the examinee was reacting. Making decision exclusively on a screening examination, without adequate follow up, is not a best practice and is strongly discouraged.

A total of −3 or lower on any one question means the test is labeled as SR (significant responding) while a +3 or greater on every question leads to an NSR (no significant responding) during the screening phase of the examination.

AIR FORCE MODIFIED GENERAL QUESTION TECHNIQUE
The Air Force Modified General Question Technique (AFMGQT) is a flexible technique for conducting multiple-issue and multiple-facet polygraph testing such as applicant screening, post-conviction sex offender testing, and impaired drivers on

probation testing. It can accommodate two, three, or four relevant questions. The AFMGQT is also suitable for single-issue criminal investigative examinations.

The AFMGQT is an improvement over the older Modified General Question Technique (MGQT). The MGQT has been found to have excellent sensitivity to deception but does not detect truthfulness at a rate greater than chance (see Krapohl, 2006). The MGQT is a derivative of the Reid Technique in structure, whereas the AFMGQT is most similar to the Zone approach. The AFMGQT is a good tool to guide investigators where to question the examinee further, or to identify prime areas for single-issue testing. In the single-issue mode it can stand on its own.

There are versions of the AFMGQT to handle two, three, and four relevant questions, and each of these versions has two variations in question sequence. It is helpful to note that there is no version of the AFMGQT for just one relevant question.

In all formats the relevant and comparison questions should be rotated systematically. Rotation allows each relevant question to be scored against a different comparison question, and it mitigates to some extent the effect of habituation that might occur to a relevant question when it is positioned only at the end of the test. It is also good practice to include additional irrelevant questions during the pretest interview in case they are needed during testing.

Each of these formats requires a minimum of three charts. Four or even five may be collected to resolve Inconclusive results. Once the results are definitive, however, testing should stop.

The next section shows the sequence of the various versions of the AFMGQT as they relate to criminal testing.

VERSIONS OF THE AFMGQT

See Tables 7.4–7.6.

AFMGQT SCORING

The 3-position, 7-position, and ESS scoring systems can be used (see Chapter 5 for a complete description). If a relevant question is bracketed by comparison questions, it is scored channel by channel against the stronger of the two comparison questions.

Table 7.4 Two relevant questions for the AFMGQT

Position	Variation 1	Variation 2
1	Irrelevant	Irrelevant
2	Sacrifice relevant	Sacrifice relevant
3	Comparison 1	Comparison 1
4	Secondary relevant	Secondary relevant
5	Comparison 2	Primary relevant
6	Primary relevant	Comparison 2
7	Comparison 3	

Table 7.5 Three relevant questions for the AFMGQT

Position	Variation 1	Variation 2
1	Irrelevant	Irrelevant
2	Sacrifice relevant	Sacrifice relevant
3	Comparison 1	Comparison 1
4	Secondary relevant	Secondary relevant
5	Comparison 2	Primary relevant
6	Primary relevant	Comparison 2
7	Comparison 3	Evidence-connecting or knowledge
8	Evidence-connecting or knowledge	Comparison 3

Table 7.6 Four relevant questions for the AFMGQT

Position	Variation 1	Variation 2
1	Irrelevant	Irrelevant
2	Sacrifice relevant	Sacrifice relevant
3	Comparison 1	Comparison 1
4	Secondary relevant	Secondary relevant
5	Comparison 2	Primary relevant
6	Primary relevant	Comparison 2
7	Comparison 3	Evidence-connecting
8	Evidence-connecting	Knowledge
9	Comparison 4	Comparison 3
10	Knowledge	

For variations 2 of the AFMGQT, where there are two adjacent relevant questions, either of them can be scored against the comparison questions that immediately bracket the relevant question pairs. If a relevant question is not bracketed by comparison questions, it is scored against the comparison question immediately preceding it.

AFMGQT DECISION RULES

When the AFMGQT is used in a multiple-facet mode (i.e., the examinee may be truthful to some crime questions and deceptive to others), it is not appropriate to consider the grand sum of all scores in the final decision. In Federal scoring, when the examinee has achieved a spot score (total score for a relevant question) of −3 or lower, the decision for the multiple-facet test is DI. For a decision of NDI, every spot score must be +3 or greater. All else is Inconclusive. When using ESS the cut-scores for DI are the same (−3 or lower at any spot), but the required spot score at every question for the decision of NDI becomes a +1 or greater.

The general rule of the AFMGQT is when an examinee is found DI or Inconclusive to one question, he is considered DI or Inconclusive to the test. Split decisions within a series are not permitted. For example, in a series where the spot scores for three relevant questions are +9, −3, +7, the test would be called DI in 3-position and 7-position scoring even though the total score would be quite high. One could not make a call of NDI to the first and third relevant questions despite the scores because split calls are not allowed. With the AFMGQT there are only decisions for the whole test. To make different decisions for each question, they must be individually tested with single-issue tests.

If the examinee is tested with the AFMGQT on a specific event, and each question covers exactly the same act, calls of DI, NDI, and Inconclusive can be made. Under those circumstances, both spot scores and total scores can be considered. A DI decision is warranted if the grand total is −6 or lower, or a spot score is −3 or lower. An NDI requires a positive spot score for every relevant question, and a total of +6 or more. An Inconclusive decision is made for everything else. The AFMGQT is virtually identical to the ZCT but without symptomatic questions. Because there is no practical, empirical or theoretical reason to base decision rules upon the presence or absence of these questions, it is reasonable to use the FZCT decision rules.

REFERENCES

Amsel, T.T., 1999. Exclusive or nonexclusive comparison questions: a comparative field study. Polygraph 28 (4), 273–283.

Bell, B.G., Raskin, D.C., Honts, C.R., Kircher, J.C., 1999. The Utah numerical scoring system. Polygraph 28 (1), 1–9.

Bradley, M.T., Janisse, M.P., 1981. Accuracy demonstrations, threat, and the detection of deception: cardiovascular, electrodermal, and pupillary measures. Psychophysiology 18 (3), 307–315.

Capps, M.H., Knill, B.L., Evans, R.K., 1993. Effectiveness of the symptomatic questions. Polygraph 22 (4), 285–298.

Elaad, E., Kleiner, M., 1986. The stimulation test in polygraph field examinations: a case study. J. Police Sci. Adm. 14 (4), 328–333.

Honts, C.R., 1996. Testimony in United States v. Gilliard, US District Court, Southern District of Georgia, Augusta Division, Case No. CRI9E-19. Full text found at: http://truth.boisestate.edu/polygraph/honts01.html.

Honts, C.R., Amato, S., Gordon, A., 2004. Effects of outside issues on the comparison question test. J. Gen. Psychol. 131 (1), 53–74.

Horvath, F., 1988. The utility of control questions and the effects of two control question types in field polygraph techniques. J. Police Sci. Adm. 16 (3), 198–209.

Horvath, F., Palmatier, J.J., 2009. Effect of two types of control questions and two question formats in the outcomes of polygraph examinations. J. Forensic Sci. 53 (4), 889–899.

Kircher, J.C., Packard, T., Bell, B.G., Bernhardt, P.C., 2002. Effects of prior demonstrations of polygraph accuracy on outcomes of probable-lie and directed-lie polygraph tests. Report to the DoD Polygraph Institute. DTIC AD Number A404128, University of Utah, Salt Lake City, UT.

Krapohl, D.J., 2006. Validated polygraph techniques. Polygraph 35 (3), 149–155.

Krapohl, D.J., Ryan, A.H., 2001. A belated look at symptomatic questions. Polygraph 30 (3), 206–212.

Podlesny, J.A., Raskin, D.C., 1978. Effectiveness of techniques and physiological measures in the detection of deception. Psychophysiology 15 (4), 344–359.

CHAPTER 8

Recognition tests

I would forget it fain; But O, it presses to my memory, like damned guilty deeds to sinners' minds.
William Shakespeare in *Romeo and Juliet*

It has long been known that physiological responses can reveal what a person holds in memory. The manifestation of the physiological response can vary by individual and context. For example, Hess (1965) reported that a magician watches for enlarged pupils from his subject when turning over playing cards to detect which one the subject was thinking about. Even earlier, in his treatise on blushing Burgess (1839) recounts his encounter with a former noblewoman, now fallen into economic despair, who revealed a "flash of the soul's emotion bursting through her cheek" when touching upon recollections of her earlier life of ease. Observations on the association between the pulse and recognition have appeared in the literature for more than 1000 years (see Chapter 1). Today, with the aid of instrumentation, added to certain test protocols, the relationship between recognition and physiological reactions could be a reliable and useful method for criminal investigations.

Though there is a high degree of overlap in the theoretical underpinnings of recognition tests and deception tests, inasmuch as both rely on differential salience between test items, they do differ in the practical elements of pretest preparation, test administration, and data analysis. These elements are the focus of this chapter.

There are three general types of recognition tests, all closely related but having separate test protocols and methods of analysis. They are the Demonstration (or Acquaintance) Tests, Peak of Tension Test (two versions), and Concealed Information Test. Demonstration Tests can take on many forms, and are not further covered here. The Peak of Tension Test is one of the oldest polygraph methods in continuous use, first appearing in the literature in the 1930s. The Concealed Information Test appeared later (Lykken, 1959), and it is a unique approach to recognition testing with a number of advantages.

PEAK OF TENSION

The expression "Peak of Tension (POT)" is attributed to Leonarde Keeler (1939), who used it and his Relevant-Irrelevant technique to solve several notorious cases in the 1930s and 1940s. The POT technique became a mainstay in polygraphy since then, and has been taught at virtually all polygraph schools up to the present time. There are two types of POT: Known Solution (KSPOT) which was called Type A by Keeler and Searching (SPOT) which Keeler labeled Type B (Ansley, 1992.)

As the names suggest, the KSPOT is used in cases where investigators know the crime details, and the SPOT is used to help investigators recover evidence, loot, or bodies when they don't yet possess the details. SPOTs are also sometimes useful to identify accomplices.

The underlying principle of POT testing is that the tonic physiological pattern will shift at or just after the critical item or key has been presented. It is generally assumed that the examinee, who knows the order of the test items, will experience growing tension as the incriminating item approaches, after which he will feel relief: hence the name Peak of Tension. The building and dissipation of psychological stress is what gives the POT data its shape. What makes the POT unique from other PDD techniques is that it is the only one that formally uses tonic shifts in physiological patterns as the basis for decision making. While a large phasic response may also be elicited by the key, it is the break in the trend of the data that reveals which of the items is the most significant to the examinee. To make this change more apparent to the eye, it is helpful to place the key near the middle of the question sequence.

POTs are generally considered supplementary tests: they are almost never conducted as stand-alone methods. Of the two types of POTs, the KSPOT is used most often.

CONSTRUCTING KSPOTs

To construct a KSPOT, the polygrapher must first select a critical detail, or "key" as it is often called in the POT. For obvious reasons, the key must be something that the guilty examinee would recognize during the test. It must also be something that an innocent person would not know or could not reasonably guess. The rest of the test is made up of noncritical items, sometimes called buffers or padding. The purpose of these items is to mask the key from an innocent examinee. There are anywhere from five to eight buffers in a KSPOT, and one key.

Examinees are informed of the POT procedures before testing. The examiner tries to impress upon the examinee that his bodily responses will build to the point where the key is presented, then drop off. This is to increase the guilty examinee's anticipation of the key, and make the responses more distinct. All of the items are reviewed with the examinee, normally in some logical order so that the guilty examinee will recognize the approach of the key during testing. Sometimes the reading of the items is augmented by placing the list of them in front of the examinee to see. The goal of the pretest interview is to heighten the guilty examinee's focus upon the looming key. Care must be taken to ensure that the innocent examinee is not cued in to the key by the examiner's behavior, as well.

The testing phase of all POTs begins with a preparatory phrase. This is to establish the context for the test, what the examiner is seeking to uncover. The preparatory phrase is followed by a prefix question, then by the items. To make the terms and procedures more clear, consider the following historical vignette and KSPOT example.

Sometime between 8:00 pm and 10:00 pm on March 1, 1932, a 20-month-old child, Charles A. Lindbergh Jr., was kidnapped from the nursery in his home in Hopewell, New Jersey. An envelope was found on the window sill of the nursery with a ransom note that read: "Dear Sir! Have 50000$ redy with 2500$ in 20$ bills 1500$ in 10$ bills and 1000$ in 5$ bills. After 2-4 days we will inform you were to deliver the Mony. We warn you for making anyding public or for notify the polise. The child is in gute care. Indication for all letters are singnature and 3 holes." On March 4th a second ransom demand arrived in which the kidnappers insisted on $70,000. Sadly, the child was discovered dead nearly three months later from a blow to the head. Bruno Richard Hauptmann was found with some of the ransom money in his possession, but claimed that he was holding it for friend. He denied any involvement in the crime.

There are several potential keys in this vignette, supposing that police had managed to control the release of the details: amount of ransom money, requested denominations, room from where the baby was kidnapped, etc. For the purpose of conducting a KSPOT on the prime suspect, Bruno Hauptmann, the location of where the kidnapper placed the envelope will be used as the key.

Preparatory phrase: Regarding where the kidnapper of the Lindbergh baby left the ransom note:

Prefix: Do you know if it was left
Buffer: In the baby's crib?
Buffer: In the wardrobe?
Buffer: On the nursery floor?
Buffer: On the dresser?
Key: On the window sill?
Buffer: On the toy box?
Buffer: In the bath?
Buffer: On the bookshelf?

The presentation of the items occurs about every 25 s, and the examinee answers "no" after each item. Note that the key is placed somewhere near the middle of the sequence, though some examiners prefer it not be exactly in the center. The key must be preceded and followed by two buffers to be enable the "peak" to take place, and there is never more than one key per POT. Care must be taken so that none of the buffers could be mistaken as a key by the guilty person. Each KSPOT is repeated three times, the first two in the same order and the third in a reverse order. If three tests are not conclusive, a fourth may be conducted with the items in a mixed order that the examinee does not know. No more than four tests are run.

With the aim of reducing false positive errors (misclassifying a truthful examinee), some polygraph examiners include an item on the test that is deliberately misleading. Called the "false key" (Arther, 1970), it is an item that the examiner hints is the key, but the item is actually only a buffer. For example, if the KSPOT were discover whether the examinee knew that a particular murder weapon was a 9-mm handgun, the examiner might query the examinee in the pretest interview whether he owned a shotgun. Regardless of whether the examinee owned this type of weapon, the word "shotgun" would be included in the list of items on the KSPOT. If the examinee did not react when "9-mm handgun" was presented, but did react to the word "shotgun," this would support the conclusion that the examinee was naïve to the type of weapon used in the murder.

CONSTRUCTING SPOTs

SPOTs have much in common with KSPOTs with the exception of selection of keys. Recall that, unlike the KSPOT, the aim of the SPOT is to tell the investigator what the key is. Creation of the item list for the SPOT is not always an easy task, and requires considerable thought. Polygraphers must design the SPOT so that the items are both exhaustive and exclusive: they must cover all possibilities but not overlap one another.

One valuable use of the SPOT is to narrow the investigators' search for a missing person where there exists a strong belief of foul play and there is a suspect in custody. Cases of murder without a body are rarely pursued because they are so difficult to prove in court, creating an incentive for a murderer to dispose of the body in a location unlikely to be discovered or at least not be linked to the murderer. A suspect claiming innocence is unlikely to volunteer the location of a body, but may agree to undergo polygraph testing. If so, the SPOT may not only help investigators find the body, but also make the tie between the suspect and the victim. This is also true for cases of kidnapping, and even theft of valuable property, where investigators need to know where to look.

In constructing the SPOT the examiner must have buffer questions, possible keys, and a coverall question for a total of 9 questions. Buffer questions in the SPOT follow the same rules as buffer questions with the KSPOT. Because the examiner does not know what the key is in a SPOT, care must be taken to ensure that the buffer questions are out of the realm of possibility for keys. They occupy the first two and last two positions. The possible keys are placed in the series from position three afterward. The coverall question is in the last position after the possible keys and addresses all other possibilities using language such as "somewhere I did not mention." It is useful to add visual stimuli to further enhance responding when testing with the SPOT.

A textbook example for the potential value of the SPOT is case of the disappearance of Karen Jo Smith:

> On December 27, 2000 Smith told her former husband Steven D. Halcomb to move out of her Indianapolis home. The following day both Smith and Halcomb were gone, as was Halcomb's car. Smith had left behind her car, valuables, and her two children, and there was no evidence that she had made any preparations to travel. Police believed that she had met her fate at the hands of Halcomb who used the two weeks he spent dodging them and his parole officer to dispose of evidence. All of the evidence against Halcomb was circumstantial but strong: he had previously abused and stalked Smith, and had attempted to contract for her

murder. On December 14, 2004, Halcomb was convicted of murder based on this and hearsay evidence from jailhouse informants. Smith's body was never found.

Because it was discovered that Halcomb had traveled between Indiana and California in the 2 weeks between Smith's disappearance and Halcomb's arrest, it would be possible to construct successive SPOTs that might pinpoint the location of Smith's body. The first SPOT might divide up a US map from California to Indiana. For example, a map could be divided up into regions. The four buffer questions would cover areas that are not likely, such as Canada, Mexico, Alaska, and Caribbean Islands. The remainder of the continental United States could be sectioned into four logical regions. Finally, the coverall question would be "an area I did not mention." A map would be placed before the examinee, and there would be a rehearsal regarding the names of the regions, such as the Eastern Region, Midwest Region, Mountain Region, and Western Region. Finally, the SPOT would look like this:

Preparatory phrase: Regarding where Karen Jo Smith's body is:

Prefix: Do you know if it is in
Buffer: Canada?
Buffer: The Caribbean Islands?
Possible key: The Eastern Region?
Possible key: The Midwest Region?
Possible key: The Mountain Region?
Possible key: The Western Region?
Coverall: An area I did not mention?
Buffer: Alaska?
Buffer: Mexico?

The SPOT would be conducted like the KSPOT was: two tests in the rehearsed order, a third in reverse order, and a fourth in a mixed order if the first three do not lead to a conclusive decision. In the present example, if the examinee reacted consistently to one region, the map might be further divided into four smaller areas. The test would be repeated, using the same principles as the first SPOT in test construction and administration. Consistent reactions on the second SPOT would call for yet another. This iterative and narrowing process would continue so long as the examinee agreed to more testing, and the SPOTs were productive.

ANALYZING THE POT

POT techniques are unique among polygraph methods for their reliance on tonic physiological patterns to determine the examinee's recognition. In POTs polygraphers look for a general increase in arousal from the beginning of the test to the key, and then a decrease in arousal thereafter. It is the trend in the pattern over the entire test that polygraphers use to pinpoint which item holds the most significance to the examinee. In contrast, most other techniques use the relatively short-lived phasic responses as a cue to deception, and trend information is largely ignored. In POTs, phasic response can also occur and are considered, but the trend patterns are the primary

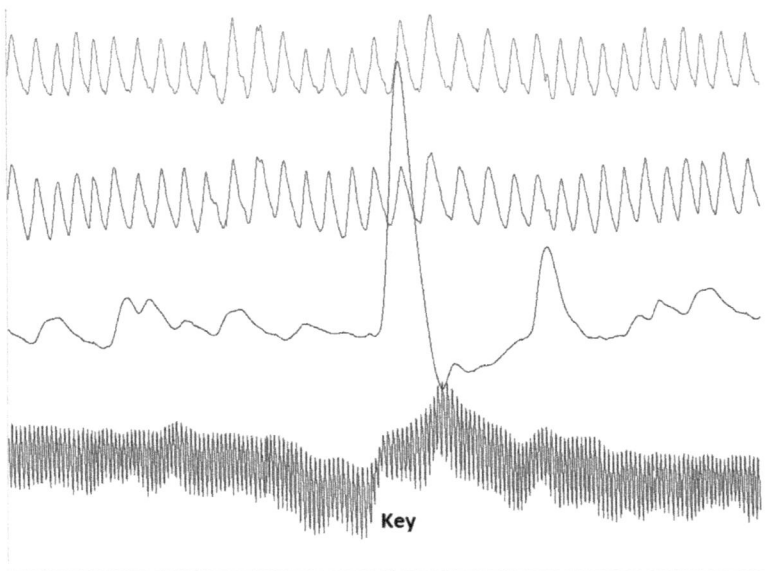

FIGURE 8.1

Pattern of responding in a Peak of Tension Test where the examinee recognized the key.

means of assessing significance of the test items. See Figure 8.1 as an example. The decision rule to conclude that the examinee has "peaked" is that the examinee must have responded in at least two of the three physiological channels on two of the three (or four) tests.

Figures 8.2 through 8.5 show the tonic response patterns for the POT. Note that there are differences in how the break in trend is manifested, but that there is a point at which the data change. When this break fails to appear, it is interpreted as the examinee having failed to recognize the key (Figure 8.5).

CONCEALED INFORMATION TEST

In 1959 Dr. David Lykken introduced a recognition test that he called the Guilty Knowledge Test (GKT; Lykken, 1959). His test was based on the premise that there would be an orienting response elicited from guilty examinees at the key that would, on average, be larger than other similar-but-unrelated items, while innocent examinees would respond to all items randomly. The method has more recently become known as the Concealed Information Technique (CIT), though some of the literature still use the older term.

The CIT has certain advantages over the POT methods. First and foremost, it is much better researched. Unlike the POT, the CIT has been conducted in scores of studies with many hundreds of subjects, resulting in a solid estimate of its accuracy.

Concealed information test **173**

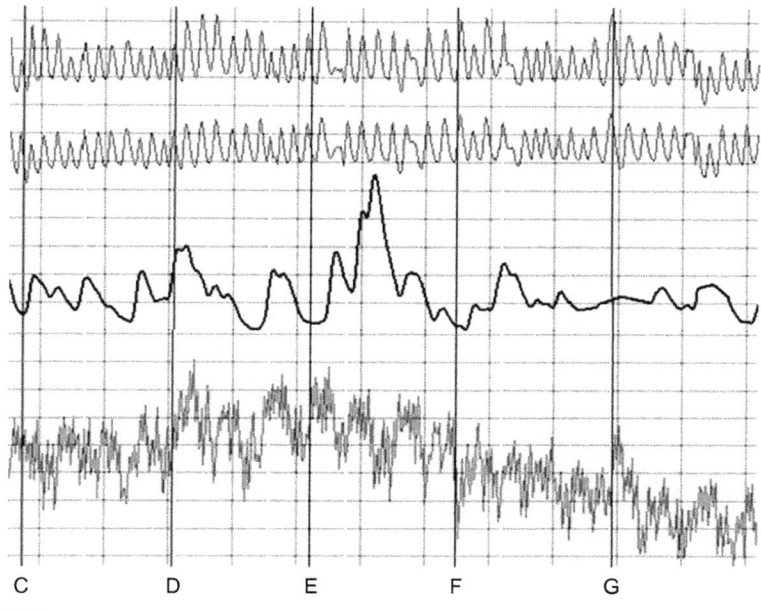

FIGURE 8.2

Peak of Tension indicating recognition of the key at item E. Note the electrodermal response at the key, the relative inactivity in that channel thereafter, and the decline of the blood pressure channel after the key has passed.

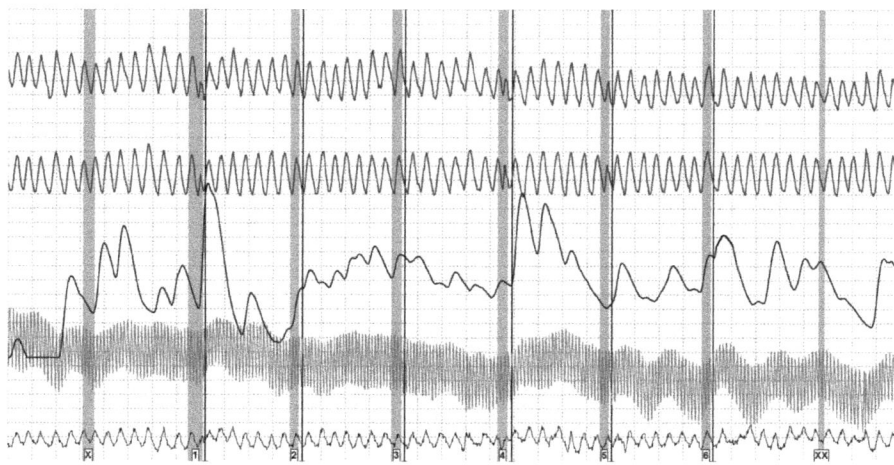

FIGURE 8.3

Peak of Tension with recognition of the key at item #4. Note the phasic response along with an increase in lability starting at the key, and a phasic response in the cardiograph tracing with a following change in tonic activity.

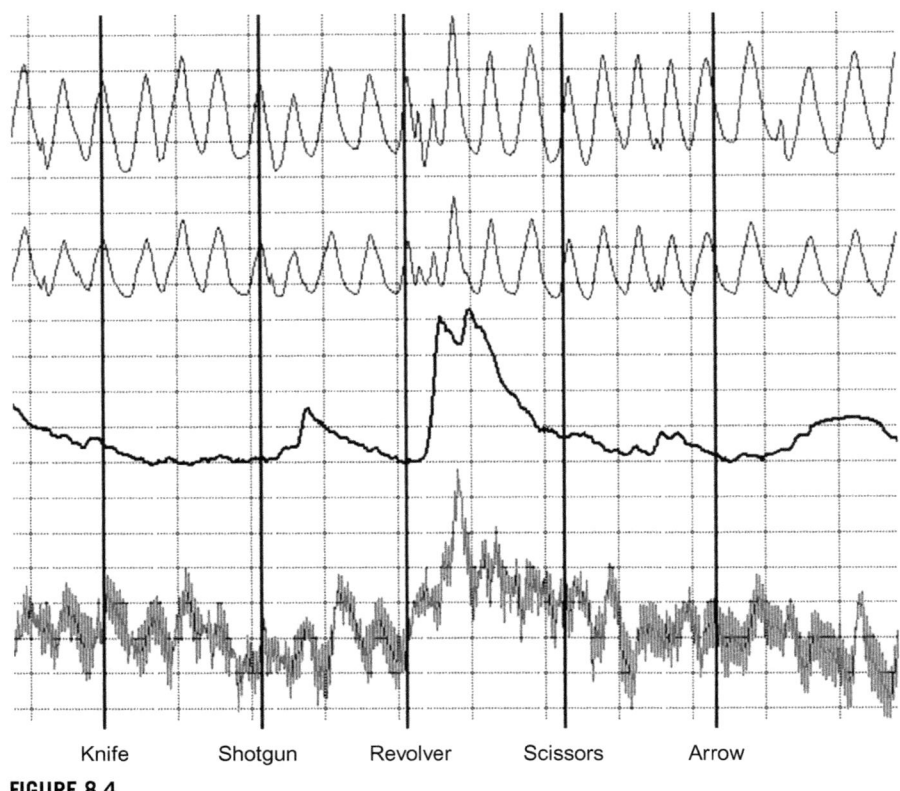

FIGURE 8.4

Peak of Tension with recognition of the key at "revolver." Note the subtle but distinct increase in tonic respiration speed after the key, and the large EDR and "peak" in the blood pressure at the key.

The National Research Council's (2003) report summarized the CIT research as showing an accuracy of 88%. This accuracy is better than what is found in the albeit-incomplete research on the POT. There is a general trend in finding higher CIT accuracy than POT accuracy (Barland, 1984; Yokoi et al., 2001).

Another important feature of the CIT is that error estimates can be calculated from the score because CIT scores map nicely over a probability distribution. For example, a score of 12 with a CIT using 7 different keys would be expected from only 1 in 1000 examinees who were truly naïve to the crime details. Said another way, it is far more likely that these scores would come from a guilty person than an innocent one. There is more about this later in the chapter. The capacity of CIT to produce sound probability-based estimates qualifies it as an excellent technique for evidentiary polygraphy.

Because the CIT relies in large part on the orienting response, it may be used in situations where the CQT is not appropriate. Take for example, where a woman is

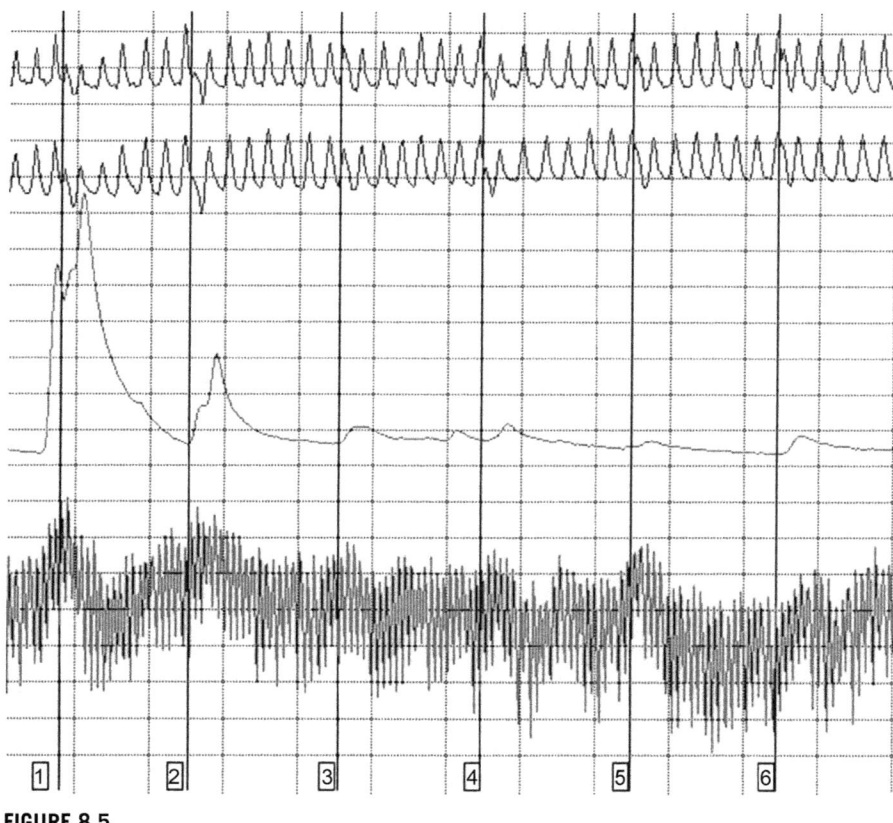

FIGURE 8.5

Peak of Tension indicating no recognition of the key at #3. Observe the lack of significant responses or patterns in any of the data channels pointing to the key.

found killed in her home and the police immediately suspect the husband who is now at his office. There may be a temptation for the police to pick up the husband and test him with the conventional CQT or even a Relevant/Irrelevant test (RI) to solve the crime or at least remove the husband as a suspect. However, the CQT and RI are believed to rely to some significant degree on emotional responses to test questions, and it seems logical that the husband, so soon upon learning of his wife's death, would have strong emotions to any question suggesting he was involved in her killing. The underlying basis of the CIT is not so dependent on emotion, and could be given to the husband as soon as he is able to sit for the test.

There are specific principles that make the CIT effective, and these principles do not constrain the technique to a singular method but permit some variation. For the sake of simplicity, only a single method will be provided here, and the principles will be discussed so that users will understand the bounds of permissible variation.

It is recommended that if both the CIT and CQT are to be conducted on the same examinee that the CIT be administered first. Giving the CIT priority is one way of ensuring that the CQT process does not reveal the kinds of details that are used in the CIT. Also, the CQT can be emotionally fatiguing to an examinee due to the necessarily dynamic and interactive pretest interview process, and the development of probable-lie material. The CIT pretest can be very brief, and there are no probable lies to develop, resulting in fewer cognitive and emotional demands on the examinee. Finally, if the CIT indicates that the examinee is concealing knowledge about the crime, an interrogation can begin immediately, producing a savings of both time and effort because the lengthier CQT has been made moot. Research has found that the CIT does better with innocent examinees than guilty examinees, so one can have more confidence when the examinee fails the CIT than when he passes it. It is only when the CIT has not found evidence of concealed information would the CQT be necessary.

The CIT uses only two types of items. The first are critical items, called keys. The second are noncritical items, called controls. Each CIT (and there can be several) contains just one key and some number of controls. The recommendation here is to use five control items per CIT, not because science has necessarily established this or some other as the ideal number, but rather in the quest for simplicity and elegance the use of five controls entails mathematics that are easier and can often be calculated in one's head.

As with all recognition tests, selection of a key demands care. Examiners must be reasonably certain that the examinee was paying attention to the detail on which the key was based, and that it is available for recall during the CIT. Examinees have an annoying habit of exercising their own preferences for what they pay attention to and remember about their crimes, and they may not be the same details that the examiner would think obvious. To help in determining what might be meaningful to guilty examinees, examiners in Japan often visit the crime scene to see firsthand what the guilty person saw, to notice the types and placement of things that catch the eye. This approach to polygraphy is not widely practiced in the United States or most other countries, but it has proven to be immensely successful in Japan. It may be the best approach to overcoming the problems inherent to the development of keys in the CIT. If this level of involvement is not possible, examiners should choose keys that cover details that a guilty examinee would find patently memorable. Most often, these are details in which the guilty examinee was behaviorally engaged during the crime.

Controls also require thoughtful consideration. They must not be evocative in themselves, lest the guilty find that they compete with the key for salience and thereby affect the scoring of the responses. For the sake of the naïve examinee controls should be roughly the same length, in the same category, and equally plausible as the key. The equivalent of a POT's false key has not been reported in the literature for the CIT. Because false positives do not appear to be a significant problem for the CIT, false keys may not be necessary.

To construct a test in the CIT, a control is always placed in the first position. When a control is in the first position, it is called an "anchor," and responses to it are ignored. The placement of the remaining controls and the key is by chance. Examiners can use a random numbers table, roll a die, or use some other method to place the key in the sequence. This means that the key may be located in the second position, the last position, or anywhere in between.

During the pretest interview it is wise to review the test items with the examinee, though not in the order that they will be presented during testing. The review will ensure the examinee understands the meaning of the items, and that the examiner's pronunciation is clear to the examinee. It also acts as a final check for the innocent examinee who may have inadvertently learned a detail of the crime, and thereby prevent an erroneous conclusion that might otherwise result from that test. Sometimes guilty examinees will claim they learned of a key from an investigator, something that can be verified by contacting the investigator. When proven untrue, the examinee's knowledge of the information can be used in later questioning. Regardless, keys for which an examinee claims to know should not be used in CITs.

Examiners must be mindful during the review of the items that one test does not reveal the key of another test. For example, if one test is about the location of a weapon found in a room (i.e., in a desk), and a subsequent test is to determine whether the examinee knew in which drawer of the desk the weapon was found, it would be necessary to test on the location of the weapon in the room first without reviewing the other tests. Under those circumstances the examiner may review and conduct each test in a sequential manner, not revealing the content of other tests until they are to be conducted.

CIT INSTRUMENTATION

The research has focused primarily on electrodermal responses (EDRs), with dozens of scientific papers supporting its use. Respiration line length (RLL) has been proposed as another diagnostic measure in the CIT (Timm, 1982, 1989; Elaad et al., 1992) and though encouraging, RLL has not moved beyond the experimental stage for the CIT. A proposed measure of vasomotor activity as recorded with a photoplethysmograph is the finger pulse waveform length (FPWL; Elaad and Ben-Shakhar, 2006). It is similar in concept to RLL. The supporting evidence for the FPWL in the CIT remains tentative at this time. There is no empirical support for scoring the cardiovascular channel in the CIT. Nevertheless, most state licensing laws, government and police policies, and professional association standards mandate minimum instrumentation standards which require recording physiological data that are designed for deception testing but not the CIT. Polygraph examiners should still abide by those laws, policies, and standards when conducting the CIT.

It is recommended that the pneumograph also be recorded during the CIT so that examiners might detect respiratory activity that could generate EDRs, and avoid presenting items when EDRs might spring from breathing behaviors. There is no reason for polygraph examiners to record other channels except to satisfy legal, licensing, or policy requirements.

CIT TESTING

Conducting the CIT is quite simple. Unlike any other technique in polygraphy, tests are given but a single time. In other words, there is one CIT per chart. During the test the examinee repeats each item back to the examiner, rather than say *yes* or *no*. Simply answering no to each item, as is done in the POT, presents an opportunity for the guilty examinee to dissociate and reduce the arousal value of the key. Repeating the items is a way of ensuring that the examinee has paid attention to them. Though having the examinee answer *no* to each item is not incorrect, and may prove effective in many cases, it would not be considered a best practice.

Each test starts with an introductory statement that establishes the context for the items to follow. For example: "If you are the person who killed John Smith, you know what the weapon was. Repeat after me each of these weapons." Finally, each item is presented to the examinee only once, with a pacing of about 25 s. When this test is completed, it is set aside, and a new test is conducted with a different key and new controls. It is recommended that a minimum of four different tests be run, and as many as 10, if possible. A test may only be repeated if there was some type of artifact that eliminated the diagnostic value of the test. When a test is re-run, the order of the items is changed according to the rules listed earlier.

To give a concrete example of how the CIT can be used, the following is a vignette on which a series of tests will be shown.

> *The body of 74-year-old Mary Smith was found in a recliner in her living room on the afternoon of July 14th. She had been dead about four hours. There was no sign of forced entry to the home, and all but one door had been found locked. Her adult children reported that Smith usually kept the back door unlocked during the day so that it was easier to let her cat in and out. Police found that the screen on the back door had been pushed out from the frame, probably by the culprit during his escape. Smith had been struck on the back of the head with a heavy stone bookend found at the scene, a blow that caused her death. There was no evidence of any other trauma to Smith's body, and it appeared she had been struck while she sat in the chair in which her body was found. Missing from the home were her Sony color television set, $16 in cash from the top of the refrigerator, and a leather jacket belonging to her grandson. The police located one suspect who had been seen in the area earlier that day, 31-year-old parolee named Doug Williams. Williams denied any knowledge or involvement in the crime, and has agreed to take a polygraph examination.*

The following tests will assume that no information about the crime had been released to the public.

Test 1: The Weapon
Introductory statement: If you killed Mary Smith, you know the object that was used to strike her. Repeat after me these objects:

Anchor: Fireplace poker
Key: Stone bookend

Control: Table lamp
Control: Steam iron
Control: Tire jack
Control: Wine bottle

Test 2: Location of the Body
Introductory statement: If you killed Mary Smith, you know which room the murder took place. Repeat these rooms after me:

Anchor: Bathroom
Control: Garage
Control: Basement
Control: Kitchen
Control: Bedroom
Key: Living room

Test 3: Theft
Introductory statement: If you killed Mary Smith, you also stole something from her home. Repeat after me these things:

Anchor: Kitchen radio
Control: CD player
Key: Television set
Control: Antique clock
Control: Laptop computer
Control: Digital camera

Test 4: The Escape
Introductory statement: If you killed Mary Smith, you damaged something when you left so we know the direction of escape. Repeat the following:

Anchor: Bathroom sliding window
Control: Double front doors
Control: Sealed bedroom window
Key: Back screen door
Control: Wooden garage door
Control: Red basement door

Only four tests are covered here, but many more are possible: the location of the victim's wound, that she had been sitting in a chair, the amount of cash stolen and where it had been located, the missing leather jacket, to name a few. It bears repeating that the examinee must be able to recognize the key.

Something that may also increase the salience of the key to the guilty is to give feedback after each test. This option is available for when the charts are relatively flat, and it does not increase the prospect of an error as it might for CQTs. If the examinee learns that he has been responding to items that implicate him, it can have an additive effect on the signal value of subsequent keys. Imagine for a moment that you are the culprit in the above Mary Smith murder, and after the first test the examiner comments, "Joe, on that test your largest reaction was to 'stone bookend.' Sit still and we'll start the next test." The examiner should not say that "stone bookend" is the key. Telling an examinee he reacted to the item indicating guilt may unnerve the innocent examinee, and perhaps cause the guilty examinee to quit the exam. It is better to simply tell the examinee of the reaction, and discourage any further conversation about it. If the examinee asks whether the reaction was on the one related to the murder, the examiner should advise the examinee that all will be covered at the end of the testing. Keep in mind that if the examinee is actually reacting to the keys, that there is no value in pointing this out between tests.

ANALYZING THE CIT

Before moving on to the mechanics of scoring, it is helpful to begin with an examination of the underlying premise on which scoring of the CIT is based. It is expected that innocent examinees, with no knowledge of the details of a crime, would react randomly to the test items. This randomness should result in scores that are different from those of guilty suspects, who tend to react to items related to the crime which they recognize. Because innocent examinees react randomly, they may at times react to a relevant item by chance. This is one reason the CIT is conducted with several different relevant items, to cancel out the effect of chance. It is also one of the benefits of the CIT over the POT, which tends to test only on a single item. Guilty suspects, in contrast to innocent examinees, continue to react to the different keys, and the persistent reactivity to several keys produces a diminishing likelihood that the reactions are random.

A good way to understand this difference is to look again at the Mary Smith murder vignette. Suppose that an examinee were being tested on this murder. Recall that there were six items presented in the first test. Because examinees are known to always react to the first item, or anchor, any reaction to the first item is ignored. The examinee, then, may have produced his largest reaction to any one of the five remaining items, including the key. If the examinee did react greatest to the key, chance has not been excluded as the possible cause. Under normal conditions, examinees knowing nothing about the crime will react to the key by chance one in five times, or 20%. Suppose for the present purposes that the examinee did react to the key on the first test, "stone bookend."

On the second test there are also six items, but ignoring the anchor, there are five to which the examinee may react the largest, just as there was in the first test. Suppose the examinee reacted to the key on this test, "living room." There is a one-in-five chance, or 20%, of this happening to an innocent person, too. However, the chance that an innocent person would react to both "stone bookend" *and* "living room" is a mere 4% (20%×20%=4%). A 4% chance is one out of 25 innocent examinees will react in this manner. Now consider the chance that the innocent person will react to "stone bookend" on the first test, "living room" on the second test, and the key on the third test, "television set." This is 20% of 20% of 20%, or only 0.8%. There is roughly one innocent person in a hundred that would react to all three keys. Add to this the fourth test where the person reacted to the key "back screen door" and the chances of the examinee being naïve to the crime details is very remote, rounding up to only 2 in 1000. Each additional test where the examinee reacts greatest to the key moves the examinee's claims of ignorance further from the realm of credibility.

The examples above have assumed that there were five scoreable items on each test. This is not the only configuration for the CIT, but merely a convenience for instruction. Examiners might employ any number of items on a test, so long as there is only a single key. If in the present murder case there had been 10 scoreable items instead of 5 on a test, and the examinee reacted largest on the key, the likelihood of this happening by chance is 10% instead of 20%. Similarly, reacting the greatest to the keys on two tests is 1% (10% of 10%), and 0.1% on three tests (10% of 10% of 10%).

It is worth repeating that examinees who react to the keys on the CIT are not necessarily guilty of the crime, though this would be the natural conclusion. These reactions only indicate the examinee has been exposed to the crime details that the guilty person would know. For this reason, the results of the CIT are Recognition Indicated (RI), and No Recognition Indicate (NRI). The use of RI and NRI makes clear that these results do not speak to the examinee's guilt or deception, only that he knows information that he denies knowing.

Returning now to the principles of scoring, in his 1959 paper Lykken proposed a simple yet effective scoring strategy. First, the reaction to the anchor is always ignored. If the largest EDR occurs at the key, the test is scored as a "2". After that, if the second largest EDR occurs to the key, the test is scored as a "1". Otherwise the score is "0". Each test receives only one score, and the scores for all tests are totaled. Referring to Figure 8.6, if item B were the key in this test, the score would be "2" because it is the largest EDR. If the key were item C, the score would be "1", being the second largest EDR. If the EDR to the key were ranked third or lower the score for that test would be "0". Reminder: always ignore the reaction to the anchor.

Lykken's (1959) decision rules were also simple: if the total score was equal to or greater than the number of tests conducted, the examinee was classified as having concealed information. Lower scores indicated that the examinee did not have this information. There were no inconclusives, though later writers have suggested that there must have been an EDR on one of the items to consider a test valid. A lack of EDRs to all items would therefore result in an inconclusive, and this is the recommended practice. To obtain exact probabilities of scores with the CIT for up to eight tests, refer to Table 8.1.

The chronic problem of all recognition tests—that guilty examinees do not always recognize the keys selected by examiners—has a potential remedy. It is recommended that as many tests be conducted as is reasonable, thereby increasing

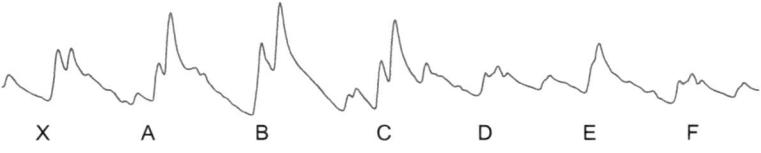

FIGURE 8.6

EDRs on a CIT test.

the likelihood that the examiner will have covered the field properly. Having larger numbers of tests not only improves the prospect for correctly identifying those with concealed information but also incrementally and simultaneously reduces the chances of a false positive result. For evidentiary examinations, it is recommended that the number of tests be conducted until a score indicates there is less than 1% chance that the examinee is ignorant of the crime details, or 10 tests, whichever comes first. Utilization of the CIT in investigative examinations, where the tests are used for less than evidentiary purposes, may permit a more lenient threshold. Users of the CIT to advance an investigation or interrogation should have confidence in a RI decision when the score indicates a probability of less than 10%.

SUMMARY OF BEST CIT PRACTICES

More than any other approach to "lie detection" the CIT has enjoyed not only a large body of research, but the strong endorsement of knowledgeable scientists. Among them are Bruno Verschuere, Gershon Ben-Shakhar, and Ewout Meijer who in 2011 (Verschuere et al., 2011) produced a text dedicated to the CIT. It is recommended for reading as it contains virtually everything known about the CIT. Their final chapter encapsulates eight best practices, a summary of which is given below.

1. The relevant CIT items should focus on salient and central details of the crime, and actions of the guilty party.
2. The CIT should be given as soon as possible after the crime.
3. As many salient items should be tested as possible. When fewer than five are available, examiners can test as few as three salient items if the tests are repeated.
4. All items should be equally plausible to one another, and maximally distinct from one another.
5. Skin conductance must be recorded, and heart rate and respiration may be recorded.
6. The Lykken scoring should be used, and a within-examinee standardization procedure can be used in conjunction or as a stand-alone method.
7. Preference should be given to quantification of responses using computer algorithms.
8. Presentation of the test items during testing should be done by someone blind to the relevant items, or automatically by computer.

Table 8.1 CIT probability table

		Score													
		3	4	5	6	7	8	9	10	11	12	13	14	15	16
Number of tests	2	12.0	4.0												
	3	28.0	12.8	3.2	0.8										
	4	43.8	24.6	10.1	3.7	0.8	0.2								
	5	57.7	37.5	19.7	9.2	3.2	1.0	0.2	0.0	0.0	0.0				
	6	68.9	49.9	30.9	16.9	7.7	3.1	1.0	0.3	0.0	0.0	0.0			
	7	77.6	60.9	42.3	26.3	14.2	6.8	2.7	1.0	0.3	0.1	0.0	0.0		
	8	84.1	70.2	53.1	36.4	22.2	12.2	5.8	2.5	0.9	0.3	0.1	0.0	0.0	0.0

The probability of an examinee achieving a particular score or higher can be determined for the number of tests. For example, if 6 tests were conducted and the examinee obtained a score of 8, the likelihood that the examinee is truly naïve of the crime details is 3.1%. Probabilities are rounded to the nearest tenth of a percent. The probabilities assume five scoreable items per test.
Table courtesy of Dr. Stuart Senter.

REFERENCES

Ansley, N., 1992. The history and accuracy of guilty knowledge and peak of tension tests. Polygraph 21 (3), 174–247.

Arther, R.O., 1970. Peak of tension: question formulation. J. Polygraph Stud. 4 (5), 1–4.

Barland, G.H., 1984. Research in electrodermal biofeedback with stimulus tests. Final report to the NSA (Contract MDA904-83-M-1150).

Burgess, T.H., 1839. The Physiology or Mechanism of Blushing. John Churchill, London.

Elaad, E., Ben-Shakhar, G., 2006. Finger pulse waveform length in the detection of concealed information. Int. J. Psychophysiol. 61, 226–234.

Elaad, E., Ginton, A., Jungman, N., 1992. Detection measures in real-life criminal guilty knowledge tests. J. Appl. Psychol. 77 (5), 757–767.

Hess, E.H., 1965. Attitude and pupil size. Sci. Am. 212, 46–54.

Keeler, L., 1939. Problems in the use of the "lie detector". In: Police Year Book 1938-1939. International Association of Chiefs of Police, Washington, DC.

Lykken, D.T., 1959. The GSR and the detection of guilt. J. Appl. Psychol. 43 (6), 385–388.

National Research Council, 2003. The Polygraph and Lie Detection. National Academies Press, Washington, DC.

Timm, H.W., 1982. Effect of altered outcome expectancies stemming from placebo and feedback treatments on the validity of the guilty knowledge technique. J. Appl. Psychol. 67 (4), 391–400.

Timm, H.W., 1989. Methodological considerations affecting the utility of incorporating innocent subjects into the design of guilty knowledge polygraph experiments. Polygraph 18 (3), 143–157.

Verschuere, B., Ben-Shakhar, G., Meijer, E., 2011. Memory Detection: Theory and Application of the Concealed Information Test. Cambridge University Press, Cambridge.

Yokoi, Y., Okazaki, Y., Kiriu, M., Kuramochi, T., Ohama, T., 2001. The validity of the guilty knowledge test used in field cases. Jap. J. Crim. Psychol. 39 (1), 15–27.

CHAPTER 9

Scientific issues

> *It is a capital mistake to theorise before one has data. Insensibly one begins to twist facts to suit theories instead of theories to suit facts.*
> Sherlock Holmes in *The Adventures of Sherlock Homes* by Sir Arthur Conan Doyle

Polygraph examiners, who provide court testimony, are involved in research, manage polygraph programs, or have an interest in advances in the field should be familiar with the published research relevant to their area of specialty. Fortunately, in this electronic age polygraph research articles are very accessible. Perhaps more than half of the research in polygraphy is available in the journal *Polygraph*, with other excellent articles appearing in publications such as the *Journal of Applied Psychology* and the *Journal of Forensic Sciences*. The body of polygraph literature is substantial, but not so impossibly great that it could not be reviewed by someone who resolves to read the most important, relevant, and interesting papers.

The purpose of this chapter is to cover not so much the research findings, but to lay out the important research issues surrounding polygraph. After decades of being largely ignored by the scientific community, the polygraph has in recent years been hotly debated by all sides. Some of the harshest criticisms directed toward the polygraph, both right and wrong, are founded on well-established scientific principles. Practitioners wanting to evaluate the merits of the criticisms, or to prepare to rebut them, will need to become conversant with the principles on which the criticisms are based.

There are scientific principles about all tests that also apply to polygraphy. The degree to which polygraph practice conforms to those principles will establish its validity and reliability. Departure from them will constrain validity and reliability to a lower limit than if practices are consistent with the principles. It seems appropriate, then, to begin with a discussion of what are validity and reliability.

VALIDITY

The term *validity* has the popular interpretation of being identical to *accuracy*, as in "This test has a validity of 90%." Though the common understanding is not incorrect, it is incomplete. There are actually several forms of validity. One may speak of construct, face, content, ecological, predictive, criterion, and criterion-related validity, in addition to others, but only one of these relates to decision accuracy.

To determine what we mean by *validity* when talking about polygraph decision accuracy, a closer examination is needed. First, what is the polygraph used for? The answer is: to discriminate between truthful and deceptive statements. However, the polygraph does not, and cannot, detect either truthfulness or deception directly. Indeed, deception and truthfulness and credibility are simply constructs: they are ideas that we may all understand, but they are not objects or physical things that can be weighed or measured. They are intangible. Constructs and other intangibles do not readily lend themselves to detection by mechanical devices, any more than an apparatus can directly detect constructs such as intelligence, personality, or moods. What a polygraph actually does is register physiological responses as part of a larger testing protocol. If the criterion for the polygraph were, say, capturing certain physiological phenomena, then one might argue the polygraph has near-perfect validity. Standard polygraphs do represent those phenomena with impressive fidelity. However, this is not the same as sorting truthteller from liar. Instead, the polygraph outputs are used to predict deception (or more correctly, postdict deception, since the results come after the act of lying). Therefore, it can be said that the polygraph and attendant processes possess *criterion-related* validity, in that the signals and analysis produce an outcome that corresponds with the construct *deception*. For the remainder of this chapter, criterion-related validity and decision accuracy will be used interchangeably.

Writers have used several and sometimes conflicting approaches to calculating polygraph decision accuracy. Some take a sample of cases, find the correct decisions, and divide that number by the number of cases in the sample (e.g., Patton, 2013). Some count inconclusive results as errors, though others do not. Still others have taken the number of confirmed errors in a sample, presume the remaining cases were all correctly decided, and estimate accuracy that way (e.g., Arther and Arther, 1998). Not surprisingly, advocates and critics of polygraph do not agree on which to use, and the choice of method can have profound influences on the calculations.

Before moving on, this might be a good point to introduce terminology regarding correct and incorrect polygraph results. A decision of deception is called a positive, whereas a truthful result is a negative. Positive and negative regard decisions. When a decision is correct, it is true, and the opposite is called false. Decisions of deception, then, can be true positive in the case of correctly detecting a liar, or false when a truthteller is called a liar. Similarly, a correct polygraph decision of truthfulness is a true negative, but a miss with a truthful examinee is a false positive.

The standard approach in polygraph research is to report accuracy both with and without inconclusive results. This circumvents intractable debates as to whether inconclusives are part of decision accuracy or only a measure of utility. Then, the accuracy with truthful cases is calculated separately from that of deceptive cases. Finally, total accuracy is determined by the average of the accuracies derived from the truthful and deceptive cases. Below is a simple formula calculating overall decision accuracy. When using inconclusive results as errors, they would be added to the number of false negatives in the case of deceptive examinees, and false positives for truthful examinees (Figure 9.1).

$$\left(\frac{\text{True positives}}{\text{(True positives + False negatives)}} + \frac{\text{True negatives}}{\text{(True negatives + False positives)}}\right)/2$$

FIGURE 9.1

Standard formula for calculating overall polygraph decision accuracy.

Here is how this might be done with actual numbers. Imagine a study of a polygraph technique using a sample of 100 truthful cases and 100 deceptive cases. In this imaginary sample, the truthful cases had 11 decision errors (false positives), 10 inconclusives, and 79 correct decisions (true negatives). The deceptive cases had 4 errors (false negatives), 7 inconclusives, and 89 correct decisions (true positives). The accuracy with the truthful cases would be reported as 79% with inconclusives (79 true negatives out of 100 cases), and 88% without them (79 true negatives out of 90 non-inconclusive decisions). These statistics might sometimes be referred to as the specificity of the test, that is, the detection of the absence of deception. Similarly, the accuracy for the deceptive cases would be 89% with inconclusives (89 true positives out of 100 cases), and 96% without them (89 true positives out of 93 non-inconclusive decisions). These statistics might elsewhere refer to the sensitivity of the test. Overall accuracy is the average of the accuracies. To calculate it, simply add the two accuracies and divide by 2. So, it would be 84% without inconclusives (average of 79% and 89%), and 92% without them (average of 88% and 96%).

Finding the ultimate criterion-related validity for the polygraph is not as easy as such a simple question might suggest. There are several factors that can influence it. A partial list would include the number of test issues, ability of the examinee to know with confidence whether he is truthful to the issue(s), number of times questions are presented, the use of valid scoring methods, what the decision rules are, whether and what type comparison questions are used, and many other technical factors. This does not even consider individual differences in examiner experience and competence, or the suitability of the examinee to undergo polygraph testing. For these reasons, polygraph decision accuracy is best calculated as a range rather than a single point. Ranges have been calculated for two major factors, the testing and the analytical techniques, and may one day be refined as research establishes the ranges imposed by other variables. Validity tables for the various polygraph methods are provided in Appendix B.

There are ways of maximizing polygraph decision accuracy that are under the control of practitioners. One is the inclusion of the most diagnostic information in their decisions. This means the use of scoring regimens that rely on validated tracing features (see Chapter 5) and optimal decision rules, the use of as many valid but independent data channels as possible, and employing valid testing protocols in a highly structured manner. There is also value in the use of automation for routine, highly repetitive tasks for what it offers toward consistency. Automation might aid in presenting certain portions of the pretest interview that does not rely on a high level of interaction, and in decision support in the analysis of the charts. Finally, examiner competency can be elevated by participation in a rigorous internship program at the start of one's professional career, standard reliance on independent quality control through one's practice, and tireless pursuit of continuing education. Taken together, these recommendations will ensure the practitioner will garner the highest accuracy, and value, possible in polygraphy.

RELIABILITY

In research, reliability denotes consistency or agreement. As with validity, there is more than one type of reliability. Three of them germane to polygraphy are test-retest reliability, intra-rater reliability, and inter-rater reliability. An evaluation of test-retest reliability might involve polygraphing the same examinee on multiple occasions on the same issues to determine the extent to which the results across those examinations agree with one another. Intra-rater reliability refers to the consistency a single scorer has with himself when looking at the same data on different occasions. Finally, inter-rater reliability is how often different scorers agree with each other on the same cases. The reliability statistic most often reported in the polygraph literature is inter-rater reliability.

Reliability is essential to validity, as it is axiomatic that a test cannot be more valid than it is reliable. In other words, without consistency a procedure cannot be accurate. Using a firearms analogy, any rifle held in the exact same position for 100 shots but producing a shot pattern all over the target is not reliable. It is producing an inconsistent result. Because it is unreliable, it cannot be accurate. The more the shots are closely grouped, the more reliable the rifle. Similarly, if there is 75% agreement among examiners on decisions for a sample of cases, the method cannot be more than 75% accurate since at least 25% of the examiners must be wrong in their decisions. Reliability does not assure validity, though, for it might be the 25% of examiners that made the correct decision. Even with 100% agreement among examiners, they still might be wrong. Using the rifle analogy again, a better weapon might produce a tightly grouped shot pattern, signaling high reliability, but the grouping may be in the corner of the target rather than the intended location at the bullseye. The weapon has high reliability but low validity. The level of reliability merely sets a limit as to what the validity might be, but does not guarantee validity.

Measures of inter-rater agreement are found in most of the better polygraph research articles. Statistical methods for calculating inter-rater reliability are beyond the scope of this chapter, however. Those who wish to familiarize themselves with reliability metrics should consult statistical texts. As background for those interested, researchers evaluating inter-rater reliability typically report Pearson's r, Cohen's kappa, and proportion of agreement.

Inter-rater reliability is improved when all examiners use the same standardized practices. Not surprisingly, police agencies and government programs with examiners trained by different schools have experienced immense challenges in finding agreement among their staff. Fortunately, the field of polygraphy has been shifting toward fewer techniques, and especially those that have published validity studies, which represents a better appreciation among practitioners for standardization. The coalescence of the field around evidence-based practices in recent years has also been a benefit.

TYPES OF VALIDITY STUDIES

There are two main types of validity studies: field and laboratory. Both have advantages and disadvantages compared to the other. Estimates of polygraph accuracy depend on the findings from both settings.

FIELD STUDIES

Among the oldest studies on polygraph testing are those using samples of field cases, usually written by practitioners (e.g., MacNitt, 1942). With immediate access to very convenient samples, mainly their own cases, researcher/practitioners undertook the task of estimating of how accurate polygraphic lie detection was. It would not be until the 1960s that investigation of the polygraph was initiated by scientists. The first, interestingly enough, had been a professional colleague of pioneer Dr. Walter Summers at Fordham University (Kubis, 1965).

Field studies permit the gathering of data affected by conditions that would be very difficult to replicate in laboratory settings. In the laboratory it is not ethically possible to induce the level of concern about the outcome of a polygraph examination similar to that a criminal suspect would feel when tested in a law enforcement setting. Field studies are said to have high ecological validity because the conditions producing the data are highly similar to real world conditions in which the test is to be used. They may also have greater external validity as a result, that is, it may be said that field studies better predict the real world accuracy of the polygraph.

One of the difficulties of field studies is the collection of representative samples of confirmed truthful and deceptive cases. This is due in large part with how polygraph results are used. In most instances, an unfavorable test result will bring about more scrutiny of the examinee than a favorable result. Examinees judged as deceptive by a polygraph examiner are more likely to be interrogated or investigated, leading to confessions or more inculpatory evidence. Conversely, a polygraph decision of truthfulness tends to redirect an investigation. If the polygraph examiner has made a false positive decision (misclassification of a truthful examinee as deceptive), it is unlikely that a confession will arise. Further investigation will not likely uncover exculpatory information owing to the common use of the polygraph near the end of an investigation. Therefore, the probability of discovery of a false positive result is reduced. Similarly, a false negative result (incorrect conclusion that the examinee was truthful) will often forestall an interrogation and redirect an investigation away from inculpatory evidence. Therefore, there is a lower but unknown probability that false positives will not be identified.

Because polygraph decision errors tend to be discovered less frequently than correct polygraph results, field samples of confirmed cases may be qualitatively different from unconfirmed cases in that the latter may harbor more errors. Field samples of confirmed cases, then, may tend to overestimate polygraph decision accuracy inasmuch as the samples consist of cases the testing examiner arrived at the right answer. Errors could be systematically filtered from the sample. The 2003 report on the polygraph by the National Research Council (NRC) did find a slightly higher accuracy reported in field studies than in lab studies, though it was not a significant difference. Nevertheless, the potential for sampling bias in field studies is a cause for concern and attention.

Another trend in the polygraph literature is worthy of comment. It has been observed that research in which examiners study their own techniques, or use their own field cases, they report accuracies substantially greater than studies by those with no personal interest in any particular technique. Studies conducted by those with demonstrable personal interest typically find decision accuracies of 100%. This is in stark relief to independent studies showing a median accuracy percentage for single-issue polygraph techniques in the high 80s to low 90s. How studies of one's own technique or cases should produce results tightly clustered near perfection is interesting in its own right, but this tendency is made more fascinating as it appears to carry beyond polygraph to most of the credibility assessment methods found in the literature. From Marston and Benussi's approaches in the early 1900s, through Walter Summer's Pathometer in the 1930s, to voice stress and brainwave devices in the more recent past, it is easy to conclude that perfect decision accuracy is achievable with almost any technique or technology (see Krapohl, 2013, for a full discussion of this phenomenon). Obviously, caution is advised. These kinds of studies fall more generally into a category called advocacy research, that is, studies used intentionally to promote an idea, service, or product. One telltale sign to watch for are studies that are subsequently used for commercial promotion by parties involved in the studies.

LABORATORY STUDIES

A second approach to polygraph research involves studies conducted in laboratory settings using mock crimes. Researchers using this paradigm program some proportion of their research volunteers to either commit a pretend crime, such as theft or vandalism, while a second group would only know about the crime but not commit it. All of the research volunteers are then given polygraph tests, and the data are analyzed by the researchers.

The ability to control variables is the chief attraction of laboratory studies. With them, experimenters can establish *a priori* the conditions that help isolate factors that might influence the results, such as experience of the examiner, pretest practices, type of polygraph testing technique, scoring method, examinee demographics, etc. By controlling the variables, or using research designs to statistically neutralize their effects, scientists are able to answer important questions about the polygraph.

Having total control also permits researchers to avoid potential confounds that can plague field research. Principal among them is establishing ground truth which, as the previous section on field studies discusses, is a virtually intractable problem for field research. Knowing with certainty the programming of the entire population of examinees avoids a source of selection bias.

The main criticism of laboratory studies lies in their dissimilarity from field conditions. It has been pointed out that in the real world, suspects choose whether to commit a crime, whereas in the laboratory the volunteers are usually assigned to guilty and innocent conditions. This difference therefore does not allow laboratory studies to capture psychological or motivational aspects that might have import to polygraph accuracy in field practice. There may also be differences in the time period between the crime and polygraph testing, where in analog studies it might be measured in minutes versus days or weeks or longer in the field. The consequences for a failed polygraph examination are also substantially different between the two settings, as well.

Whether these factors affect polygraph data is a significant question, for large disparities between settings could generate philosophical disputes as to which better represents the true accuracy of polygraph testing. In search of an answer, Pollina et al. (2004) analyzed archived samples of polygraph data gathered from the field and from the laboratory. Their analysis found differences in the profiles of physiological responding between the data from the two settings, with stronger cardiovascular responding in the field data. However, decision accuracy was not significantly different between field and lab cases. These findings are in accord with the 2003 NRC report. It would appear from the current state of the research that field and lab data, although flawed in dissimilar ways, point to similar accuracy for the polygraph.

EFFECT OF DECISION RULES

The focus on polygraph techniques and scoring systems has overshadowed interest in polygraph decision rules, which are essential to meeting consumer requirements as will be later discussed. Polygraph examiners have long regarded decision rules to be immutable components of scoring systems, if not of entire polygraph techniques. Scoring of polygraph charts were widely practiced for more than 20 years before the first tentative steps were taken to look at how different decision rules affected the sensitivity, specificity, and inconclusive rates (Honts and Driscoll, 1987). Since then they have been studied extensively by many writers in search of "optimal" decision rules. As we will learn, "optimal" can change according to conditions.

To understand the effect of decision rules, it is instructive to use the statistical standard, the bell curve. A bell curve can be constructed by the frequency of scores examinees produce in polygraph testing. In conventional 7-position scoring of, say, the Federal Zone Comparison Test, the total score for a case can hypothetically range from −81 to +81. This is because there are three data channels, three charts, three relevant questions, three possible points per question per data channel ($3^4=81$), and the points may be in the positive or negative direction.

As all examiners know, deceptive suspects virtually never get −81 points nor do truthful examinees get +81. If one were to plot on a graph how often examinees get these extreme scores, the dot marking the point would be at almost zero. Other scores happen more often. A total of +9 is fairly frequent among truthtellers. If one were to mark on a plot how often +9 happened for truthtellers, it would be higher than, say, +34 or −4. If an examiner had access to the total scores of some large number of truthful examinees, and plotted how often total scores occurred, the distribution would take on the familiar bell curve, with certain scores in the middle happening the most, and scores at the ends happening infrequently or never. The same is true if one plotted the frequencies of total scores for liars. It would also create a bell curve, but one that is to the side of the one consisting of the scores from truthful examinees. Figure 9.2 will help conceptualize the following discussion.

Figure 9.2 shows two overlapping bell curves, and three vertical lines marked A, B, and C. The bell curve to the left is meant to represent the frequency of scores of liars, and the right curve is that from truthful examinees. The two curves overlap, as sometimes do the scores from deceptive and truthful examinees (e.g., a total score of +1 could come from either group). The three vertical lines are hypothetical cutoffs for scores.

Let us look at where line A intersects the bell curves. If line A represents a cutoff score, all cases to the left would be called deceptive, and all the cases to the right truthful. For ease of discussion, inconclusive results will be ignored for a moment. If all of the cases to the left of line A are called deceptive, most of the liars would receive the correct results, as most of the bell curve for liars is to the left of line A. A small portion of the truthful examinees also fall to the left of line A, and would be called deceptive in error. Similarly, most of the truthful cases are to the right of line A, and would be

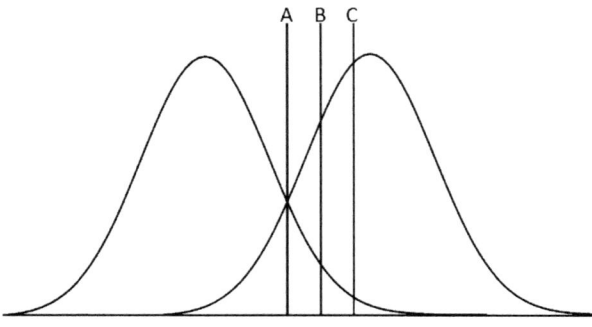

FIGURE 9.2

Idealized bell curves representing the frequency of total scores for deceptive (left) and truthful (right) polygraph examinees, with three proposed cutoff points.

correctly called truthful. A relatively smaller group of deceptive examinees also are to the right of line A, and would be mistakenly called truthful. At line A, the errors are approximately equal for deceptive and truthful cases.

Suppose that the cost of errors is higher when missing a liar than when missing a truthteller. One may then decide to use the cutoff score represented by line B. At this point on the bell curves, more of the liars' cases fall to the left of the line, and would be correctly called deceptive. The new cutoff at line B has benefitted the detection of deception. The cost is in the error rate with truthful examinees. Note that more of the truthtellers' bell curve now falls below the cutoff, and those cases would be called deceptive at line B.

Line C shows a risk-aversive cutoff score, where a miniscule proportion of liars would be missed. Note that the number of liars to the right of line C is very small, indeed. Also note, though, the increasing proportion of truthtellers falling to the right of line C. The tradeoff in correct decisions on one side and errors on the other is not equal. As the cutoff moves further to the right, the number of correct decisions begins to slow while the number of wrong decisions grows exponentially. With extreme risk avoidance, the test can no longer detect truthfulness greater than chance.

The same effect also works in reverse. Once the cutoff moves to the right of line A, the test will be better at making decisions of truthfulness, but less of deception. The total avoidance of false positive errors would move the cutoff to a level where it could no longer detect deceptiveness better than guessing.

The bell curves help illustrate that the road to improved accuracy is not in the movement of cutoff scores. Those changes only affect the kinds of errors one will make. The avoidance of errors comes with the addition of an inconclusive zone.

A tolerance for errors would permit a very narrow inconclusive area, bounded by cutoff scores that are relatively close to one another. To reduce errors, the boundaries must be moved outward. Using the bell curves of Figure 9.2 again, one can see that the expansion of the inconclusive zone begins to include more cases that would have had erroneous results. It also begins to include an increasing proportion of cases that had been correctly decided. The tradeoff becomes more imbalanced as the inconclusive zone grows. Total avoidance of errors is hypothetically possible, but at that point it is likely that most polygraph results would be inconclusive. Only cases with extreme scores would receive determinations of truthfulness or deception, but virtually all of the decisions would be correct ones. This is why many writers consider the proportion of inconclusive results a metric of utility rather than decision errors, because inconclusive rules are imposed to minimize errors.

The central theme of this thought exercise was to demonstrate that decision rules are compromises of accuracy and utility. Extreme accuracy is possible at low utility, and errors are highest when utility is maximized. Selection of a set of decision rules implicitly signals the user's tolerance for whatever utility and accuracy come with those rules.

EFFECTS OF BASE RATES

The proportion of something in a population is called the base rate. The concept of base rate is used throughout fields such as medicine and psychology. Base rates do not affect the accuracy of any test, but they do provide a very useful index for assessing how confident one can be in the test results. In polygraph testing, having knowledge of base rates can help guide decision rules. To illustrate this point, let us start with the following assumptions for a hypothetical polygraph screening program, and then look at the effect that base rates produce.

Assumptions: Polygraph decisions are 80% accurate for both detecting truthfulness and deception in a screening context. The population undergoing testing numbers 1000 persons. Inconclusive results are excluded from this exercise. The base rate will be altered according to setting. Pay attention to how base rate affects the type of error, though not the total number of errors.

We will consider three base rates of deception: the first exam of convicted sex offenders (high), of government employees in search of a spy (low), and of applicants for law enforcement positions (balanced). Tables 9.1–9.3 show how the types of errors are affected by the base rate of deception.

Base rates can also interplay with decision rules. In the preceding examples, the presumed accuracy of the polygraph was 80% for both truthtellers and liars. This balanced accuracy need not be the rule, however. With polygraph scores available,

Table 9.1 Crosstabs of hits and misses for deceptive and truthful offenders with a base rate of 95%, 80% polygraph decision accuracy, and 1000 offenders

Decision	Deceptive examinees	Truthful examinees	Total number	Wrong decisions	False positive	False negative
Deceptive	760	10	770			
Truthful	190	40	230			
Total	950	50	1000	200	10	190

Table 9.2 Crosstabs of hits and misses for deceptive and truthful employees with a base rate of 0.1%, 80% polygraph decision accuracy, and 1000 employees

Decision	Deceptive examinees	Truthful examinees	Total number	Wrong decisions	False positive	False negative
Deceptive	1	200	201			
Truthful	0	799	799			
Total	1	999	1000	200	200	0

Table 9.3 Crosstabs of hits and misses for deceptive and truthful applicants with a base rate of 50.0%, 80% polygraph decision accuracy, and 1000 applicants

Decision	Deceptive examinees	Truthful examinees	Total number	Wrong decisions	False positive	False negative
Deceptive	400	100	500			
Truthful	100	400	500			
Total	500	500	1000	200	100	100

decision rules (cutoff scores) can be adjusted to avoid errors that decision-makers consider more costly. Reminder: Adjusting the decision rules will not make the polygraph more accurate. The adjustments will only change the proportions of false positive and negative errors. It is possible to avoid certain types of errors, but at a cost of increasing errors of another kind.

Expanding on the earlier illustration regarding base rates of deception for sex offenders, suppose decision-makers found 150 false negatives per 950 deceptive sex offenders to be intolerably high. The population of concern poses a continuing threat to innocent citizens. After due deliberation, decision-makers express the desire for a more risk-averse approach, reducing false negatives to fewer than 30 per 950 deceptive examinees (assuming the remaining 50 examinees per 1000 are truthful). The thoughtful and responsive examiner, using a scoring system that allows her to calculate errors at each cutoff score, finds the appropriate new decision rule. Being statistically literate, she uses the probability information available with her scoring system, and redoes the crosstabs to determine the effect on her error rate. She finds she can achieve the target of 3% false negative (or <30 per 950 deceptive examinees) with the new cutoff scores, but to do so her false positive rate increases to 48%. Table 9.4 displays the impact of the new decision rules.

Note in this example that the examiner's overall error rate appears to have decreased from a total of 200 under the original decision rules (Table 9.1) to only 53 with the new cutoff scores (Table 9.4). At first blush the lower number of errors

Table 9.4 Crosstabs of hits and misses for deceptive and truthful examinees with a base rate of 95.0%, 97% accuracy with deceptive examinees, 52% with truthful examinees, and 1000 examinees

Decision	Deceptive examinees	Truthful examinees	Total number	Wrong decisions	False positive	False negative
Deceptive	921	24	942			
Truthful	29	26	58			
Total	950	50	1000	53	24	29

suggests the polygraph technique has increased its accuracy. This is a false assumption. Returning to the formula for calculating polygraph accuracy found in Figure 9.1, accuracy with the original decision rules were balanced at 80%. The accuracy for the new decision rules is the average of 97% and 52%, or about 75%. In other words, decision accuracy declined with the new decision rules even though the number of errors also declined. How can this be?

It is because the test has been made sensitive to the category of examinee that has the highest base rate. In other words, there is an overwhelming number of examinees in the category that the test is good at identifying, and not many in the group where the test does poorly.[1] The real cost has come with the increase of false positives, going from 10 to 24, or from 20% to 48% of truthful examinees. However, if decision-makers are aware and accepting of the tradeoff, the new decision rules may be better in those specific circumstances. A key consideration is the relative cost of errors, which in most investigative contexts, is more heavily weighted in avoiding false negatives. It also speaks to an advantage that might come from reporting error likelihoods in polygraph reports, so the end user can ensure the decision rules result in proportions of errors that are aligned with their tolerances.

The risk-aversive decision rules used for Table 9.4 would not be appropriate in settings with low base rates or higher costs for false positives. For example, where the test is looking for a single spy among 1000 employees, a false positive rate of 48% would mean that 480 out of 999 truthful government employees would fail the test. US government employees are not sanctioned for failed polygraph tests, but such outcomes do trigger other more expensive investigative processes, which would quickly be overwhelmed by the sheer number of employees requiring investigative focus. Other decision rules better fit these conditions.

Adjusting of decision rules according to the base rates and cost of errors is a new concept in polygraph screening, and would seem to run contrary to efforts to standardize polygraph procedures. Other fields have found the fine-tuning of decision rules to be advantageous for just those reasons, though. An excellent model can be found in the medical screening for tuberculosis. The test indicator for tuberculosis is an induration (skin reaction, inflammation) a few days after an injection of a purified protein derivative made from tuberculosis bacteria. The size of the induration, measured in millimeters, is used to evaluate the skin response at the injection site. If the size of the induration is sufficiently large, it is judged to be a positive result, suggesting tuberculosis infection.

The size used to make a determination is not a single value, however. There are three different recommended thresholds: 15, 10, and 5 mm, corresponding with low-, medium- and high-risk patients (Curley, 2003). That is, the threshold is the most

---

[1] An extreme example of this effect might be illustrated as follows. Suppose the base rate of deception is 100%. The tool to make decisions of deception is not a polygraph, but a two-headed coin. The decision rule is that when the flipped coin lands on heads, the decision will be that the examinee lied. Since the decision rule guarantees a deceptive result, and all of the examinees are deceptive, the "accuracy" of the coin could be misapprehended as perfect. It is not until the coin is assessed against a truthful population can a true estimate of the coin's accuracy be calculated.

liberal (easily met) for those in high-risk categories, and the most conservative for those in the lowest risk groups. High-risk categories are those who may have had the disease previously, or those with compromised immune systems from diseases such as HIV or cancer. Low-risk patients are those who have no known risk factors, and medium risk has a corresponding list of certain risk factors. The application of the different decision rules is not arbitrary, but subject to well-specified conditions. Medical professionals are not free to apply different decision rules simply on personal preferences. Similarly, if adjustable polygraph decision rules were to be adopted by agencies or departments, they must be internally consistent and based on rational factors that can be both articulated and justified.

Base rates, combined with a careful consideration of the cost of errors, are essential to optimizing decision rules. Neither one is constant across settings in polygraphy, and much work remains to be done to develop standards on which to establish sensible decision rules.

Some initial steps have begun in this regard. An innovative approach has been developed which helps determine the value of polygraph testing across a range of base rates for a fixed accuracy. In doing so, it provides a statistical mechanism that can be applied to different sets of decision rules.

The concept is called information gain (IG) and was proposed by Wells and Olson (2002) as a method quantifying the value of eyewitness identifications in police line ups, or "not there" decisions, as a function of base rate of guilt over simply guessing. The method was astutely recognized by others as having implications for polygraphy. Honts and Schweinle (2009) were the first to reanalyze published accuracy findings of lab, field, screening, and forensic polygraph examinations, subjecting the data to IG analysis. In doing so they were able to demonstrate how confidence in polygraph results varied along with the prior likelihood of guilt. It therefore circumscribed where polygraph results added the most, and the least, value.

The computational steps in calculating IG are described by Honts and Schweinle (2009) and are not repeated here. The resultant values are plotted on a graph to represent the increase in information about the credibility of individuals over chance, or over another method if the interest is in incremental validity. For purposes of illustration we will use the IG analysis of Handler et al. (2013) of the directed lie screening test (DLST), a law enforcement variation of the Test for Espionage and Sabotage (DoD Polygraph Institute Research Division Staff, 1997). Decisions in the Handler et al. (2013) analysis had been based on the empirical scoring system (ESS; Nelson et al., 2011).

Handler et al. first gauged the IG for professional lie catchers unassisted by technology. Using decision accuracy calculated by Vrij (2008, p. 161) from several published studies, Handler et al. first showed the IG of the professional lie catcher decisions over chance alone (Figure 9.3). Figure 9.4 displays IG for the DLST with ESS.

The graphs reveal two important aspects of the use of the DLST in applicant processing. The first is that the inclusion of polygraph results in an applicant screening

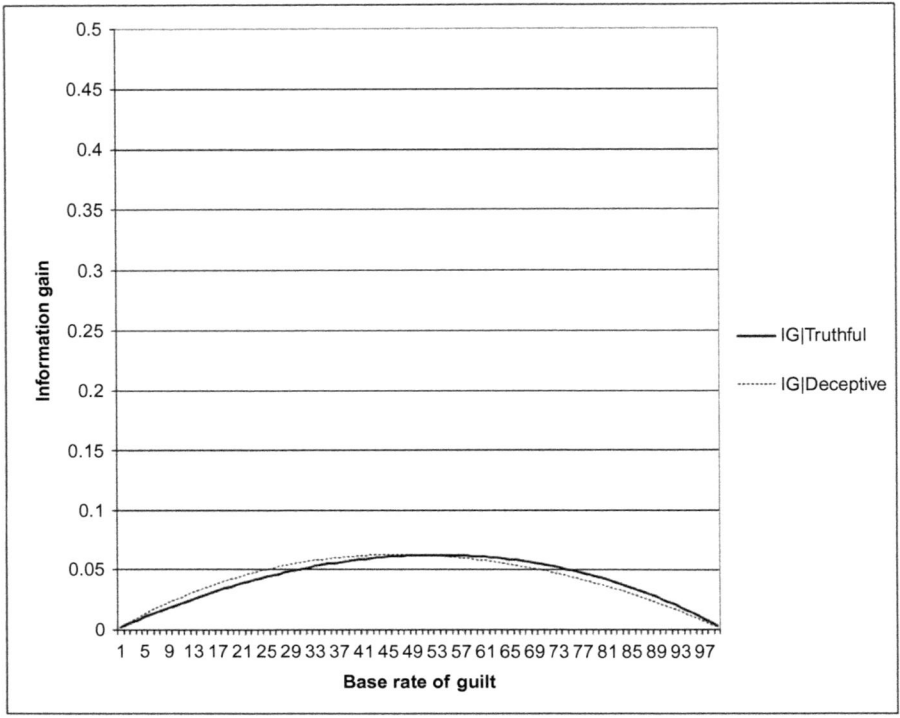

FIGURE 9.3

Information gain (IG) for professional lie catchers for detecting deception and truthfulness across base rates.

From Handler et al. (2013). Used with permission.

process is value-added over decisions of credibility without those results. There will be an elaboration of this observation later in this section as it applies to screening applicants for a limited number of positions. The second is that at extreme base rates, polygraph decisions do not provide useful information substantially better than unassisted lie detection. If this latter interpretation is true, the base rate has implications for the topics tested by the polygraph: testing on topics with very high or very low incidence may be contraindicated.

To convert this concept to practical terms, we will return to an earlier example. Readers may recall that previously we referred to a low base-rate example, wherein 1000 government employees were to be polygraphed to uncover any involvement in espionage. The presumed base rate of deception was one-tenth of a percent, an estimate that most would hope is high. At this extreme base rate, there is not greater confidence in polygraph decisions than of decisions of a trained investigator conducting an interview without the polygraph. In other words, the use of a polygraph test question solely about espionage would likely be wasteful of polygraph resources, and the test results would provide no IG over simple adroit interviewing.

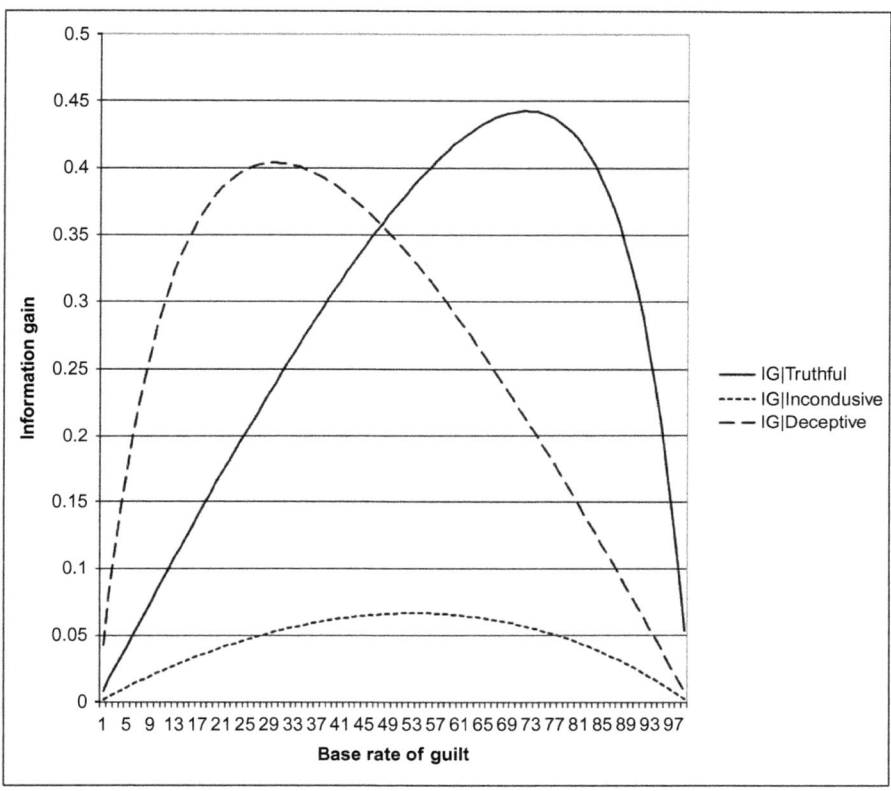

FIGURE 9.4

Information gain (IG) for the directed lie screening test with the empirical scoring system across base rates.

From Handler et al. (2013). Used with permission.

Decision-makers generally believe that polygraph vetting is vitally important to national security, as witnessed by the expansion of governmental polygraph screening both in the US and much of the Western world. These expectations may lead polygraph programs to consider dedicating test questions to topics decision-makers consider vital, but are about rare behaviors. Given what is now known about the IG of this methodology, however, it may be appropriate to consider a different way.

One way is to boost the base rate captured by the test question, and thereby increase the IG. Let us look again at the espionage question, which is directed toward a vanishingly small target. Polygraphers can expand the coverage of the test question to address behaviors of interest that also includes espionage, and collectively enlarge the base rate of behaviors encompassed by the question. For example, examinees who undertake betrayal of their country share behaviors with those who are preparing to do so, and with those who violate security practices out of convenience, error, accident, or low conscientiousness. Instead of asking about espionage, a question might be expanded to cover all disclosures of classified information to unauthorized persons. The definition of "unauthorized persons" could include family members, friends, acquaintances, disclosures though social media, to news outlets, and of course, foreign governments and terrorist organizations. A question phrased in this way magnifies the base rate, and increases the potential IG of the polygraph results. Because polygraph results are used to guide further interviewing in this setting, and are not arbiters of employee fate, the cost of error remains unchanged while the value of polygraph results increases.

In contrast to looking for spies, broad questions work against IG at exceedingly high base rates, such as in certain types of sex offender testing. It should be self-apparent that if history demonstrates that virtually all offenders lie during their first polygraph examination, polygraph results of deception are redundant, and do not add useful information. There may be sound reasons for withholding IG analysis from sex offender testing, however. In the PCSOT context, the principal goal is the development of information about the offender's behavior. Polygraph results play a role in guiding the polygraph examiner toward the topic(s) about which the examinee is withholding information. Polygraph is used iteratively, that is, examiners seek to gain more information from the examinee after a failed polygraph, and follow up with more testing using narrower test questions and more powerful polygraph techniques. This process tends to yield more self-disclosure from offenders regarding illegal and precursor behaviors. Treatment providers who use polygraph services appreciate the self-disclosure that polygraph testing prompts, and use the information to shape the offender's treatment. Polygraph results are a means to an end, but not an end in themselves. Unless the polygraph questions can capture the range of behaviors of interest to treatment providers, the value of polygraph testing is reduced.

As mentioned earlier in this section, IG analysis displayed in Figures 9.3 and 9.4 also speak to the value of including polygraph results in applicant screening. Note that decisions of credibility are incrementally better using polygraph results than using professional judgments of deception without the polygraph. As such, polygraph decisions would seem to assist hiring officials choosing among candidates. An underappreciated advantage is that the polygraph could benefit the qualified candidate, as well. This is demonstrated using a common example of a police candidate selection process.

When openings are announced for opportunities to attend an agency's police academy to prepare to become sworn officers, the ratio of applicant to selectee is very high. It is common to have 10 applicants for each position. From these 10 aspirants, 9 will not be chosen because the number of positions available is limited. Regardless of the tools used in selection, 9 of 10 applicants will not get the job. Suppose that there are 100 openings at the police academy, and 1000 applicants. Let us also suppose that on average 500 applicants are suitable for the position, and 500 are not suitable owing to involvement in criminal activity, domestic abuse, illicit drug use, excessive traffic offenses, or other past behavior. As Figure 9.3 shows, reliance on professional interviewers' skills in deception detection to sort the 500 qualified from the 500 unqualified applicants would prove to be a failure. Optimistically, perhaps 56% of the unsuitable candidates could be caught in their deception, but about half of the suitable candidates would be misclassified as deceptive. The pool of candidates judged truthful by the professional interviewers would be roughly half suitable and half unsuitable.

Let us now change the hiring process to include polygraph screening, and take a very conservative accuracy estimate of 67% for the testing methodology. The pool of candidates resulting from polygraph screening versus professional interviewers would consist of two-thirds suitable candidates instead of one-half. For the suitable applicant, the chances of entering the selection pool increases from 50% to 67%. In other words, for the suitable candidate the likelihood of being chosen for the police academy increased by about a third. Therefore, adding polygraph to the screening process works in favor of the qualified applicant. When a polygraph screening program is well developed and employs only best practices, suitable candidates will have an advantage over the chances of selection where the polygraph is not used. The test topics must be chosen so that they are useful in predicting future success as police officers, and of course, base rates of the behaviors must be considered.

POLYGRAPH THEORIES

One of the chief criticisms aimed at polygraph is that it is atheoretical, that is, its research and practice are not founded nor guided by a theoretical framework. The problem may not be that that there is *no* theory, however, but that there are too many theories offered to explain how the polygraph functions in deception detection. In the early days of scientific interest in polygraphy, Barland and Raskin (1973) summarized five proposed theories alone, some that better explained certain aspects while other theories accommodate other aspects. Several other theories have been offered since. The equivalent to physics' Unified Field Theory for polygraph on which there is universal agreement has not yet appeared, however. There are currently four ideas that have moved to the fore, and though some may not meet the current understanding of what fully constitutes a "theory," they have at least taken on placeholder status for the purposes of elucidation and testing.

PSYCHOLOGICAL SET

According to Matte and Grove (2001), the concept of *psychological set* is attributed to polygraph pioneer Cleve Backster, but they explained that Backster himself claimed to have taken it from a 1948 introductory psychology textbook. In the Backster definition, psychological set specifies that:

> *A person's fears, anxieties, and apprehensions are channeled toward the situation which holds the greatest immediate threat to his self-preservation or general well being. He tunes in that which indicates trouble or danger by having his sense organs tuned for a particular stimulus, and he tunes out that which is of a lesser threat to his self-preservation or general well being. In other words, he establishes psychological set (Matte and Grove, 2001).*

Backster's psychological set was almost universally adopted by polygraph practitioners, and has been a part of the instruction in nearly all polygraph schools for more than 40 years. Backster introduced other neologisms, as well, including "anticlimax dampening," "superdampening," "zone," "total chart minute concept," and others. All were offered to name and explain phenomena examiners saw in their polygraph data.

Backster's concepts had face validity and were convenient and easily understood. There were efforts by advocates to root psychological set in existing and respected concepts such as the double-bind effect and cognitive dissonance. There have been no consistent challenges to psychological set in polygraphy by outside scientists. Most scientists have not considered it a theory at all.

Psychological set had come to incorporate and enlarge an earlier theory called *fear of detection*. Polygraph pioneer John Reid and others suggested that the physiological responding on the polygraph chart had little to do with guilt or shame, but simply that the guilty person's concern about getting caught generated the response. This view did seem to be supported by field experiences of examiners who reported that guilty examinees who had given up defending themselves often failed to react to their lies on the polygraph.

The psychological set theory did meet challenge within the field beginning in 2001. In a rejoinder article to Matte and Grove (2001), it was pointed out by Krapohl (2001) that mainstream psychology defines psychological set in a very different way from Backster's definition, that its use in polygraphy had no equivalent in the larger scientific community. Krapohl also challenged them on the relationship of the selective-attention research as regards polygraphy and psychological set. Left with no alternative, however, Krapohl conceded that the field should not change to a new term until the appropriate one was found.

The *fear of detection* aspect of psychological set also came under additional fire as directed-lie techniques became more popular. Directed lies appear to be effective, but an examinee's concern about being detected is not involved in causing reactions to them as had been supposed with probable-lies. There was also laboratory research showing that reactions during deception took place in low- and no-motivation conditions. Fear did not appear to be a necessary condition. Taken together, the previous assumptions about psychological set were in increasing doubt.

In 2006 the new challenge to psychological set was raised by Handler and Nelson. First, they determined that the expression never appears in the 1948 textbook in which Backster claimed he found it, nor any other editions of the book. With the elimination of that text as the source, and the passing of Backster, the origin of psychological set may be lost to history. Handler and Nelson also determined that the many references to psychological set in publication indexes of psychological research had nothing in common with how polygraphers were using the expression. Handler and Nelson offered a more general but well-established concept in its place to explain the differential responding that appears in polygraphy. They suggested the concept of *salience* as an alternative expression. This concept appears to resonate with competing theories to be taken up next.

In sum, psychological set is not as an attractive theory as it was once regarded, though it is still taught in some polygraph schools.

RELEVANT ISSUE GRAVITY

In 2009 polygraph researcher Dr. Avital Ginton proposed an alternate theory he termed relevant issue gravity (RIG). It is attention-based, and is conceptualized as the compelling force arising from the qualities of the relevant question to capture and bind an examinee's attention. Relevant questions, according to the theory, have a stronger RIG strength for guilty examinees than they do for innocent examinees. As a consequence, comparison questions can divert the attention of innocent examinees more easily than they can for deceptive examinees. This trend is in accord with the generally accepted finding that deceptive examinees tend to react greatest to relevant questions and innocent examinees respond more to comparison questions.

Ginton's theory is relatively new, and has not been formally tested as of yet. It is not encumbered with the fear-of-detection assumption central to psychological set, and therefore may address the laboratory findings that comparison question testing seems to work even under no-fear conditions. The RIG theory also seems to suggest that reactivity shifts from the relevant questions to the comparison questions as a continuum in proportion to the RIG strength, as opposed to the all-or-none assumptions of psychological set. Such a prediction is consistent with the known distribution of polygraph scores.

RIG theory could require additional refinement as experiments deem necessary. One area of immediate interest may be the focus on selective attention as the principal component. In polygraph testing the questions are posed sequentially, not simultaneously. The test questions do not compete for finite attentional resources *per se* as they would in, for example, classic split-attention paradigms. RIG theory suggests that attention bound to relevant questions for deceptive examinees interferes with their capacity to attend to comparison questions, at least less so than for truthful examinees. However, examinees are required to answer each test question appropriately, and their relatively routine ability to do so indicates that attention is being granted to every question. As such, there appear to be processes beyond attention that are evoking responses to different categories of question as a function of truthfulness. It may be that attention is necessary, but not sufficient, and that a multi-component process is at play. Until the studies are completed, it remains unknown.

DIFFERENTIAL SALIENCE

A year following the publication of RIG theory came a second challenge to psychological set. Senter et al. (2010) suggested that the relative salience of each test question was the operating mechanism that brings about the physiological responding used in polygraphy. They coined the expression differential salience (DS) to denote the subjective importance an examinee gives to a test question, as indexed by the response intensities for test questions, and it was the difference in response magnitudes that permits inferences of deception or recognition. This idea, that salience was the key factor, had been proposed by others (Handler and Nelson, 2007; Krapohl, 2001), but had not previously been fully explored. Like Ginton's RIG, Senter's DS did not rely on the fear of detection, though it is implicit that this fear could mediate salience, and thereby augmenting response sizes. DS was not based on attention, and was conceived as to explain differential reactivity for both the comparison question test and the concealed information test.

As a new theory, DS is awaiting empirical testing. It was initially proposed to incorporate and explain findings across existing studies and field observations. Research will be needed to determine whether DS is viable. There are unanswered questions as to whether salience alone is sufficient to explain the phenomenon, or if additional components also play a part. It may be that there is a sequence of important processes, and that the overall system only works when each critical component functions properly. Much work remains to be done to test DS.

The idea of a multi-component process has more recently been proposed, called preliminary process theory (PPT).

PRELIMINARY PROCESS THEORY

Palmatier and Rovner (2015) have proposed the adaptation of an existing theory, PPT, to explain polygraphy. Palmatier and Rovner argue that PPT underlies not only the differential responding of the comparison question test, but the concealed information test, as well. There are two advantages to the Palmatier et al. representation: the grounding of polygraphy in an established theory outside of the polygraph field, and the description of a series of processes within the theory rather than a single component.

PPT evolved from decades of work by Dr. Robert Barry (see Barry, 1990, for a summary) who conducted a series of studies on, among other variables, phasic physiological responding and attentional processing. Barry determined that the orienting response was not a unitary concept in terms of physiological responding. His work with electrodermal, respiratory, and cardiovascular measures made his work specifically relevant to polygraphy, which shares these physiological data channels.

PPT is predicated upon the orienting response, and encompasses stimulus appraisal and other highly automated cognitive functions of which stimulus salience plays a key role. It makes certain predictions about phasic physiological responding that have not been tested in the context of credibility assessment, but easily could be. Future testing of PPT in the polygraph setting will determine whether it is sustainable.

REFERENCES

Arther, R.O., Arther, C.A., 1998. Truths about the proven truth verifier—the polygraph. J. Polygr. Sci. 33 (3), 1–4.

Barland, G.H., Raskin, D.C., 1973. Detection of deception. In: Prokasky, W.F., Raskin, D.C. (Eds.), Electrodermal Activity in Psychological Research. Academic Press, New York.

Barry, R.J., 1990. Preliminary process theory: towards an integrated account of the psychophysiology of cognitive processes. Acta Neurobiol. Exp. 56, 469–484.

Curley, C., 2003. New guidelines: what to do about an unexpected positive tuberculin skin test. Cleve. Clin. J. Med. 70 (1), 49–55.

DoD Polygraph Institute Research Division Staff, 1997. A comparison of psychophysiological detection of deception accuracy rates obtained using the Counterintelligence Scope Polygraph and the Test for Espionage and Sabotage question formats. Polygraph 26 (2), 79–106.

Ginton, A., 2009. Relevant Issue Gravity (RIG) strength—a new concept in PDD that reframes the notion of psychological set and the role of attention in CQT polygraph. Polygraph 38 (3), 204–217.

Handler, M., Nelson, R., 2007. Polygraph terms for the 21st century. Polygraph 36 (3), 157–164.

Handler, M., Honts, C.R., Nelson, R., 2013. Information gain of the directed lie screening test. Polygraph 42 (4), 192–202.

Honts, C.R., Driscoll, L.N., 1987. An evaluation of the reliability and validity of rank order and standard numerical scoring of polygraph charts. Polygraph 16 (4), 241–257.

Honts, C.R., Schweinle, W., 2009. Information gain of psychophysiological detection of deception in forensic and screening settings. Appl. Psychophysiol. Biofeedback 34, 161–172.

Krapohl, D.J., 2001. A brief rejoinder to Matte & Grove regarding "psychological set". Polygraph 30 (3), 203–205.

Krapohl, D.J., 2013. Polygraph principles: a literature review. Polygraph 42 (1), 35–60.

Kubis, J.F., 1965. Analysis of Polygraph Data. Final Report, U.S. Air Force, contract RADC-TDR-64-101, AF30(602)2634.

MacNitt, R.D., 1942. In defense of electrodermal response and cardiac amplitude as measures of deception. J. Crim. Law Criminol. Police Sci. 33 (3), 266–275.

Matte, J.A., Grove, R.N., 2001. Psychological set: its origin, theory and application. Polygraph 30 (3), 196–202.

National Research Council, 2003. The Polygraph and Lie Detection. Committee to Review the Scientific Evidence on the Polygraph. Division of Behavioral and Social Sciences and Education, The National Academies Press, Washington, DC.

Nelson, R., Blalock, B., Handler, M., 2011. Criterion validity of the Empirical Scoring System and the Objective Scoring System, version 3 with the USAF Modified General Question Technique. Polygraph 40 (3), 172–179.

Palmatier, J.J., Rovner, L., 2015. Credibility assessment: Preliminary Process Theory, the polygraph process, and construct validity. Int. J. Psychophysiol. 95 (1), 3–13.

Patton, C.A., 2013. The Integrated Zone Comparison Technique: a field utility study in a deceptive population. Eur. Polygr. 7 (3), 113–120.

Pollina, D.A., Dollins, A.B., Senter, S.M., Krapohl, D.J., Ryan, A.H., 2004. Comparison of polygraph data obtained from individuals involved in mock crimes and actual criminal investigations. J. Appl. Psychol. 89 (6), 1099–1105.

Senter, S.M., Weatherman, D., Krapohl, D.J., Horvath, F.S., 2010. Psychological set or differential salience: a proposal for reconciling theory and terminology in polygraph testing. Polygraph 39 (2), 109–117.

Vrij, A., 2008. Detecting Lies and Deceit, Pitfalls, and Opportunities, second ed. Wiley & Sons Ltd, Chichester, England.

Wells, G.L., Olson, E.A., 2002. Eyewitness identification: information gain from incriminating and exonerating behaviors. J. Exp. Psychol. Appl. 8 (3), 155–167.

CHAPTER 10

Polygraph legal issues

Gordon L. Vaughan

"Even if this evidence was 100% accurate, would you still say ... [polygraph evidence] should be excluded?"
"Yes."
Exchange between Supreme Court Justice John Paul Stevens and Deputy Solicitor General Michael R. Dreeben during oral argument in *United States v. Scheffer*, November 3, 1997.

Courts and lawmakers in the United States have, for decades, struggled with issues regarding the use of polygraph. Such issues have included: should the results of polygraph testing be admissible as evidence in courts of law and under what conditions; are *Miranda* warnings required before administering a polygraph examination; are statements made by a person faced with or following a polygraph considered voluntary; should polygraph be used to assist in the treatment and monitoring of sex offenders released into the community; should the use of polygraph be restricted in the workplace; and are polygraph examiners required to be licensed. This chapter will address these and other legal issues involving polygraph.

ADMISSIBILITY OF EVIDENCE OF POLYGRAPH EXAMINATION RESULTS
FROM *FRYE* TO *DAUBERT*

At approximately 8:45 p.m. on Saturday evening, November 27, 1920, began the case that would be the first to consider the admissibility of polygraph evidence in court—and as it turns out, the case that for over seven decades would govern the admissibility of scientific evidence in general in most United States courts. It was on that date and time that Dr. R. W. Brown, a well-known Washington, D.C. physician and president of the National Benefit Life Insurance Company, was shot and killed at his home office.[1] Dr. Julian Jackson, a houseguest of Dr. Brown visiting from

---

[1] Weiss, K., et al., 2014. Frye's Backstory: a tale of murder, a retracted confession, and scientific hubris. J. Am. Acad. Psychiatry Law 42 (2), 226.

Virginia, was able generally to describe the suspected gunman, though it was not until 9 months later that James Alphonzo Frye confessed to the shooting during interrogation for an unrelated check forgery. Frye later retracted his confession, alleging he had an alibi and that he had been tricked into confessing.[2] When the alibi witness failed to materialize, Frye's attorneys turned to Dr. William Moulton Marston, a psychologist and lawyer who was a vocal champion for the use of his recently developed systolic blood pressure deception test. This test, bearing little resemblance to the modern polygraph instrument or technique, consisted only of periodic blood pressure measurements taken with a standard sphygmomanometer during a dialog with the examinee in which there was no formal questioning technique.[3]

According to Marston, his sphygmomanometer testing demonstrated that Frye was truthful in his claim of innocence, and Frye's attorneys sought admission of Marston's opinion at Frye's trial for the murder of Dr. Brown.[4] Judge Walter I. McCoy, Chief Judge of the D.C. District Court, denied admissibility of the test results, and Frye was convicted of second degree murder. Frye appealed his conviction, arguing that the trial court erroneously refused to admit the systolic blood pressure deception test evidence.

D.C. Circuit Court Judge Josiah Alexander Van Orsdel, writing for a unanimous three-judge panel, announced what became known as the "Frye" or the "general acceptance" test for admissibility of scientific evidence.[5] Judge Van Orsdel's opinion was brief, even by 1923 standards, and free of citation to any prior case authority. After describing Marston's test, Judge Van Orsdel moved quickly to the point and noted:

> *Just when a scientific principle or discovery crosses the line between the experimental and demonstrable stages is difficult to define. Somewhere in this twilight zone the evidential force of the principle must be recognized, and while courts will go a long way in admitting expert testimony deduced from a well-recognized scientific principle or discovery, the thing from which the deduction is made must be sufficiently established to have gained general acceptance in the particular field in which it belongs.*[6]

Judge Van Orsdel concluded that the systolic blood pressure deception test had not gained sufficient acceptance among physiological and psychological professionals to be admissible.

---

[2] Legal historians have debated Frye's reason for confessing. Compare Weiss, *supra* (stating that the confession was a result of a promise made to Frye that he would be able to collect a reward posted by the family, but be exonerated by the alibi witness) *with* Stern, B.A., Krapohl, D.J., 2003. The infamous James Alphonzo Frye. Polygraph 32, 188 (chronicling that Frye agreed to discuss Dr. Brown's murder on the promise that the check fraud charge would be dropped—he confessed after lengthy interrogation). In any event, Frye continued to deny killing Dr. Brown for the rest of his life.

[3] Honts, C.R., Quick, B.D., 1995. The polygraph in 1995: progress in science and the law. N. D. Law Rev. 71 (3), 987.

[4] Weiss, *supra* at 227.

[5] Prior to *Frye*, a court's typical inquiry regarding admissibility of scientific evidence was only whether the expert was "qualified." Osborn, A., 1935. Reasons and reasoning in expert testimony. Law Contemp. Probs. 2, 488, 489.

[6] *Frye v. United States*, 293 F. 1013, 1014 (D.C. Cir. 1923) (emphasis added).

The emergence of the *Frye* "general acceptance" test was, initially, gradual, but eventually came to be the dominant standard for admissibility of scientific evidence.[7] In the years following *Frye*, while courts deemed other forms of scientific forensic evidence admissible under the *Frye* general acceptance standard, polygraph evidence, despite significant advances in its development and science, continued to be generally excluded.[8]

There were occasional exceptions to the general exclusion of polygraph evidence by the courts.[9] A prominent example of such a case came in the 1989 Eleventh Circuit decision of *United States v. Piccinonna*.[10] There, Julio Piccinonna was indicted on several counts of making intentional false statements to a federal grand jury investigating allegations of price-fixing violations in the southern Florida waste disposal industry. In his defense, Piccinonna offered to take and stipulate to the admissibility of a not-yet-administered polygraph and, when the prosecution declined that offer, commissioned his own polygraph, the results of which were reported as nondeceptive to the relevant questions.[11] When Piccinonna offered this polygraph evidence at his trial, the Trial Court Judge Jose A. Gonzales, Jr. refused to admit it as prior Eleventh Circuit case precedent had installed a *per se* ban on evidence of polygraph test results. Although denying the requested polygraph evidence, Judge Gonzales observed that polygraphs were now more widely used and the Eleventh Circuit may want to reconsider its exclusionary position. Judge Gonzales allowed that if Piccinonna was convicted, he would permit him, posttrial, to present his polygraph evidence for the purposes of making a record for his appeal. Piccinonna was convicted on two counts of giving false testimony, and Judge Gonzales permitted Piccinonna to present, for the record on appeal, his polygraph evidence.

On appeal, a three-judge panel of the Eleventh Circuit upheld Judge Gonzales' denial of the admission of Piccinonna's polygraph evidence. However, Piccinonna requested that the entire twelve judges of the Eleventh Circuit hear the case—a procedure known as an "en banc" hearing and one typically reserved for particularly important cases or cases in which there have been inconsistent positions taken among three-judge panels of the court. The request for *en banc* consideration was granted, and the panel decision was set aside. Judge Peter T. Fay, writing for a clear eight-judge majority of the full court, overturned the prior *per se* ban of polygraph evidence and Piccinonna's conviction and observed:

---

[7] Bernstein, D., 2001. Frye, Frye, again: the past, present, and future of the general acceptance test. George Mason Law & Economics Research Paper No. 01-07. Available at SSRN: http://dx.doi.org/10.2139/ssrn.262034.

[8] McCall, J.R., 1996. Misconceptions and reevaluation—polygraph admissibility after Rock and Daubert. Univ. Ill. Law Rev. 363 (25).

[9] Daniels, C.W., 2003. Using polygraph evidence after Scheffer—the law of polygraph admissibility in American jurisdictions and suggestions for dealing with the recurring legal obstacles. Champion 27, 12, 13.

[10] *United States v. Piccinonna*, 885 F.2d 1529 (11th Cir. 1989).

[11] *Id.* at 1531.

> *Since the Frye decision, tremendous advances have been made in polygraph instrumentation and technique. Better equipment is being used by more adequately trained polygraph administrators. Further, polygraph tests are used extensively by government agencies. Field investigative agencies such as the FBI, the Secret Service, military intelligence, and law enforcement agencies use the polygraph. Thus, even under a strict adherence to the traditional Frye standard, we believe it is no longer accurate to state categorically that polygraph testing lacks general acceptance for use in all circumstances. For this reason, we find it appropriate to reexamine the per se exclusionary rule and institute a rule more in keeping with the progress made in the polygraph field.*[12]

Judge Fay went on to hold that polygraph evidence would be admissible in two circumstances. First, it would be admissible when both parties stipulate, in advance of the test, to its admissibility. Second, it may be admitted when used to impeach or corroborate the testimony of a witness at trial whose credibility has been challenged. The effect of this requirement was that unless the witness (including a defendant) put his or her credibility at issue by testifying at trial, the witness' unstipulated polygraph evidence would not be admissible. In such instance, the party planning to use the evidence must give the opposing party both adequate notice of the intent to use the evidence and a reasonable opportunity to have their own expert administer a polygraph to the witness.[13] Judge Fay also noted that the trial judge retained wide discretion to admit or deny polygraph evidence and that, absent an abuse of discretion, the trial court's decision would not be altered on appeal.

While *Piccinonna* appeared to portend a friendlier environment for admissibility of polygraph evidence in the Eleventh Circuit, any euphoria in the polygraph community was diminished when Judge Garcia, on consideration of Piccinonna's polygraph evidence at his retrial, still ruled it inadmissible and the Eleventh Circuit upheld, on further appeal, Judge Garcia on that decision.[14] In the years subsequent to *Piccinonna*, Eleventh Circuit trial courts have overwhelmingly exercised their discretion to disallow admissibility of polygraph evidence.[15]

Over time, the *Frye* general acceptance test was severely criticized by courts and commentators as too conservative. The standard was considered difficult to apply as it was not always easy to define when a scientific theory had become generally accepted and what professional discipline constituted the "relevant scientific community." Many complained that the standard deprived parties from the use of important

---

[12] *Id.* at 1532.
[13] *Id.* at 1536.
[14] *United States v. Piccinonna*, 729 F. Supp. 1336 (S.D. Fla. 1990) *aff'd,* 925 F.2d 1474 (11th Cir. 1991).
[15] See, for example, *United States v. Gilliard,* 133 F.3d 809, 812 (11th Cir. *1998*); *United States v. Pavlenko*, 845 F. Supp. 2d 1321, 1324 (S.D. Fla. 2012) [quoting *United States v. Carroll*, 450 F. App'x 937, 940 (11th Cir. 2012)]. ("While *Piccinonna* did away with the *per se* ban on admissibility, it did not in any way limit the trial court's discretion to exclude polygraph evidence 'on other grounds under the Federal Rules of Evidence.'")

scientific evidence while the question of general acceptance gestated within the scientific community.[16]

The Supreme Court of the United States expressly replaced the *Frye* test for determining admissibility of scientific evidence in 1993 in *Daubert v. Merrell Dow Pharmaceuticals, Inc.*[17] *Daubert* arose out of a products liability action brought by several families who alleged that Bendectin, a prescription drug intended to mitigate pregnancy morning sickness, caused birth defects. In the trial court, Judge Earl B. Gilliam had excluded expert opinion testimony from experts hired by the families linking birth defects to the drug as such opinions were not based on epidemiological study and statistical correlation between the drug and birth defects—which Judge Gilliam concluded was the generally accepted scientific means to establish a required causal link.[18] Judge Gilliam also observed that the families' experts' opinions were contrary to the unanimous findings of all published peer reviewed epidemiologic studies of Bendectin, each finding no demonstrated link between the drug and birth defects.

The Ninth Circuit, in a three-judge panel decision written by Judge Alex Kozinski, affirmed Judge Gilliam's decision. Judge Kozinski noted that expert opinions must be "based on a given scientific methodology to be admissible" and that opinions based on use of scientific methodology that diverges significantly from such procedures cannot meet the general acceptance requirement of *Frye*.[19] Judge Kozinski went on to observe that the nonepidemiological based opinions offered by the families that Bendectin caused birth defects were derived from methodology too far removed from scientifically reliable technique.

The Supreme Court, in an opinion written by Justice Harry Blackmun and joined by six other justices, concluded that the *Frye* approach of relying on general acceptance in the scientific community was too restrictive—particularly given the more liberal approach to admissibility of the modern federal rules of evidence in general and, in particular, Federal Rule of Evidence 702 which had been adopted in 1975 by the federal courts to address admissibility of expert testimony. Justice Blackmun, noted:

> *The inquiry envisioned by Rule 702 is ... a flexible one. Its overarching subject is the scientific validity and thus the evidentiary relevance and reliability—of the principles that underlie a proposed submission. The focus, of course, must be solely on principles and methodology, not on the conclusions that they generate.*[20]

Justice Blackmun called on trial courts to act as the evidentiary "gatekeeper" responsible for determining the admissibility of scientific testimony. To fulfill this

---

[16] Faigman, D.L., et al., 2012. Modern Scientific Evidence: The Law and Science of Expert Testimony § 1:6.
[17] *Daubert v. Merrell Dow Pharm., Inc.*, 509 U.S. 579, 587 (1993).
[18] *Daubert v. Merrell Dow Pharm., Inc.*, 727 F. Supp. 570, 575 (S.D. Cal. 1989).
[19] *Daubert v. Merrell Dow Pharm., Inc.*, 951 F.2d 1128, 1130 (9th Cir. 1991).
[20] *Daubert.*, 509 U.S. at 594-595.

gatekeeping function, the *Daubert* court placed considerable discretion in the trial court and suggested guidelines for the trial courts to determine whether the offered evidence is based on reliable scientific knowledge. The guidelines suggested by the *Daubert* court were: (1) whether the theory or technique on which the testimony is based is capable of being tested; (2) whether the theory or technique has a known rate of error in its application; (3) whether the theory or technique has been subjected to peer review and publication; and (4) the level of acceptance in the relevant scientific community of the theory or technique.[21] As was later verified in *Kumho Tire Co. v. Carmichael*,[22] none of the four factors suggested in *Daubert* was to be rigidly applied in every case, and courts were to keep in mind the competing needs of keeping untrustworthy pseudoscience from the jury and of keeping the courts open to scientific developments.

A majority of states have adopted the *Daubert* standard.[23] In practice, trial courts often hold "Daubert" hearings, outside the presence of a jury, to assess whether the tendered scientific evidence meets *Daubert* and Rule 702 standards. A failure to provide an opportunity for such hearing might, under certain circumstances, constitute an abuse of discretion.[24] Whether a *Daubert* hearing is held or not, the trial court must create a sufficient record so that the decision on whether the court abused its discretion in admitting or not admitting the evidence can be reviewed.[25]

POST-DAUBERT ADMISSIBILITY OF POLYGRAPH EVIDENCE
United States V. Scheffer
The only time the United States Supreme Court has considered an issue regarding the admissibility of the results of a polygraph examination was in 1998 in the case of *United States v. Scheffer*.[26] *Scheffer* did not consider whether polygraph evidence was admissible under *Daubert* but, rather, considered the constitutionality of a codified evidentiary rule that imposed a *per se* ban imposed on military courts' use of polygraph evidence.

Historically, United States armed forces had studied and used the polygraph, and military courts, unlike their civilian counterparts, had formally recognized the scientific reliability of the polygraph and its admissibility as evidence in court-martial

---

[21] This factor was, of course, the familiar *Frye* test. In *Daubert*, however, it was but one consideration to be factored into a larger inquiry on admissibility of scientific evidence.
[22] *Kumho Tire Co. v. Carmichael*, 526 U.S. 137, 152-153 (1999).
[23] Approximately 33 states follow *Daubert* or a similar standard for accessing admissibility of scientific evidence. Many states, however, continue to follow the *Frye* general acceptance standard. See Dooley, J.A., 1977. Modern Tort Law: Liability and Litigation, 2nd ed., § 15:64.
[24] See, for example, *United States v. Smithers*, 212 F.3d 306 (6th Cir. 2000).
[25] See, for example, *Goebel v. Denver and Rio Grande Western R.R. Co.*, 215 F.3d 1083, 1088 (10th Cir. 2000).
[26] *United States v. Scheffer*, 523 U.S. 303 (1998).

proceedings.[27] President George H.W. Bush, through his executive power to establish rules of evidence for military courts, responded to the military courts' acceptance of polygraph evidence by issuing a new military rule of evidence that imposed a *per se* exclusion on polygraph evidence.[28] That ban had the effect of eliminating even the chance of a proponent of polygraph evidence to have such evidence considered for admissibility under a *Daubert* analysis.

The defendant, Edward Scheffer, an airman stationed at March Air Force Base in Riverside County, California, had volunteered as an informant for the Air Force Office of Special Investigations (OSI). As an informant, Scheffer was obligated to submit to periodic urinalysis and polygraph examinations by an OSI examiner. In April 1992, Scheffer tested positive on one such urinalysis for traces of methamphetamine, but in an OSI polygraph administered after the urinalysis and before the results of the urinalysis had been determined, Scheffer was deemed not deceptive on the question of drug use. Scheffer was charged, in part, with illegal use of methamphetamine and tried by general court-martial. At his trial, Scheffer testified that he had not knowingly used methamphetamine and suggested that the drug may have surreptitiously been given to him while at the residence of persons from whom he was seeking to develop information on criminal activity.

Scheffer offered as evidence the nondeceptive results of the OSI polygraph. However, as a result of the military's new polygraph exclusionary evidence rule, the court-martial panel was not allowed to consider the evidence. Scheffer was convicted, and he appealed to the Court of Appeals for the Armed Forces, arguing that the *per se* exclusion violated his Sixth Amendment guarantee to have his defense evidence heard. A similar Sixth Amendment argument had previously been the basis for striking down *per se* evidentiary bans on the ability of an accused to introduce exculpatory, hearsay statements; accomplice testimony; and hypnotically refreshed testimony.[29] The Court of Appeals, in a 3 to 2 decision written by Judge H.F. Gierke, III, agreed that the military's *per se* ban of polygraph violated Scheffer's Sixth Amendment right to present a defense and reversed Scheffer's conviction. Judge Gierke stated that a *per se* polygraph ban went too far as it barred an entire class of evidence without consideration of relevant scientific advances. Judge Gierke observed that whether polygraph had made sufficient technological advances in the "seventy years since Frye" to meet the evidentiary requirements of *Daubert* would never be known "unless we give appellant an opportunity to lay the foundation."[30]

Polygraph proponents' hopes that *Scheffer* might be a watershed case for polygraph admissibility were dashed when the Supreme Court reversed the Court of Appeals' decision and upheld President Bush's evidentiary ban of polygraph in military courts. While the court was able to garner eight justices who agreed that the

---

[27] See, for example, *United States v. Gipson*, 24 M.J. 246 (C.M.A. 1987).
[28] Mil. R. Evid. 707.
[29] Dery, G.M., III, 1999. Mouse hunting with an elephant gun: the Supreme Court's overkill in upholding a categorical rejection to polygraph evidence in *United States v. Scheffer*. Am. J. Crim. Law 26, 227.
[30] *United States v. Scheffer*, 44 M.J. 442, 446 (C.A.A.F. 1996).

ban was not unconstitutional, there was a pronounced divide among the justices on the basis of the decision—with no group gaining a majority.

The principal holding in *Scheffer* was authored by Justice Clarence Thomas and joined by Chief Justice Rehnquist and Justices Scalia and Souter (the "Thomas four").[31] The Thomas four believed that the *per se* exclusion was supported for three primary reasons: (1) ensuring that only reliable evidence is introduced at trial; (2) polygraph evidence usurped the jury role in determining credibility; and (3) avoiding litigation that is collateral to the primary purpose of the trial.[32] As to the reliability issue, the Thomas four stated: "there is simply no consensus that polygraph evidence is reliable. To this day, the scientific community remains extremely polarized about the reliability of polygraph techniques."[33]

Justice Anthony Kennedy wrote an opinion joined by Justices O'Connor, Ginsburg, and Breyer (the "Kennedy four"). The Kennedy four reluctantly joined the Thomas four, finding that, based on the current good-faith dispute regarding the validity of polygraph evidence, the *per se* rule of exclusion "is not so arbitrary or disproportionate that it is unconstitutional."[34] The Kennedy four went on to say, however, that they did not agree that the *per se* exclusion was wise and that a later case might cause them to reexamine their agreement on the constitutionality of such an exclusionary position. The Kennedy four also acknowledged the tension between the *Scheffer* result and the *Daubert* doctrine, as well as the inconsistency between the government's oppositionist position to the use of polygraphs by the accused while, at the same time, extensively using polygraph testing in conducting its own business.

Justice John Paul Stevens, in his separate dissent, stated that the Sixth Amendment does prohibit a *per se* exclusion of polygraph evidence and courts should be open for the admission of polygraph results. Justice Stevens conceded "within the broad category of lie detector evidence, there may be a wide variation in both the validity and the relevance of particular test results" noting that:

> *Questions about the examiner's integrity, independence, choice of questions, or training in the detection of deliberate attempts to provoke misleading physiological responses may justify the exclusion of specific evidence. But such questions are properly addressed in adversary proceedings; they fall far short of justifying a blanket exclusion of this type of expert testimony.*[35]

Often overlooked in *Scheffer*, but significant to the resolution of questions of admissibility in jurisdictions that do not have a codified *per se* exclusion of polygraph, a majority of the justices did resolve favorably for polygraph proponents two issues often associated with justification for polygraph evidence exclusion: the questions of usurpation of the jury function and avoiding collateral litigation.

---

[31] Daniels, *supra* at 16.
[32] *Scheffer*, 523 U.S. at 309.
[33] *Id.*
[34] *Id.* at 318.
[35] *Scheffer*, 523 U.S. at 333-34.

As to the issue of usurpation of jury function, the Kennedy four in their concurrence and Stevens in his dissent rejected the argument. Justice Kennedy characterized the notion of jury usurpation as "overreaching" and "empty rhetoric" and wrote that he "had thought this tired argument had long since been given its deserved repose as a categorical rule of exclusion."[36] Justice Stevens agreed, writing that "fear that the average jury is not able to assess the weight of [polygraph] testimony reflects a distressing lack of confidence in the intelligence of the average American."[37] Thus, a majority of the Supreme Court has rejected the usurpation argument.[38]

As to the issue of the burden of collateral litigation, both the Kennedy four and Stevens refused to agree with the Thomas four's endorsement of this argument as a basis for polygraph evidence rejection. Justice Stevens observed that such collateral proceedings "are a routine predicate for the admission of any expert testimony, and may always give rise to searching cross-examination." Justice Stevens believed that if testimony could be excluded for the reason that it is "collateral," the right to a "meaningful opportunity to present a defense would be an illusion."[39] Thus, a majority of the Supreme Court also rejected the collateral litigation argument.

While *Scheffer* is, technically, a holding limited to consideration of the constitutionality of a codified *per se* ban of polygraph, the Thomas four's observations that "there is simply no consensus that polygraph evidence is reliable" has resonated in lower courts' subsequent consideration of polygraph admissibility under *Daubert*.[40] Despite frequent attempts by proponents of polygraph to admit polygraph results, the overwhelming majority of post-*Daubert/Scheffer* federal court opinions continue to express reluctance to change their general exclusionary positions on nonstipulated polygraph evidence. Similarly, while many state courts accept stipulated polygraph evidence, state courts share their federal counterparts' reluctance to accept polygraph evidence in trials.

Lee v. Martinez

New Mexico has been the exception to the general rule of polygraph evidence exclusion, having for over 40 years generally permitted the introduction of unstipulated polygraph evidence. The New Mexico Supreme Court initially found in favor of the admissibility of unstipulated polygraph evidence in 1975 in *State v. Dorsey*.[41] There, in reversing the trial court's exclusion of a defendant's tendered polygraph examination, the New Mexico Supreme Court held that the rule of polygraph inadmissibility was

---

[36] *Id.* at 318, 319.

[37] *Id.* at 336, 337.

[38] Shniderman A., 2012. You can't handle the truth: lies, damn lies, and the exclusion of polygraph evidence, Albany L.J. Sci. Tech. 22, 433, 465 (noting that many courts have failed to note or ignored "the fact that a majority of the justices rejected the usurpation argument").

[39] *Scheffer*, 523 U.S. at 337.

[40] Bush, J.C., 2006. Warping the rules: how some courts misapply generic evidentiary rules to exclude polygraph evidence. Vand. Law Rev. 59, 539, 556 ("Other opinions similarly cite *Scheffer* as dispositive in their Rule 702 analysis. *Scheffer*, however, only addressed a *per se* inadmissibility rule and thus never needed to conduct a *Daubert* analysis.").

[41] *State v. Dorsey*, 539 P.2d 204 (N.M. 1975).

mechanistic in nature and inconsistent with the concept of due process. The court also found such exclusion incompatible with the purpose and scope of the modern trend of evidentiary rules to focus on whether the evidence will offer any help to the trier of fact in deciding the issue. Later, the New Mexico Supreme Court codified admissibility of polygraph evidence in New Mexico Rule of Evidence 11-707, wherein strict provisions for polygraph examiner qualifications and testing protocols were established.

In 2004, the New Mexico Supreme Court was, in *Lee v. Martinez*,[42] called upon to consider whether to repeal New Mexico Rule of Evidence 11-707. The issue found its way to the court through a petition by several criminal defendants seeking an order compelling district courts to admit polygraph evidence by a showing of compliance with Rule 11-707 rather than also requiring application of a *Daubert*-style consideration of the evidence.[43] It was the position of the petitioners that Rule 11-707 dispensed with the need also to demonstrate admissibility under a *Daubert*-style analysis. The court remanded the case to District Court Judge Richard J. Knowles to conduct an evidentiary hearing as to the scientific reliability of polygraph evidence and to make recommendations, to include a recommendation as to whether New Mexico should repeal Rule 11-707.[44]

Judge Knowles held 7 days of hearings in which nationally recognized experts testified on issues of polygraph reliability as well as other issues relevant to potential repeal of Rule 11-707. Following receipt of the evidence, Judge Knowles recommended to the New Mexico Supreme Court that Rule 11-707 be repealed.

The New Mexico Supreme Court, after review of the evidence presented to the district court, rejected Judge Knowles' recommendation. In a unanimous opinion written by Justice Pamela B. Minzner, the court concluded that "the control question polygraph examination [was] sufficiently reliable" and that admissibility need meet only the requirements of Rule 11-707.[45] The court concluded that so long as the expert is qualified and the examination was conducted in accordance with Rule 11-707, polygraph evidence would be presumptively admissible.

The *Lee v. Martinez* Court reached its decision only after an exhaustive consideration and rejection of the various criticisms of polygraph.[46] Acknowledging that polygraph testing was not problem free, the court observed:

> *We are cognizant of a number of potential problems with polygraph results, such as the use of physical and mental countermeasures to "beat the polygraph" and the influence on results of examiner expectancies ... However, any doubt about the admissibility of scientific evidence should be resolved in favor of admission.*

---

[42] *Lee v. Martinez*, 96 P.3d 291 (N.M. 2004).

[43] New Mexico follows a *Daubert*-style analysis for admissibility of expert testimony. *See State v. Alberico*, 861 P.2d 192 (N.M. 1993).

[44] *Lee*, 96 P.3d at 293.

[45] *Id.* at 298.

[46] In Bush, *supra*, the author provides an even more in-depth consideration of the various arguments and evidentiary rules often used (and as is the thesis of the author—misused) as an alternative to *Daubert*-style challenges to polygraph evidence, including Federal Rules of Evidence 403 and 608.

The remedy for the opponent of polygraph evidence is not exclusion; the remedy is cross-examination, presentation of rebuttal evidence, and argumentation.[47]

Justice Minzner further observed that, like the Kennedy four and Justice Stevens in *Scheffer*, "a categorical exclusion of polygraph results would be unwise" and also unfair "where the same government officials who vigorously oppose the admission of exculpatory polygraphs of the accused find polygraph testing to be reliable enough to use in their own decision making."[48]

STIPULATED POLYGRAPH EVIDENCE

It will be recalled that in *Piccinonna*, the 11th Circuit held that an acceptable method for introducing evidence of polygraph results was through the stipulation of the parties. A stipulation is, for the purposes of a judicial proceeding, an agreement, admission, or some other evidentiary concession made by the parties or their attorneys to some matter in the case.[49] Courts typically encourage stipulations and, unless manifest injustice would result from their enforcement, are generally bound to enforce them.[50]

Stipulations are sometimes characterized as a contract. While stipulations do not require, as do contracts, mutual consideration, such consideration is typically present where the stipulation is to admit yet-unknown polygraph results. With the possible exception of consideration, however, stipulations operate under similar contract interpretation and enforcement rules. As such, vague stipulations—like vague contracts—are subject to court rejection or limited enforcement.

There are many advantages to evidentiary stipulations to polygraphs. First, arguments regarding the collateral effect of litigating the admissibility of polygraph evidence are minimized. Second, unlike a polygraph examination unilaterally commissioned by an attorney who will opt not to disclose the result should the client be determined deceptive, the outcome will be known and available for use by all parties.[51] Third, as there will be no or limited need to call expert witnesses other than the polygraph examiner to testify regarding the science supporting polygraph, the expense of presenting the polygraph evidence is reduced. Fourth, when confronted

---

[47] *Lee*, 96 P.3d at 306.

[48] *Id.*

[49] 73 Am. Jur. 2d, *Stipulations* §1.

[50] See, for example, *United States v. Kanu*, 695 F.3d 74 (D.C. Cir. 2012); *In re Needham*, 354 F.3d 340 (5th Cir. 2003).

[51] The reasonable assumption in unilateral polygraph examinations made under the protection of attorney work product privilege is that the results of an examination will not be disclosed by the attorney unless his client is found to be nondeceptive. In such circumstance, of the nondeceptive polygraph results reported by the attorney to the prosecutor or adverse party, the ratio of false negatives (wrongly calling a deceptive subject nondeceptive) to true negatives (properly calling a nondeceptive subject nondeceptive) increases—thus rendering the cases disclosed by the attorney as having a much higher likelihood of being a wrong call than the ratio of wrong calls across all disclosed and undisclosed examinations. The New Mexico Supreme Court considered this argument in *Lee v. Martinez*, 96 P.3d at 302-303.

with the results of the polygraph, the parties are better positioned to evaluate the merits of their case and resolve the matter by plea agreement, settlement, or dismissal.[52]

The first reported decision regarding stipulated polygraph evidence came from Wisconsin in 1943 in the case of *LeFevere v. State*.[53] There, the Wisconsin Supreme Court upheld a trial court's rejection of a stipulation to admit polygraph evidence. In 1947, the Kansas Supreme Court, in rejecting nonstipulated polygraph evidence, suggested that were the evidence stipulated to by the parties, it would have been received.[54] That suggested result was realized in subsequent decisions of the Kansas Supreme Court.[55] Other states followed and, presently, there are approximately 19 states that permit stipulated polygraph examinations—though some place more restrictions on such stipulations than others. A caveat, however, is that several state appellate courts have not considered whether they would admit stipulated polygraph evidence and, as such, it is reasonable to assume that at least some of those states, on considering the issue, would agree to accept such evidence. Even in those states that admit evidence from stipulated polygraphs, courts maintain varying degrees of discretion to reject them.

The form of a stipulation is, of course, important. Oral stipulations will almost never be upheld.[56] Where a party fails to comply with the terms of a stipulation, the court will likely not enforce the agreement. For example, in *People v. Wheeler*, a Michigan intermediate appellate court found unenforceable a stipulation to admit polygraph evidence where the agreement called for the defendant to be examined by a police-administered exam, but the defendant sought and was given an examination by a private examiner.[57] As such, great care should be given in drafting a stipulation to address potential contingencies that may impact the admissibility of the examination results.[58]

---

[52] Anecdotally, in consulting with an experienced prosecutor regarding the potential use of stipulated polygraph evidence, the author was advised that when approached by criminal defense counsel with an argument of innocence, he will offer that the defendant submit to a stipulated polygraph examination. Typically, the prosecutor has observed that when that offer is conveyed to the defendant, it is rejected—but followed by plea discussions better grounded in the defendant's implied acknowledgement of criminal responsibility.

[53] *LeFevre v. State,* 8 N.W.2d 288 (Wis. 1943).

[54] *State v. Lowry*, 185 P.2d 147 (Kan. 1947).

[55] See, for example, *State v. Lassley*, 545 P.2d 383 (Kan. 1976).

[56] See, for example, *Wingfield v. State*, 796 S.W.2d 574 (Ark. 1990).

[57] *People v. Wheeler*, 2010 WL 1790441 (Mich. App. 2010) (unpublished opinion).

[58] The provisions of a stipulation may vary based on the circumstances in which the stipulation is presented—such as whether the stipulation is entered into with an uncharged suspect or witness or with a represented defendant. Stipulation agreements might include but not be limited to provisions considering the: admissibility of the results; admissibility of any conclusion of use of countermeasures; admissibility of examinee's failure to attend the examination; admissibility of the results in retrials or collateral litigation; selection and qualifications of the polygraph examiner; instrumentation and technique to be used; location and conditions of the examination; recording of the examination; whether the examination will be quality controlled and the impact and admissibility of the results of the quality control; whether there will be a posttest interview; a *Miranda* waiver; a waiver of liability; and responsibility for payment for the costs of the examination.

There is some debate on whether a polygraph stipulation for unrepresented suspects requires advice and consent of an attorney to be enforceable. While many states considering this issue have not imposed such requirement,[59] a minority of jurisdictions permitting stipulated polygraph evidence require advice and consent of an attorney.[60] New Jersey's experience serves as an example of what may occur when courts perceive that investigators and/or polygraph examiners attempt to overreach in the polygraph stipulations they present to unrepresented suspects. In *State v. A.O.*, the stipulation provided, in addition to stipulating to the admissibility of the polygraph results, that the suspect could not present any rebuttal witness evidence to the results of the polygraph.[61]

Polygraphs of represented suspects and defendants—stipulated or otherwise—should, ordinarily, not include a posttest interview without the presence of the attorney or written consent of the attorney that his client can be interrogated following the examination.[62]

POLYGRAPH EVIDENCE IN SENTENCING

Polygraph results are sometimes offered as evidence at sentencing hearings. Federal and most state courts impose far fewer restrictions on the types of evidence admissible in such hearings compared to criminal trials.[63] As to nonprivileged evidence, federal evidentiary rules are inapplicable at sentencing hearings[64] with federal law expressly providing that "no limitation shall be placed on the information concerning the background, character, and conduct of a person convicted of an offense … for the purpose of imposing an appropriate sentence."[65]

Because of these relaxed evidentiary standards, sentencing authorities are free to consider a wide range of evidence that may otherwise be inadmissible at trial.[66] As such, prosecutors and defense counsel routinely offer broad-ranging sentencing evidence; such as the defendant had a "difficult family history"[67] and victim impact statements.[68]

---

[59] See, for example, *Beaudoin v. State*, 714 S.E.2d 624 (Ga. App. 2011); *Davies v. State*, 730 N.E.2d 726 (Ind. Ct. App. 2000).

[60] *State v. A.O.*, 965 A.2d 152 (N.J. 2009).

[61] *Id.* at 164.

[62] *United States v. Leon-Delfis*, 203 F.3d 103 (1st Cir. 2000) (represented defendant's waiver of counsel for polygraph examination did not include waiver for postexam interrogation).

[63] State court evidentiary sentencing standards may differ from federal standards.

[64] Fed. R. Evid. 1101(d)(3); U.S. Sentencing Guidelines, 6A1.3 ("the court may consider relevant information without regard to its admissibility under the rules of evidence applicable at trial, provided that the information has sufficient indicia of reliability to support its probable accuracy").

[65] 18 U.S.C.A. § 3661.

[66] *Witte v. United States*, 515 U.S. 389, 398 (1995) ("[a]s a general proposition, a sentencing judge may appropriately conduct an inquiry broad in scope, largely unlimited either as to the kind of information he may consider, or the source from which it may come") (internal quotation marks omitted).

[67] *Eddings v. Oklahoma*, 455 U.S. 104, 115 (1982).

[68] *Payne v. Tennessee*, 501 U.S. 808, 820–821 (1991).

Significantly, as the expert admissibility standards of *Daubert v. Merrill Dow Pharmaceuticals, Inc.* are based on federal rules for admissibility of expert testimony, *Daubert* is inapplicable to federal sentencing.[69] Federal courts, however, retain considerable discretion in determining whether to admit polygraph evidence for sentencing considerations.[70] Pursuant to United States Sentencing Guidelines, evidence, including expert evidence, is subject to the requirement that it "possess sufficient indicia of reliability to support its probable accuracy."[71] Thus, courts continue—though not nearly as routinely—to reject polygraph evidence at sentencing hearings.[72]

Capital sentencing cases provide for even more relaxed evidentiary considerations, with federal law providing that evidence in such proceedings "is admissible regardless of its admissibility under the rules governing admission of evidence at criminal trials except that information may be excluded if its probative value is outweighed by the danger of creating unfair prejudice, confusing the issues, or misleading the jury."[73] The United States Supreme Court has stated that in capital sentencing considerations, with "only minimal exceptions," the sentencing authority should be permitted to consider "any relevant mitigating factor."[74]

Federal circuit courts are split, however, on the admissibility of polygraph evidence in capital case sentencing.[75] At least one commentator has argued that, under the more liberal evidentiary sentencing considerations, polygraph results should be admissible in capital cases.[76]

---

[69] *United States v. Fields*, 483 F.3d 313, 342 (5th Cir. 2007) ("[n]o Circuit that we are aware of has applied *Daubert* to sentencing").

[70] *United States v. Givens*, 767 F.2d 574, 585 (9th Cir.1985) *cert. denied*, 474 U.S. 953 (1985).

[71] U.S.S.G., 6A1.3, *supra*. *See generally*, Claudia G. Catalano, *Admissibility of Testimony at Sentencing, Within Meaning of U.S.S.G. § 6A1.3, Which Requires Such Information Be Relevant and Have "Sufficient Indicia of Reliability to Support its Probable Accuracy,"* 45 A.L.R. Fed. 2d 457 (2010).

[72] Sarno, G.G., 1986. Admissibility of Expert Testimony as to Appropriate Punishment for Convicted Defendant, 47 A.L.R.4th 1069, § 15.

[73] 18 U.S.C.A. § 3593.

[74] *Eddings v. Oklahoma*, 455 U.S. at 112.

[75] See *Paxton v. Ward*, 199 F.3d 1197 (10th Cir. 1999) (defendant's rights under the Eight and Fourteenth Amendment were violated where he was precluded from introducing exculpatory polygraph evidence in capital case sentencing); *Rupe v. Wood*, 93 F.3d 1434 (9th Cir. 1996) (exclusion of polygraph evidence in sentencing hearing of capital case violated defendant's due process rights to present relevant, mitigating evidence). But see *United States v. Fulks*, 454 F.3d 410 (4th Cir. 2006) (defendant did not have a constitutional right to present polygraph evidence during sentencing in capital case that he was truthful in statement that accomplice killed victim); *United States v. Catalan-Roman*, 368 F. Supp. 2d 119, 123–124 (D.P.R. 2005) (polygraph evidence failed to meet the "precondition of relevance" as it was not relevant to aggravating or mitigating factors in capital case sentencing).

[76] Domin, C., 2010. Mitigating evidence? The admissibility of polygraph results in the penalty phase of a capital trial. U.C. Davis Law Rev. 43, 1461, 1478–1479.

POLYGRAPH ADMISSIBILITY IN OTHER PROCEEDINGS

Polygraph evidence has often been accepted for the purposes of assisting in establishing probable cause.[77] It has also enjoyed some, though only marginally more, admissibility success in administrative proceedings[78] as, similar to sentencing hearings, administrative hearings typically do not adhere to strict rules of evidence. Some courts have permitted introduction of polygraph test results, not for the purposes of establishing whether the subject was deceptive or nondeceptive, but rather to establish a nonpretextual reason for an adverse employment decision.[79]

USE OF POLYGRAPH IN INTERROGATION
GENERAL RULE

With only narrow exceptions,[80] confessions obtained in anticipation of, during, or following polygraph examinations are admissible so long as they otherwise meet constitutional standards. As such, and all other factual circumstances being equal, a confession that would be admissible as a result of an interrogation *without* the use or threat of a polygraph would also admissible where it was obtained *with* the use or threat of a polygraph.[81] Because the court will, absent special circumstances, not permit testimony that the confession was obtained as part of a polygraph examination, the court will instruct that the examiner/interrogator not be referred to as a polygraph examiner but, rather, as an "investigator" or some other generic description.

---

[77] See, for example, *Craig v. Singletary*, 127 F.3d 1030, 1046 (11th Cir. 1997); *Bennett v. City of Grand Prairie, TX*, 883 F.2d 400, 405–406 (5th Cir. 1989).

[78] See, for example, *Evans v. DeRidder Mun. Fire*, 815 So. 2d 61 (La. 2002).

[79] Ruzicho, A.J., Jacobs, L.A., 2014. Employment Practices Manual 1, § 6A:8 ("Unless exposed as pretextual, an employer may negate an inference of discrimination by asserting the employee's refusal to submit to a lawful polygraph. Similarly, a discharge for flunking the test will rarely be deemed pretextual."); *Eddings v. City of Hot Springs, Ark.*, 323 F.3d 596, 600 (8th Cir. 2003); *Richardson v. Dougherty County, Ga*, 185 F. App'x. 785, 788 (11th Cir. 2006) (*per curiam*).

[80] Wisconsin is an extreme outlier to this general rule of admissibility—taking the position that postpolygraph statements are not admissible unless the interview eliciting the statement was totally discrete from the preceding polygraph examination. *State v. Harris*, 757 N.W.2d 849 (Wis. Ct. App. 2008). As such, to guard potential inadmissibility of an incriminating statement following a polygraph, Wisconsin law enforcement polygraph examiners separate the polygraph examination from the posttest interrogation in location and time and sometimes by using a different interrogator than the polygraph examiner.

[81] See, for example, *State v. Dressel*, 765 N.W.2d 419 (Minn. Ct. App. 2009) ("evidence obtained in connection with a polygraph examination is not inadmissible merely because the evidence was obtained in connection with a polygraph examination"); *Lagan v. State*, 656 S.E.2d 879 (Ga. Ct. App. 2008) (statements made prior and subsequent to the administration of a polygraph examination are admissible).

MIRANDA CONSIDERATIONS

Because there is little debate that a polygraph examination, whether pretest, test, or posttest is an interrogation,[82] polygraph examinations often raise the question of whether the examinee requires "Miranda rights"[83] admonitions. To trigger a requirement to provide *Miranda* admonitions, there must be three elements present: (1) police; (2) custody; and (3) interrogation. If any one of the three elements is absent, *Miranda* admonitions are not required.[84] As a polygraph examination is an interrogation, whether a polygraph examinee requires *Miranda* admonitions depends on whether the examination is a "police" examination and whether the examinee is "in custody." These are fact-specific inquiries, and a detailed consideration of these issues is beyond the scope of this chapter. However, generally, absent acting as an employee, contractor, or agent for law enforcement, a private polygraph examiner is not required to warn a suspect of his or her *Miranda* rights.[85] Additionally, the question of custody generally turns on whether a reasonable person, under the totality of the circumstances, would have felt that he or she was at liberty to terminate the interrogation and leave.[86] It has been held that attachment of polygraph components does not render a polygraph examination as being custodial.[87]

Where *Miranda* warnings are required, the United States Supreme Court has held that such a warning and a subsequent waiver of those rights need be given only at the onset of the examination and remain effective through postpolygraph questioning, at least as to interrogations conducted closely following the examination.[88]

Incriminating statements made during or on threat of a polygraph examination must, like such statements made without the use or threat of polygraph examination, be voluntary. Courts have overwhelmingly held that polygraph examinations are not inherently coercive but may be a factor in considering the issue of voluntariness under the totality of the circumstances.[89] It is improper and may render a statement involuntary where it is

---

[82] *Rhode Island v. Innis*, 446 U.S. 291 (1980) (an "interrogation" refers to any words or action, other than those normally attendant to an arrest, that the police should know are reasonably likely to elicit an incriminating response from the suspect).

[83] *Miranda v. Arizona*, 384 U.S. 436 (1966).

[84] *Id.* at 477; see generally, The Miranda Rules—Custody, Interrogation, and Exceptions, Fed. Prac. Proc. Crim. 1, § 75 (4th ed.) (2014).

[85] See, for example, *People v. Coblentz*, 176 Cal. Rptr. 516, 123 Cal. App. 3d 477 (Cal. App. 1981).

[86] *United States v. Boslau*, 632 F.3d 422, 427 (8th Cir. 2011).

[87] *United States v. Lee*, 315 F.3d 206, 212 (3d Cir. 2003).

[88] *Wyrick v. Fields*, 459 U.S. 42 (1982).

[89] See, for example, *State v. Monroe*, 711 A.2d 878 (N.H. 1998), *cert. denied*, 525 U.S. 1073 (1999) (use of polygraph results in questioning suspect is not inherently coercive, but merely a factor to be considered in examining the circumstances surrounding voluntariness of a confession); *United States v. Black Spotted Horse*, 120 F. Supp. 2d 802 (D.S.D. 2000) (defendant's confession after having been confronted with failed polygraph examination was not coerced and was voluntary where defendant was given proper *Miranda* warning prior to beginning the polygraph examination); *State v. Blank*, 955 So. 2d 90 (La. 2007) (threat and ultimate administration of polygraph examination did not render defendant's subsequent confession to murder involuntary). But see *Cole v. State*, 923 P.2d 820 (Alaska Ct. App. 1996) (threat of getting court-ordered polygraph among considerations that led to finding that confession was coerced).

represented to the examinee that the results of a polygraph examination are admissible as evidence in court in a jurisdiction in which they are not generally admissible.[90]

One circumstance in which polygraph evidence may be admissible is for the limited purpose of rebutting a defendant's allegation that his confession was coerced when, in fact, it was obtained as a result of being confronted with a deceptive examination.[91] Such limited admissibility permits the prosecution to contextualize the circumstances in which the incriminating statement was obtained.

POSTCONVICTION SEX OFFENDER TESTING

The United States Supreme Court has observed that "sex offenders are a serious threat in this Nation" in large part because "the victims of sexual assaults are most often juveniles" and because "convicted sex offenders are much more likely than any other type of offender to be rearrested for a new rape or sexual assault."[92] Polygraph testing has been increasingly used in postconviction monitoring of probationers and parolees—particularly sex offenders—who have been released into the community.[93] Polygraph testing is used as part of a comprehensive approach in which the probation/parole officer, therapist, polygraph examiner, and others work together toward risk assessment, treatment planning, and monitoring of the sex offender.[94]

In the treatment role, the polygrapher tests the offender regarding their personal history, relevant to their sexual offending, in an effort to break through denial—which is believed to be a barrier to effective treatment.[95] Polygraph testing has been shown to be an effective method to break through this denial.[96] In the monitoring role, the

---

[90] *Dressel*, 765 N.W.2d at 426.

[91] *People v. Montgomery*, 704 N.E.2d 816 (Ill. App. 1998) (testimony by a polygraph examiner that defendant confessed after being confronted with his exam results was admissible for the limited purpose of showing that the confession was obtained due to the polygraph examination and not obtained by unconstitutional coercion).

[92] *McKune v. Lile*, 536 U.S. 24, 32-33 (2002) (plurality opinion). See also Maiano, M.A., 2006. Sex offender probationers and the fifth amendment: rethinking compulsion and exploring preventative measures in the face of required treatment programs. Lewis Clark Law Rev. 10, 989, 995–996 ("Sex crimes are a serious problem in the United States. Although some researchers are concerned that statistical methods used to determine sex offender recidivism do not accurately capture the full breadth of the problem, even the 'best case' scenarios are troubling.").

[93] See, for example, English, K., 2004. The containment approach to managing sex offenders. Seaton Hall Law Rev. 34, 1255; Kebrick, A., 2009. Polygraph testing in sex offender treatment: a constitutional and essential tool for effective treatment. Ariz. St. Law J. 41, 429.

[94] Kim English, *supra* at 1259-1260.

[95] Hindman, J., Peters, J.M., 1988. Research disputes assumptions about child molesters. Nat'l. Dist. Attorneys Ass'n Bulletin 7, 1.

[96] *Id.*; Ahlmeyer, S., Heil, P., McKee, B., English, K., 2000. The impact of polygraphy on admissions of victims and offenses in adult sexual offenders. Sexual Abuse: J. Res. Treatment 12, 123; Angela Kebrick, *supra at* 1262 ("[t]he criminal justice supervision activity… is informed and improved by the information obtained during a well-conducted postconviction polygraph").

polygrapher assists in determining whether the offender is potentially re-offending or engaging in conduct inconsistent with his or her conditions of release. In this role, polygraph testing of sex offenders has been likened to urinalysis of drug offenders.[97]

Most states have programs which permit some form of Postconviction Sex Offender Testing (PCSOT)[98] and courts have almost uniformly upheld the use of PCSOT testing in such programs.[99] Offenders who refuse to participate in court-ordered polygraph testing may face revocation of their probation or parole.[100] Courts, however, have properly become increasingly sensitive that an offenders' Fifth Amendment right against self-incrimination may be implicated by PCSOT testing. Most recent decisions considering the issue have held that a probationer or parolee may not be compelled to answer questions that might lead to or support uncharged crimes.[101]

Where an offender is not obligated to answer questions that may lead to evidence of uncharged crimes and does not face adverse consequences for refusal to answer, courts have held that the Fifth Amendment self-incrimination right is not offended.[102] Additionally, the Fifth Amendment right against self-incrimination is not self-executing—that is, an individual who is faced with a question that solicits incriminating information must assert the privilege.[103]

Fifth Amendment self-incrimination is not implicated where, through polygraph testing or otherwise, inquiries are made of the parolee or probationer regarding conduct that would not constitute an uncharged crime but, rather, is related to a condition of release.[104] As examples, while an offender could not be compelled to answer

---

[97] English, *supra at* 1261.

[98] *Id.* at 1266.

[99] Blum, G.L., 2015. Validity and application of therapeutic polygraph examinations in sex offender treatment. 101 A.L.R.6th 545, § 1 ("Supervised release conditions, imposed as part of a defendant's sentence for sexual predation against minors, requiring sex offender treatment using polygraph testing to obtain information necessary for risk management and treatment, is typically permissible and constitutional.")

[100] See collected cases, *id.* at II, A § 4.

[101] See, for example, *United States v. Antelope*, 395 F.3d 1128 (9th Cir. 2005) (offender could not be compelled to reveal his full sexual history as part of postconviction treatment program, despite the potential treatment benefit, as the risk of self-incrimination was real and appreciable); *Commonwealth v. Fink*, 990 A.2d 751 (Pa. 2010) (revocation of offender's parole based on refusal to complete a questionnaire that made inquiries regarding offender's past sexual conduct violated offender's privilege against self-incrimination as the questionnaire had the potential to reveal essential links in a chain of evidence that could support prosecution on uncharged crimes).

[102] See, for example, *Doe v. Massachusetts Parole Bd.*, 979 N.E.2d 226 (Mass. App. 2012).

[103] *Minnesota v. Murphy*, 465 U.S. 420 (1984).

[104] See, for example, *United States v. Lee*, 315 F.3d at 213 ("A polygraph examiner, however, may still ask other questions that pertain to appellant's compliance with supervised release conditions without implicating the Fifth Amendment"). *See also* Vance, S., 2011. Looking at the law: an updated look at the privilege against self-incrimination in postconviction supervision. Fed. Probation 75, 33 ("If noncompliance [with a condition of probation] might result in revocation but not in criminal prosecution, the offender may not validly invoke his Fifth Amendment right.").

whether he or she had sexually assaulted a minor (as such offense would be an uncharged crime), the offender could be compelled to answer whether he or she had been within a prohibited distance of a minor under the conditions of release (as this would be a violation of the conditions of release, but not a crime). Similarly, where viewing pornography would constitute a violation of probation, questions asked during a polygraph examination regarding viewing pornography do not implicate the Fifth Amendment, as, while the answer could serve as a basis of a probation violation, it could not serve as a basis for future criminal prosecution.[105]

POLYGRAPH IN THE WORKPLACE

Prior to the enactment of the Employee Polygraph Protection Act of 1988 ("EPPA")[106] United States private-sector employers extensively used polygraphs for the purposes of prescreening job applicants, periodic employee testing, and investigating specific instances of wrongdoing.[107] Pre-EPPA surveys indicated that approximately one-fourth of all major United States businesses used polygraph and, of those who did not, approximately 40% reported that they might use it in the future.[108] Employer demand for polygraph, and the absence of few or any effective polygraph licensing laws, resulted in many polygraph examinations being performed by untrained or poorly trained examiners. During this time, there were wide reports of unprofessional and abusive polygraph examinations.[109]

On June 27, 1988, President Ronald Reagan signed into law the Employee Polygraph Protection Act of 1988. Absent an exclusion or exemption under the act, EPPA prohibits "employers" from "directly or indirectly" requiring, requesting, suggesting, or causing any employee or prospective employee to take a lie detector test; using, accepting, or inquiring about the results of a lie detector test; discharging, disciplining, discriminating against, denying employment or promotion, or threatening to take adverse employment action against an employee or prospective employee based on the results of a lie detector test or for refusing to take a lie detector test; and discriminating against an employee or prospective employee for filing a complaint under the act or otherwise exercising rights under the act.[110]

Excluded from the act are the United States government, any state or local government, and any political subdivision of a state or local government acting in the

---

[105] *United States v. Locke*, 482 F.3d 764 (5th Cir. 2007).
[106] 29 U.S.C. § 2001, *et seq*. (See Appendix A).
[107] Natale, A.J., 1989. The Employee Polygraph Protection Act of 1988—should the Federal Government regulate the use of polygraphs in the private sector? U. Cin. L. Rev. 58, 559, 571–572.
[108] Belt, J.A., Holden, P.B., 1978. Polygraph usage among major U.S. corporations. Personnel J. 57, 80.
[109] Brown, R.K. Specific incident polygraph testing under the Employee Polygraph Protection Act of 1988. Wash. L. Rev. 64, 661.
[110] 29 U.S.C. § 2001, *et seq*.

capacity of an employer. There are also limited exemptions from the act for the federal government to administer polygraph tests to private employees of employers and private contractors who provide services in certain areas of national defense and security. There are also limited exemptions to certain employers authorized to manufacture, distribute, or dispense controlled substances and certain employers providing security services. In addition, the act permits, under limited and extremely controlled conditions, polygraph examinations for the investigation of certain economic losses or injuries.[111]

Navigating exemptions under EPPA is often difficult and the penalties for violation of the act are harsh. The act, in addition to the statutory penalties, provides an offended employee a private, civil cause of action against the employer, which includes monetary damages and recovery of attorney fees and costs for successful prosecution. Additionally, a polygraph examiner may be considered an "employer" and subject to the act where the examiner goes beyond acting as an independent examiner and instead acts in the interest of an employer in relation to the employee. Factors that may be important to determine whether a polygraph examiner acts as an independent examiner or in the interest of the employer are:

> *(1) Who determined the employees to be examined; (2) under what circumstances the tests were to be administered; and (3) whether the examiner decided if an employee was to be disciplined as a result of the test, or whether he just reported the test results to the employer.*[112]

Some states have imposed more restrictive requirements than EPPA on the use of polygraph in the workplace.[113] There has also been a growing popularity of "Peace Officer Bills of Rights" which sometimes include provisions limiting circumstances in which a law enforcement officer must submit to a polygraph examination.[114] These "bills of rights" do not, however, typically prevent the use of polygraph for prescreening law enforcement applicants for these positions.

---

[111] 29 U.S.C. § 2006.

[112] Syferth, P.D., 2001. An overview of the employee polygraph protection act. J. Mo. B. 57, 226, 227 (citing *Fallin v. Mindis Metals, Inc.*, 865 F. Supp. 834, 840 (N.D. Ga. 1994). *See also Calbillo v. Cavender Oldsmobile, Inc.*, 288 F.3d 721 (5th Cir. 2002) (polygraph examiner retained by an employer may be an "employer" under EPPA where the examiner goes beyond the role of an independent examiner and, as a matter of "economic reality," exerts control over the employer's compliance with EPPA).

[113] See, for example, Hebert, L.C. 1 Employee Privacy Law, Vol. I §§ 6:21-6:65 (Clark, Boardman, Callaghan, Supp. 2014) (noting that "the state statutes regulating the use of polygraph examinations by employers vary widely" and discussing the various state statutes).

[114] Keenan, K.M., Walker, S., 2005. An impediment to police accountability? An analysis of statutory law enforcement officers' bills of rights. B.U. Pub. Int. Law J. 14, 185, 223 (citing as examples the prohibition of certain police polygraph testing in such statutes in California, Illinois, and Maryland).

Before embarking on a private employee polygraph examination, the employer and the polygraph examiner would do well to consult an attorney familiar with EPPA and state laws that impact employee polygraph testing and publications and which provide a more comprehensive treatment of EPPA and related legislation and regulation.[115]

LICENSING OF POLYGRAPH EXAMINERS

There are no United States federal polygraph examiner licensing laws. There are, at the time of writing this chapter, approximately 26 states that require polygraph examiners to be licensed, though state licensing requirements vary dramatically. Many of the licensing laws restrict detection of deception to instruments that record channels that are traditional polygraph channels. Such laws have been held to meet constitutional requirements and convictions for violations of such laws have been upheld.[116] Courts have also upheld polygraph licensing laws that establish polygraph examiner training requirements[117] and/or require continuing education of polygraph examiners.[118]

Federally employed examiners are, so long as they are acting in the scope of their federal employment, not subject to state licensing requirements on the basis of supremacy of federal regulations and considerations of federal preemption. Otherwise, examiners who travel outside their resident state to administer a polygraph examination must be careful to ensure that they are not conducting an examination in violation of the other state's licensing laws.

THE FUTURE OF POLYGRAPH AND THE LAW

United States Supreme Court Justice Potter Stewart stated that, "any rule that impedes the discovery of truth in a court of law impedes as well the doing of justice."[119] Justice Stewart's sentiment has not translated in United States courts to acceptance

---

[115] Syferth, P.D., 2001. *supra*; Pellicciotti, J.M., 2005. The employee polygraph act of 1988: a focus on the act's exemptions and limitations. Loy. Law Rev. 51, 911.

[116] See *Clark v. State*, 665 S.W.2d 476, 480 (Tex. Crim. App. 1984) (upholding a defendant's conviction for conducting a voice stress deception test, finding that a Texas licensing law that limited detection of deception devices to polygraph instruments was not an equal protection violation); *Illinois Polygraph Soc. v. Pellicano*, 414 N.E.2d 458, 462 (Ill. 1980) (upheld licensing law that required recording of cardiovascular and respiratory patterns); *Heisse v. State of Vt.*, 519 F. Supp. 36 (D. Vt. 1980) (upholding detection of deception licensing law as rationally limited to polygraph operators even to exclusion of psychological stress evaluator operators (PSEs) as the validity of PSEs is questionable and PSEs can violate privacy interest as they can be administered without the knowledge of the examinee).

[117] *Illinois Polygraph Soc.*, 414 N.E.2d *at* 145.

[118] *Costain v. State Regulation & Licensing Dep't*, 989 P.2d 443 (N.M. App. 1999).

[119] *Hawkins v. United States*, 358 U.S. 74, 81 (1958) (Stewart, J. concurring).

of the results of polygraph evidence. Many reasons have been given to justify this judicial reticence, including that: polygraph evidence is not sufficiently reliable; it usurps the role of a jury in determining witness credibility; it confuses the jury; and it creates litigation which is collateral to the primary purpose of the trial. Beneath these objections likely lies a more visceral opposition to the admissibility of polygraph evidence—an opposition not grounded on traditional evidentiary considerations but, rather, on fears that a scientifically validated means of detection of deception foretells of dystopian government intrusions into privacy and of ascendance of technology over human judgment.[120] As noted by one polygraph critic, "there is only one thing worse than a lie detector that doesn't work, and that's a lie detector that does work."[121]

It is not anticipated that the visceral objection to polygraph will abate in the near future and, accordingly, despite steady and significant improvements in the science of polygraph, gains toward the general admissibility of unstipulated polygraph evidence should be expected to be minimal. Indeed, other detection of deception technologies face similar issues. As noted by a recent commentator regarding the admissibility of fMRI as a detection of deception tool:

> *One need only examine the history of polygraph evidence to see that an important cultural prejudice against devices that betray the brain's private workings provides a further obstacle toward acceptance. The bold courtroom aspirations of fMRI advocates will hinge on their ability to distinguish it from the polygraph and quell Orwellian fears, as much as it will on proving the technology's validity.[122]*

Gains for admissibility of polygraph evidence may, however, reasonably be predicted for stipulated polygraph examinations, as the will of the parties and the current state of polygraph science should tip the scale to admissibility. To realize this result, however, a proponent of admissibility of stipulated polygraph will need to present to the court a thoughtful and thorough presentation of the current status of polygraph science through a polygraph examiner and a psychophysiological expert familiar with the science of polygraph.

Until the United States Supreme Court weighs in on the use of polygraph evidence in sentencing hearings, it is expected that the debate regarding polygraph use

---

[120] See, for example, *People v. Lyon*, 744 P.2d 231, 238 (Or. 1987) (Lind, J. concurring) ("I doubt that the uneasiness about electrical lie detectors would disappear even if they were refined to place their accuracy beyond question"); Wittenberg, K.A., Simmons, K.L., 1997. Truth or consequences—the changing dynamics of polygraph tests. Or. St. B. Bull. 58, 23, 24 (Some opponents of polygraph view them as "reminiscent of Orwell's 'Big Brother'"); Hebert, L.C., 2014. *supra* at § 6:6 (Opponents "have called polygraph testing 'strip searches of the mind'" and an "insidious Orwellian instrument of torture").

[121] Loviglio, J., 2003. New technology detects a lie before it's spoken. Associated Press, Pittsburgh Post-Gazette, May 25, available at: http://old.post-gazette.com/healthscience/20030525brainsci2p2.asp.

[122] Kittay, L., 2007. Admissibility of fMRI lie detection the cultural bias against "Mind Reading" devices. Brook. Law Rev. 72, 1351, 1354.

in sentencing will continue to occupy the attention of trial and lower appellate courts. It is not unreasonable to expect that, in the near future, the Supreme Court will confront this issue—likely in the context of whether an exclusion of polygraph in a capital sentencing matter violates a right to present a defense or due process. While it should be expected that some hostility to polygraph evidence will remain with courts that consider the issue, the relaxed sentencing evidentiary standards—coupled with the improvements in the science and application of polygraph—should result in a favorable decision for admissibility of polygraph evidence in capital sentencing hearings.

With the exponential growth of polygraph in the international community, courts around the world will confront their own questions of legal implications of polygraph. While the United States' experience may provide some precedent for international considerations of polygraph legal issues, differences in legal systems and cultural considerations will likely have an equal or more important impact.

Inevitably, science will produce a means for the detection of deception with demonstrable accuracy that courts and society will be unable to dismiss cavalierly as "unreliable." Such an instrument may not resemble the current polygraph. It will be then, however, that we will be forced to confront the legal, social, ethical, and political dilemmas that accompany the scientific ability to identify liars, a confrontation that most courts and society have thus far taken great pains to avoid.

ACKNOWLEDGMENTS

The author gratefully acknowledges the influence of Justice Charles Daniels to this chapter's section on admissibility of polygraph evidence. Prior to Justice Daniels' appointment to the New Mexico Supreme Court, he and this author served on an American Polygraph Association committee tasked to draft a sample brief supporting the admissibility of polygraph evidence. Justice Daniels' insightful contribution to that brief, as well as a two-article series he authored for the May and June 2003 issues of Champion that is cited herein, provided a point of reference for the admissibility discussion in this chapter.

ABOUT THE AUTHOR

Gordon L. Vaughan, J.D. is a shareholder in the law firm of Vaughan & DeMuro, a Colorado law firm with offices in Colorado Springs and Denver, Colorado. He has been General Counsel to the American Polygraph Association ("APA") since 1997. He has litigated and provided consultation services on dozens of cases involving issues of polygraph. He has authored a number of articles and publications regarding polygraph legal issues and has represented the APA as amicus curiae counsel in many cases, including *United States v. Scheffer* and *Lee v. Martinez*. He has been a frequent national and international lecturer regarding polygraph legal issues. He may be contacted at www.vaughandemuro.com.

CHAPTER 11

Advanced topics

I may be a despicable person, but when Truth speaks through me I am invincible.
Mahatma Gandhi

As examiners transition from their initial polygraph education program to their internship and field practice they will encounter situations or special applications that may not have been part of their initial education. In this chapter, we augment primary examiner skills with advanced material designed to assist those who will eventually face these challenges in the field.

PHYSICAL CONDITIONS REQUIRING ACCOMMODATION

Most polygraph testing is fairly routine and can be accomplished using standard procedures. There are many examinees with physical conditions, however, that will require accommodation if these individuals are to be tested successfully. Some of the conditions are health related, others congenital, and still others may be injuries. They extend from the transitory to the permanent, mild to severe, and the merely inconvenient to the highly challenging. In this section are suggested methods to assist examiners with special-needs examinees. All of the conditions discussed here are physical in nature, and there is no attempt to cover the wide range of emotional and psychological factors an examiner may encounter in the course of a career in polygraphy.

The eight categories of conditions addressed here are, alphabetically: amputations/injuries, blindness, cardiovascular disorders, dwarfism, hearing impairment, obesity, pregnancy, and stuttering.

AMPUTATIONS/INJURIES

Examinees may be missing limbs due to accident or injury, and their absence could require the examiner to seek alternate sites to place the polygraph sensors. Similarly, chemical burns, scarring, joint pain, some skin diseases, and even sunburns can sometimes prevent examiners from traditional sensor placements. Factors to consider when contemplating an alternate site are:

1. Is the physiological phenomenon sufficiently detectable at the new site?
2. Will the sensor cause pain or injury at the new site?

3. Would the placement of the sensor at the alternate site cause the examinee to become embarrassed or make the examiner vulnerable to accusations of inappropriate touching?[1]

Electrodermal

The most common recording sites for electrodermal are the fingers and palms (~240 eccrine glands per cm^2). If those sites are not possible or are undesirable, electrodermal activity (EDA) can be detected on the bottom of the feet (~180 cm^2), and the forehead (~240 cm^2). Some individuals may produce adequate EDA responses at other sites: arm or forearm (~115 cm^2), leg (~80 cm^2), or abdomen (~100 cm^2). Remember, the detectability of the EDA response arises from the number of eccrine glands *between* the sensors, not *under* the sensors: sensor placement may need to be further apart or the gain setting may need to be higher for sites with a lower concentration of eccrine glands. Selection of the sensor site should also allow for a good coupling between skin and sensor (not blocked by hair or thick callous).

Cardiovascular

Placement of the cardiograph cuff on the upper arm is the preferred approach. That site should always be used unless a documented medical condition or pain sensitivity would make it unadvisable. The second possible position is the forearm, followed by the wrist. Under truly exception circumstances the leg is an option, beginning at the calf. Respect, sensitivity, and good judgment are crucial if the cuff is to be placed anywhere on the leg. Also, be mindful that the Velcro fastener on the cuff can quickly shred sheer sockings. For all of these alternate sites, cuff pressure should be increased until the tracing is comparable to that seen when the cuff is on the upper arm. Finally, thick layers of clothing between the cuff and the skin (i.e., jackets and sweaters) interfere with getting a good signal from the cardiovascular system.

Pneumograph

Other than the abdomen and chest, there are not any good sites for the pneumograph sensors currently in use. Technologies exist for placement of flowmeters at the nostrils, but they are not available with any of the field polygraphs.

Photoplethysmograph (PPG)

The PPG sensor works best on the fingers. In unusual situations they can also be placed on the toes. The vasomotor response for detection of deception is not as well documented at sites beyond the hands.

There are field reports from examiners conducting testing of veterans of combat who have been fitted with prosthetic legs due to the loss of their own. Many of these examinees have commented that they sit with ease for a longer time when they remove the prosthetic. If it can be accomplished with sensitivity, examiners may invite these examinees to take off their artificial limb if it would make them more comfortable.

---

[1] This last consideration provides yet another basis to use audio-video recording of all polygraph examinations.

BLINDNESS

Testing sight-impaired examinees is fairly straightforward, and there are only a few points to remember. First, it is helpful early on to determine whether the examinee is totally blind or partially sighted. If the examinee has some vision, determine to what extent he can see. Depending on the degree of blindness, the examiner may need to read the consent, waiver, and other documents to the examinee, and to guide his hand to the signature line. It may also require some adjustment to the test room to avoid tripping hazards.

If the examiner is responsible for guiding the examinee into the test room, and wants to lead him by the arm, it is courteous for the examiner to verbally offer his own arm to the examinee rather than to grab the arm or hand of the examinee.

Also helpful is to let the examinee touch and hold the polygraph sensors during the explanation of what they are, what they do, and where they will be placed. This is to avoid catching the examinee off guard when the sensors are placed on his body, and to help secure and maintain rapport.

The examinee will also be attentive to sounds coming from the examiner, such as those generated by examiner movements, changes in the direction from which the examiner's voice is coming, even turning his head away. It is polite for the examiner to inform the examinee of examiner movements that might be obvious to a sighted examinee, but could be distracting or disconcerting to the sightless. The examinee may also be distracted by other sounds that occur during the testing phase: real-time printing or kymograph motor, key presses on computer polygraphs or pen scratching on analog instruments, the sound of clothes rustling, voice inflections during the reading of the test questions, even unconscious examiner behaviors such as scratching, throat clearing, and swallowing.

Here are some additional suggestions:

1. Be clear and precise in conversation.
2. Expect the examinee to have normal hearing. Do not talk louder than one would with a sighted person.
3. Do not assume the person needs help with all tasks. Ask before taking over the task.
4. "Person who is blind" is preferred over "blind person."
5. Always speak directly to the individual, not to the person who may be escorting him.

Finally, a word of caution about service animals. If the examinee brings a seeing-eye dog to the session, it is strongly recommended to have the animal penned in an area outside of the test room. Their movements or sounds may distract the examinee during testing. These animals are also very protective of their masters. Moving too close to the examinee or too quickly, acting in any way threatening, or even placing the sensors on the examinee may trigger protective behaviors in the animal and cause it to become aggressive.

CARDIOVASCULAR DISORDERS

With a wide range of cardiovascular conditions among examinees, there is no single solution to problems that examiners may encounter. Those most likely encountered are below.

Heartbeat Irregularities

Arrhythmias are fairly common. Some, such as premature ventricle contractions (PVCs, or "skipped heartbeats") are experienced by virtually everyone at least occasionally. If they become too frequent, the patient may be prescribed beta blockers to reduce the arrhythmias. These medications tend to flatten the cardiovascular channel, both in terms of blood pressure dynamics and pulse changes. Blood pressure reactions are still possible for examinees taking beta blockers, but the reactions tend to be subdued.

In some cases, the course of treatment is a pacemaker. The purpose of the pacemaker is to regulate the heartbeat when the body's own internal regulatory mechanisms have become unreliable. Polygraph charts of examinees with pacemakers will show a heartbeat that is very stable. However, blood pressure responses are generally similar to those seen with individuals without pacemakers. There is no reason to be concerned about the diagnosticity of the cardiovascular tracing simply because the examinee has a pacemaker. Algorithms that use pulse rate information will be affected, though minimally.

Heart Attacks

Examinees having heart attacks during polygraph examinations are so rare as to not to have been reported in the literature. Nevertheless, if the examinee has a serious heart condition, it is prudent to ask the examinee prior to testing to obtain a letter from his physician indicating that a polygraph examination poses no threat to the health of the examinee.

Some examinees who have experienced heart attacks are prescribed medication to improve blood flow. One side effect of a few of these medications is excessive bleeding and bruising. Examiners must be cautious with the blood pressure cuff with examinees taking such medications as even normal cuff pressure can break small vessels in the arm and cause bruising and petechial hemorrhages. Another common medication, the diuretic, is associated with poor electrodermal signals.

Respiratory Blood Pressure Fluctuations (RBPFs)

Previously and incorrectly referred to as *vagus* in the polygraph field, RBPF represents the influence of breathing on the cardiovascular system. RBPF is manifested on the charts as a cyclical rise and fall of the blood pressure tracing, typically accompanied by constrictions of the pulse amplitude, that match the pace of the examinee's breathing, but delayed by about 3 s. RBPFs can be caused by physiological factors such as cardiovascular health, age, obesity, medications, or fatigue. They can also be induced if the examinee overrides his homeostatic mechanisms by taking over breathing voluntarily in a manner that does not match his body's requirements, typically breathing too deeply or too slowly or both. Voluntary breathing should be discouraged if observed, as it significantly reduces the diagnostic value of the respiratory data channel, and it can also induce very noisy blood pressure and electrodermal patterns.

Except when RBPFs are caused by over breathing, there are few options available to the examiner to dampen them. If fatigue is suspected as the cause, simply allowing the examinee to sleep before the next polygraph session can remedy the problem. If the examinee's prescriptions are a possible cause of the RBPFs, the examiner must *not* tell the examinee to discontinue his medications, but must simply do the best possible to conduct the examination.

The most common approach to mitigating RBPFs is to place the cuff on the calf of the leg, and use additional cuff pressure. Higher cuff pressure is less uncomfortable at the calf, and 90-100 mmHg is easily tolerated by most examinees. This approach does not eliminate the RBPFs, but in some cases will diminish their magnitude. Examiners must still be cautious about chart interpretation to ensure scores are not based on RBPFs.

A cautionary note: RBPFs are sometimes mistaken for fluctuations caused by the cuff coming into contact with the examinee's chest during testing. The expansion and contraction of the chest against a cuff too close to the body can also cause cyclical rises and falls in the blood pressure tracing that mimics RBPFs. While RBPFs tend to be delayed about 3 s after the breathing cycle, changes from the cuff against the chest are not delayed, but correspond temporally precisely with respiration. The examiner can avoid this problem by ensuring the cuff does not touch the chest during testing.

DWARFISM

Dwarfism is not a disorder, but with it sometimes come maladies that require adjustments to the polygraph examination process. Some examinees with dwarfism may have chronic joint pain due to abnormal bone growth or alignment. This is especially the case when it entails the spine. The examinee's discomfort may be reduced by support cushions or adjustments to the test chair. At a minimum, the examinee should be afforded something on which to place his feet so that they are not unsupported while in the test chair.

An examinee with a smaller trunk size will also have a reduced lung capacity, which may affect the pace of breathing. Pneumograph tracings may show a more rapid, but shallower, breathing cycle than is typical with adults.

The only polygraph sensor affected by the smaller body size is the cardiograph cuff. Smaller versions of the cuff are available from all of the polygraph manufacturers.

The generally accepted terms for these individuals are: "little person," "dwarf," or "person of short stature." For more information on dwarfism, go to http://www.lpaonline.org/.

HEARING IMPAIRMENT

About 8% of the adult population is deaf or hard of hearing, a percentage that is smaller among the young and increases to about 30% of those age 65 and older. Demographically, some groups are more affected than others. For example, whites are more than two times as likely to be hearing impaired as blacks, and non-Hispanics have twice the prevalence of hearing impairments as Hispanics.

For examinees hard of hearing, it is typical for them to wear hearing aids. If, for some reason, the examinee does not have or did not bring a hearing aid, examiners with computer instruments will find that they can use the computer, along with a microphone and headphones, to amplify the sounds for the examinee. This takes a little preparation time, but once in place the system can always be available if needed.

While most of the hearing impaired can perceive some sounds, especially when using technology, a small number of examinees cannot hear at all. Special procedures are called for when an examinee is not able to adequately perceive the statements of the polygraph examiner. Below are two possible solutions to this challenge.

Interpreter

If the examinee is capable of reading sign language, an interpreter competent in sign language can be brought into the session. The procedures for working with a sign language interpreter are similar in many respects to those for using a foreign language interpreter (see section "Working with Foreign Language Interpreters"), with a couple differences.

One is that the sign language interpreter must remain in line of sight of the examinee for all phases of the examination, including test phase. As a result, the interpreter must learn to mask any emotion that might leak from his demeanor. This will require practice and preparation prior to the session. Also, as a point of good manners the examiner should speak directly toward the deaf person during the interview phase rather than toward the interpreter. This also goes for eye contact. A second difference from the typical polygraph examination is that the examinee may be permitted to answer either verbally (if possible) or by the brief shaking or nodding of the head during the testing. Having the examinee answer in sign language may interfere with physiological recording, and should not be done.

In the interest of clarity, portions of the pretest dialog may be done directly through the use of writing between the examiner and examinee. This process can give the examiner more confidence that the pretest information is being correctly conveyed to the examinee unless he understands the sign language used by the interpreter. If this is done the examiner and examinee should write on the same line pad, one after another, and use different color pens if the written conversation is to become part of the evidence record.

Technology

If the examiner uses writing to communicate with the examinee during the pretest interview, the next task is to communicate during testing. Obviously, writing is not a workable solution for this phase. Instead, examiners can opt to use a second computer screen to present the test questions to the examinee. Some of the computer polygraphs already have the capability to display content on a second screen which is controlled by the computer polygraph. The screen can be placed in front of the examinee, and the examiner would control which questions are presented and for how long. Again, examinees can answer with a brief nod or shake of the head.

Here are some additional suggestions:

1. Among the deaf it is considered rude to break eye contact when communicating. If a translator is used, he or she should look at the examinee when signing, but look down after presenting each test question.
2. Pointing and staring at people is proper, even necessary, in the deaf culture.
3. Examinees may refer to themselves as deaf, hard of hearing, or hearing impaired. Ask them what they prefer.
4. To get the attention of a deaf person, it is acceptable to slightly wave a hand or tap him lightly on the shoulder or arm. Do not throw an object to get his attention.
5. Use transitional phrases during conversations when moving to new topics. Abrupt shifts in topics can be confusing.
6. Be patient during conversation. Shouting or exaggerated speech is not helpful.

OBESITY

With obesity on the rise in most of the industrialized countries, examiners are increasingly faced with testing individuals who require adaptations of the examination process. These examinees are more likely to be taking medications that will affect the tonic behavior of the physiological recordings. They may require different polygraph sensors, and even different test furniture. Fortunately, even the morbidly obese examinees can be successfully tested with the proper preparations.

Examiners should know in advance the weight limit and dimensions of their polygraph test chair. If the chair cannot safely hold the examinee, an alternative must be found. Living room furniture, such as couches or chairs, may provide both space and weight capacity. If the examinee is in a wheelchair, this too could be used so long as the wheels are locked to prevent accidental movement. As a firm rule, an examinee should never be tested in a chair unless the examiner can prove it can support the examinee's weight.

Two types of polygraph sensors are most affected by large body masses: the pneumograph sensors and the blood pressure cuff. The standard size pneumograph sensor and chain can handle a circumference of about 60 in. (~1.5 m). Polygraph manufacturers sell chain extenders that can add as much length as needed. Because the body landmarks used for placing pneumograph sensors can be more difficult to pinpoint for obese individuals, it may be necessary to move the sensors to different locations to obtain a good signal.[2]

---

[2] In their book on polygraph, Reid and Inbau (1977) commented that obtaining a satisfactory pneumograph tracing from obese examinees is a frequent problem. They recommended placing a ruler or similar object under one of the pneumograph sensors, oriented vertically, to increase the amplitude of the signal. Though the text was published before electronic enhancement of signals was standard on polygraphs, the approach may still have value with modern instrumentation upon occasion.

The standard cardiograph cuff is designed for arms with a circumference of up to about 12 in. (~30 cm). Larger cuffs are also sold by the polygraph manufacturers. If the examinee requires a larger cuff, and one is not immediately available, a second-best location for the cuff is the forearm. When using the forearm site, cuff pressure will have to be increased. Note that RBPFs are almost always present with highly overweight examinees.

Seriously overweight examinees are virtually certain to be taking prescription medications. Most of these medications (e.g., blood pressure medications, blood thinners, and appetite suppressants) are unlikely to affect the polygraph tracings. Diuretics can significantly reduce electrodermal responses, however, and beta blockers can diminish the reactivity in the cardiograph channel. Reduced reactivity may require additional test charts in order to formulate a final decision for the examination. Using a PPG may help recapture the reduced diagnostic information in the charts. Examinees must never be told to discontinue prescription medications for the polygraph examination.

PREGNANCY

Examiners are often in a dilemma as whether to recommend the testing of pregnant examinees. Agencies vary significantly in their policies. Some will not test a pregnant female under any conditions, others will conduct the test if the examinee's doctor approves in writing, and still others will test up to the third trimester after which they will not conduct testing. There is no ultimate "true" answer to this question. The final answer for any agency is usually based on legal and medical considerations, with only minor input from polygraph examiners. Below are a few factors to consider as a policy is formulated.

There is no published evidence that pregnant examinees as a group cannot be safely and effectively tested at any point in their pregnancies. There are individual cases where the pregnancy is at risk, and polygraph testing would, therefore, be ill-advised. In other circumstances, such as testing applicants, the refusal to conduct polygraph testing on a pregnant applicant would impose a delay (and some may say a discriminatory delay) on the employment processing of the applicant. This postponement could have implications for insurance coverage and other second-order effects of interest to the applicant and possibly her attorney.

If the decision is made to conduct the testing, it is helpful for the examiner to recall that pregnancy can carry with it back pain, nausea, mood swings, discomfort when sitting too long or in the wrong position, chronic stomach issues, sensitivities to touch, sudden urinary urges, and a host of other pregnancy-related conditions including the occasional kick in the examinee's ribs by the unborn child. Examiners must carefully monitor the examinee for signs of distress, and be prepared to take breaks more often than normal.

STUTTERING

While virtually all people stutter occasionally, those classified as stutterers have breakdowns in speech fluency that are more frequent, have longer duration, and for whom the production of nonstuttered speech requires much more effort and concentration. There are no unique personality characteristics or level of intelligence association with stuttering, and though stress may increase its intensity and frequency, stress is not the driver for stuttering for the stutterer: it happens even in nonstressful settings. The tendency to stutter is mitigated when whispering, singing, repeating another's speech, talking to one's self, or speaking in unison with others.

Polygraph examinees have been known on occasion to feign stuttering in order to buy more time to think about their answers or to avoid the testing altogether. Examiners should be on guard against this tactic. If the stuttering continues even when using some of the approaches in the previous paragraph, there is cause for suspicion. Also, any stuttering during testing should occur at the end of the inhalation cycle. If it takes place elsewhere, it is probably not genuine.

In the pretest interview of examinees with extreme cases of stuttering, the examiner can have the examinee respond to his questions in writing, especially when the answers are expected to be short. For longer answers, the examinee may have to revert to speaking, in which case whispering the words may be advantageous.

Very few stutterers have difficulty answering *yes* or *no*. Consequently, stuttering during testing happens infrequently. In those rare instances, the examinee can be instructed to whisper the answers to the test questions, or use head nods and shakes to indicate his answers.

ETHICS

First, we must acknowledge that everyone lies; you, me, and everyone. Many people consider the act of lying *per se* an evil, but is it really? Lying can serve many functions, both good and bad, from hiding heinous crimes to preserving cherished relationships, from protecting national security to imposing political oppression, from false tax filings to appeasing creditors, practical jokes, business negotiation, political propaganda, legal defense, commercial advertising, and many others. Deception is as much a part of the human experience as any other. As Leonard Saxe observed: "Lying has long been a part of everyday life. We couldn't get through the day without being deceptive" (Komet, 1997).

Polygraph examiners are in the business of identifying some of those lies. The unique role served by polygraph examiners in the performance of their professional duties comes with great responsibility. Polygraph results, and examinee disclosures, can have significant and lasting consequences for clients, communities, departments, agencies, national security, and most often, the examinee. Consider that the polygraph, in various settings, can contribute substantially to high-stakes decisions in hiring, firing, probation, release, prosecution, offender management, intelligence and counterintelligence, and investigations. It is not uncommonly the case that winners and losers are decided in some part by polygraph results. Because polygraph examiners can have this power bestowed upon them, they must give rigorous attention to responsible behavior and decision making. Examiners who fail to uphold the highest ethical principles do more than betray the profession: their actions can potentially have devastating real world consequences for those who rely upon them.

This section covers ethical standards pertinent to the polygraph profession, and draws upon examples of the ethical failings by a few that highlight how challenges and pressures that accompany this field can at times lead to an unfortunate compromise. From the experiences of others, examiners may gain a greater appreciation for the basis for standards, and the need to attend to them.

REASONS FOR ETHICAL LAPSES

In a field spanning nearly 100 years, with tens of thousands of practitioners in nearly 100 countries, cataloging all documented and suspected ethical violations is well beyond the ambitions of this section. There will always be some who represent themselves as polygraph examiners, but show a cavalier disregard for the profession's ethical standards when they become inconvenient or unprofitable. Their values become obvious in a relatively short time. This section is dedicated to the other type of examiners, the professional, to help sensitize them to potential ethical pitfalls that perhaps they had not considered previously.

Even the most ethical examiners have their trials. Polygraph examiners, like all human beings, can fall prey to influences that can cloud their judgment, and bring about bad decisions. Because their decisions can affect so many people, examiners must be aware of these influences, and be on guard against their compromising effects. Those influences can be either external or internal.

External Pressures

Those who hold interests in the exam are known to try to influence the conduct of the exam, or shape the results. It may range from the obvious, such as bribes or threats, to the more subtle. There may be an investigator who conveys that there is conclusive evidence that the examinee is the culprit, and that the test of the examinee will determine whether the polygraph can really detect lies. Sometimes police chiefs will insist the examiner conduct a test though the examinee is clearly unsuited due to youth, fatigue, intoxication, mental disability, or a high emotional state. Examinees may try to exploit their social stature, sexual allure, or relationships with powerful figures to sway the examiner in their favor. In the private sector, an employer might impose an unreasonable number of tests on the examiner per day, for which the examiner must decide whether to take risky shortcuts or jeopardize his employment. Client companies have been known to exert economic pressure on examiners to screen out individuals of certain ethnic groups under the guise of polygraph testing.

Internal Pressures

The cause of ethical failings can come from examiners themselves. Lazy or incompetent examiners are responsible for a host of problems: manipulating tracings, discarding polygraph charts, deliberately mislabeling questions, using voice inflections to induce reactions on certain questions, and fabricating examinee statements. In screening examinations, this kind of examiner may create disincentives for examinees to self-report relevant information because the new information may result in additional examiner effort in testing and reporting. Or, conversely, some examiners have used the polygraph as a prop for the sole purpose of securing confessions, not all of them true, or out of scope of the examination. Some examiners commit even more egregious violations for want of money, such as testing for criminal organizations, teaching examinees to defeat polygraph testing, or basing decisions upon the size of the fees. Others, driven by desire for money or notoriety, use the polygraph for television programs in ways that misrepresent polygraphy and denigrate the profession.

ETHICAL PRINCIPLES

All professions have core ethical principles. They are part of what distinguishes a profession from simply a job. These principles underlie an implicit contract wherein the collective body of professional practitioners commits to certain types of behaviors and practices in exchange for public trust. The national polygraph associations all have ethical standards, and though not identical, they have common threads that reveal shared conclusions regarding what it means to be ethical as a polygraph examiner.

What is a good beginning point for ethics in this very special field? As it happens, polygraphy has principles in common with other fields that may help guide selection of ethical practices. Two good examples are the professions of clinical psychologist and court judge. Psychologists, for their part, engage in complex interactions with their clients, use valid testing methods, and make best assessments of individuals with those methods. Their ethical core focuses most often on the best interest of the client, or at least to do them no harm.

Judges, on the other hand, need to be independent of individual interests, and serve the cause of justice, though their decisions often have adverse consequences for individuals. Their ethical principles regard impartiality highest. Judges are bound by precedent and protocol, but these are not required to be scientifically validated.

Clinical psychologists are often called upon to form decisions about individuals that can affect them in profound ways, decisions that might run contrary to the patient's preferences, but clinicians have an array of validated tools on which to refer. Impartiality, though important, is secondary to the needs of the patient.

Polygraphy straddles both of these fields: though it involves assessment processes not entirely dissimilar from those of psychologists, the polygraph examiner is seeking the cause of truth rather than the interest of the examinee. And, unlike judges, they have sophisticated and valid assessment tools to guide their decisions. So, polygraph examiners must be impartial, but can also guide their practices with the body of scientific evidence.

The demands of fulfilling one's duty can give rise to potential conflict for the examiner, having a responsibility to use valid methods while ensuring the proper treatment of an examinee in a process that may lead to a bad outcome for the examinee who has volunteered to undergo the examination. Consequently, the ethical values of the polygraph profession do not map perfectly to other professions.

When distilled to their essence, virtually all possible polygraph ethical lapses might be subsumed within four general categories: Regard for the Examinee, Competence, Integrity, and Impartiality. Below are recommendations for four commonsense pillars of polygraph ethics, and their meanings.

Regard for the Examinee
The rights of the examinee are fundamental. Examiners must not conduct testing without the examinee's informed consent. Confidentiality of the examinee's statements must be consistent with the examinee's informed consent, and other disclosures should not be made except as required by law. Examiners must only test suitable examinees and on justifiable issues. Examiners should refrain from discussing with the examinee sensitive topic areas that are out of scope of the investigation, and are not necessary for the conduct of the examination.

Competence
All parties affected by polygraph results have a reasonable expectation that the testing examiner is proficient in polygraphy in general, and when appropriate, the specialty in particular. Competence is achieved through a quality educational program and a period of supervised field practice, and maintained through relevant readings and regular continuing education participation. Examiners must remain current with best practices, and their testing and analytical methods must be supported by independent research.

Integrity
An examiner's professional actions shall comply with governing laws and regulations, as well as with any of their contracts and agreements with examinees and clients. Examiners shall never conduct testing that circumvents the law, or provide assistance to others for that purpose. Examiners shall not alter testing or analysis protocols to affect test results, and must account for all the recorded data. Unless valid methods are used under proper conditions, examiners performing demonstrations of the polygraph for the public are not justified in offering veracity opinions.

Impartiality
A polygraph examiner's judgment must be sound, independent, and based solely on the available data. The manner in which examiners conduct, analyze, and report an examination must be consistent and fair in all cases regardless of the demands, expectations, or incentives from others. Polygraph examiners must not conduct testing on individuals with whom they have a personal relationship, nor on matters in which they have a personal interest.

CONCLUSION
These general ethical principles are intended to address most situations polygraph examiners may encounter, with the goal of protecting individuals and society against consequences of poor professional practices. Polygraph examiners are committed to

the pursuit of truth, using the best techniques and technologies available, to ensure the cause of justice. They continuously exercise professional discipline that assures all parties that they will diligently employ fair and best practices. They remain personally committed to ethical conduct, and demand the same for all their fellow practitioners.

REPORT WRITING

With very rare exception, polygraph examiners must provide a written summary of polygraph examinations they conduct. This may even be a requirement established by certain licensing laws and professional associations. Some of the structure and details in polygraph reports will vary according to the needs of the client, but there are core elements that are included in almost all polygraph reports. Here are some suggested areas. Examiners may choose to include other information not listed, and to adjust the order to fit their clients' requirements. Samples of field reports can be found in Appendix C. In addition, some providers of computer polygraph software offer report templates that may be useful.

IDENTIFICATION

The identity of the examinee must be verified before testing, and the report should list the examinee's name, along with any other names by which he might be known. The report needs to make clear who the examinee is. Listing the types of identification documents the examinee provided might prove important should the examiner anticipate being called upon to testify about the session. Some examiners also include the examinee's date of birth, and if the examiner uses a coding system in their practice for administrative purposes, it is often convenient to make it part of the report, as well. Examiners should be mindful of their responsibility to protect personally identifying information, especially when a security breach could allow to identify theft or misuse of examinee's personal information. The type of identity information retained and reported by the examiner should be well considered.

BACKGROUND

In the Background section, the examiner relates all of the history relevant to the polygraph exam. It can identify the client, as well. In a criminal case, this section might be a condensed summary of the crime and subsequent investigation. For routine applicant screening a statement can be made about the position to which the examinee has applied, and when test coverage differs according to position, the type of test issues used in that applicant's session. In sex offender management testing, the report can relate the category of testing (e.g., maintenance, instant offense, etc.) and when appropriate, the precipitating events that triggered the exam. When the exam is a continuation of an earlier session, a short summary of the previous exam might be added to provide context. The reader of the report should be left with a clear understanding of *what* happened that brought the examinee to be tested.

PURPOSE

Some examiners combine Background and Purpose under a single heading. What is important is to convey what the test topics are. This information verifies for the client that the examination focused on the requested issues. It is the central *why* of the examination. For example: the purpose of this examination was to assess the veracity of the examinee's denial of being involved in any of the Svobodniki arsons. Or: Attorney John Smith requested the examination test his client's denial of killing Pierre Laporte on October 17, 1970. Or: the examination was conducted at the request of the examinee to support his assertions of having bribed Rod Blagojevich in May 2007.

THE EXAMINATION

The examiner should document the *when* and *where* of the session. This will include the start and ending times along with the date. Also statements can be made regarding the use of electronic recording and the type of instrumentation.

When the examination or reporting process deviates from normal practice, it can be prudent to add those details to the report. Here are a few examples of situations the examiner may want to ensure is documented:

- Testing for an attorney who does not want the examinee to be informed of the results.
- When the examiner accommodates an examinee who has a relevant medical issue (changes in seating, lower lighting, adjustment to room temperature, alternate sensor placement, frequent restroom breaks, etc.)
- It is necessary to use an interpreter for an examinee who is hearing impaired or does not communicate in the language of the examiner.
- The examiner is prohibited by the client from following up a deceptive result with more questioning.
- Someone is in the test room to serve as a witness to the session.
- The use of special equipment (e.g., visual presentation of the test questions via computer monitor, examinee wore sound-canceling headphones through which test questions are presented aurally).
- The examinee imposes time constraints on his availability to remain in the session.
- The examination takes place in a nontraditional setting (e.g., prison, client's or examinee's home, hotel or motel, outdoors, etc.)

PRETEST

Here the examiner reports the most important aspects of the pretest interview. Included can be statements about the examinee's rights disclosure, assessment for suitability for testing, and the examinee's admissions, alibis, or recollections regarding the issue at hand.

Examiners must be circumspect about reporting information that is out of scope of the purpose of the examinations. Examiners with mandatory reporting responsibilities certainly must document criminal admissions from examinees; however, there is little to gain in any type of examination to report minor transgressions that have no value in making hiring, prosecutorial, or adjudicative decisions, and that may only serve to embarrass the examinee. Examinees often offer this type of information during the discussion of probable-lie comparison questions, or they volunteered it without prompting as they try to get all of their concerns off their chest. Generally, unless the information meets the intent of the examination, it should be documented, if at all, only in technical notes kept by the examiner.

TEST PHASE

The final wording of the relevant questions is listed, along with the examinee's answers. The examiner may identify the testing technique if it is informative to the consumer, but even if the technique is not placed in the report, at least report (truthfully) the chosen technique has been scientifically validated. Research citations supporting the testing technique can be included if the consumer wishes, but this information is not otherwise reported.

ANALYSES AND RESULTS

For multiple-issue screening examinations, the recommended results are Significant Responses (SR), No Significant Responses (NSR), or Inconclusive. Some programs use No Opinion[3] in place of Inconclusive. For specific-issue testing, the results are Deception Indicated (DI), No Deception Indicated (NDI), and Inconclusive or No Opinion.

Decisions are made by test, not by test question. That is, an examinee is deceptive to a test, or truthful to a test. Rendering a deceptive decision to one relevant question and one of no deception to another relevant question given in the same test is not supported by the scientific literature, and is a risky practice.

A statement as to how an examiner arrives at these decisions has increasingly been added to polygraph reports. In situations where the consumer is versed in statistics and decision theory, examiners have included details about the scores, references

---

[3] The replacement of Inconclusive for No Opinion began in the US Government in the 1990s. In practical terms the two labels are interchangeable, though some officials thought the newer label would be useful in countering critics' claims that an Inconclusive result was a decision error when calculating polygraph accuracy. A No Opinion was intended to denote a suspension of judgment, and by extension No Opinions could not be decision errors because they were not decisions at all. This labeling legerdemain subsequently did little to change how such statistics are calculated: critics still consider No Opinions as decision errors and proponents do not. Most dispassionate writers began to report decision accuracy both ways, with and without Inconclusives, thereby not taking sides as to whether Inconclusives were a metric for utility or for validity. By way of comparison, practitioners of other forensic sciences prefer the term Inconclusive, not No Opinion, and do not regard them as errors.

to normative data against which these scores have been compared, and a metric for uncertainty such as error likelihood or confidence intervals (see the following example).

> *Criterion Accuracy/Probability of Errors:*
> *Event-specific examinations with alpha = 0.05 for deceptive classifications and alpha = 0.05 for truthful classifications can be expected to produce a false-positive error rate for which the 95% confidence interval is from 0.007 to 0.093, with an expected confidence interval of 0.007 to 0.093 for false negative errors when interpreted with an assumption of non-independent criterion variance (calculated using binomial approximation to the standard normal distribution using a nominal sample space of 100 cases). The 95% confidence interval for unweighted mean decision accuracy is 0.907 to 0.993.[4]*

Professionals who understand test theory, such as psychologists, can find value in these additional details, and when these professionals are the client, the underlying statistical information is value added. There are also examiners who report the results from one of several polygraph algorithms. When doing so, examiners should at least be conversant of the research supporting those algorithms, and the confidence intervals for the results they produce.

In most other circumstances, where consumers are less interested in the statistical underpinnings of the examiner's decision, a simple result may be sufficient. It can be useful to report (truthfully) that the analysis system had been scientifically validated. As the polygraph profession begins to raise the expectations of the consumer community, a decision to use methods other than validated testing and analysis protocols can make an examiner appear unprofessional.

There is another category of results beyond the conventional ones directly addressing the examinee's veracity. When there is clear evidence that the examinee has attempted to defeat testing by the use of countermeasures which have rendered the physiological data uninterpretable or unreliable, an examiner should report those findings in lieu of decisions of deception or no deception. If there is sufficient data to make a decision of deception, even in the presence of countermeasures, examiners can do so. However, making a decision of no deception indicated when countermeasures are indicated should be avoided. Truthful examinees have been known to try to manipulate polygraph testing, and a retest of an examinee who then cooperates with the examiner's instruction will provide a much better foundation for a result of truthfulness.

There is no generally accepted expression in the field when reporting an examinee's use of countermeasures. Historically, John Reid preferred the expression Purposeful Non-cooperation (PNC). PNC did not speak to the examinee's guilt or innocence, but only to the degree to which the examinee complied with an examiner's instructions. Reid took a number of steps to ensure the behavior was intentional (see section Yes Test as an example). Polygraph results regarding countermeasures should be based on unequivocal evidence, or by the examinee's acknowledgement of having used them.

---

[4] We are grateful to Mr. Milton (Skip) Webb for providing this example.

POSTTEST STATEMENTS

Polygraph examiners normally advise an examinee of the examination results, and solicit an explanation if those results suggested deception. In polygraph reports, posttest statements are summarized to include the central details. In sex offender management testing, as well as applicant screening, information derived during the posttest interview can be used develop a new set of test questions to determine whether the examinee has fully disclosed information on the topic. In criminal settings an examiner may shift roles from tester to interrogator, and seek a confession and supporting details from the suspect. Confessions are written in a separate document, but may be appended to the report.

OTHER INFORMATION

Depending on the circumstances, there is other information examiners have incorporated into their standard reports. These details will depend upon the needs of the client. They can include the results of a quality control review, instrument calibration information, the examiner's state license number, and citations of scientific research supporting the examiner's methods. When testing for attorneys, the examiner can state that the report is the attorney's work product to help afford the attorney-client privilege to the polygraph documents.

There is also information that should *not* appear in a polygraph report. For example, examiners should not offer opinions or recommendations for which they are not professionally qualified to make. These might be psychological assessments and sentencing recommendations. Also, it is not recommended that examiners list test questions other than the relevant questions. They are not informative to clients, and tend to confuse those not trained in polygraphy. The documentation of all technical questions should be in notes examiners maintain for future reference.

POSTCONVICTION SEX OFFENDER TESTING (PCSOT)

Polygraph saw its first formal use in the postconviction arena in the 1960s when Judge Clarence E. Partee from Illinois began to utilize polygraph in probation settings (Abrams and Ogard, 1986; Bromberg and O'Donohue, 2014). Once the precedent had been set, it was only a few short years later, in the early 1970s, when a more widespread use of polygraph surfaced, oftentimes via judicial decree, in the treatment and supervision of sex offenders (Abrams and Abrams, 1993). The implementation of polygraph, as a part of supervision and treatment, continues to evoke in-depth discussions and debate as to polygraph's utility, effectiveness in reducing recidivism, as well as the surrounding legal concerns involving an examinee's constitutional rights. Research over the past couple of decades seems to majoritively favor the use of polygraph among sex offenders, but detractors highlight the need to show a more direct link to recidivism, to see more independent projects and case studies, as well as the need to include larger sample sizes for those cases. Despite the debates, probation officers and treatment professionals that have been utilizing polygraph as part of managing sex offenders have largely found polygraph to be a useful tool and believe it would be difficult to now do their jobs as effectively without it (Cooley-Towell et al., 2000; McGrath et al., 2007; Tubman-Carbone, 2009).

Indeed, the use of polygraph among various jurisdictions in the United States is ever increasing. A 2009 survey demonstrated a growth trend in the use of polygraph in adult postconviction programs from 30% in 1996, 63% in 2000, 70% in 2002, to 79% in 2009 (McGrath et al., 2010). Outside of the US, adoption of the use of polygraph in postconviction settings is also being evidenced in Canada and England, as well as other European and Asian countries.

The prevailing model for managing sex offenders has been the Containment Approach, or otherwise named the Containment Triangle, which entails a collaborative multidisciplinary approach. The containment team typically consists of a supervision officer, treatment provider, and polygraph examiner, but additional credentialed professionals are included as available and/or necessary, such as psychiatrists, social service workers, school officials, medical doctors, prison personnel, researchers, etc. The model recognizes that diverse professionals can contribute in unique, significant ways to the management of sex offenders, but these contributions are magnified by fostering a team approach with open communication and sharing of available resources.

As a result, polygraph's use in sex offender management is not intended as a stand-alone tool, but rather as a resource that can be integrated within the collective efforts of treatment providers and supervision officers. Specifically, the role of the polygraph is to: detect an offender's level of involvement or abstinence from problem behaviors; increase disclosures of problem behaviors, and; deter offenders from engaging in problem behaviors. The overarching goal of any sex offender management program is community safety, and ultimately, the reduction of new victims or continued impact to prior victims. The polygraph examiner becomes part of the containment team by assisting to limit or identify re-offenses or problem behaviors by the offender. Though the role of the supervision officer, treatment provider, and polygraph examiner are uniquely different, there are situations in which one member of the containment team may possess the professional credentials of multiple roles. Because of incompatible roles and responsibilities, examiners who also provide supervision or treatment of offenders should not administer examinations to persons they directly or indirectly supervise or treat.

While the basic phases of a polygraph examination are the same for this kind of testing as for others, the implementation of polygraph as a tool after an individual has been convicted brings with it some unique circumstances. This is in part due to the fact that there is generally more than one entity that may request a polygraph, and each entity may have a different objective that needs to be accomplished. As a result, exams can at times necessitate a diagnostic approach, while at other times require a screening approach. Because of this variance, a categorization of various test types in PCSOT has evolved. A thorough description of each exam type and additional polygraph considerations in the area of PCSOT was published in 2009 by the American

Polygraph Association in a document titled *Model Policy for Postconviction Sex Offender Testing*. It is recommended that readers consult this document as an additional reference. What follows is a brief description of each test type along with its identified frame of reference (relevant question topic areas) and time of reference (the period of time in the examinee's life that test questions can target). The frame of reference typically refers to the specific behaviors or acts that are to be addressed during testing, while the time of reference typically identifies the exam's orientation to pre- or postconviction activities.

INSTANT OFFENSE

A specific-issue exam is designed to investigate the examinee's involvement in the crime for which they were convicted. This exam is typically administered when an offender denies all or some significant aspects of their instant offense crime. Resolving issues of denial in all or part of their involvement in the crime is considered essential for the greatest success in treatment and/or if there are requests to reunite with the victim. The frame of reference is the nature of the crime itself and examination targets should address the offender's denial of participation in specific, significant allegations made in the police report, presentencing investigation report, victim impact statement, or other such documentation. The time of reference is defined by the time of the crime, and consequently will always focus on acts prior to their date of conviction.

INSTANT OFFENSE INVESTIGATIVE

A specific-issue exam also addresses the crime(s) of the instant offense, but allows for further inquiry of additional or unreported sexual contact with the victim, levels of force or violence with the victim, or frequency of contact with the victim. The time of reference for this exam is identical to the instant offense exam, and while the frame of reference covers the extent or type of contact with the victim, the targets are considered exploratory.

PRIOR ALLEGATION

A specific-issue exam designed to target allegations of sexual misconduct for which the examinee may or may not have been already convicted. The time of reference for this examination encompasses any alleged sexual criminal acts prior to the examinee's date of conviction for the current crime.

SEXUAL HISTORY (I & II)

These two screening examinations are designed to encompass an examinee's lifetime of behaviors prior to the date of their current supervision. The targets addressed are the examinee's unreported victims, sexual deviant behaviors, compulsivity and/or paraphilias. Both exams are of particular interest to the multidisciplinary team to assist in risk assessment, treatment planning, risk management and decision support.

Generally speaking, a Sexual History Exam I addresses issues of force and/or hands-on sexual contact with victims. Target areas of concern will typically address forced sexual contact, sexual contact with minors, sexual contact with family members, or sexual contact with individuals that are incapacitated, sleeping, or unconscious.

A Sexual History Exam II addresses behaviors of sexual deviancy, compulsivity, or preoccupation. Generally speaking, this examination is considered a means to address noncontact offenses and the frequency of those behaviors. Examples of target behaviors are exhibitionism, voyeurism, frottage, theft of undergarments, viewing child pornography, masturbation in public, sexual contact with animals, use of computers to solicit minors, stalking, etc.

SEX OFFENSE MONITORING

A screening exam intended to specifically identify new victims or the offender's involvement in sexual re-offense behaviors since being placed on supervision, or since their previously passed monitoring exam. This exam is typically requested whenever a member of the containment team has an escalated concern of reoffending behaviors. The prior listed exam types focus on events in the offender's life before being placed on supervision. This exam and the one following are the only two exam types centered on the offender's actions since being on supervision. The time of reference for the sex offense monitoring examination may also be adjusted to address a period of time since their last previously passed monitoring examination. Though the time of reference is different from the formerly listed exams, the targets for this exam are similar to identified targets for sexual history examinations. Examples of monitoring exam targets include sexual contact with minors, forced sexual contact with a person of any age, viewing of child pornography, exhibitionism, voyeurism, stalking, etc.

MAINTENANCE

Also a screening exam, but one that attempts to discover if the offender has been following the technical terms of their established treatment and supervision guidelines. Examples of exam targets would be the prohibited use of alcohol or drugs, unauthorized contact with minors, grooming behaviors, violating travel or housing restrictions, masturbation activities to include fantasies, having contact with victim(s), unauthorized computer use, violating curfew, unreported sexual partners, viewing pornography, etc. The frame of reference for this exam centers on possible violations of their supervision or treatment guidelines, while the time of reference involves any behaviors since being placed on supervision or since their last passed polygraph examination. The time of reference should be consistent for all targets addressed in the exam. The frequency of administered maintenance exams varies from program to program. Some program administrators prefer a random assignment while others establish a more regimented schedule ranging from every 4 to 6 months, or annually at a minimum.

An additional target that may be addressed in a maintenance exam is a question about criminal sexual acts, sexual acts of deviancy, compulsivity, or preoccupation. Though these targets are specifically addressed in a monitoring exam, it is recognized that reoffending is also a violation of the treatment and supervision guidelines. Furthermore, with the routine administration of maintenance exams, the ability to incorporate a monitoring question during the test may prove beneficial to ensure a more continuous observance of the offender to ensure the ultimate program goal of public safety. Given the exploratory, multi-issue structure of a maintenance examination, examiners choosing to incorporate a monitoring question on a maintenance exam should follow-up with a single-issue monitoring examination when there is an unresolved issue on a previously failed maintenance exam.

Regardless of the type of exam being administered, examiners should adhere to the fundamental practices discussed in earlier chapters of this text in regards to pretest, test operations, and test data analysis procedures for the corresponding format used. Additionally, examiners should ensure that examinees are suitable candidates prior to administering a polygraph test and that great care is taken to always respect the rights and dignity of each examinee.

Examiners should also be aware of local laws pertaining to mandatory reporting requirements as well as being mindful not to violate the right against self-incrimination held by examinees being asked to answer questions about criminal behaviors. Additional information on each of these issues can be found in Chapter 10.

ASSET FORFEITURE TESTING

Success in criminal enterprises in which immense profits are garnered, such as drug trafficking, traditional organized crime, and white collar securities fraud requires the criminal to use very advanced methods for concealing assets. Finding those assets is not always easy, and can sometimes be impossibly difficult in this increasingly electronic age. Criminals have found methods that defy the most aggressive investigation, lengthy surveillance, paid informants, and forensic accountants. The polygraph may be the only means of identifying and locating assets under these circumstances.

The first step for introducing the polygraph into a plea agreement is the crafting of the agreement itself. Those interested in the legal aspects of asset forfeiture can obtain more information through the US Department of Justice, and many salient and essential principles are reported by Bryant (1989). The details of a successful plea agreement are beyond the scope of this section, however, the most essential points suggested by Bryant (1989) are summarized below:

- The defendant must agree to cooperate with federal, state, and/or local authorities.
- The defendant must agree to submit to debriefings by authorities.
- The defendant must agree to voluntarily turn over any requested physical evidence (i.e., documents).

- The defendant must agree to provide truthful testimony, as necessary, at all legal proceedings.
- The defendant must agree to waive venue.
- The defendant must agree to submit to a polygraph examination to identify co-conspirators and assets, and to forfeit assets under their control.
- With regard to the polygraph portion of the agreement, the best language would require the examinee to "submit to polygraph testing to the satisfaction of the government." It should not specify that the examinee has to pass the polygraph. There are occasions where an inconclusive result could be adequate, especially if the defendant's admissions were deemed sufficient by the government.
- Generally, open-ended plea agreements should be avoided due to the increased potential of perjury.
- The government must be prepared to honor the agreement, even if only struck orally.
- It is sometimes also useful to include a notification that defendants may be prosecuted for obstruction of justice, with imprisonment for 1 year, if they destroy or remove property to prevent seizure. Not only might this inspire more candor from the defendant, but it can also provide a motivation for better cooperation from attorneys or others who may be secretly holding illicit assets for the defendant.

Once the polygraph is involved, investigators must provide the examiner with a detailed accounting of the defendant's assets well before testing is scheduled. This, combined with the conditions of the plea agreement, will aid in the development of the test coverage for the issues of interest to the government.

Polygraph testing for asset forfeiture can be long and challenging due to the breadth and complexity of the issues. Asset forfeiture cases normally have two or three topic areas. They are the identification of concealed criminal collaborators, hidden assets, and at times, seizable assets. Each of these is managed in separate tests. It is commonplace for a defendant to be tested over more than one session with many hours per session. Investigators should be available to assist in sorting out whether new information provided by the defendant is significant, and to suggest lines of inquiry.

To help investigators determine whether others were involved in the criminal activity beyond what the defendant has disclosed, below are examples of some possible relevant question types:

- Other than who you mentioned, was there anyone else helping you transport people across the border?
- Did you receive sensitive law enforcement information from anyone other than XX?
- Is there someone else you have not told me that helped you smuggle those weapons?
- Was someone you are not telling me involved in your smuggling operation?
- Are you withholding any information to protect someone?

It is important to be mindful that there are defendants who may try to withhold the name of a family member whom he has drawn into the criminal enterprise, and may never provide this information even at the risk of additional prison time. Experienced prosecutors are aware of this possibility, and in the interest of seeing the plea agreement succeed, will often agree that the defendant need not disclose family members' names. Examiners, therefore, must adjust their test questions accordingly.

The most common use of the polygraph in asset forfeiture cases is in the verification that the defendant has disclosed all of his assets to investigators. In those cases, polygraph test questions target hidden assets. Examples of relevant questions are below:

- Do you have any illegal assets you have not told the FBI?
- Are you deliberately hiding any illegal assets?
- Other than what you told me, are you now concealing any illegal assets?
- Are you now concealing any assets from the Nevada Investigation Division?
- Do you have any offshore assets?

The third most common use of the polygraph in plea agreements is to help prosecutors determine whether certain property can be legally seized. If the property was used in the commission of, or paid for by the profits of an illegal enterprise, it generally can be confiscated by the government. Knowing what that property is, therefore, can become important. For example, suppose a defendant has a legal business that provides income in addition to his illegal business. If the defendant's boat or car, as examples, were paid for through profits of his legal business, they may be exempt from seizure, depending on the plea agreement. Conversely, if they were purchased with ill-gotten gains, the government can take them. Similarly, if the boat or car were used in the commission of crimes, they can be seized. Below are some hypothetical relevant questions:

- Did you ever use your Cigarette Marauder boat to transport illegal drugs?
- Have you ever illegally smuggled anyone into the US using your Kenworth tractor-trailer.
- Was any part of your house at 1234 Cherry Lane, Myrtle Beach, paid for by drug money?
- Have you ever deposited drug money into your account at Smith Savings and Loan?
- Was your land in Humboldt County paid for with profits from illegal drug sales?

Use of validated polygraph techniques, preferably those with high sensitivity to deception, should be used along with valid chart interpretation methods. Though polygraph evidence is rarely tendered as evidence in these cases, the use of defensible methodologies avoids a basis for challenge. There is a greater awareness among attorneys that there are polygraph techniques with stronger empirical foundations, and examiners who choose to depart from those techniques can potentially introduce difficulties into the execution of the plea agreement.

As a general rule, defendants will disclose information during the polygraph examination that was not previously known to investigators, especially if the examiner is experienced. Admissions totaling millions of dollars are relatively common, as are revelations of involvement of multiple co-conspirators. Information is one of the chief advantages of polygraph testing for asset forfeiture, and adverse test results without actionable information are of limited value. In pursuit of this information examiners should be prepared to use their best elicitation and interrogation skills. There may also be occasions where techniques such as the Searching Peak of Tension may give clues to the examiner where to focus attention.

CONCLUSION

One of the unfortunate facts about organized crime and narcotics trafficking is that they are lucrative. With such large stores of money, criminals can use a portion to conceal the rest so that it may be impractical or impossible to track. Well-crafted plea agreements, combined with well-executed polygraph testing, enable the justice system to ensure crime does not continue to pay.

WORKING WITH FOREIGN LANGUAGE INTERPRETERS

The frequency of the use of interpreters during polygraph examinations is in proportion to size, number, and variety of foreign-language ethnic groups in the larger society. In the US, for example, Spanish is the number one spoken language after English (12% of population and growing); however, there exist significant American communities where the primary languages are Polish, Cambodian, Arabic, Croatian, Hmong, French Creole, Cantonese, Russian, Tagalog, several Native American languages, Armenian, and scores of dialects. Many countries similarly have international communities where nonnative languages are spoken, or where there is more than one official language. Ideally, a polygraph examiner could competently conduct the examination in the language of the examinee. Many countries have bi- and trilingual polygraph examiners. However, there are occasions when an interpreter may be required to interview suspects, and to polygraph them. The purpose of this section is to guide examiners through the important steps for testing through an interpreter.

STEP 1: THE INTERPRETER

The most important avoidable error comes with the selection of the interpreter. Language competency is extremely important, but by no means the only consideration. For example, complications are virtually assured if there is an existing personal relationship between the interpreter and the examinee. The use of the examinee's coworkers, family, or fellow members of social organizations is simply bad practice. It can introduce unconscious biases, and make it infinitely more difficult to develop information from the examinee that he does not want the interpreter to know. Interpreters may be tempted to protect an examinee by refusing to convey faithfully what the examiner is saying, or by filtering one or both sides of the interview. Or the opposite might be true, where a previous bad relationship could prompt the interpreter to misrepresent what the examinee is saying more in the negative direction. The baggage of a previous relationship between interpreter and examinee must be strenuously avoided unless there is no alternative.

Finding an interpreter with no ties to the examinee may prove challenging in some circumstances, especially where the ethnic community is small and most of the members know one another. Nevertheless, examiners should recognize the risk if they must use an interpreter with a personal relationship with the examinee.

Examiners should also be mindful of the demographics of the examinee and interpreter. For example, in some societies the status of women is very low. Using a woman as an interpreter for testing a male examinee from certain cultures can prove problematic, especially if an interrogation is required. There are also ethnic and religious sensitivities to consider, where sometimes generations-long conflicts have created imposing social and psychological barriers between groups despite a shared language. These challenges to the examination process may not be insurmountable if skillfully handled, but they should never catch the examiner unprepared.

STEP 2: PREPARATION

The central consideration when using interpreters is the control of the polygraph session. The inclusion of a third person in the examination process adds a significant dynamic that can disrupt or even derail the examination process. Interpreters are almost always tempted to edit what is said, either to help or otherwise, creating a filter that can distort the true meaning of the examiner and examinee statements. Miscommunication can confuse the interview and possibly erode the validity of the polygraph results. Consequently, an inviolable ground rule when using interpreters is that they interpret exactly what is said on both sides of the interview: no filtering, no editing, and no sidebars with the examinee. This message must be communicated to the interpreter in a manner that is both clear and firm, but also polite and respectful. Always remember that the interpreter must be a willing collaborator with the examiner.

The interpreter should arrive well before the examination. This will allow time to help the interpreter become familiar with the examination process. During this time the interpreter should be given a full description of the process, including the proposed test questions and their purposes. The more the interpreter understands about the examination, the more accurate the communication of it can be to the examinee.

On the topic of the test questions, examiners should strive to simplify them as much as can be done without jeopardizing their meaning. The test questions should be written out in advance because the interpreter will need time to translate them, and it is better done as much as possible before the examination begins. The examiner will provide the question list to the interpreter, complete with labels, who will then write them on another sheet of paper in the language to be used during testing. The interpreter should ask for clarification from the examiner when needed, to ensure the correct interpretation of the questions. The examiner should take back his question list once the translation is complete.

The preparation time is also the opportunity for the examiner to learn what he can from the interpreter about the language and customs of the examinee. At a minimum the examiner should learn to recognize the foreign words for *yes* and *no*. This will enable him to properly annotate the examinee's answer during testing. It will also permit him to grasp some of the examinee's verbal responses during the interview. If the interpreter can explain some of the cultural sensitivities to the examiner, this is also very useful. Can the examiner ask about the examinee's family? Are there certain gestures to avoid? What does direct and indirect eye contact mean? How does that culture view deception? What about interpersonal space, physical contact, etc.? This information may help the examiner avoid social pitfalls that can interfere with rapport.

One vital step in the preparation phase is practice: the live polygraph test should not be the time to discover that the interpreter is confused about the procedures. Before the examinee arrives the examiner should place the interpreter in the chair reserved for the interpreter, and the examiner will take his place in his interview chair. The two should then practice portions of the pretest and testing phase for about 10-15 min. The interpreter must be able to imitate the examiner's tone and emphasis, and produce a monotone voice for the testing phase.

Once the practice is complete, the examiner explains to the interpreter that for quality control purposes he wants the interpreter to translate the test questions back to the examiner's language. Oftentimes interpreters will resist this step, but if it is explained that the second translation is essential to the evidentiary process, they may be more willing to comply. Once the interpreter has retranslated the questions the examiner should compare them to his original list. The two lists should match one another precisely, at least in terms of question content. If there are some that are not equivalent, the interpreter needs to retranslate until they are.

When the questions have been translated properly they can be written on index cards, one question to a card, with the question label at the top. The reason for index cards is that the examiner can easily adjust the sequence of the questions between charts by sorting the cards into the order he prefers. It is helpful to have an additional card with an irrelevant question written on it in case it is needed for insertion during testing to allow time for recovery from a reaction or artifact. It is also handy to have index cards prepared for statements such as; please sit still, the test has begun, and the test is over. If a demonstration or acquaintance test is to be conducted, index cards must be prepared for that test as well.

STEP 3: PRETEST

The examinee must understand early in the pretest interview that all discussions are between the examiner and the examinee. The role of the interpreter is only to interpret, not to explain. All of the examinee's statements are to be directed to the examiner. Likewise, the examiner always addresses his remarks to the examinee. This process is facilitated when the examiner keeps eye contact with the examinee, not the interpreter.

Some examinees may feign an ignorance of the examiner's language, and request an interpreter when one is really not needed. This may be attempted by deceptive examinees to create a psychological barrier between himself and the examiner, or to gain additional time before answering questions. The examiner needs to be on guard for this ruse. An examiner may informally test the examinee's language ability by asking questions of him when he first arrives at the office, such as who he is looking for, or telling him (without gestures) to hang up his coat. If it appears he does not need an interpreter, the session can begin without one. Otherwise the interpreter should be brought into the examination.

Seating during the examination must be thought out well. During the pretest interview the examiner and interpreter must be able to see each other, and the examiner and examinee should face one another, but the examinee ought not to be able to see the interpreter without effort. This can be accomplished by having the interpreter behind, but slightly to the side of the examinee during the interview (Figure 11.1).

FIGURE 11.1

Placement of the polygraph examiner, examinee, and interpreter during the pretest interview.

Photo courtesy of the National Polygraph Academy. Setting posed by members of the Singapore Polygraph Association.

The pretest interview should proceed normally, with adaptation for the cultural factors relevant to the examinee. Because each statement is said twice during the interview (once by the speaker and the other by the interpreter) the pretest interview will be longer than those conducted without an interpreter. In view of the extended time requirement, the examiner may build in a break during the pretest interview that he would not ordinarily do.

Examiners must continually monitor the interpreter's statements to have more confidence that he is not altering the exchange. Almost all interpreters at some time will begin to edit the discussions. For example, it is quite common for an examinee to provide a 2-min answer to an examiner's pretest question, and for the interpreter to distill it down to 10s when he passes the statement to the examiner. This is a sure sign that the interpreter has begun editing. When this happens, the examiner should take the interpreter to another room to review and reinforce the instructions for interpreting for the examination. Another method is to establish a ground rule where both the examiner and examinee will speak only one, or parts of one sentence at a time, and wait for those statements to be interpreted before moving on to the next statement. This process helps ensure the interpreter is not condensing the statements.

There are instances where the examinee will make statements which require changes to the test questions.[5] The changes should be noted in the examiner's question sheet, and the interpreter will work from that sheet to change the wording on the index cards. Once the final wording is agreed upon, the examiner will place the index cards in the order he wants them presented, and return them to the interpreter.

STEP 4: TESTING

During testing, the examinee should not be able to see either the interpreter or the examiner without turning his head or body, but they both should be able to view the examinee. The interpreter's seat is placed behind the examinee's seat, while the examiner sits in a position that lets him observe the examinee (see Figure 11.2).

As the examiner is preparing to conduct the testing he will speak to the examinee through the interpreter, but once the test has begun only the interpreter will speak. Cued by the examiner using a hand signal out of the view of the examinee, the interpreter reads each test question to the examinee in the order the examiner

---

[5] There are various field reports that examinees in some cultures resist, or cannot grasp, the "symptomatic" or "outside issue" question. This should not be surprising inasmuch as the "symptomatic" question was invented in a purely American context. Because a cardinal rule of polygraphy is that no question is ever tested without the understanding and consent of the examinee, examiners may have to replace these questions on an individual basis with irrelevant questions, or choose a technique that does not call for them. Research in recent years has not shown "symptomatic" questions to be scientifically valid, but examiners must be aware that some quality control reviewers may challenge a Zone-type test that does not use these questions as policy or doctrine requires.

FIGURE 11.2

Placement of the polygraph examiner, examinee, and interpreter during testing.

Photo courtesy of the National Polygraph Academy. Setting posed by members of the Singapore Polygraph Association.

has placed the index cards. The interpreter remains silent otherwise, and awaits the next signal from the examiner. It is important that any movement of the interpreter or examiner, or any communication between them, be undetected by the examinee.

If there is a need to insert an additional irrelevant question, or to give other instructions to the examinee during testing, the examiner should hand the appropriate index card to the interpreter and signal for it to be read. This procedure will entail some movement on the part of the examiner, but it must be done as discretely as possible.

Modern technology has given examiners a tool that would allow more control over the presentation of the test questions. Most computer polygraphs have the capability for recording audio files for presentation during testing. Using this capability, the interpreter can record his reading of the test questions into the computer where it can be stored until needed. The examiner can then call up the audio file in whatever order and pace he prefers during the test. Using the audio files would free up the interpreter to watch the examinee more closely, or even to leave the testing room to reduce distractions.

CONCLUSION

Testing through an interpreter can be an awkward but often necessary approach to polygraph testing. The suggestions in this article cover the most common problems examiners will encounter, and potential solutions to those problems. If examiners follow these recommendations, are diligent, and follow best practices they can have full confidence in their results.

SILENT ANSWER TEST

The Silent Answer Test (SAT) is a specialty procedure that has been found to be useful in many polygraph cases. For some techniques, the SAT is used only as circumstances require. For others, a SAT is incorporated into the examination as a standard method (i.e., Marcy Technique, Integrated Zone Comparison). The first published description of the SAT was by Frank Horvath and John Reid in 1972.

The SAT can satisfy a number of purposes, but a primary use for the SAT is to collect respiration tracings that are minimally artifacted (see Figures 11.3 and 11.4). The SAT can eliminate answering distortions in the respiration data, and it may also serve to reduce artifacts associated with throat clearing, coughs, or swallows that are sometimes triggered by the vocal response. It can also provide an exemplar against which to compare respiration tracings that are suspected of having been deliberately manipulated.

Instructions for preparing the examinee for the SAT can vary, but one possible script is provided here:

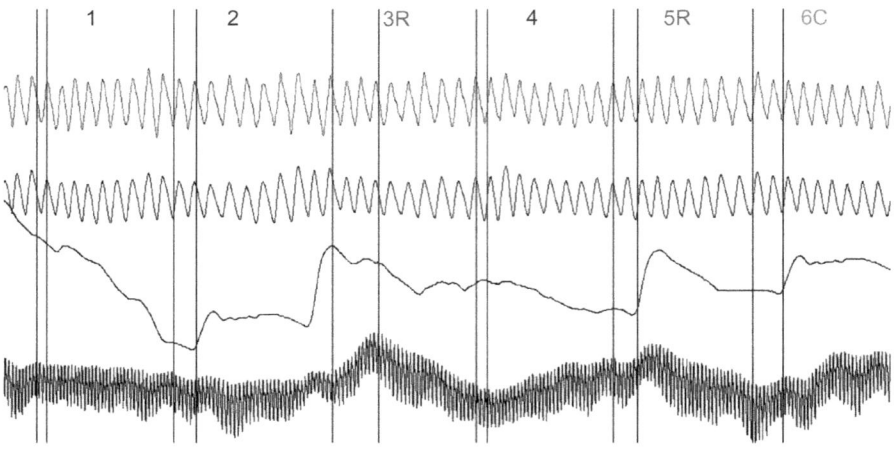

FIGURE 11.3

Silent Answer Test of an examinee. (We are grateful to Cholan Kopparumsolan for providing the chart segments seen here. The polygraph method is the Marcy Technique where the first chart is normally a SAT.)

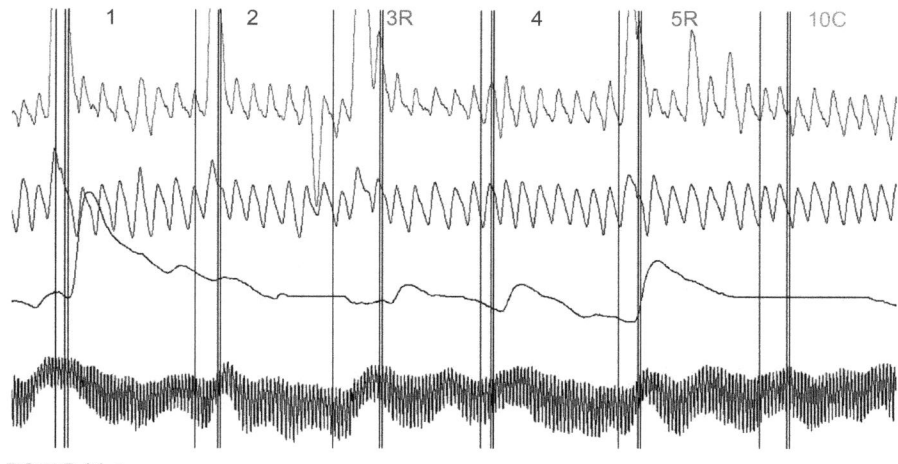

FIGURE 11.4

Chart of the same examinee answering verbally.

> *Fred, for this next test we're going to do something a little different. I'm going to read to you all of those questions again, but instead of answering each question aloud like you have been, I would like you to answer them silently in your mind. For example, when I ask you if today is Monday, instead of saying the word yes I'd like you to think the word yes. In other words, answer correctly, but silently, with all of the questions. Do you understand? (Wait for acknowledgment.) Just remember to listen to the questions and answer them to yourself. If you have been truthful to all of the questions, this test will be a little easier than the other tests. It is only when people try to lie to themselves, which they would be doing with this particular test, that we see much larger reactions on the questions they are lying to. Again, if you've been truthful to all of the questions, as you promised me you would be, you have nothing to worry about.*

The test is then conducted in the usual manner, and the data are scored as with any other test.

Some examiners are concerned that the examinee may silently answer *yes* to the relevant questions on the test, and because he would not be lying with the *yes* answer there would not be a reaction on the test. It is helpful, though, to remember that the polygraph is not a lie detector, but a salience detector. If the relevant questions are threatening to the examinee it would not matter how, or whether, he answers in his head. However, if the examiner is still uncomfortable when the examinee gives no outward sign of his answer, he can have the examinee nod or shake his head once to give his answer. This requirement also ensures that the examinee is paying attention during the SAT. The examinee is admonished not to move his head more than one-half inch, though, to reinforce the need to remain still during testing.

YES TEST

In their classic polygraph text, Reid and Inbau (1977) offered a method to determine whether the examinee has tried to defeat the polygraph examination. Called the "Yes Test," it is designed to entice potentially countermeasuring examinees to reveal themselves. It is not a test of deception, but rather a test of cooperation, and is typically only administered when an examiner already has an indication that the examinee has done something to alter the physiological data. It is often the last chart in an examination. It is not scored.

In the Yes Test an examinee answers all of the test questions with a *yes* answer. Because relevant questions are normally phrased to be answered no, the examinee would be answering the opposite way from all previous tests. Probable-lie questions are not given in a Yes Test, and the examinee is made aware of this. A possible narrative to the examinee before the Yes Test might be like the following:

> *Fred, we're going to set aside these earlier tests for the moment, and the next test I'm going to give you is a little different from what we've been doing up to this point. First, I won't be asking you any of those questions about (the probable-lie comparison questions), but I will be asking you all of the rest of the questions. On this test I'd like to you to answer yes to all of the questions, even the ones you've been saying no to all along. Do you understand? Answer yes to every question, including the ones you said no to before. The reason for doing it this way is that I already have test charts where you've been saying no on certain questions, and I would like to compare them to this next test where you'll be answering yes and see whether there is anything different about the reactions. I'm sure you've already noticed that for some of the questions your answers can't be truthful on this test and the other tests. Just remember, answer yes to all of the questions this time.*

In cases where the answers had already been *yes*, such as in confirmatory testing of victims and witnesses, the test can be turned around so that the examinee would now answer all questions *no*. It would then be a "No Test." The irrelevant questions would then be modified so that the truthful answer is *no*.

The Yes Test is conducted only once. Reactions to the relevant questions are not meaningful in the Yes Test, but substantial changes in tonic physiology or movements are. About two-thirds of deceptive examinees will try to manipulate the tracings. Truth-tellers, in contrast, rarely try to affect the tracings.

If the results from the rest of the testing would be DI, the predominant call would be DI irrespective of the Yes Test. If the charts had been uninterpretable or suggest truthfulness, and the Yes Test indicated the examinee had tried to manipulate it, a result indicative of countermeasures, such as PNC, can be issued. Otherwise, the results of the initial testing stand.

See the following chart segments[6] for examples of manipulations on the Yes Test.

---

[6] We are grateful to Cholan Kopparumsolan for providing the chart segments seen here. The polygraph method is the Marcy Technique.

CASE 1

Standard Chart

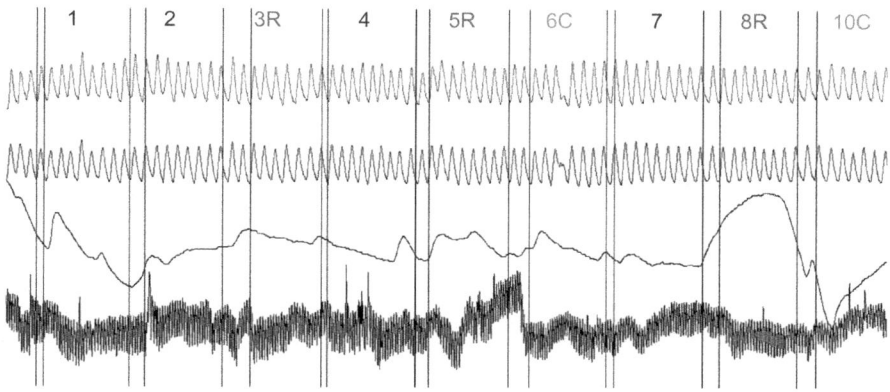

Yes Test Chart

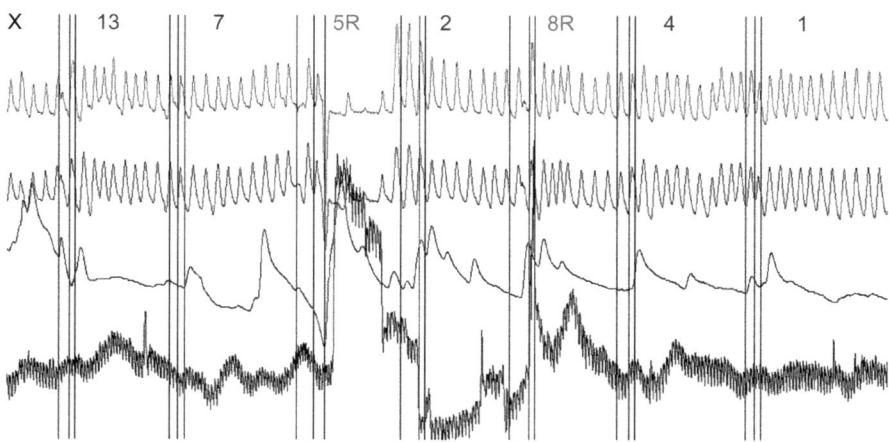

Note the movements in the cardiograph, and exaggerated breathing on the relevant questions.

CASE 2

Standard Chart

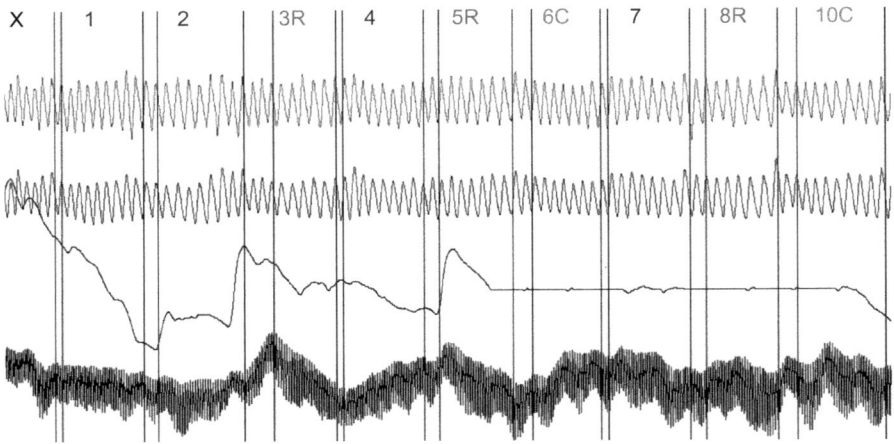

Yes Test Chart

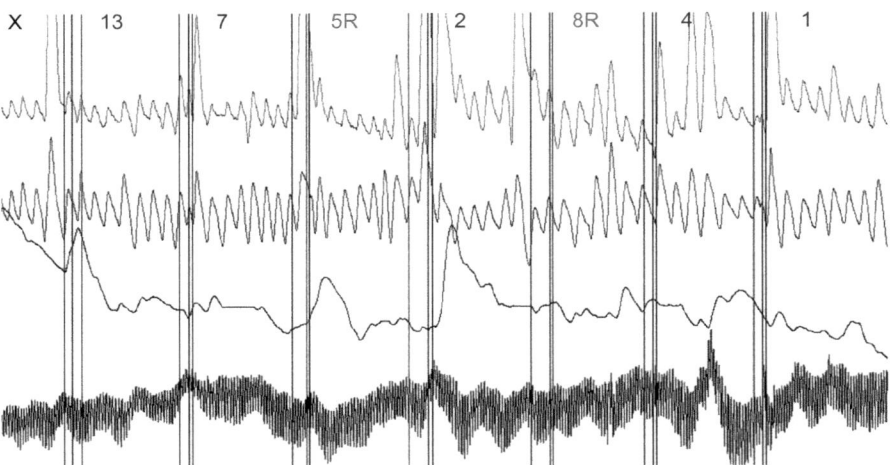

Note the exaggerated breathing on almost all of the questions.

Yes test **265**

CASE 3
Standard Chart

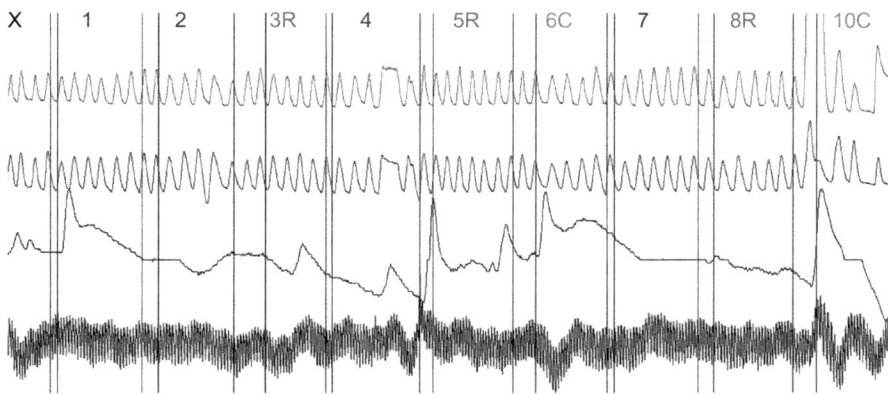

Yes Test Chart

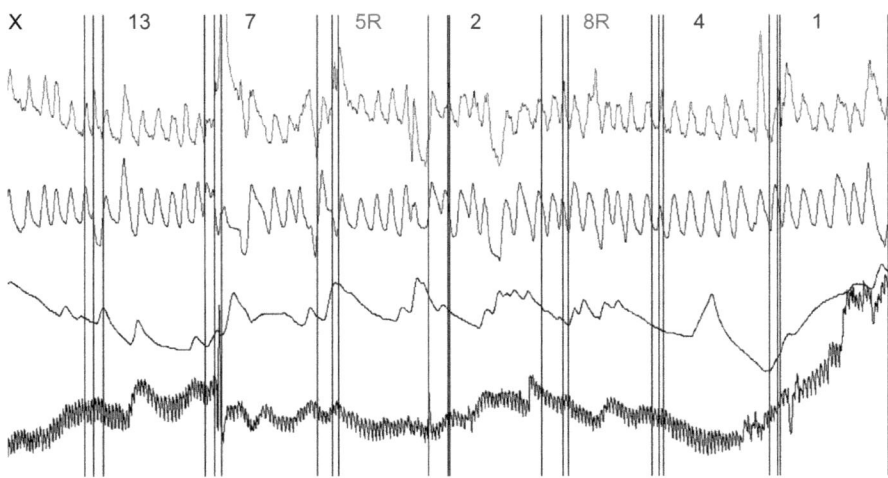

Note the pronounced irregularity in the breathing compared to the earlier chart, and evidence of movements during irrelevant questions.

CASE 4

Standard Chart

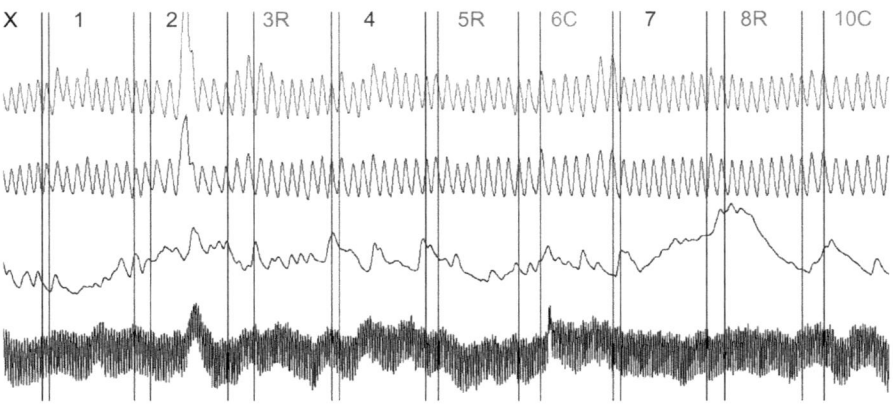

Yes Test Chart

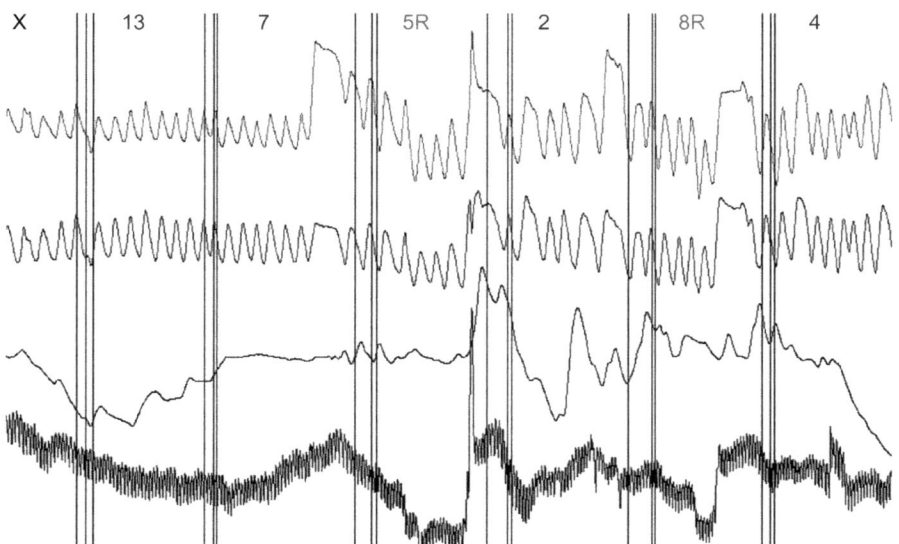

Note the exaggerated breathing accompanied by apparent movements in the cardiograph.

PAIRED TESTING: THE "MARIN PROTOCOL"

With the unassuming title *Standard Guide for PDD Paired Testing*, the "Marin Protocol" as it has come to be known was established as a standard with the American Society of Testing and Materials (ASTM, 2011a,b). The Marin Protocol is perhaps one of the most innovative and misunderstood concepts in polygraphy in recent years. It was proposed by Jonathan Marin, a nonpolygrapher statistician in two little known, but insightful articles in the journal *Polygraph* (2000, 2001). In his paper, Marin introduced a method that could reduce polygraph decision errors using a simple and elegant mathematical principle. That principle, called joint probabilities, paved the way for the polygraph to be used in special circumstances where established polygraph accuracy may not ordinarily be sufficiently high. The purpose of this section is to explain why and how the protocol works, and to outline the essential requirements. Included are recommendations that are not unique to the Marin Protocol, but are part of the body of best practices. Those who may be called upon to conduct testing under the Marin Protocol are encouraged to obtain a copy of the standard by contacting ASTM directly at ASTM.org.

To have a better understanding of the principle of joint probabilities that undergirds the Marin Protocol, it is best to start with a commonly recognized example. In this case, we shall use a coin flip. As everyone knows, the likelihood of a fair coin landing on heads (H) is 50/50, or expressed here as 0.5: likewise, there is a 0.5 chance of it landing on tails (T). If one had two coins, and flipped them simultaneously, there are four possible combinations: HH, HT, TH, and TT. The chance of tossing both coins and obtaining, say HH, is one in four, or 25%. This can be calculated mathematically by multiplying the individual probabilities. For example, the probability of obtaining one H is 0.5, and the probability of the second H is also 0.5. By multiplying these individual probabilities together the final answer is 0.25, or 25% ($0.5 \times 0.5 = 0.25$). This principle also applies to conditions where there are more than two possible outcomes, such as a toss of a die or drawing cards from a deck.

Let us now substitute the coin flips with something with a different proportion; polygraph decision accuracy. According to the National Research Council's report (2003), polygraphy in field and laboratory studies had a median accuracy of 0.86 for specific-issue examinations. This means that the polygraph can be expected to have a median error rate of 0.14 (setting aside inconclusive results). Using this value in place of the 0.5 from the coin flip, we can now calculate the likelihood of two independent polygraph examinations both resulting in an error ($0.14 \times 0.14 = 0.02$). In other words, if there are circumstances where polygraph examinations are given to two individuals, only one of whom is lying, then the likelihood of a wrong call on both individuals is a mere 2%. An error rate so small would be the envy of any of the behavioral sciences. The rate would also be 2% when two individuals are tested from the same side of the litigation and are telling the same story. The proportion of error becomes even smaller when more than two individuals are polygraphed. For three examinees the likelihood of a combined error is three-tenths of one percent ($0.14 \times 0.14 \times 0.14 = 0.003$). As each new individual is tested in this scenario the error rate is multiplied by 0.14 and that the potential combined error rate approaches 0. The power of the Marin Protocol becomes apparent.

Obviously, the multiexaminee conditions described earlier do not arise often for polygraphers. Usually there is a single suspect, and the question for the examiner is whether this suspect is lying or truthful, and there is no opportunity to exploit the advantages that come with joint probabilities. However, this limitation does not prevail everywhere. There are settings where conflicting statements between two or more individuals are abundant, incentives for lying are strong, verification of truthfulness is exceptionally difficult, and the consequences for error are potentially dire. These settings include civil and family court, administrative hearings, and arbitrations. Here the majority of the evidence is testimonial, and in a disturbing proportion of the cases one of the protagonists is probably lying out of self-interest, spite, or revenge. How often there is perjury is an unknowable, of course, but one can feel confident that it is more than a rarity. Consider allegations of abuse leveled by one parent against another in a disputed child custody case. Or, the conflicting claims of culpability between partners in a murder case. Or, accusations and counter-accusations regarding contractual fulfillment. Contradictory claims in personal injury suits. The list is long, and among many of these cases the polygraph and the Marin Protocol might be brought to bear for the cause of justice.

It should be clearly understood that the Marin Protocol was not devised as a mechanism for polygraph results to be introduced as evidence before a court or judge, though the courts may benefit from its principles if they chose to avail themselves of them. Rather, it can be simply stated that the goal of the Marin Protocol is to reduce perjury. It does so by agreement of the contesting parties so that, if the polygraph results of both sides point to the same conclusion about an issue (one party is deceptive and the other truthful), the deceptive party is prohibited from testifying about the issue. The deceptive party may testify regarding other issues, but the fact that there is a 98% chance of the testimony to the tested issue was false, that option should be eliminated for the person. The polygraph results are never entered into evidence, nor does the polygraph examiner testify.

The standards are rigorous in the conditions in which the protocol can be invoked, in the competency of the testing examiners, in the testing techniques that may be employed, and in the manner in which the results may be used. It may be the most stringent requirements in all of polygraphy. The following are the requirements for the litigants, examiner, test issues, and test protocol.

REQUIREMENTS

When there are differences in testimony between two parties, the difference must be substantial, so that honest mistakes on the part of one of the testifiers can be ruled out. For example, in a dispute between spouses regarding who took a valuable piece of jewelry from their joint safety deposit box, it is reasonable to conclude that each spouse knows for certain about his or her own guilt in the matter. The Marin Protocol is probably suitable for those instances, but other cases may not be so clear. For example, there is far less certainty when the playful spousal give-and-take turns violent and both spouses subsequently contend that the other threw the first real blow. In this case, there is much more room for personal interpretation as both partners may believe themselves to have been the victim. This type of case may not lend itself to a solution involving the Marin Protocol.

Another factor to consider for selection of the Marin Protocol is the real importance of the contested issue: the difference in testimony must also be over something truly central to the case, not just a tangential point that does not directly bear on a core issue. It is a waste of time and effort to conduct testing over something that really does not matter to the case. Similarly, if other irrefutable evidence exists that resolves the subject, there is little to gain by polygraphing on the same subject. To polygraph on issues that have little relevance or added value to the case might be considered an abuse of the Marin Protocol. Returning again to the example of the missing jewelry from the safety deposit box, if this incident were central to a household property contest between spouses, the Marin Protocol may help settle the matter. However, if this were a child custody dispute, polygraph testing on missing jewelry is not justified and should not be considered. Likewise, when there is irrefutable evidence such as bank records and video recording that shows that only one spouse visited the safety deposit box at the time the jewelry disappeared, the Marin Protocol would not be useful.

Examiner competency is also essential, and should not be taken for granted. Since the National Research Council has determined that the median accuracy for the polygraph is 86%, and it is probable that not all examiners are equally gifted, there must be some examiners whose personal best is somewhere below 86%. Polygraphers such as these, or for whom no meaningful accuracy data exists, should not be used for the Marin Protocol because their involvement will not satisfy the assumption of adequate accuracy. As in many other fields, verification of the proficiency of polygraph examiners can be somewhat difficult. Longevity in the profession is not a reliable indicator of competence, nor is the source of training, number of examinations, academic title, current or former agency employment, or membership in professional organizations. Verification requires a careful and independent test of the examiner's real skills.

One source is where examiners have participated in a published polygraph study and individual decision accuracy was reported and found to meet the minimum. To be a fair test of competency, the data set must be large enough to give a reliable estimate, and the examination protocol must match field practices. There are only a small number of polygraphers who have undergone this test.

Another essential requirement is the manner in which the polygraph examination is conducted. To ensure that the examiner can achieve the minimum level of accuracy, the testing must use one of the single-issue techniques. This means that the relevant questions must all cover the same issue so that truthfulness to one relevant question ensures truthfulness to all relevant questions, and deception to one is deception to all. Multiple-issue or multiple-facet examinations do not satisfy this condition. Using the safety deposit box example again, the relevant question should cover only whether the examinee took the jewelry. Including a relevant question regarding the knowledge of who did steal the jewelry would violate the single-issue requirement. For example, if only one person *could* have stolen the jewelry, then they both know who did it, reducing any value this question might offer.

Not only does the examiner have to use a single-issue technique, but he or she must also use one that has been subject to replicated and published scientific research that shows that the technique can achieve the required level of accuracy (see ASTM standard *Conduct of Research in Psychophysiological Detection of Deception*). This is an exclusive list. In 2011 the American Polygraph Association established a committee to evaluate the state of the evidence up to that time, and the association published the committee report in *Polygraph* in December of that year. It has been updated since, and a summary is found in Appendix B.

Once the test method has been properly chosen and conducted, the examiner must employ a numerical scoring system appropriate for this application. Because of the unique nature of the setting for the Marin Protocol, the numerical scoring systems in common practice requires adjustment to ensure fairness. Most polygraph scoring systems have decision rules that show better sensitivity for detecting deception than for detecting truthfulness. This is not a shortcoming of the polygraph or the techniques, but simply that the decision rules were established for criminal investigations rather than for paired testing applications. It is important in criminal investigations that the culprit does not fall off the radar, so the threshold for decisions of deception is set lower than in other settings. For the quasievidentiary conditions of the Marin Protocol, a different set of decision rules are needed to provide an evenhanded accuracy for both truthful and deceptive examinees. Various scoring and decision methods are discussed in Chapter 5.

In terms of instrumentation, it is recommended that a computer polygraph be used. It is not a requirement of the Marin Protocol, but these instruments permit analyses of the physiological data that are more difficult or not possible with older analog instrumentation. This includes evaluation by specialized software and decision algorithms. Moreover, some inadequacies in the initial recording, such as improper gain settings or out-of-range tracings can be corrected offline only with computer polygraphs. Because Marin Protocol cases are usually subject to independent quality control evaluation, there are advantages to having the physiological recordings in digital form for the instantaneous electronic transmission of the data to reviewers, and the printing of high-fidelity copies. Computer polygraphs have been in examiners' hands since 1980s, and the older analog instrumentation are currently used by a very small and shrinking minority of practitioners.

Regardless of whether the instrumentation is analog or digital, the following data channels should be recorded:

1. Breathing, monitored by two strain gauges.
2. Electrodermal conductivity or resistance using silver/silver chloride sensors.
3. Cardiovascular activity, recorded with a blood pressure cuff.
4. Motion sensor, for the detection of covert movements.
5. (Optional) Photoplethysmograph, to record vasomotor activity.

As in all polygraph examinations, the testing room must be quiet, free of distractions, and comfortable. The Marin Protocol does not prohibit attorneys or other representatives from sitting in the examination room, but it is recommended that advocates for either side not be present during testing to reduce any appearance of undue influence on the process. If advocates insist that they witness the examination, they may monitor the session remotely by closed circuit television. An additional requirement of the Marin Protocol is the audiovisual recording of the session, intended for use by the independent quality control, but the same camera can also provide live feed to a monitor for parties interested in viewing the examination. In this way, the integrity of the examination can be maintained.

CONCLUSION

The Marin Protocol cannot solve all instances of false courtroom testimony. The current perjury detection system is weak, relying to a large extent on the deterrent effects of oaths under God. This method has fallen far short of ensuring truthful testimony from witnesses who are motivated to protect self-interests.

The Paired Testing process is a carefully crafted procedure that can be put into play only under very narrow conditions. When circumstances permit, it is a powerful tool for those who would speak the truth in court.

TESTING VICTIMS OF TRAUMATIC EVENTS

Seasoned polygraph examiners will agree that some of the more challenging tests they have performed are confirmatory testing of claimed victims of violence. The most frequent victims seen by law enforcement are those of sexual assault, women (and men) who have been brought to the polygraph because there is at least some evidence that the reported crime did not occur, or happened differently from what the alleged victim claims. Unlike testing of virtually all other criminal suspects, in these cases the question is what the crime is and who the criminal is: either the victim's allegation is true and the police must pursue the culprit, or the allegation is false and the complainant has committed the crime of submitting a false report.

In this section we will use the term "victim" to characterize the examinee who has made an allegation of criminal physical harm. We do so recognizing that some who purport victimization are reporting falsely. It is our view that the victim only converts to a suspect when evidence or an admission supports this change in status. The preponderance of the empirical field studies bolsters the view that most rape allegations are true. False reports range from 2% to 8%, depending on the criteria used to assess their veracity. For this reason, all self-reported victims must be treated with sensitivity until it is confirmed that they are making a false allegation.

In Chapter 3 it was explained that good relevant questions evoke an associated memory in the examinee. This memory establishes the salience of the relevant test questions. When testing suspects this is the best approach. When testing victims, the use of relevant questions that stimulate recollections of a traumatizing event has a fairly obvious problem: was the subsequent physiological response a consequence of deception or the recall of the disturbing crime? The very nature of victim testing, therefore, can call for a deviation from the standard approach.

That said, it is helpful to note that not all victims are traumatized by the reported event. Some may have exceptional coping skills, or sufficient time has passed so that the recollection of the assault is not unsettling. The recommendations found here apply best to where trauma is suspected or evident.

It may be helpful to look at these kinds of tests from a different perspective: the examiner is not testing the victim regarding the event, as one would when testing a suspect, but only her statement about the event. The central issue, then, is whether the statement is true or false. It is from this vantage that many of our recommendations follow.

RECOMMENDATIONS

Testing of victims should never be the first choice. In point of fact, testing of the victim should never be undertaken unless there is strong evidence that the allegation is false. When possible the first test should be of the suspect, if known. Only if the suspect agrees to testing, and the results prove favorable to the suspect, should polygraph be considered for the victim. It may also be very helpful to the investigation if testing of the suspect included a form of recognition testing, such as the Peak of Tension or Concealed Information Test.

Virtually all police polygraph examiners recommend a reasonable period between the incident and the victim's polygraph examination. There is no research on what the optimal period should be, and it primarily would be a function of the physical and emotional state of the victim. The standard delay is often 72 h, but it should be recognized that any fixed period would be arbitrary. Each case should be thoughtfully weighed according to the circumstances.

One method of mitigating the emotional baggage that comes with testing on a traumatizing event is to have the victim provide a brief written statement about the incident, and conduct the polygraph testing about the veracity of the statement. Keep in mind that victims may leave out details that are embarrassing to them, and may not remember every detail. This written statement is not the same as the official complaint to police, but merely a tool to aid the polygraph process in assessing whether the crime occurred. Statements for the purpose of testing should be kept short, and deal as much as possible with the core issue.

For victims of sexual offenses, examiners should not use probable- or directed-lie questions on the topic of sex. Not only are sex questions less effective in this context, they leave the impression that the victim's previous sexual history is at issue. Rather, inasmuch as the main issue is the validity of the statement the victim has given, comparison questions should address lying in nonsexual matters, such as to persons in authority or to avoid trouble.

For polygraph testing of female victims where the examiner is male, arrangements should be made to have second female present during the examination. The female witnessing the examination should be mature, have no connection to the examinee, and be neutral as regards the case. This third party should not participate in the examination process.

If the examination is to be monitored in an observation room, only the investigating personnel and legal representation should view the session. None of the victim's family or friends should ever observe.

Unlike suspect testing, relevant questions can be constructed to be answered "yes" for victims. Examiners should use a testing technique with a minimum of relevant questions. Given the scrutiny these types of examinations can attract, examiners should strictly adhere to the protocols of validated testing and scoring methods.

REFERENCES

Abrams, A., Abrams, J., 1993. Polygraph Testing of the Pedophile. Ryan Gwinner Press, Portland, OR.

Abrams, S., Ogard, E., 1986. Polygraph surveillance of probationers. Polygraph 15 (3), 174–181.

American Polygraph Association, 2009. Model policy for post-conviction sex offender testing. Polygraph 38, 167–183.

American Society for Testing and Materials, 2011a. Conduct of research in psychophysiological detection of deception. Available at http://www.astm.org.

American Society for Testing and Materials, 2011b. Standard guide for paired PDD testing. Available at http://www.astm.org.

Bromberg, D.S., O'Donohue, W.T., 2014. Toolkit for Working with Juvenile Sex Offenders. Academic Press, Waltham, MA.

Bryant, W.G., 1989. Disclosing hidden assets: plea bargains and use of the polygraph. Police Executive Research Forum, No. 87-DD-CX-K090.

Cooley-Towell, S., Pasini-Hill, D., Patrick, D., 2000. The value of post-conviction polygraph: the importance of sanctions. Polygraph 29 (1), 6–19.

Horvath, F.S., Reid, J.E., 1972. The polygraph silent answer test. J. Crim. Law Criminol. Police Sci. 63 (2), 285–293.

Komet, A., 1997. The truth about lying. Psychology Today. Available at http://www.psychologytoday.com/articles/199704/the-truth-about-lying.

Marin, J., 2000. He said/she said: polygraph evidence in court. Polygraph 29 (4), 299–304.

Marin, J., 2001. The ASTM exclusionary standard and the APA "litigation certificate" program. Polygraph 30 (4), 288–293.

McGrath, R.J., Cumming, G.F., Hoke, S.E., Bonn-Miller, M.O., 2007. Outcomes in a community sex offender treatment program: a comparison between polygraphed and matched non-polygraphed offenders. Sex. Abuse J. Res. Treat. 19 (4), 381–393.

McGrath, R.J., Cumming, G.F., Burchard, B.L., Zeoli, S., Ellerby, L., 2010. Current Practices and Emerging Trends in Sexual Abuser Management: The Safer Society 2009 North American Survey. Safer Society Press, Brandon, VT.

National Research Council, 2003. The Polygraph and Lie Detection. National Academies Press, Washington, DC.

Reid, J.E., Inbau, F.E., 1977. Truth and Deception: The Polygraph ("Lie Detection") Technique. Williams & Wilkins, Baltimore, MD.

Tubman-Carbone, H., 2009. An Exploratory Study of New Jersey's Sex Offender Polygraph Policy: Report to the New Jersey State Parole Board. New Jersey State Parole Board, Trenton, NJ. Retrieved from http://media.nj.com/ledgerupdates_impact/other/11.18.09%20polygraph%20report.pdf.

CHAPTER

Alternate technologies

12

> *The known is finite, the unknown infinite; intellectually we stand on an islet in the midst of an illimitable ocean of inexplicability. Our business in every generation is to reclaim a little more land.*
> **Thomas Henry Huxley**

With the rapid advance in sensor technology, computer power, and algorithms, the field of credibility assessment has witnessed a procession of technologies and devices over recent years touted as a replacement for the polygraph. These methods are often portrayed as being more modern, and by implication they are better than the polygraph.

The characterization of the polygraph as old technology has a ring of truth. With the exception of computerization, the device has not changed substantially since Keeler's polygraph patent in the 1920s. That said, no other technology has successfully competed against the polygraph for the dominant position in all that time, despite recurring predictions that its days were numbered. One may wonder how that can be.

The polygraph may seem simple and old fashioned, but it has also proven remarkably resilient to challenges posed by newer technologies that aim to push it aside. This durability has surprised most observers, frustrated dozens of competitors, and confounded generations of critics. The reasons for the polygraph's longevity may be difficult to nail down precisely, but it may speak to the simple power to consistently deliver what it is designed to do. The polygraph is certainly not the first technology to enjoy an extended life. A parallel example might be found in the automobile engine. Karl Benz developed a reliable internal combustion engine for automobiles in the 1870s. Many years and many inventions have since come and gone, and despite the dedication of immense fortunes to develop alternatives, experts do not see a viable substitute for the gas-powered car emerging for a while. From this, one might conclude that the age of a technology alone does not necessarily imply obsolescence.

The invention of a better "lie detector" technology is inevitable in the long run, of course, and the polygraph will one day be replaced as assuredly as will be the gasoline engine. It is axiomatic that the new will always replace the old (witness the long-delayed but ultimate fate of Edison's phonograph and incandescent light bulb). It is helpful to note, though, that not every "new" becomes *the* replacement for the old. Indeed, most do not. In the field of credibility assessment, "new" has not yet translated to "better." The daunting complexity involved in assessing human veracity is underestimated by those not well grounded in the field. Unfortunately, the majority of new methods introduced to the market have been the product of businessmen, field practitioners, engineers, or others who do not have the skills, or independence, to determine whether their methods are actually valid and reliable. Added to these conditions, there are really no checks and balances to protect the public from bogus lie detectors, and there have been more than a few. Inevitably, invalid methods are revealed and discarded, but often not before some form of human suffering was experienced. There are sound reasons for viewing with skepticism any approach to credibility assessment that was developed outside the bounds of good science.

Even with a solid scientific foundation, most new credibility assessment technologies will fail to gain broad acceptance. This is due in large part to unfamiliarity with the needs of investigators and the nature of investigations: what seems like a good idea to scientists is often not all that useful to those in the field. It may be helpful, then, to review some of the critical characteristics of a useful credibility assessment technology for the benefit of those who would venture into research and development for the instrument that will supersede the polygraph.

- For the widest applicability, the technology must be useful in deception detection, not just recognition detection. Despite the validity of paradigms such as the Concealed Information Test, recognition testing cannot be used in areas such as applicant screening or offender monitoring where the polygraph is commonly used. Recognition testing fits best in criminal investigations, a subset of all polygraph applications.
- It must be easily accessible. Restrictions imposed by the technology's expense, portability, significant manpower requirements, or costly training will work against its fielding.
- There are additional challenges with physiologically based methods. Because physiological signals are noisy, and can be influenced by environmental factors acting on the examinee, the degree of control exercised over the examinee's environment will set the upper bounds for how much validity the technology can deliver. Unconstrained settings offer the greatest challenges, where reliable deception detection will be severely limited.
- To be effective in the long run, the technology must be valid and reliable; its ability to prompt confessions alone is insufficient. Interrogation props may initially be effective, especially those with an aura of science, but validity shortcomings are ultimately discovered by users. Only valid methods are sustainable.
- Invasiveness, real or perceived, will reduce the number of individuals willing to undergo testing by the technology.
- Credibility assessment is not simply a hardware/software project. The link between the detected signal and the act of deception must be established. New sensors, even

those with exquisite sensitivity or remarkable standoff range, are not useful without a test and analysis protocol for deception detection.[1]

There is one final comment that addresses the utility of credibility assessment tools. There has been an understandable emphasis among scientific endeavors to automate as much of the process as possible, and in most cases, completely. One heretofore neglected problem has to do with the limits of automated credibility assessment methods in general: They can better handle the detection of deception than uncovering the truth. Said more simply, the good ones may be able to determine that an examinee's statement is false, but getting at the truth often involves a less structured interaction with the examinee after the testing to find out what the single truth actually is. After all, the opposite of a falsehood may be another falsehood. A purely automated test is limited in the flexibility required to educe the truth. This might better be illustrated with an example from a typical polygraph screening examination.

Suppose that a police candidate is taking a polygraph examination and wishes to hide the fact that she had tried an illicit drug once about 2 years earlier. During the pretest interview of the polygraph examination, she denies ever trying any illegal drug, and during the screening test, she physiologically responds to the corresponding question. From the polygraph response, it is reasonable to conclude that there is information the examinee is withholding, but the polygraph result does not reveal what the information is. It may be significant or minor, disqualifying or irrelevant to a hiring decision. The mere detection of deception, therefore, is insufficient. The standard polygraph procedure would be for the examiner to tell the examinee of her reaction to the drug question, and to solicit an explanation. A good interviewer would be successful in obtaining the minor admission about what the examinee is hiding, and then retest her to determine whether this new detail represents the whole truth. The information, combined with the test results, can be very useful to hiring officials. It is this iterative process leading to new information that adds value over the results alone.

Returning to the use of completely automated systems, the same scenario with another valid technology would lead to the conclusion that the applicant had been untruthful to the drug topic. Unless there is a follow-up with a skilled interviewer, plus the opportunity for additional tailored testing, the initial test results indicating deception becomes the end of the process. It is unknowable, therefore, whether the

---

[1] By way of example, in the 1990s, a vendor of a technology that could detect thermal changes on the inner ear approached the US government advocating its potential for lie detection, despite the absence of any research suggesting a link between deception and eardrum heat. Ideas from other vendors have included sensors placed in furniture for lie detection during unstructured interviews, and the aiming of thermal cameras in the face of suspects during free-flowing interrogations. Another offered a video game where the examinee would try to guide a ball through a virtual maze while undergoing questioning. In an unsolicited proposal for terrorist detection at airports, a vendor suggested the showing of pictures of cartoon characters carrying guns, bombs, and other weapons while the ticketing agent monitored the electrodermal activity of ticket purchasers. A fatal error of each of these proposals was the misapprehension that technology alone was the key to lie detection.

examinee is hiding a trivial drug experimentation or a lifetime of addiction. The examinee's location in this continuum of possible behaviors can make a substantial difference to hiring officials. Some levels of drug involvement are regarded as acceptable, and others as instantly disqualifying. Simply reacting to a polygraph test question about drugs is not fully informative, therefore. Similarly, in the national security domain, inadvertent disclosures of government secrets to one's spouse are viewed much less seriously than wholesale delivery of highly sensitive documents to a foreign power or terror group. Reacting to the test question about revealing classified information is not adequate in itself to answer which of these behaviors, or others, took place. Some automated systems can develop information offered by examinees (e.g., automated interviews, self-report instruments, etc.) while others can validate it through testing, but currently none can do *both*. An inability to perform both functions iteratively may impose a practical limit on automated credibility assessment systems to testing only on questions where test results are sufficient in themselves (e.g., specific events where it is known what happened), or perhaps as an initial screening tool for large populations to help prioritize individuals for other screening or investigative methods.

There are encouraging lines of research that could satisfy many of the requirements listed earlier, and this chapter covers those that would seem to be the most promising. Some are in their earliest stages, existing only as demonstration systems that can track physiological events. Others have gone through validation and some fielding, and are awaiting the proper problem set before achieving wider use. Most, though not all, are at a stage where a single physiological phenomenon (e.g., pulse, electrophysiological potentials, and pupillary dilation) is monitored using a single sensor or several sensors of the same type. As such, they are not projected to function in the role currently served by the polygraph, though they may be better suited than the polygraph for other, perhaps niche, applications.

EVENT-RELATED POTENTIALS

The brain is a bioelectric organ. It is composed of about 80-90 billion neurons, more or less, each communicating with other neurons through the transmission of electrical impulses down the length of the cell. Some sources suggest that the human brain has upward of 100 trillion connections among these cells. The sheer number of connections combined with the level of activity of individual neural cells produces an unimaginable number of miniscule electrical impulses. All psychological activity is based on these impulses in extraordinarily complex ways that scientists are trying to decipher.

HOW IT WORKS

When groups of neurons fire together, they create a signal, or brainwave, that can sometimes be detected with sensors placed on the scalp. The strength of the brainwave can depend on the number of neurons, their orientation, the co-occurrence of their firing, and their distance from the sensors. Since their discovery in the late 1920s, brainwaves have offered scientists a very useful view of how the brain processes internal and external stimuli, and how the brain gives rise to the mind. The timing, scalp distribution, and possible brain sources of these waves can be used to explore psychological processes, some of which could be implicated in the act of deceiving.

Researchers began testing the idea of using event-related potentials (ERPs; brainwaves) as early as the 1980s for recognition testing in the lie detection context (Miyake et al., 1986; Rosenfeld et al., 1987). The most promising of them is the P300, which derives its name from the positivity of signal occurring about 300 ms after presentation of the stimuli.

The P300 is evoked by relatively rare but salient stimuli. Laboratory studies of the P300 in credibility assessment use visual or auditory stimuli of three types—irrelevant, target, and probe. Subjects are presented stimuli at a regular pace of 2-3 s, and are instructed to press one button when the stimulus is irrelevant and a second button when the stimulus is a target. The target stimuli are established before testing and represent 20% of the stimulus presentations or less in most studies. They are intentionally placed among the stimulus presentations to evoke a P300 response inasmuch as they are given salience by virtue of the task of identifying them with a different button press. The relative rarity of target items has led scientists to dub the procedure the "oddball paradigm." The probe stimuli are the concealed details related to the crime which the experimenter wants to determine whether the subject recognizes. They are also shown 20% of the time, or less. To the innocent examinee, the probe would be interpreted as an irrelevant item, whereas the guilty examinee would recognize the probe and produce a P300. The stimuli are presented dozens of times, and the signals are averaged for the three types of stimuli. Averaged neutral items do not evoke a sizeable P300 response while the target items normally do. The ERPs for the probe items are compared to those from the neutral and target items to determine which of the two they most closely resemble. This involves very intense calculations only possible with computers. In commercially available systems, statistical decisions are produced by algorithms in the software.

POTENTIAL IN LIE DETECTION

Discrimination between individuals with concealed information and those who do not is quite high. Laboratory research typically reports accuracy between 85% and 95%, and higher accuracy reported in the research by developers of commercial systems. These accuracies are generally better than those that rely upon responses from the peripheral nervous system (e.g., polygraph), and for concealed-information approach, the P300 may be a preferred method in some settings. The placement of sensors and the activation of the instrumentation are teachable to nonspecialists, removing one barrier to fielding the technology. There are no known health or safety hazards to either operators or examinees when used properly.

There are only a few disadvantages with the use of brainwaves in criminal investigation. First, the existing approaches are restricted to only tests of concealed information. Cases in which this approach is possible represent a very small minority of all cases where the polygraph is currently used. Combining this limitation with the substantial cost of ERP systems, their perceived value to departments and agencies could be affected. Second, brainwave techniques are no more immune to countermeasures than are polygraph techniques. Hopes that a shift to a central nervous system method would make them resistant to examinee manipulation have not been realized. Simple muscular movements of the eyes or jaw can produce electrical signals that obscure the much more subtle ones from the brain. Finally, advocates of a method that entails sensors that directly monitor the brain using scalp electrodes will face a significant public relations challenge. The image of being crowned with a wire-laden skull cap or band does little to reassure those who may find the method intrusive.

The P300 test remains a viable method in criminal investigation owing to its solid scientific foundation and relative ease of use. So long as it is limited to tests of concealed information, however, it may remain only a niche technology, suited to special circumstances. The prospect remains that brainwave research will uncover an approach that satisfies the field's need for a deception detection technology.

FUNCTIONAL MAGNETIC RESONANCE IMAGING

Another central nervous system approach to credibility assessment was made possible with the development of the functional magnetic resonance imaging (fMRI). One method showing progress is called blood oxygen level dependent (BOLD) method, which uses the concentration of oxygenated blood as a marker in the brain. While the science underlying the BOLD method is substantial, its transition as a credibility assessment tool from laboratory demonstration to field deployment has been plagued by technical limitations, premature commercialization, and excessive extrapolation by public media and critics. The fMRI in lie detection is yet immature, though it will not always be so.

HOW IT WORKS

It has long been known that oxygenated and deoxygenated blood have different effects on magnetic fields. Pioneering work in the 1990s demonstrated that the fMRI could exploit these effects to create a three-dimensional image that showed which brain structures were activated by certain tasks. Active neurons require additional energy, but because the brain cannot store glucose, the vascular system transports nutrients and oxygen to feed the neurons. The relatively greater amount of oxygenated blood in activated brain structures allows researchers to detect those structures from surrounding brain tissues containing less oxygenated blood. By imaging the brain with the fMRI system, scientists are able to locate those regions associated with a cognitive task or overt behavior.

POTENTIAL IN LIE DETECTION

If the act of deception is a unique and distinct cognitive process, it is reasonable to hypothesize that specific areas of the brain would be involved. In this light, the fMRI's potential in credibility assessment becomes obvious. Scientists merely need to identify those areas in someone's brain that are activated by deception but are not involved in preparing truthful statements. Though simple in concept, it has proven a stubbornly difficult feat to realize. If the remaining substantial technical hurdles can be overcome, fMRI could become the ultimate "lie detector" owing to its unique ability to reveal the construction of lies at the source. It is from this perspective that scientists began exploring the potential of fMRI for credibility assessment.

Initial indications from group data were the basis for optimism (Kozel et al., 2005; Langleben et al., 2002), with classification accuracies meeting or exceeding those of the polygraph. Significant challenges have arisen with regard to individual differences, countermeasures, nonoverlapping processes for different kinds of lies, and going beyond veracity decisions for groups and obtaining them for single individuals. Once resolved, cost pressures, the limited number of possible testing sites, and the technology's lack of portability will impose more constraints than experienced by the polygraph and make it less competitive as a replacement. Moreover, thorny legal and public policy issues await if the method is to be turned to purposes where it might offer the most benefit: courtroom evidence, selection of public safety employees, and granting access to national secrets.

These difficulties notwithstanding, functional brain imaging is considered by many as the technology that could achieve the greatest accuracy in detecting deception. Reaching this level will take much more time and funding to accomplish and is not expected in the near term. Due to limits discussed earlier, the fMRI is also not a strong candidate to replace the polygraph. It may fulfill its greatest potential in settings where the higher costs and lower availability of the fMRI are offset by the exceptional accuracy ultimately anticipated from the technology.

THERMAL IMAGING

The detection of infrared radiation has a long scientific genealogy going back to the latter part of the nineteenth century, when inventor and astronomer Samuel Pierpont Langley devised a mechanism so sensitive that it could detect the thermal radiation of a cow at a distance of 400 m. Advances in the field a few years later were directed toward such problems as long-distance detection of icebergs, steam ships, and forest fires. In more recent times, thermal imaging with sophisticated cameras has found a broad range of uses, including energy conservation, rescue operations, medical diagnostics, and countless industrial, law enforcement, and military applications.

HOW IT WORKS

Activation of the sympathetic nervous system can trigger several body responses; among them are increased sweating, greater contractile force in the heart, shunting of blood from the extremities to the major muscles, changes in respiration, and increased cutaneous blood perfusion. Some of the responses alter the heat signature emitted by the body. Thermal imaging can identify differences in temperature with impressive sensitivity as well as with great temporal and spatial resolution. Tracking temperature differences over time and over area can reveal certain physiological processes, some of which may be useful in inferring physiological states, and by extension, deception.

POTENTIAL IN LIE DETECTION

In a test of concept, Pavlidis et al. (2002) conducted analyses of temperature changes about the eyes of examinees undergoing polygraph testing regarding a mock crime and reported an accuracy with thermal data that exceeded those of the experienced polygraphers conducting the exams.[2] See a typical thermal image in Figure 12.1. Subsequent work found that thermal imaging can be used to derive pulse (Garbey et al., 2007) and breathing (Fei and Pavlidis, 2010). There is further research interest in developing a thermal capability to monitor pore openings, an analog to the electrodermal response (SBIR/STTR, 2012). This field is in its infancy, and detection of other heat-related physiological responses may be discovered in future research.

Current research trends show that thermal imaging can monitor different physiological systems. It has the additional attractive feature of being able to do so without contact sensors. If remaining technical challenges can be overcome, thermal imaging may find a role in traditional "lie detection" settings, or in other applications where its unique capabilities make it a better choice than the polygraph or other technologies, especially in less structured circumstances.

Disadvantages attendant to thermal imaging may include the significant cost of thermal cameras and analysis software, though these may abate over time. There are also complex technical hurdles in accommodating aspect changes (head turning), ambient temperature, individual differences, and the prospect of signal degradation caused by metabolic factors.

---

[2] The findings of this study warrant closer examination. Pavlidis et al. (2002) reported an average decision accuracy of 83% for the thermal approach, and 70% for the polygraphers on the same 20 laboratory subjects. Absent from the report, however, is that there were actually 32 cases in which thermal and polygraph data were collected, not 20. Five cases were subsequently excluded because the examinee fell asleep or failed to properly complete the mock crime, leaving 27 usable cases. For the polygraph, there was one false positive and no false negatives among these 27 cases, for an overall decision accuracy of 95% if seven inconclusive results are not counted as errors. If the seven cases excluded by the thermal analysis can similarly be considered inconclusive, the inconclusive rate for the two technologies was identical. Given these assumptions and including all usable cases, the decision accuracy of the polygraph would actually have been higher than that of the thermal approach. The thermal data from seven cases were not used by the researchers because the subjects had not been sufficiently responsive in the thermal spectrum, possibly due to metabolic factors resulting of having eaten lunch before their tests were conducted. Pavlidis (personal communication) indicated the above information was included in their original manuscript, but had been redacted by the publication editors.

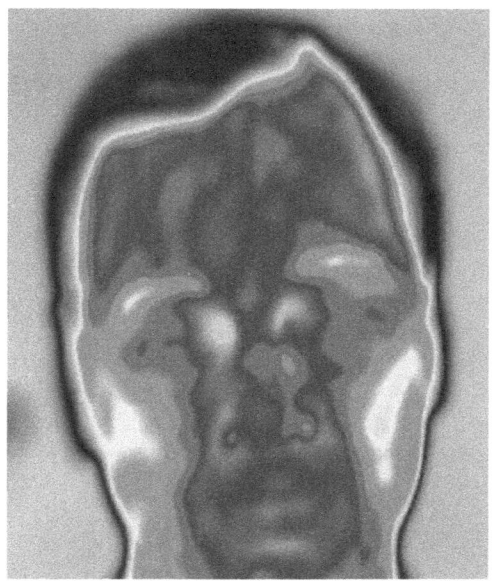

FIGURE 12.1

Thermal image of the principal author. Areas of interest in deception detection appear in this image as bright spots near the inside corner of each eye.

SACCADIC EYE MOVEMENT

Rapid individual eye movements are called saccades. In humans and many animals, saccades are used to gather visual information in the most efficient way, by moving from interesting point to interesting point, allowing the construction of mental maps of the salient segments of the visual scene. As you read this text, your eyes are not smoothly scanning over the words at an even pace, but rather they are jumping rapidly between fixation points. Your eyes may jump back to reread certain portions, then move ahead after the information requirement has been satisfied. The speed of those jumps cannot be controlled: saccades occur at the quickest speed the eyes can manage. And, you do not perceive visual information between saccades. Though your eyes continue to function during the jumps, neural mechanisms inhibit the otherwise blurred images from being perceived.

HOW IT WORKS

The least intrusive means for eye tracking involves directing an infrared illuminator toward the eye and registering the reflection with a special camera. As the eye moves, the angle of the reflection changes in a corresponding way. The subject is shown images or videos, and by triangulation the gaze and fixation points of the subject can be calculated using the reflected infrared light. Plotting the pattern over the original image shows researchers the areas of interest, the sequence of the fixation points, and the amount of time at, and between, fixation points.

Saccades are not under conscious control once they have been initiated. This feature of saccades can therefore be exploited as an avenue to assess a subject's informational needs, visual efficiency strategies, and possible pathologies. Saccades have been studied extensively in psychology and play a key role in research regarding driver fatigue, ergonomics, immersive virtual reality, and to facilitate communication for the physically handicapped, among many other areas. With the growth of the Internet, saccades have also attracted enormous commercial interest as they can be used to determine optimal placement of advertising.

One area of particular interest to credibility assessment scientists is whether familiar and unfamiliar images produce differences in visual efficiency strategies. If so, eye tracking may be useful as a recognition test, determining whether a suspect has previously seen a crime scene or victim despite his denials.

POTENTIAL IN LIE DETECTION

There are several types of eye behavior: pupillary response, saccadic movements, fixation selection, fixation time, etc. A declassified 1974 research report to the US government pointed to differences in the number of fixations on visual material for guilty and innocent groups (Hall and Rosenberger, 1974). The chief limitations at that time were computer power and exploration of other phenomena that could improve discrimination to the individual level.

As technology improved, the US government again took an interest in eye movement for deception detection. Cohen et al. (1992) completed a series of five experiments wherein they were able to classify individual subjects significantly better than chance as to whether they were viewing familiar or unfamiliar faces. Similar results were found when showing them familiar and unfamiliar buildings. These findings were the basis of new hope that a standoff technology might be effective in deception detection. Research interest has since waned in this area, however.

Because eye tracking is minimally intrusive, and requires only that the examinee look at a series of images, it is an attractive technology. Compared to other alternatives, it is neither costly nor difficult to operate. There are few disadvantages though the drawbacks may be significant to many field users. One is that images must be carefully prepared. This entails photo editing to remove any secondary information in the key and neutral images beyond what the subject is to be tested for. The editing can be time-consuming, and would very difficult to automate. In addition, all images should show the same aspect of the object of interest inasmuch as changing the point of view can alter the gaze pattern. Creating a bank of images may offset the per-use cost of image development, but would require a commitment from a department or agency to invest in it. Complicating the matter is that investigators must have proper images of the person or thing to be used during the test, which is not always easily accomplished.

The principal shortcoming that may be insurmountable is that this approach is inescapably a recognition test, and as with other technologies in this category, cannot be used nearly as often as a deception test. Also, there has been no countermeasure research published for eye tracking, and it is not yet known how resistant it is to subject manipulation. However, eye tracking has been shown to be effective using another paradigm, in the oculomotor deception test (ODT) which is taken up next.

OCULOMOTOR DECEPTION TEST

Advances in instrumentation that captured multiple channels of eye behavior simultaneously (e.g., gaze trace, fixation duration, pupil size) along with better computers introduced the possibility of creating a fully automated deception test. If this approach proved to be valid, it would be one of the most useful of the emerging approaches to credibility assessment. In the screening context, it might be added to existing vetting processes for security clearances, visa applications, and informant validation, among other law enforcement and government functions.

HOW IT WORKS

Two forms of eye behavior are used, saccades and pupil responses, in a reading and responding paradigm. Tracking of saccades (see previous section) has been used for many years to help scientists understand reading behavior and its underlying cognitive processes. Pupillary responses have long been known to be associated with fear, attraction, interest, workload, and the orienting response. Better technologies have allowed for the simultaneous recording of these eye behaviors, and to correlate them with deception.

POTENTIAL IN LIE DETECTION

The relationship between anxiety and pupillary dilation was established more than a century ago (Bumke, 1904), and the value of the pupillary response in "lie detection" was recognized before and during World War II (Berrien, 1940; Berrien and Huntington, 1943). In later years, the pupillary response was investigated by polygraph researchers (Bradley and Janisse, 1979; Webb et al., 2009) as an additional data channel to conventional polygraphy. Similarly, saccades have attracted intermittent interest by other lie detection researchers (Baker et al., 1990; Berrien, 1942; Hall and Rosenberger, 1974; Pennebaker and Chew, 1985). While all of the research was encouraging, validities of the approaches were not sufficient for fielding the technologies.

It was not until more recently that a novel paradigm was devised using reading of text, which showed more promise (Cook et al., 2012). Anne Cook and her colleagues developed and tested an approach using eye movements, pupillary responses, fixations, blinks, and reaction time while subjects silently read true-false questions and then clicked an answer on a computer screen. The paradigm and measures were then assessed in a variety of laboratory studies to refine the procedures and maximize

FIGURE 12.2

Commercial oculomotor deception test.

Photo courtesy of Converus, Inc.

accuracy, and then the device was placed in field settings to test against polygraph screening. Laboratory studies pointed to a classification accuracy similar to the polygraph, and field studies showed a correlation between the results of the two technologies.

The ODT could be fully automated, thereby limiting human involvement to introducing examinees to the system and fulfilling administrative functions. The testing protocol is completed within 1 h in most circumstances, and because there are no sensors attached to the examinee, perceptions of intrusiveness of the technology are mitigated. The ODT system is portable, relatively inexpensive, and satisfies the requirement to be considered a deception test. It is among the strongest candidate technologies to compete with the polygraph, though it may fit other non-polygraph applications better. See Figure 12.2 for an example of the system setup.

One drawback of the ODT system is that a minimum degree of reading fluency is necessary, a requirement not universally met. Another is that there remains work to be done to adjust the system for the sentence structure and reading behaviors attendant to non-Western languages. Also, it is yet unknown how vulnerable the method would be to countermeasures. There could be additional problems in capturing pupil data as the result of droopy eyelids, excessive blinking, or overuse of makeup. Finally, the implementation of ODT in an iterative fashion to elicit and validate information following the initial test series has not been demonstrated.

LASER DOPPLER VIBROMETRY

Noncontact and standoff systems for detection of deception have been proposed and studied for decades. They are expected to be perceived as less invasive by examinees, and in the case of the polygraph blood pressure cuff, more comfortable. There has also been hopefulness that it might be useful in non-polygraph settings, perhaps even covertly. Interest in noncontact physiology was boosted in the years following the terror attacks of September 11, 2001, with proposals to include successful systems in passenger screening at airports.

Among the candidate noncontact systems is the Laser Doppler Vibrometer (LDV). It uses laser light reflected from the human body to detect several possible indices of physiological stress.

HOW IT WORKS

Certain biological processes produce vibrations or movements on the body's surface (e.g., breathing, heart sounds). It is possible to detect them using the Doppler Effect with laser light.

Research has progressed furthest in the detection of the pulse at the carotid artery in the neck. To do so, a video camera is used to detect the face of the examinee, and through software, the system calculates the location of the carotid artery. An eye-safe laser beam is shown against this artery from a distance of a meter or more, and the wavelength of the reflected light is compared to that of the original. A shorter wavelength (higher frequency) occurs when the object is moving toward the sensor, and longer when it is moving away. In the case of the carotid, the arterial wall pushes outward during systole and returns to resting position during diastole. The light's wavelength, therefore, can register the pulsing action of the carotid artery. The same process might be applied to the movement of the chest during breathing, or even to gestures using the limbs.

POTENTIAL IN LIE DETECTION

Initial work by Rohrbaugh et al. (2006) has explored various stress indices detectible by LDV that might be applicable to credibility assessment. They include blood pressure, pulse, respiration, body tremor, and muscle tension. Because LDV can monitor multiple channels of physiological data, it is a stronger candidate than many other polygraph alternatives. As a noncontact system, it may reduce the physical discomfort some polygraph examinees experience, thereby permitting longer periods of data collection. The lack of wires and hoses connecting the examinee to the technology can reduce psychological aversion to the testing process for some. There may also be additional diagnostic signals that can be extracted from the LDV data stream that are not available with the current polygraph sensors.

There is little research supporting the LDV in credibility assessment, however, and its validity in that application is still an open question. Some physiological activity known to be diagnostic, such as the electrodermal response, may not be available using this approach. There is also the question of cost and whether the advantages of a noncontact system warrant a greater expense that comes with it.

In a classic text on polygraph testing, Reid and Inbau (1977) discussed the use of a radio-based Doppler system to record respiration and arm movement. From this it is clear that noncontact Doppler has been available for many decades. Despite its

FIGURE 12.3

In front of the subject is a laser Doppler vibrometer noncontact system for the measurement of the pulse at the carotid artery. The sensors on the subject's fingers are photoplethysmograph and electrodermal sensors, the signals which go to the A/D converter on his forearm, part of the Preliminary Credibility Assessment Screening System. Posed by Dr. Frank Horvath, Professor Emeritus of the School of Criminal Justice of Michigan State University, now with the National Center for Credibility Assessment. Compare image in page 376 of Reid and Inbau's (1977) *Truth and Deception* text.

Photo credit: Todd Vinson.

advantages, the Doppler approach has never moved beyond a laboratory demonstration. Developers of other Doppler approaches may profit from examining why it has historically failed to gain wider acceptance. Figure 12.3 shows the setup for the LDV system.

VOICE-BASED SYSTEMS

The analysis of human speech would seem to offer an easily obtained and unobtrusive means of detecting emotional states, including stress, and possibly by inference, attempts at deception. Practical applications of an accurate system could include real-time stress assessment for certain occupations (e.g., pilots, warfighters, astronauts), as an adjunct to clinical diagnosis and treatment of anxiety-related disorders, as a standoff capability for high-stakes exchanges such as hostage and treaty negotiations, and as a tool for interviews and interrogation in a range of settings. As such, voice stress has attracted intermittent scientific attention.

The earliest scientific use of instrumentation to deconstruct the vocal spectrum in a deception paradigm was reported by Friedhoff et al. (1962), who were interested in its application in psychological assessment. Their results pointed to differences in loudness variations as a function of emotion. Later, the US Army funded a contract to examine whether a voice-based lie detector could be useful in interrogations (Decision Control Inc., 1972). Across various tests in that contracted assessment, the results were inconsistent. Despite early encouragement, a subsequent independent assessment for the US Army casts doubts on this approach to credibility assessment (Mortland, 1974).

Since that time, various devices have entered the commercial market with claims of exceptional accuracy in detection of deception. Scientific research on the commercial approaches has been almost universally disappointing with, at best, intermittent mixed results (see Eriksson and Lacerda, 2007). Most claims of effectiveness rely on anecdotes or rudimentary analyses of field samples of favorable cases.[3] There is scarce evidence to contradict the US National Research Council's (2003) conclusion that there is "little or no scientific basis for the use of the computer voice stress analyzer or similar voice measurement instruments as an alternative to the polygraph …"

One consequence of the commercialization of voice stress analysis (VSA) devices, and their subsequent debunking, has been a general impression that pursuit of a voice-based method for credibility assessment could be fruitless. This is an unfortunate conclusion, and possibly erroneous, as there are components in the human voice found by independent researchers to provide reliable, if modest, indices of emotional states. Among these components are fundamental frequency mean and range (Bulut and Narayanan, 2008), and high frequency energy, none of which would seem to have been exploited by commercial devices. Continued interest in this avenue may reveal other VSA approaches to provide viable data channels for stress and deception detection.

AUTOBIOGRAPHICAL IMPLICIT ASSOCIATION TEST

In recent years, there has been a resurgence of interest in reaction time for the detection of deception. Reaction time garnered great attention in the early years of psychoanalysis (Jung, 1919) as a means of revealing hidden "complexes," but its application in lie detection has been marked by inconsistent research results. A new paradigm called the autobiographical Implicit Association Test (aIAT) (Agosta and Sartori, 2013) has given new promise to reaction time. A relative flurry of deception-detection studies since 2008 has suggested the aIAT to be a promising method for

---

[3] An example of the latter can be found in a 2012 report by Chapman and Stathis, an article used extensively in advertising one of the commercially available voice stress analysis (VSA) devices. The report's principal author, a community college professor, examined the incidence of confessions from his own field cases. His data found an extremely high correspondence between confessions and the results of the VSA. From this, the authors concluded that VSA can significantly increase confession rates by the detection of voice stress. Questions soon arose about the validity of the article, however. For example, the journal in which it reportedly appeared is not found in any of the standard indexes used by US libraries. Indeed, no other articles could be located that came from this journal. Multiple editing errors, including a graph using Cyrillic text, raised further questions. The untimely passing of Professor Chapman prevented interested researchers from asking for clarification, and the coauthor has not filled in the gaps. Taken in toto, the article's value in assessing the validity of VSA is questionable.

determining within individuals which of two details is true. The research has even ventured into the domain of future intentions, an area where more lie-detection paradigms have feared to tread. If proven effective in additional research, the aIAT could be effective in criminal investigation, or even as a prescreening tool for applicants to positions of public trust.

Much of the research on the aIAT has been conducted by a single lab, and the question of examinees faking their reaction times is as-yet unresolved. At this time, the aIAT appears to be minimally intrusive, inexpensive, entirely automated, and potentially useful. It is a method warranting more research interest.

REFERENCES

Agosta, S., Sartori, G., 2013. The autobiographical IAT: a review. Front. Psychol. 4, 1–12 (Article 519).
Baker, L., Stern, J.A., Goldstein, R., 1990. The gaze control system and the detection of deception. Final report to the US Government for Contract #90–F131400.
Berrien, F.K., 1940. Pupillary responses as indicators of deception. Psychol. Bull. 39, 504–505.
Berrien, F.K., 1942. Ocular stability in deception. J. Appl. Psychol. 26, 55–63.
Berrien, F.K., Huntington, G.H., 1943. An exploratory study of pupillary responses during deception. J. Exp. Psychol. 32 (5), 443–449.
Bradley, M.T., Janisse, M.P., 1979. Pupil size and lie detection: the effect of certainty on detection. Psychology 16 (4), 33–39.
Bulut, M., Narayanan, S., 2008. On the robustness of overall F0-only modifications to the perception of emotions in speech. J. Acoust. Soc. Am. 123 (6), 4547–4558.
Bumke, O., 1904. Die Pupillenstörungen bei Geistes- und Nervenkrankheiten. Verlag von Gustav Fisher, Jena.
Chapman, J.L., Stathis, M., 2012. Field evaluation of effectiveness of VSA (voice stress analysis) technology in a US criminal justice setting. Criminal. Court Expert. 57, 238–251.
Cohen, N.J., McConkie, G.W., Webb, J.M., Althoff, R.R., Holden, J.A., Noll, E.L., 1992 (October). Detecting guilty knowledge using eye monitoring data. Final report to the US Government.
Cook, A.E., Hacker, D.J., Webb, A.K., Osher, D., Kristjansson, S., Woltz, D.J., Kircher, J.C., 2012. Lyin' eyes: ocular-motor measures of reading reveal deception. J. Exp. Psychol. Appl. 18 (3), 301–313.
Decision Control Inc., 1972. Detection of emotional stress by voice analysis: final report. Technical Report to the US Army Land Warfare Laboratory, No. LWL-CR-03B70.
Eriksson, A., Lacerda, F., 2007. Charlatanry in forensic speech science: a problem to be taken seriously. Int. J. Speech Lang. Law 14 (2), 169–193.
Fei, J., Pavlidis, I., 2010. Thermistor at a distance: unobtrusive measurement of breathing. IEEE Trans. Biomed. Eng. 57 (4), 988–998.
Friedhoff, A.J., Alpert, M., Kurtzberg, R.L., 1962. An effect of emotion on voice. Nature 193, 357–358.
Garbey, M., Sun, N., Merla, A., Pavlidis, I., 2007. Contact-free measurement of cardiac pulse based on the analysis of thermal imagery. IEEE Trans. Biomed. Eng. 54 (8), 1418–1426.
Hall, R.J., Rosenberger, M.A., 1974. Summary and analysis of recent Elk River experimentation, vol. 2. Report to the US Government (declassified).

Jung, C.G., 1919. Studies in Word-Association. Moffat, Yard & Co., New York.

Kozel, F.A., Johnson, K.A., Mu, Q., Grenesko, E.L., Laken, S.J., George, M.S., 2005. Detecting deception using functional magnetic resonance imaging. Biol. Psychiatry 58 (8), 605–613.

Langleben, D.D., Schroeder, L., Maldjian, J.A., Gur, R.C., McDonald, S., Ragland, J.D., O'Brien, C.P., Childress, A.R., 2002. Brain activity during simulated deception: an event-related functional magnetic resonance study. Neuroimage 15 (3), 727–732.

Miyake, Y., 1978. A study of skin resistance response, photoplethysmographic vasomotor response and eye movement indices of lie detection. Rep. Nat. Res. Inst. Pol. Sci. 31 (2), 18–24 (In Japanese).

Miyake, Y., Okita, T., Konishi, K., Matsunaga, I., 1986. Kyogi kenshutsu shihyo to shite no jisho kanren nodeni [Event-related brain potentials as in index of detection of deception]. Sci. Pol. Res. Inst. Rep. 39, 18–24 (In Japanese).

Mortland, J.E., 1974. Report Prepared for the Army Land Warfare Laboratory, vol. 2, Appendix B. Task Sheets. Battelle Columbus Laboratories. AD/A-002 573.

National Research Council, 2003. The Polygraph and Lie Detection. Committee to Review the Scientific Evidence on the Polygraph. Division of Behavioral and Social Sciences and Education, The National Academies Press, Washington, DC.

Pavlidis, I., Eberhardt, N.L., Levine, J., 2002. Human behavior: seeing through the face of deception. Nature 415, 35.

Pennebaker, J.W., Chew, C.H., 1985. Behavioral inhibition and electrodermal activity during deception. J. Pers. Soc. Psychol. 49, 1427–1433.

Reid, J.E., Inbau, F.E., 1977. Truth and Deception: The Polygraph ("Lie Detector") Technique, second ed. Williams and Wilkins, Baltimore, MD.

Rohrbaugh, J.W., Serevaag, E.J., Stern, J.A., Ryan, A.H., 2006. The physiology of threat: remote assessment using laser Doppler vibrometry. J. Credib. Assess. Witness Psychol. 7 (2), 135–145.

Rosenfeld, J.P., Nasman, V.T., Whalen, R., Cantwell, B., Mazzeri, L., 1987. Late vertex positivity in event-related potentials as a guilty knowledge indicator: a new method of lie detection. Int. J. Neurosci. 37, 125–129.

SBIR/STTR, 2012. Solicitation: standoff counter human deception detection device. http://www.sbir.gov/sbirsearch/detail/395491.

Webb, A.K., Honts, C.R., Kircher, J.C., Bernhardt, P., Cook, A.E., 2009. Effectiveness of pupil diameter in a probable-lie comparison question test for deception. Legal Crim. Psychol. 14 (2), 279–292.

Glossary[1]

0-10

3-Position scale Abbreviated form of the 7-position scale for polygraph test data analysis. The major difference is that the range of values for each comparison is from −1 to +1, rather than the range of −3 to +3 in the 7-position scoring system. This process is based on the simple and robust principle that physiological reactions of greater magnitude are caused by stimuli that are more salient to the examinee due to emotional, cognitive, or behaviorally conditioned factors.

7-Position scale System of assigning values to individual physiological responses, based on differential responding to relevant and comparison questions. The values in 7-position scoring are whole numbers between −3 and +3. By convention, negative values represent greater responding to relevant questions, while positive values indicate greater responses to comparison questions. There are three major versions of the 7-position scoring system: Backster, Utah, and Federal.

A

Acquaintance test A single test using numbers, one of which the examinee has chosen, normally conducted as the first test in an examination. The acquaintance test serves several purposes: to familiarize the examinee with the test procedures; to properly set the gains and centerings; to help detect countermeasures; and to assess the range of responsiveness of the examinee.

Adrenergic Neurons that release the neurotransmitter norepinephrine. Also, substances that mimic norepinephrine in its physiological effects.

Afferent nerves Nerve fibers that carry impulses from the periphery toward the central nervous system. Also called sensory nerves.

Air Force Modified General Question Test (AFMGQT) Polygraph comparison question testing format, used primarily within the US Government, with flexible question orderings and numbers of relevant questions. The AFMGQT can be used in single-issue, multiple-facet, and multiple-issue polygraph examinations. The AFMGQT uses relevant, probable-lie, sacrifice relevant, and irrelevant questions. Symptomatic questions are not used.

Aorta Main systemic artery from the heart. The aorta receives blood from the left ventricle through the aortic valve, normally tricuspid and having three leaflets. The upward extending portion is considered the ascending aorta, followed by a downward bend, the arch of the aorta. The portion passing through the chest is the thoracic aorta, from where the blood flows to all parts of the body.

Apnea Temporary cessation of breathing. Apnea is considered the ultimate manifestation of respiratory suppression. When they are specifically associated with certain questions during a polygraph examination, they are considered significant physiological reactions and

---

[1] These terms are derived from the 2012 *Terminology Reference for the Science of Psychophysiological Detection of Deception* (PDD) by Donald Krapohl, Mark Handler, and Shirley Sturm, and is reprinted by permission of the American Polygraph Association.

strongly diagnostic of deception. True involuntary apneas almost always take place near the bottom of the exhalation cycle.

Autonomic nervous system (ANS) In vertebrates, the system of nerves that regulates all innervated tissues and organs except striated muscle fibers. The ANS is divided into the sympathetic and parasympathetic portions. The ANS performs the vegetative functions and regulates arousal levels. All conventional polygraph methodologies monitor ANS activity. See sympathetic and parasympathetic nervous systems.

Axon The long central process of a neuron. A single axon extends from each cell body of the neuron to the synapse or end organ and is responsible for the transmission of the nerve impulse. In humans and other vertebrates, most peripheral axons are sheathed in a fatty layer called myelin, which acts to insulate the axon from the surrounding tissue. There are regular breaks in the myelin sheathing, called the nodes of Ranvier, that allow the electrical impulses to jump from node to node (saltatory transmission) rather than transit in the axon via the slower chemical depolarization process.

B

Baseline arousal Term used in polygraphy to characterize a marked upward shift in the entire respiration tracing. Baseline arousals do not always occur during deception; however, when they are observed they are reliable indicators of stress. Some baseline arousals are relatively short-lived, lasting only a few respiration cycles, while others may continue much longer.

Blind chart analysis Evaluation of polygraph recordings without the benefit of extrapolygraphic information, such as subject behavior, case facts, pretest admissions, base rates of deception, etc.

Blood pressure The force the blood exerts against the walls of the blood vessels, usually measured in millimeters of mercury, is called blood pressure. Polygraph examiners evaluate only relative blood volume changes, as current polygraphs are not capable of providing absolute blood pressure measurements.

Brachial artery Major blood vessel located in upper arm. Occlusion blood pressure sensors are frequently placed there, and it is the preferred placement site for the blood pressure cuff in polygraph testing.

Bradycardia Heart rate of less than 60 beats per minute. Brachycardia is common among athletes and those with hypothyroidism. Slow heart rate can also indicate the influence of medications.

Bradypnea Very slow and abnormal respiration, longer cycle time. The term does not distinguish between autonomic and deliberate respiration slowing.

Brain stem Includes the adult brain structures, i.e., midbrain, pons, and medulla (mesencephalon) region structures including the thalamus, third ventricle, and hypothalamus. These structures are essential for the automatic control of respiration and cardiovascular systems.

Breakdown (or breakout) test Polygraph test in which a single issue is addressed, and is always given after a multiple-issue test has indicated that the examinee has consistently responded to that issue. The rationale for this two-stage approach to polygraph testing is that, while multiple-issue screening examinations are very useful in identifying which among several issues the examinee is concerned with, they lack the power of these single-issue formats in making correct determinations of deception or truthfulness. This approach is used in many polygraph screening programs to maximize both utility and accuracy of the polygraph in preemployment and other applications.

C

Cardiograph General term for any recording of the heart's activity. In polygraph testing, the use of a blood pressure cuff to monitor relative arterial blood pressure changes and pulse wave is more precisely described as sphygmography (recording of the arterial pulse) or occlusion plethysmography (partial blockage of circulation to measure volume changes in a body part).

Central nervous system (CNS) That portion of the nervous system consisting of the brain and spinal cord. CNS activity, although closely integrated with autonomic nervous system (ANS) activity, is not separately considered in traditional polygraph approaches. It has been used with event-related potentials (ERPs) in concealed information tests.

Chart Graphical record of phenomena. In polygraphy, it refers to the polygram on which is recorded the physiological activity during testing. The term chart is sometimes used interchangeably with *test*.

Comparison question Type of question used to elicit responses that are compared with the responses to relevant questions. There are two main types: directed lie (DLC) and probable lie (PLC). Subtypes for the DLC are the trivial and the personal. For the PLC, they are the exclusive (exclusionary) and the nonexclusive (inclusive). Historically called control question, comparative response question, and emotional standard.

Comparison question technique (CQT) An umbrella term for standard testing formats that use probable-lie or directed-lie comparison questions. Included are the Reid, the MGQT, the zone comparison, the positive control, the Utah, the Arthur, the quadri-track, and the test for espionage and sabotage. None of the following are considered CQTs: relevant/irrelevant, peak of tension, and concealed information tests.

Concealed information test (CIT) Otherwise known as the guilty knowledge test. The CIT is actually a series of tests in which there is only one critical item in each series, much like the better-known peak of tension tests. The tests are constructed so that the order of the item presentations is randomly selected. The theoretical operating mechanism of the CIT is that there is greater signal value in the critical item for guilty examinees than in the irrelevant items. The CIT is believed to rely on cognitive processes, and is therefore not subject to false positives from nervous examinees.

Confirmatory testing Polygraph examination used to verify the statements of suspects, witnesses, and victims.

Conspecnificance Mnemonic device used in the instruction of polygraphy. It stands for *con*sistency, *spec*ificity, and sig*nificance*, three characteristics of a physiologic response indicative of deception. In order for response patterns to support a polygraph outcome of deception, they must appear regularly to the same questions, manifest themselves uniquely to those questions, and be of a magnitude to be distinguishable from baseline variability.

Constant current method Measurement of skin resistance, where the current applied to the skin is held constant.

Constant voltage method Measurement of skin conductance, where the voltage applied to the skin is held constant.

Control question Superseded term, now called the comparison question.

Countermeasures In polygraph research, it has been labeled as actions taken by the examinee to influence the physiological responses to produce a truthful test outcome. There are several typologies for countermeasures, depending on the definition used. Under some circumstances, polygraph countermeasures have been found to be effective, such as when an examinee receives special training and feedback. Most spontaneous attempts are ineffective.

Craniosacral division of autonomic nervous system An anatomical division of the autonomic nervous system (ANS) that represents the sites for outflow from the parasympathetic division of the ANS, that is, some of the cranial and sacral nerves carry parasympathetic nerves.

Credibility assessment An umbrella expression for the multiple disciplinary field that relies on physiological and behavioral measures to test the agreement between an individual's memories and statements. Credibility assessment approaches have included reaction time tests, word association tests, polygraph, central nervous system measures, and behavioral analysis, among others.

D

Deception indicated (DI) Along with NDI (no deception indicated) and inconclusive, a conventional term for a polygraph outcome. A decision of DI means that (1) the physiological data are stable and interpretable, and (2) the evaluation criteria used by the examiner led him to conclude that the examinee is not wholly truthful to the relevant issue under investigation. The DI and NDI decision options are used primarily in single-issue testing, and they correspond with SR (significant response) or SPR (significant physiological responses) and NSR (no significant response) or NSPR (no significant physiological responses) in multiple-issue, or screening, examinations with the US Government.

Deception test These methods ask directly about the matter to be assessed, are capable of addressing multiple behavioral issues of concern, and may or may not depend on the existence of a known incident or known allegation. There are two broad categories of deception tests, the historically older relevant-irrelevant and the comparison question tests (CQT). This term is used in contrast to recognition test.

Dendrite Process of a neuron specialized to function as a postsynaptic receptor region of the neuron.

Diastole Portion of the heartbeat cycle when the heart muscles have relaxed and the chambers are filled with blood. The left ventricular diastole is represented in the polygraph sphygmograph tracing as the descending limb of the pulse wave.

Dicrotic notch A regular feature in diastolic limb of the pulse wave. It occurs between the systole and subsequent diastole of the waveform, and its proximity to either of these two cardiac events is a function of the air pressure in the recording system. The greatest contributor to the dicrotic notch is the rebounding of the blood against the closed aortic semilunar valve after systole.

Differential salience Expression that characterizes the positive correlation between the degree of psychological significance and intensity of the physiological response. The concept of differential salience is based on the premise that responsivity can reveal underlying mental processes which can be exploited to detect deception or recognition under controlled and structured conditions. It is proposed as a substitute for the older "Psychological Set" hypothesis.

Directed-lie comparison (DLC) question Type of question used to elicit a response that is compared with the response evoked by the relevant question. The DLC question is different from the probable-lie comparison (PLC) question in that the examinee is instructed by the examiner to answer the DLC question untruthfully, whereas the principle of the PLC requires the examiner to lead the examinee to be untruthful to that question without revealing the purpose. The true strengths of the DLCs are that they can be standardized much easier than the PLCs, they are less intrusive, and their effectiveness is less subject to examiner skill. DLCs are being used in many quarters of the polygraph profession.

Directed lie screening test (DLST) A screening test for law enforcement based on the technique and procedures for the test for espionage and sabotage (TES). The DLST uses a repeated series of two relevant and two directed-lie comparison questions, and the conventional 7-position scoring system.

Dyspnea Labored or difficult breathing, generally resulting from disease.

E

Eccrine glands One of the two types of sweat glands, the eccrine glands influence electrodermal activity. They are found throughout the skin surface of the body, but in highest concentration on the hands and feet.

Efferent nerves Neurons that carry nerve impulse from the central nervous system to the effector organ or muscles. Also called motor nerves.

Electrodermal activity (EDA) All exosomatic and endosomatic changes in the electrical properties of the skin.

Electrodermal response (EDR) Reaction of skin measured by changes in its electrical properties, including skin resistance (SR), skin conductance (SC), and skin potential (SP).

Empirical scoring system An evidence-based numerical scoring system similar in many respects to 3-position scoring, with the exception that the electrodermal scores are doubled and the decision rules can be adjusted to match risk tolerance.

Eupnea Normal quiet respiration.

Evidentiary examination A polygraph examination in which the written and stated purpose agreed to by the parties involved is to provide a diagnostic opinion as an evidence in a pending judicial proceeding.

Examination The entirety of the polygraph process, including pretest, test, and posttest elements, from onset to completion.

Exclusive (exclusionary) comparison question Probable-lie comparison questions that do not overlap the event covered by the relevant issue questions.

F

False negative The failure to detect the presence of a particular event or item. A false negative in polygraph testing refers to the incorrect decision that deception was not practiced by the examinee. Also called a Type-2 error.

False positive The false detection of something that is not actually present. In polygraph testing, it is the incorrect decision that deception was practiced by the examinee. Also called a Type-1 error.

Feature In polygraphy, the term refers to a specific aspect of a waveform, pattern, or measurement in a tracing.

Fight, flight, freeze Three stereotypic behavioral responses to threat, sometimes simply called F3. The physiological responses concomitant to these behaviors are the same, namely, mobilizing bodily resources for an expenditure of energy and narrowing attentional focus to the features of the threat. This preparation activity of the body has been used as a rudimentary explanation for the pattern of arousal responses that are recorded during a polygraph exam.

Finger pulse amplitude (FPA) Cardiographic measure of the pulse wave recorded by plethysmograph (both occlusion and photo type) at the finger. Constrictions in amplitude are associated with sympathetic nervous system arousal.

Format A particular order of question presentations, or rules that govern the order, along with the types of questions. "Format" is sometimes incorrectly used interchangeably with "technique," a broader term that encompasses not only the format but also all practices in the pretest and test phases.

"Friendly polygrapher" hypothesis A hypothesis proposed by Martin Orne in 1973 that a deceptive examinee would not be as detectible by an examiner who conducts a polygraph examination on behalf of the examinee's attorney because the examinee has no fear of adverse consequences. There are no studies supporting this hypothesis with the comparison question technique, and all field studies that have investigated it have failed to find the effect.

G

Galvanic skin response (GSR) A superseded term for the electrodermal response measured exosomatically by the change in the electrical resistance of the skin. GSR is sometimes erroneously called galvanic skin resistance or galvanic skin reflex. The modern term is electrodermal response (EDR).

Ganglion A cluster of nerve cell bodies (pl. ganglia).

General nervous tension (GNT) Expression used in the practice of polygraphy to characterize recorded physiological patterns that suggest the examinee's basal level of arousal is high. This arousal is not indicative of deception in itself. GNT is sometimes indicated by very fast heart rates, unusually labile electrodermal activity, and uneven respiration cycles. Polygraph examiners try to bring examinee's arousal state nearer to a median level to optimize the interpretability of the test charts.

Global analysis Evaluation of the polygraph recordings as a whole, as opposed to making systematic comparisons among questions. Global evaluation can also represent the use of extra-polygraphic information such as subject behavior and case facts when rendering a polygraph decision.

Guilty knowledge test (GKT) A test published by Dr. David Lykken and is based on a concealed information paradigm. While similar tests are described in the literature as early as 1904, and Hugo Munsterberg outlines a comparable approach in his 1908 book *On the Witness Stand*, Lykken formalized the procedures, and advocated its use in place of the comparison question technique. Recent writers have renamed this method as the Concealed Information Test.

H

Habituation Adaptation to a stimulus over time. As an organism habituates to a stimulus or environment, its response diminishes both in intensity and frequency. In polygraphy, habituation has been found within tests, but little or none between tests.

Homeostasis Homeostasis is a term used within the scientific community to describe the maintenance of the internal viability of organisms. The historical concept of homeostasis is the basis of modern concepts of autonomic regulation and control. Also, see allostasis.

Hypothenar eminence Prominence on the palm corresponding with the musculature of the little finger. One of the most productive recording sites, along with the thenar eminence, for electrodermal activity.

I

Inclusive (inclusionary, nonexclusionary) comparison question Comparison question that potentially encompasses the activity of interest in the relevant questions. While contemporary practice tends to favor exclusionary comparison questions, no research has found them to increase decision accuracy over inclusive comparison questions.

Incomplete Polygraph outcome used in some sectors that indicates that testing was terminated before sufficient physiological information was collected. This may be due to the sudden onset of health problems, extreme emotional distress, or the examinee's unwillingness or inability to remain for further testing. It may also signify that the examinee provided information after initial testing that necessitated subsequent testing, but it was not completed due to examinee fatigue, time limits, or equipment problems.

Inconclusive Polygraph outcome where testing was completed, but neither deception nor truthfulness can be diagnosed because the physiological data are inconsistent, inadequate, artifacted, or contaminated. Alternate term is indefinite, or no opinion.

Inspiration (inhalation)/expiration (exhalation) ratio (I/E ratio) The duration of inhalation compared with that of exhalation. Normally the ratio is about 1:2 in a resting human and changes during stress. It was first reported by Benussi in 1914. Changes in the I/E ratio are considered by some to be a diagnostic criterion in polygraph data analysis.

Inter-chart stimulation Examiner-examinee interaction that takes place in a few minutes between individual tests. The interaction might include general reminders for the examinee to answer all questions truthfully (in the case of probable-lie techniques), or further emphasizing the comparison questions. Some research suggests that inter-chart stimulation may improve the validity of polygraphy though it remains a controversial procedure in the field.

Investigative examination A polygraph examination which is intended to supplement and/or assist an investigation and for which the examiner has not been informed and does not reasonably believe that the results of the examination will be tendered for admission as evidence in a court proceeding. Types of investigative examinations can include applicant testing, counterintelligence screening, community safety examinations (e.g., postconviction sex offender testing, domestic violence testing, intoxicated drivers on probation, etc.), as well as routine specific issue and single issue or multiple-facet diagnostic testing.

Irrelevant question A question designed to be emotionally neutral to examinees. Irrelevant questions are most often placed in the first position of a question list because an orienting response usually follows the presentation of the first question and is of no diagnostic value. In CQT formats, it is also used after a relevant or comparison question that has elicited a strong response so as to permit physiologic arousal levels to return to baseline before presenting another question. Irrelevant questions are used in nearly every type of polygraph test.

K

Key The critical item in a series of similar-but-neutral items used in peak of tension (POT) tests. In a known solution POT, the key is the relevant question that contains the incriminating information that only a guilty person should know. A key in a searching POT is the test item that holds information that only the guilty person knows and the polygraph examiner is trying to uncover. In stimulation tests, the key is the question to which the examiner directs the examinee to lie.

Key word method Procedure employed during polygraph testing in which the examinee is instructed to provide not only a yes or no reply but also repeat an important word from the test question. The key word in the test question is associated with the concept it is supposed to represent. The key word method is used to neutralize dissociation countermeasures.

Kircher features Ensemble of measurable physiological features found in traditional polygraph recordings that correlate highest with deception. They are respiration line length, electrodermal response amplitude, relative blood pressure amplitude, and finger pulse amplitude.

Known solution peak of tension (KSPOT) test Peak of tension test in which the critical item, or key, is known only to the investigator, polygraph examiner, a guilty person, or a person with incriminating knowledge. The key is placed in a question series among other items equally plausible to an innocent examinee and presented to the subject to determine if a consistent physiologic arousal occurs to the key.

L

Labile Unstable, inconsistent, or dynamic. Polygraph tracings that display a high degree of responsivity or broad amplitude changes are referred to as labile.

Latency The delay between stimulus presentation and some aspect of the response. Onset latency relates to the delay between the stimulus presentation and the beginning of the response, while the peak latency uses the time of the maximum amplitude of the response as the second point. Latencies of specific physiologic responses vary. A significant departure from typical latencies can indicate that a given response is unrelated to the stimulus, that there are problems in attention for the subject, or that countermeasures are being engaged. Because of individual differences, within-subject analyses are warranted.

Lykken scoring System of scoring electrodermal responses in the concealed information test (formerly the guilty knowledge test) and establishing the threshold for decisions. The Lykken scoring system compares the responses of the critical test items in a rank-order method against those of the neutral items. One variant uses averaged ranks.

M

Medulla oblongata A part of the brain stem responsible for automatic control of respiratory and cardiovascular activity. The medulla oblongata is closely associated with physiological events relating to polygraph test data analysis.

Mental countermeasures A class of countermeasures in which the examinee attempts to affect the polygraph recordings through self-manipulation of attention, memory, emotion, cognition, semantics, or arousal.

Motor nerves Neurons that carry nerve impulses from the central nervous system to the effector organ or muscles. Also called efferent nerves.

Movement sensor Mechanical sensor that detects covert movements. The movement sensor is used to detect certain types of physical countermeasures.

Multiple-facet test Test format in which the relevant questions are targeted toward different elements of the same crime. For example, in a counterfeiting case, the polygraph examiner might use three relevant test questions with a suspect. One could cover printing the bills, the second, passing the bills, and the third, knowing where the printing equipment is.

Multiple-issue examination Test typically used in screening; it allows the polygraph examiner to determine which of several areas should be followed up with further questioning. It is somewhat uncommon to make decisions of truthfulness or deception in these types of tests. Such decisions are generally made after subsequent testing on the isolated issue in a single-issue test format. Among the more common multiple issue test formats are the Relevant/Irrelevant screening test and the test for espionage and sabotage.

N

Neuron Structural unit of the nervous system and is the conducting cell. The typical neuron consists of a soma body, dendrites, and axon.

Neurotransmitter Chemical involved in the transport of the neural signal to another neuron or effector organ. Neurotransmission has six stages: synthesis of the neurotransmitter, storage, release, receptor interaction, re-uptake, and inactivation. There are many pharmacological agents that influence neurotransmission, and they are of interest in polygraph research due to their effects on tonic and phasic arousal levels.

No deception indicated (NDI) In conventional polygraphy, NDI signifies that (1) the polygraph test recordings are stable and interpretable and (2) the evaluation criteria used by the examiner led him to conclude that the examinee was truthful to the relevant issue. The NDI and DI (deception indicated) decision options are used in specific-issue testing and correspond to NSPR (no significant physiological responses) and SPR (significant physiological responses) in multiple-issue, or screening, examinations.

Nonexclusive (inclusive or inclusionary) comparison question Comparison question that overlaps the relevant issue by time, location, or issue. Also called Reid, inclusionary, or inclusive comparison question. As an example, if the relevant issue were the robbery of a particular bank on a specific date, the comparison question might be, "Have you ever stolen anything in your life?"

No opinion Alternate form of an inconclusive call, especially in the US Government. Sometimes used to denote an incomplete call in other sectors.

No significant physiological responses (NSPR or NSR) Accepted verbiage in the US Government for polygraph screening examination outcomes equivalent to no deception indicated in single-issue tests. The alternate language comes from an acceptance that screening exams do not produce the high validity of single-issue tests, and, therefore, the results are better reported as the absence of physiologic arousals rather than inferring truthful intent on the part of the examinee.

Numerical analysis Systematic assignment of numbers to physiologic responses, along with decision rules, so that polygraph data analysis is more objective and standardized.

O

Orienting response (OR) Heightened sensitivity to specific stimuli that is characterized by increased information processing, narrowed attentional concentration, and physiologic excitation. Polygraph test question series never begin with a relevant question because the physiological pattern of an OR can be easily confused with a response indicative of deception.

Overall truth question Polygraph test question that addresses the examinee's overall truthfulness or intention to be truthful during testing. Used in some multiple-issue screening tests.

P

Parasympathetic nervous system One of the three divisions of the autonomic nervous system also referred to as the craniosacral system because the preganglionic neurons lie in those areas. Parasympathetic ganglia anatomically lie in or near the organs they innervate, thus allowing for more localized control. Functionally, it is involved in conservation and restoration of energy. The parasympathetic and sympathetic divisions of the autonomic nervous system function to maintain homeostasis.

Peak of tension (POT) Recognition testing procedures, including known solution and searching (probing). A known solution POT (KSPOT) is used to determine whether the examinee is aware of details of a crime that have been kept from the general public and would presumably only be known to the perpetrator of the crime or those with incriminating knowledge. A searching POT (SPOT) is used to determine details of a crime that are not known to officials, such as the location of an unrecovered body, but would be known to a participant in the crime. Peak of tension tests are not generally used to determine truth or deception, but rather to assist in the investigation or interrogation.

Peripheral nervous system Portion of the nervous system resident primarily outside of the brain and spinal cord. The cell bodies of the preganglionic sympathetic neurons lie in the spinal cord and those of the parasympathetic branch are situated in the brain stem.

Phasic response A relatively rapid reaction, characterized by a short-term change and return toward baseline.

Photoplethysmograph (PPG) The PPG uses the reflection of a red light emitted into the skin to detect changes in the volume of blood in the upper layers of skin, typically recorded at the finger when using a polygraph. Physiological arousal is marked by a constriction in the pulse amplitude as blood is shunted from the extremity during activation of the sympathetic nervous system.

Pneumograph A device that records respiration, and one of the three traditional channels of the modern polygraph. Most contemporary polygraphs use two pneumograph recordings: abdominal and thoracic. The types of sensors include the traditional corrugated rubber tube, the mercury strain gauge, and the piezoelectric.

Polygraph By definition, an instrument that simultaneously records two or more channels of data. The term now most commonly signifies the instrument and techniques used in "lie detection," though polygraphs are also used in research in other sciences. The polygraph traditionally records physiologic activity with four sensors: blood pressure cuff, electrodermal sensors, and two respiration sensors. Some instruments also record finger pulse amplitude using a photoplethysmograph.

Posttest Final portion of a polygraph examination. The posttest could include a debriefing of an examinee who passed the examination, or an interview or interrogation of an examinee who failed the examination. The posttest may or may not be a part of any given polygraph technique, and plays no part in the formulation of the results in any polygraph technique.

Premature ventricle contraction (PVC) Term loosely applied to distortion in the cardiograph waveform resulting from an ectopic heartbeat. More precisely, it is a ventricular contraction between two sinus cycles without a compensatory pause.

Pretest interview The earliest portion of the polygraph examination process during which the examinee and examiner discuss the test, test procedure, examinee's medical history, and the details of the test issues. The pretest interview also serves to prepare the examinee for the testing. The length of the pretest interview ranges from 30 min to 2 h or longer, depending on the complexity of the case, examiner-examinee interactions, and testing technique. All polygraph techniques use pretest interviews.

Probable-lie comparison question (PLC) One of the two major types of comparison questions. PLCs are questions to which it is likely that the examinee is untruthful or unsure of his or her answer. Their intended purpose is to create a competition of salience such that the anxious innocent examinees will expend more of their physiologic responses on them than the relevant questions, but the guilty examinee will still find the relevant questions more arousing than the PLCs. Two main types of PLCs are the exclusionary (Backster type) and the nonexclusionary (Reid type).

Psychophysiological detection of deception (PDD) Common scientific term to denote the use of the polygraph to diagnose deception.

Purposeful noncooperation (PNC) An expression first reported by John Reid to denote a polygraph examination outcome in which examinees had used physical countermeasures in an attempt to defeat the polygraph examination. Reid did not consider PNC to be synonymous with the practicing of deception though he wrote that it was a fairly reliable indicator of the examinee's motives to deceive.

R

Recognition test The recognition test family of polygraph techniques includes peak of tension tests, acquaintance tests, and concealed information tests. They attempt to determine if the examinee has knowledge only available to persons directly involved in an incident of concern.

Relevant/irrelevant (RI) technique Family of polygraph test formats in which traditional lie comparison questions are not employed. While originally used in criminal testing, RI tests currently are more often found in multiple-issue screening applications.

Relevant issue gravity (RIG) A theory proposed by Avital Ginton in 2009. It represents the force induced by aggregation of qualities that the relevant issue possesses which attracts and bounds the examinee's attention to the relevant issue. It is manifested in preoccupation of the examinee's mind with the relevant issue and its derivatives and in difficulties to divert attention to other topics or issues. It is postulated in the RIG strength theory that the RIG strength for the guilty examinees on average is stronger than the RIG strength for the truth-tellers. Therefore, it is harder to divert the attention of the guilty examinee to the comparison question and relatively easier to do that with the truth-tellers. This is compatible with the basic decision rule of the CQT, namely, stronger reactions to comparison questions compared to the reactions to the relevant questions indicates a relatively weak RIG strength which means a nonguilty examinee. And of course the opposite outcome indicates a relatively strong RIG which means a guilty examinee.

Relevant question A question that deals with the target issue of concern to the investigation. In addition to "did you do it" types of questions, relevant questions also include evidence-connecting and "do you know who" questions. Strong relevant questions address the "did you do it" type of questions, while moderate-strength relevant questions address evidence connecting and prior knowledge, such as participation in planning, providing help to the perpetrators, or knowing the identity of the perpetrators. Moderate-strength relevant questions also address the examinee's alibi or place him at the scene of the crime.

Respiration One of the standard physiological signals in polygraph testing. Respiratory data are generally obtained via a pneumograph transducer placed around the thorax and abdomen of the test subject.

Respiratory blood pressure fluctuations (RBPF) An undulating waveform observed in the cardiograph channel during polygraph testing, erroneously called "vagus" in the past. When an examinee engages in a deliberate attempt to control his or her breathing, it will frequently trigger a cyclic waveform in the cardiovascular channel.

Respiration line length (RLL) Feature in a respiration tracing that changes during arousal. It is a linear measure of the respiration waveform over a specified period of time. It was first reported in the polygraph literature by Dr. Howard Timm, who credited Dr. Frank Horvath with the idea. Several studies have since supported the use of this measure in deception tests.

S

Sacrifice relevant question Question introduced by Cleve Backster and used in most forms of the ZCT as well as other types of tests. The sacrifice relevant is a question that asks the examinee if he intends to answer truthfully to every question related to the relevant issue. The sacrifice relevant question is not numerically scored. Its value has been disputed in independent research.

Salience The state or quality of standing out relative to other stimuli. In learning theory, salience refers to the strength of the relationship between a response and a reinforcer or outcome. In general, as the intensity of the outcome increases, the intensity of the response increases. In the framework of polygraph testing, the intensity of arousal will increase commensurate with perceived salience of stimuli (test questions).

Screening examination A polygraph examination conducted in the absence of a reported issue or allegation to investigate whether an examinee has withheld information regarding engagement in behaviors encompassed by relevant questions that cover specified periods of time. Screening examinations may be designed to investigate multiple types of behaviors or multiple aspects of a single kind of behavior.

Searching (or probing) peak of tension (SPOT) Peak of tension test in which the testing examiner does not know the critical item, and it is used to determine information concealed by a guilty examinee. Applications of this format include determining the location of stolen goods or the bodies of murder victims, the amount of cash stolen, or the name of an accomplice. In practice, SPOT tests are not often used alone, but rather are a *post hoc* procedure once deception has been established with comparison question or relevant/irrelevant tests.

Senter rules Also called two-stage rules, Senter rules are used for single-issue testing. The Senter rules begin by basing a decision on the total score for the case. If a decision would be inconclusive from the total score rule, the second stage is used in which the spot scores are considered. The net effect of the Senter rules is to decrease the proportion of inconclusive results while not affecting the proportion of correct decisions.

Significant physiological responses (SPR or SR) Accepted verbiage in the US polygraph screening programs, and is equivalent to Deception Indicated in specific-issue tests.

Silent answer test (SAT) Specialized procedure in which the examinee is directed to answer to himself instead of making a verbal response. Proposed by Dr. Frank Horvath in 1972 to help avoid distortions to the pneumograph tracings attributable to speech disorders, or to uncover certain countermeasures.

Single-issue examination An event-specific or a screening polygraph examination conducted in response to a single known or alleged incident for which the examinee is suspected of involvement or to investigate the examinee's possible involvement in a single behavioral concern for which there is no known or alleged incident. When used in screening, a single-issue examination typically follows a multiple or mixed issue screening examination in the successive hurdles model.

Skin conductance (SC) Broad term for two exosomatic electrodermal phenomena, skin conductance level and skin conductance response.

Skin conductance level (SCL) Basal conductance of the skin. SCL is the tonic measure of SC.

Skin conductance response (SCR) A change in the electrical conductance of the skin elicited by a stimulus. SCR is a phasic response.

Skin potential level (SPL) Basal electro-potential of the skin. SPL is the tonic level.

Skin resistance (SR) General term for the phenomena of skin resistance level and skin resistance response. SR is recorded exosomatically and was the primary means of detecting electrodermal activity throughout much of polygraph history until the introduction of computerized instrumentation with SC.

Skin resistance level (SRL) Tonic level of electrical resistance of the skin.

Skin resistance response (SRR) Phasic response measured by electrical resistance of the skin.

Specific issue polygraph examination A single-issue polygraph examination, almost always administered in conjunction with a criminal investigation, usually addressing a single issue.

Specific physiological response (SPR) Accepted verbiage in the Federal Government and elsewhere for polygraph screening examination outcomes equivalent to Deception Indicated in single-issue tests.

Spot A permanently assigned location of a relevant question in a CQT question series.

Spot analysis The numerical evaluation of a relevant question by comparing it to a comparison question no further than one position to the left or right of that spot location. A "spot" represents the location of a relevant question in a question series; the physiological data at the relevant question (spot) are compared with those of an adjacent comparison question.

Spot score Total score for a particular relevant question. Sometimes called a subtotal score.

Successive hurdles approach In the successive hurdles approach, each examinee in a multiple-issue examination would begin with a screening test that contained several different relevant questions. Though multiple-issue examinations have a higher false positive rate (incorrect decision of deception) than do single-issue examinations, they have a very small rate of false negatives. If no significant responses were noted during the multiple-issue examination, the polygraph session would be over. However, if there were significant responses during the multiple-issue examination, the polygraph session would continue. Next, a single-issue examination would be administered in the area the examiner observed significant responses during the multiple-issue examination. The single-issue examination has much better discrimination power and would help to elucidate physiological arousal more specifically. In this way, the more resource-intensive single-issue examinations would be reserved for the smaller subset of applicants who did not pass the multiple-issue examination. The net effect of the two-stage screening process is a better accuracy without increased resources.

Suppression One respiratory response pattern indicative of orienting and arousal, characterized by breathing that is shallower and slower than tracing average. The polygraph respiration tracing of suppression will manifest in a decrease in amplitude, a slower rate, or a temporary increase in the baseline of the waveform. Suppression has been found to be a reliable indicator of salience since the first part of this century, and it is a primary reaction criterion for diagnosing deception.

Sympathetic nervous system Thoracolumbar portion of the autonomic nervous system centrally involved in responding to arousing stimuli. Most sympathetic nerves are adrenergic and prepare the body to respond to increased demands. Sympathetic nervous activation increases blood flow from the heart, triggers the release of glucose and epinephrine, dilates the pupils, and initiates other responses in preparation for action. Unlike most of the sympathetic nervous system, sympathetic nerves to the eccrine sweat glands are cholinergic.

Symptomatic question A question type developed by Cleve Backster that was once thought to identify whether an examinee is fearful; the examiner will ask an unreviewed question about an outside issue. In this construct, the examinee's mistrust would dampen his responses to other test questions, and the symptomatic question could determine whether the lack of responsivity was attributable to the outside issue. Symptomatic questions are widely used, though the trend in the research finds they have no meaningful effect.

Synapse Junction between neurons. Site where the nervous impulse is transferred from one neuron to another. Neurotransmitters reside in vesicles of one neuron and are released by the axon into the synapse to chemically induce the next neuron or organ to respond.

Systole Contraction of the cardiac muscles. Left ventricular systole results in movement of blood out of the heart into the aorta. Systoles can be subdivided into three primary components: pre-ejection, ejection, and relaxation periods. The left ventricular systolic peak is represented on a conventional polygraph as the highest vertical point in the pulse wave of the cardiovascular tracing.

T

Tachycardia Abnormally rapid heartbeat, greater than 100 beats per minute. Tachycardia can result from poisoning, medications, certain illnesses, and during states of anxiety or excitement.

Tachypnea Rapid breathing, usually shallow.

Technique All practices taking place in a polygraph examination including pretest procedures, question formulation, format, number of tests, test sequencing, and scoring and decision rules.

Test In polygraphy, the test is used to differentiate a single running of a question series (sometimes also called a chart) during physiological recording from the examination, which is considered to be the totality of the polygraph process. It can also refer to specialized procedures within techniques, such as the yes test and acquaintance test. Other times it refers to a technique, such as the test for espionage and sabotage.

Test for espionage and sabotage (TES) Multiple-issue testing format employed by some US Government agencies for screening purposes. The TES uses a repeated series of relevant and directed-lie comparison questions, and the conventional 7-position scoring system. An identical format has been devised for police candidate screening called the directed lie screening test (DLST).

Thenar eminence Prominence on the palm at the base of the thumb. One of the optimal recording sites for electrodermal activity and a preferred location in psychophysiological research.

Time bar One method of restricting the coverage of the comparison question so that it will not include the time in which the incident under investigation took place. Time bars generally predate the crime. A typical time bar for the comparison question might be phrased "Before the age of X, did you ever…" or "Prior to 1998, did you ever…" There is a school of thought that examinees may confuse the relevant questions with the comparison questions unless these two types of questions are designed to avoid any degree of overlap.

Tonic level Baseline level. This terminology in polygraphy is frequently used to delineate basal waveform levels from short-term responses induced by stimuli. Tonic levels change slowly compared to phasic activity.

Tonic response Shifting of tonic level, typically in response to changing conditions. For example, the adjustment of electrodermal tonic levels due to temperature changes, reduction of pulse rate between standing and reclining, and faster breathing that accompanies an increase in walking speed. Tonic responses take several seconds or minutes to occur, unlike phasic responses which tend to be very rapid.

True negative Correct decision that the variable of interest is not present (i.e., an accurate polygraph outcome of truth telling).

True positive Correct decision that the variable of interest is present (i.e., an accurate polygraph outcome of deception).

U

Utah probable lie technique (UPLT) A technique developed by researchers at the University of Utah beginning in the 1970s, and was initially influenced by the Backster zone comparison test. Unique characteristics of the UPLT that separate it from other zone approaches are: the inclusion of the photoplethysmograph; rotation of the probable-lie questions; recording of five charts when the test would be inconclusive at three charts; and symmetrical cutoffs of +/−6. More recently, the developers of the Utah technique have also endorsed the use of directed-lie questions in place of probable-lie questions.

V

Vasoconstriction Narrowing of blood vessels, especially arterioles, thereby reducing blood flow to a region of the body. During sympathetic nervous system activation, vasoconstriction takes place in some parts of the body, shunting blood supplies to major muscles in preparation for defense or flight. Some medications influence vasoconstriction.

Vasodilation Expansion of blood vessels, especially arterioles, which deliver increased blood flow to a region of the body. Vasodilation and vasoconstriction are regulated by the autonomic nervous system and can be affected by some medications.

Vasomotor Relating to the influences of the smooth muscles on the internal diameter of a blood vessel.

Y

You phase One of the most commonly used formats in the Backster zone comparison technique. The standardized test addresses a single issue and single degree of involvement in the issue. The format provides for two or three relevant questions, worded slightly differently from one another, addressing the single issue and degree of involvement. It also requires a repeat of the relevant question wording in the sacrifice relevant question.

Z

Zone comparison technique (ZCT) Polygraph technique developed by Cleve Backster that contains three Zones (black, red, green) with comparison of responses between two of the zones (red and green) for a determination of truth or deception. The ZCT was the first modern polygraph technique in general use to incorporate numerical analysis. There are several alternate forms of the ZCT and they are used more often in forensic applications than any other technique.

APPENDIX

Public Law 100 – 347
100th Congress

An Act

To prevent the denial of employment opportunities by prohibiting the use of lie detectors by employers involved in or affecting interstate commerce.

Be it enacted by the Senate and House of Representatives of the United States of America in Congress assembled,

SECTION 1 SHORT TITLE

This Act may be cited as the "Employee Polygraph Protection Act of 1988."

SECTION 2 DEFINITIONS

As used in this Act:

(1) COMMERCE. – The term "commerce" has the meaning provided by section 3(b) of the Fair Labor Standards Act of 1938 (29 U.S.C. 203(b)).
(2) EMPLOYER. – The term "employer" includes any person acting directly or indirectly in the interest of an employer in relation to an employee or prospective employee.
(3) LIE DETECTOR. – The term "lie detector" includes a polygraph, deceptograph, voice stress analyzer, psychological stress evaluator, or any other similar device (whether mechanical or electrical) that is used, or the results of which are used, for the purpose of rendering a diagnostic opinion regarding the honesty or dishonesty of an individual.
(4) POLYGRAPH. – The term "polygraph" means an instrument that –
  (A) records continuously, visually, permanently, and simultaneously changes in cardiovascular, respiratory, and electrodermal patterns as minimum instrumentation standards; and
  (B) is used, or the results of which are used, for the purpose of rendering a diagnostic opinion regarding the honesty or dishonesty of an individual.
(5) SECRETARY. – The term "Secretary" means the Secretary of Labor.

SECTION 3 PROHIBITIONS ON LIE DETECTOR USE

Except as provided in sections 7 and 8, it shall be unlawful for any employer engaged in or affecting commerce or in the production of goods for commerce –

(1) directly or indirectly, to require, request, suggest, or cause any employee or prospective employee to take or submit to any lie detector test;

(2) to use, accept, refer to, or inquire concerning the results of any lie detector test of any employee or prospective employee;

(3) to discharge, discipline, discriminate against in any manner, or deny employment or promotion to, or threaten to take any such action against –
   (A) any employee or prospective employee who refuses, declines, or fails to take or submit to any lie detector test, or
   (B) any employee or prospective employee on the basis of the results of any lie detector test; or

(4) to discharge, discipline, discriminate against in any manner, or deny employment or promotion to, or threaten to take any such action against, any employee or prospective employee because –
   (A) such employee or prospective employee has filed any complaint or instituted or caused to be instituted any proceeding under or related to this Act,
   (B) such employee or prospective employee has testified or is about to testify in any such proceeding, or
   (C) of the exercise by such employee or prospective employee, on behalf of such employee or another person, of any right afforded by this Act.

SECTION 4 NOTICE OF PROTECTION

The Secretary shall prepare, have printed, and distribute a notice setting forth excerpts from, or summaries of, the pertinent provisions of this Act. Each employer shall post and maintain such notice in conspicuous places on its premises where notices to employees and applicants to employment are customarily posted.

SECTION 5 AUTHORITY OF THE SECRETARY

(a) IN GENERAL. – The Secretary shall –
   (1) issue such rules and regulations as may be necessary or appropriate to carry out this Act;
   (2) cooperate with regional, State, local, and other agencies, and cooperate with and furnish technical assistance to employers, labor organizations, and employment agencies to aid in effectuating the purposes of this Act; and
   (3) make investigations and inspections and require the keeping of records necessary or appropriate for the administration of this Act.

(b) SUBPOENA AUTHORITY. – For the purpose of any hearing or investigation under this Act, the Secretary shall have the authority contained in sections 9 and 10 of the Federal Trade Commission Act (15 U.S.C. 49 and 50).

SECTION 6 ENFORCEMENT PROVISIONS

(a) CIVIL PENALTIES. –
- **(1)** IN GENERAL. – Subject to paragraph (2) any employer who violates any provision of this Act may be assessed a civil penalty of not more $10,000.
- **(2)** DETERMINATION OF AMOUNT. – In determining the amount of any penalty under paragraph (1), the Secretary shall take into account the previous record of the person in terms of compliance with this Act and the gravity of the violation.
- **(3)** COLLECTION. – Any civil penalty assessed under this subsection shall be collected in the same manner as is required by subsections (b) through (e) of section 503 of the Migrant and Seasonal Agricultural Worker Protection Act (29 U.S.C. 1853) with respect to civil penalties assessed under subsection (a) of such section.

(b) INJUNCTIVE ACTIONS BY THE SECRETARY. – The Secretary may bring an action under this section to restrain violations of this Act. The Solicitor of Labor may appear for and represent the Secretary in any litigation brought under this Act. In any action brought under this section, the district courts of the United States shall have jurisdiction, for cause shown, to issue temporary or permanent restraining orders and injunctions to require compliance with this Act, including such legal or equitable relief incident thereto as may be appropriate, including, but not limited to, employment, reinstatement, promotion, and the payment of lost wages and benefits.

(c) PRIVATE CIVIL ACTIONS.
- **(1)** LIABILITY. – An employer who violates this Act shall be liable to the employee or prospective employee affected by such violation. Such employer shall be liable for such legal or equitable relief as may be appropriate, including, but not limited to, employment, reinstatement, promotion, and the payment of lost wages and benefits.
- **(2)** COURT. – An action to recover the liability prescribed in paragraph (1) may be maintained against the employer in any Federal or State court of competent jurisdiction by an employee or prospective employee for or on behalf of such employee, prospective employee and other employees or prospective employees similarly situated. No such action may be commenced more than 3 years after the date of the alleged violation.
- **(3)** COSTS. – The court, in its discretion, may allow the prevailing party (other than the United States) reasonable costs, including attorney's fees.

(d) WAIVER OF RIGHTS PROHIBITED. – The rights and procedures provided by this Act may not be waived by contract or otherwise, unless such waiver is part of a written settlement agreed to and signed by the parties to the pending action or complaint under this Act.

SECTION 7 EXEMPTIONS

(a) NO APPLICATION TO GOVERNMENTAL EMPLOYERS. – This Act shall not apply with respect to the United States Government, any State or local government, or any political subdivision of a State or local government.

(b) NATIONAL DEFENSE AND SECURITY EXEMPTION –

   (1) NATIONAL DEFENSE. – Nothing in this Act shall be construed to prohibit the administration, by the Federal Government, in the performance of any counterintelligence function, of any lie detector test to –

   (A) any expert or consultant under contract to the Department of Defense or any employee of any contractor of such Department; or

   (B) any expert or consultant under contract with the Department of Energy in connection with the atomic energy defense activities of such Department or any employee of any contractor of such Department in connection with such activities.

   (2) SECURITY – Nothing in this Act shall be construed to prohibit the administration, by the Federal Government, in the performance of any intelligence or counterintelligence function, of any lie detector test to –

   (A)

   (i) any individual employed by, assigned to, or detailed to, the National Security Agency, the Defense Intelligence Agency, or the Central Intelligence Agency,

   (ii) any expert or consultant under contract to any such agency,

   (iii) any employee of a contractor to any such agency,

   (iv) any individual applying for a position in any such agency, or

   (v) any individual assigned to a space where sensitive cryptologic information is produced, processed, or stored for any such agency; or

   (B) any expert, or consultant (or employee of such expert or consultant) under contract with any Federal Government department, agency, or program whose duties involve access to information that has been classified at the level of top secret or designated as being within a special access program under section 4.2(a) of Executive Order 12356 (or a successor Executive order).

(c) FBI CONTRACTORS EXEMPTION – Nothing in this Act shall be construed to prohibit the administration, by the Federal Government, in the performance of any counterintelligence function, of any lie detector test to an employee of a contractor of the Federal Bureau of Investigation of the Department of Justice who is engaged in the performance of any work under the contract with such Bureau.

(d) LIMITED EXEMPTION FOR ONGOING INVESTIGATIONS – Subject to sections 8 and 10, this Act shall not prohibit an employer from requesting an employee to submit to a polygraph test if –
  (1) the test is administered in connection with an ongoing investigation involving economic loss or injury to the employer's business, such as theft, embezzlement, misappropriation, or an act of unlawful industrial espionage or sabotage;
  (2) the employee had access to the property that is the subject of the investigation;
  (3) the employer has a reasonable suspicion that the employee was involved in the incident or activity under investigation; and
  (4) the employer executes a statement, provided to the examinee before the test, that –
    (A) sets forth with particularity the specific incident or activity being investigated and the basis for testing particular employees,
    (B) is signed by a person (other than a polygraph examiner) authorized to legally bind the employer,
    (C) is retained by the employer for at least 3 years, and
    (D) contains at a minimum –
      (i) an identification of the specific economic loss or injury to the business of the employer,
      (ii) a statement indicating that the employee had access to the property that is the subject of the investigation, and
      (iii) a statement describing the basis of the employer's reasonable suspicion that the employee was involved in the incident or activity under investigation.
(e) EXEMPTION FOR SECURITY SERVICES. –
  (1) IN GENERAL – Subject to paragraph (2) and sections 8 and 10, this Act shall not prohibit the use of polygraph tests on prospective employees by any private employer whose primary business purpose consists of providing armored car personnel, personnel engaged in the design, installation, and maintenance of security alarm systems, or other uniformed or plainclothes security personnel and whose function includes protection of –
    (A) facilities, materials, or operations having a significant impact on the health or safety of any State or political subdivision thereof, or the national security of the United States, as determined under rules and regulations issued by the Secretary within 90 days after the date of the enactment of this Act; including –
      (i) facilities engaged in the production, transmission, or distribution of electric or nuclear power,
      (ii) public water supply facilities,

(iii) shipments or storage of radioactive or other toxic waste materials, and
(iv) public transportation, or
(B) currency, negotiable securities, precious commodities or instruments, or proprietary information.
(2) ACCESS. – The exemption provided under this subsection shall not apply if the test is administered to a prospective employee who would not be employed to protect facilities, materials, operations, or assets referred to in paragraph (1).
(f) EXEMPTIONS FOR DRUG SECURITY, DRUG THEFT, OR DRUG DIVERSION INVESTIGATIONS. –
(1) IN GENERAL. – Subject to paragraph (2) and sections 8 and 10, this Act shall not prohibit the use of a polygraph test by any employer authorized to manufacture, distribute, or dispense a controlled substance listed in schedule I, II, III or IV of section 202 of the Controlled Substances Act (21 U.S.C. 812).
(2) ACCESS. – The exemption provided under this subsection shall apply –
(A) if the test is administered to a prospective employee who would have direct access to the manufacture, storage, distribution, or sale of any such controlled substance; or (B) in the case of a test administered to a current employee, if –
(i) the test is administered in connection with an ongoing investigation of criminal or other misconduct involving, or potentially involving, loss or injury to the manufacture, distribution, or dispensing of any such controlled substance by such employer, and
(ii) the employee had access to the person or property that is the subject of the investigation.

SECTION 8 RESTRICTIONS ON USE OF EXEMPTIONS

(a) TEST AS BASIS FOR ADVERSE EMPLOYMENT ACTION. –
(1) UNDER ONGOING INVESTIGATIONS EXEMPTION. – Except as provided in paragraph (2), the exemption under subsection (d) of section 7 shall not apply if an employee is discharged, disciplined, denied employment or promotion, or otherwise discriminated against in any manner on the basis of the analysis of a polygraph test chart or the refusal to take a polygraph test, without additional supporting evidence. The evidence required by such subsection may serve as additional supporting evidence.
(2) UNDER OTHER EXEMPTIONS. – In the case of an exemption described in subsection (e) or (f) of such section, the exemption shall not apply if the results of an analysis of a polygraph test chart are used, or the refusal to take a polygraph test is used, as the sole basis upon which an adverse employment action described in paragraph (1) is taken against an employee or prospective employee.

(b) RIGHTS OF EXAMINEE. – The exemptions provided under subsections (d), (e), and (f) of section 7 shall not apply unless the requirements described in the following paragraphs are met:
  (1) ALL PHASES. – Throughout all phases of the test –
     (A) the examinee shall be permitted to terminate the test at any time;
     (B) the examinee is not asked questions in a manner designed to degrade, or needlessly intrude on, such examinee;
     (C) the examinee is not asked any question concerning –
        (i) religious beliefs or affiliations,.
        (ii) beliefs or opinions regarding racial matters,
        (iii) political beliefs or affiliations,
        (iv) any matter relating to sexual behavior; and
        (v) beliefs, affiliations, opinions, or lawful activities regarding unions or labor organizations; and
     (D) the examiner does not conduct the test if there is sufficient written evidence by a physician that the examinee is suffering from a medical or psychological condition or undergoing treatment that might cause abnormal responses during the actual testing phase.
  (2) PRETEST PHASE. – During the pretest phase, the prospective examinee –
     (A) is provided with reasonable written notice of the date, time, and location of the test, and of such examinee's right to obtain and consult with legal counsel or an employee representative before each phase of the test;
     (B) is informed in writing of the nature and characteristics of the tests and of the instruments involved;
     (C) is informed, in writing –
        (i) whether the testing area contains a two-way mirror, a camera, or any other device through which the test can be observed,
        (ii) whether any other device, including any device for recording or monitoring the test, will be used, or
        (iii) that the employer or the examinee may (with mutual knowledge) make a recording of the test;
     (D) is read and signs a written notice informing such examinee –
        (i) that the examinee cannot be required to take the test as a condition of employment,
        (ii) that any statement made during the test may constitute additional supporting evidence for the purposes of an adverse employment action described in subsection (a),
        (iii) of the limitations imposed under this section,
        (iv) of the legal rights and remedies available to the examinee if the polygraph test is not conducted in accordance with this Act, and
        (v) of the legal rights and remedies of the employer under this Act (including the rights of the employer under section 9(c)(2); and
     (E) is provided an opportunity to review all questions to be asked during the test and is informed of the right to terminate the test at any time.

(3) ACTUAL TESTING PHASE – During the actual testing phase, the examiner does not ask such examinee any question relevant during the test that was not presented in writing for review to such examinee before the test.

(4) POST-TEST PHASE – Before any adverse employment action, the employer shall –
  (A) further interview the examinee on the basis of the results of the test; and
  (B) provide the examinee with –
    (i) a written copy of any opinion or conclusion rendered as a result of the test, and
    (ii) a copy of the questions asked during the test along with the corresponding charted responses.

(5) MAXIMUM NUMBER AND MINIMUM DURATION OF TESTS. – The examiner shall not conduct and complete more than five polygraph tests on a calendar day on which the test is given, and shall not conduct any such test for less than a 90-minute duration.

(c) QUALIFICATIONS AND REQUIREMENTS OF EXAMINERS. – The exemptions provided under subsections (d), (e), and (f) of section 7 shall not apply unless the individual who conducts the polygraph test satisfies the requirements under the following paragraphs:

(1) QUALIFICATIONS. – The examiner –
  (A) has a valid and current license granted by licensing and regulatory authorities in the State in which the test is to be conducted, if so required by the State; and
  (B) maintains a minimum of a $50,000 bond or an equivalent amount of professional liability coverage.

(2) REQUIREMENTS. – The examiner –
  (A) renders any opinion or conclusion regarding the test –
    (i) in writing and solely on the basis of an analysis of polygraph test charts,
    (ii) that does not contain information other than admissions, information, case facts, and interpretation of the charts relevant to the purpose and stated objectives of the test, and
    (iii) that does not include any recommendation concerning the employment of the examinee; and
  (B) maintains all opinions, reports, charts, written questions, lists, and other records relating to the test for a minimum period of 3 years after administration of the test.

SECTION 9 DISCLOSURE OF INFORMATION

(a) IN GENERAL – A person, other than the examinee, may not disclose information obtained during a polygraph test, except as provided in this section.

(b) PERMITTED DISCLOSURES – A polygraph examiner may disclose information acquired from a polygraph test only to –
  (1) the examinee or any other person specifically designated in writing by the examinee;
  (2) the employer that requested the test; or
  (3) any court, governmental agency, arbitrator, or mediator, in accordance with due process of law, pursuant to an order from a court of competent jurisdiction.
(c) DISCLOSURES BY EMPLOYER – An employer (other than an employer described in subsection (a), (b), or (c) of section 7) for whom a polygraph test is conducted may disclose information from the test only to –
  (1) a person in accordance with subsection (b); or
  (2) a governmental agency, but only insofar as the disclosed information is an admission of criminal conduct.

SECTION 10 EFFECT ON OTHER LAW AND AGREEMENTS

Except as provided in subsections (a), (b), and (c) of section 7, this Act shall not preempt any provision of any State or local law or of any negotiated collective bargaining agreement that prohibits lie detector tests or is more restrictive with respect to lie detector tests than any provision of this Act.

SECTION 11 EFFECTIVE DATE

(a) IN GENERAL – Except as provided in subsection (b), this Act shall become effective 6 months after the date of enactment of this Act.
(b) REGULATIONS. Not later than 90 days after the date of enactment of this Act, the Secretary shall issue such rules and regulations as may be necessary or appropriate to carry out this Act.

Approved June 27, 1988.

APPENDIX B

2015 Update to the APA 2011 meta-analytic survey of validated polygraph techniques

Raymond Nelson

In 2007 the Board of Directors of the American Polygraph Association (APA) resolved to require the use of validated polygraph techniques as a standard of practice for its members beginning January 2012. Since that time polygraph examiners and other professionals who work within and alongside the various polygraph testing milieu have become increasingly aware of the importance of evidence-based practices. In response to anticipated questions about which polygraph techniques would be regarded as compliant with the APA Standards of Practice, an ad hoc committee was tasked with surveying the published literature. The results of that survey were published in the *Report of the Meta-analytic Survey of Validated Polygraph Techniques* (APA, 2011). With that publication, the APA attempted to provide examiners and other professionals with a convenient reference to summarize the current knowledge about polygraph techniques and polygraph accuracy. As is sometimes the case, information can begin to become obsolete almost as quickly as it is published. In the four years since the publication of the meta-analytic survey some new information has become available, meaning that the 2011 report, although still useful, was already becoming incomplete. This update to the meta-analytic survey will serve to orient the reader to a few new developments that should be considered part of our present knowledge-base regarding validated polygraph techniques. However, this update is intended to be brief, and will only summarize information, both old and new, in the context of the design of the 2011 meta-analytic survey.

APA Standards of Practice require that polygraph techniques used for evidentiary purposes, in which the test is conducted with the intention that the results will be used in an evidentiary proceeding, should have demonstrated accuracy at .9 or greater with an inclusive rate under .2. Polygraph techniques use in paired-testing contexts should have accuracy at .86 or greater with an inconclusive rate under .2, while polygraph techniques used for investigative purposes should have an accuracy rate of at last .8 with an inconclusive rate under .2. Lastly, APA requires that polygraph techniques used in screening programs should minimally have a demonstrated accuracy level that is significantly greater than chance.

APPENDIX B Meta-analytic survey of validated polygraph techniques

The design of the 2011 report was intended primarily to answer questions about which polygraph techniques satisfied the APA requirement for validity. A valid polygraph technique must have been supported by publication and replication of validity that conformed to the requirements of the APA Standards of Practice. Minimally, this meant that any polygraph technique described in two research publications might suffice. It became apparent in the context of completing the initial survey that this very minimal requirement would become quickly unsatisfactory. It was also apparent that the context of the survey could also provide insight into our present knowledge of polygraph accuracy. For these reasons, it was decided to complete the survey task with the incorporation of some of the principles of meta-analysis, namely the declaration, in advance of any data analysis, of what kinds of publications and what kinds of information would merit inclusion in the survey, and the weighting of aggregated reported accuracy effect sizes.

Requirements for inclusion in the meta-analytic survey were based on a definition of a polygraph technique as consisting of those core structural elements required to study criterion validity or test accuracy. In practical terms this meant that polygraph techniques must have been supported by published description of the procedures for test administration and test data analysis. Publications of this type support additional studies and quality assurance activities intended to ascertain whether an individual exam was conducted properly. Peer-reviewed research publications were included, as were government publications which were subject to independent review. Academic texts would be included. Self-published texts and self-published manuscripts would not be included, nor would un-reviewed articles that provided information that was insufficient for analysis. It was also determined that publications polygraph techniques should be supported by published statistics including the mean and standard deviations of numerical scores for guilty and innocent cases, from which different studies can be compared with the assumption that scores from various studies involving the same polygraph technique should not differ significantly if the exams were conducted and scored using the same procedure and if the study samples were drawn from or representative of the same population. Required statistics would include information about test sensitivity, specificity, false-positive and false-negative error rates. From these statistics all others of interest could be calculated including positive and negative predictive value, unweighted accuracy and inconclusive rates. A requirement for published information about the reliability of test scores was also declared, thereby requiring the judicious attachment of caveats regarding one of the techniques included in the survey despite the absence of any published information on test reliability.

For some purposes, questions about polygraph validity may be better or more broadly addressed in the report from the National Research Council (NRC; 2003) of the National Academy of Sciences. Upon reading the meta-analysis it becomes apparent that the APA conclusions do not differ from those of the NRC. The value of the APA 2011 survey is not that it provided a different or a better answer to questions about criterion validity of polygraph techniques today; the value of the meta-analysis is that it more directly addressed our present knowledge about polygraph techniques in use in field settings, administered, scored and interpreted using techniques that represent those used by present-day polygraph examiners who are compliant with the APA requirement to use validated techniques. The present report will serve to update the reader to new developments since the publication of the 2011 report. It does not differ substantially from that report, and readers are directed to it and other publications for more complete discussion and information regarding the individual polygraph techniques.

Two additional techniques are included in this update. One is the Michigan State University Modified General Question Technique (MSU-MGQT). This technique was extant but remained unrecognized at the time of the 2011 report. However, it is now apparent that the two publications serve to anchor, in the form of a publication and material replication, that the technique is capable of rendering accurate decisions that are consistent with other validated polygraph techniques. The second inclusion is the Relevant-Irrelevant Screening Test, for which only one publication was available during 2011, while a second one was added in 2014.

Two polygraph techniques, included in both this analysis and the 2011 report, deserve additional discussion. These are the Matte Quadri-Track Zone Comparison Technique (MQTZCT) and the Integrated Zone Comparison Technique (IZCT), both of which are outliers to the distribution of other results, and both of which are supported by research of a character that may warrant caution. A more satisfactory approach would be to include only those studies for which it was reasonable to believe the results would be replicable and representative of what can be expected in field testing. More complete information regarding the scientific and methodological confounds pertaining to these techniques can be found in the various footnotes of the original 2011 report. However both the MQTZCT and IZCT were incorporated in the 2011 meta-analysis after meeting very broad inclusion criteria, and likewise are included here.

Overall polygraph accuracy should not be considered different from what it was in 2011. Event specific diagnostic exams are shown to have a mean unweighted accuracy rate of .89 (95% CI=.82 to .95), while exams interpreted with the assumption of independent response variance are shown to have a mean accuracy rate of .82 (95% CI=.74 to .90). Table 1 shows an alphabetical listing of validated techniques, including information on test sensitivity, test specificity, false-positive and false-negative error rates, along with overall unweighted accuracy and unweighted inconclusive rates. Table 2 lists the studies included in this updated survey, while Table 3 shows the study sample sizes. Mean accuracy of the included studies, weighted for sample size, was .88 (95% CI=.81 to .94). One of the benefits of the availability of statistical information regarding polygraph accuracy and error rates is that it encourages readers to think probabilistically, and resist the impulse to engage in false hopes of a test that offers either deterministic perfection or physical measurement of the amorphous behavioral and epistemological constructs of human deception and truth-telling.

In general, this update will suffer from the same limitations as the 2011 report. Namely, there may be an overemphasis on named techniques, and there may be a

Table 1 Estimated performance of validated techniques with (Standard error) and {95% confidence intervals}

Technique (Scoring System)	Sensitivity	Specificity	False Negative	False Positive	Inconclusives for Deceptive Cases	Inconclusives for Truthful Cases	Unweighted Accuracy	Unweighted INC
AFMGQT (7-position)	.784 (.058) {.671 to .898}	.555 (.068) {.421 to .689}	.078 (.050) {.001 to .175}	.202 (.057) {.089 to .314}	.121 (.033) {.055 to .186}	.261 (.049) {.164 to .357}	.822 (.042) {.738 to .905}	.191 (.030) {.132 to .249}
AFMGQT (ESS)	.784 (.058) {.671 to .898}	.555 (.068) {.421 to .689}	.078 (.05) {.001 to .175}	.202 (.057) {.089 to .314}	.121 (.033) {.055 to .186}	.261 (.049) {.164 to .357}	.875 (.039) {.798 to .953}	.170 (.036) {.1 to .241}
Backster You-Phase (Backster)	.835 (.063) {.712 to .958}	.562 (.080) {.406 to .719}	.013 (.013) {.001 to .039}	.197 (.066) {.068 to .326}	.152 (.062) {.032 to .273}	.240 (.067) {.109 to .372}	.863 (.042) {.781 to .944}	.196 (.046) {.107 to .286}
CIT (Lykken)	.815 (.048) {.721 to .910}	.832 (.067) {.700 to .963}	.185 (.048) {.09 to .279}	.168 (.067) {.037 to .3}	–	–	.823 (.041) {.744 to .903}	–
DLST/TES (7-position)	.748 (.062) {.626 to .869}	.792 (.060) {.674 to .909}	.156 (.050) {.058 to .255}	.127 (.052) {.026 to .229}	.096 (.041) {.016 to .175}	.081 (.037) {.008 to .153}	.844 (.039) {.768 to .920}	.088 (.028) {.034 to .142}
DLST/TES (ESS)	.809 (.069) {.674 to .945}	.751 (.031) {.691 to .811}	.112 (.057) {.001 to .224}	.146 (.027) {.093 to .200}	.078 (.052) {.001 to .18}	.102 (.014) {.075 to .130}	.858 (.037) {.786 to .930}	.090 (.026) {.039 to .142}
Federal You-Phase (7-position)	.841 (.050) {.742 to .939}	.632 (.069) {.497 to .768}	.028 (.023) {.001 to .073}	.161 (.051) {.061 to .261}	.131 (.046) {.041 to .221}	.205 (.057) {.093 to .318}	.883 (.035) {.813 to .952}	.168 (.037) {.096 to .241}
Federal You-Phase (ESS)	.845 (.052) {.742 to .948}	.757 (.064) {.633 to .882}	.034 (.026) {.001 to .085}	.138 (.050) {.039 to .236}	.128 (.046) {.037 to .219}	.255 (.044) {.170 to .341}	.904 (.032) {.841 to .966}	.192 (.033) {.127 to .256}
Federal ZCT (7-position)	.858 (.051) {.759 to .957}	.581 (.073) {.438 to .723}	.033 (.029) {.001 to .090}	.188 (.051) {.089 to .287}	.110 (.044) {.023 to .196}	.232 (.064) {.106 to .358}	.860 (.037) {.788 to .931}	.171 (.040) {.093 to .249}
Federal ZCT (7-position - evidentiary)	.800 (.054) {.693 to .907}	.815 (.057) {.704 to .926}	.115 (.044) {.029 to .202}	.123 (.044) {.036 to .209}	.085 (.039) {.008 to .162}	.064 (.040) {.001 to .143}	.867 (.048) {.773 to .961}	.075 (.029) {.018 to .131}
IZCT (Horizontal)	.977 (.02) {.937 to .999}	.946 (.035) {.878 to .999}	.012 (.015) {.001 to .041}	.001 (.005) {.001 to .010}	.012 (.014) {.001 to .040}	.054 (.035) {.001 to .122}	.994 (.008) {.978 to .999}	.033 (.019) {.001 to .069}
MQTZCT (Matte)	.967 (.021) {.926 to .999}	.963 (.033) {.899 to .999}	.011 (.021) {.001 to .052}	.001 (.015) {.001 to .03}	.022 (<.001) {.022 to .022}	.037 (.029) {.001 to .094}	.994 (.013) {.968 to .999}	.029 (.015) {.001 to .058}
MSU-MGQT (Utah 7-position)	.853 (.068) {.720 to .987}	.770 (.072) {.629 to .911}	.125 (.064) {.001 to .251}	.104 (.060) {.001 to .222}	.062 (.047) {.001 to .155}	.166 (.073) {.022 to .309}	.877 (.049) {.781 to .972}	.114 (.043) {.029 to .198}
RI-Screening (Global)	.825 (.062) {.703 to .947}	.419 (.060) {.302 to .536}	.132 (.058) {.019 to .246}	.506 (.047) {.414 to .597}	.050 (.036) {.001 to .121}	.083 (.044) {.001 to .169}	.657 (.040) {.579 to .735}	.067 (.028) {.011 to .123}
Utah-ZCT combined (Utah 7-position)	.853 (.049) {.757 to .948}	.809 (.056) {.699 to .918}	.051 (.031) {.001 to .112}	.074 (.038) {.001 to .148}	.096 (.040) {.017 to .176}	.117 (.046) {.027 to .207}	.930 (.028) {.875 to .984}	.107 (.030) {.048 to .165}
ZCT (ESS)	.829 (.056) {.719 to .940}	.820 (.051) {.72 to .92}	.095 (.037) {.021 to .168}	.088 (.034) {.022 to .154}	.082 (.044) {.001 to .168}	.093 (.042) {.012 to .175}	.901 (.028) {.845 to .956}	.088 (.030) {.029 to .147}

Appendix B Meta-analytic survey of validated polygraph techniques

Table 2 Summary of validity statistics for studies included in this analysis

Technique (Scoring System)	Study (Year)	Sensitivity	Specificity	False Negative	False Positive	Inconclusives for Deceptive Cases	Inconclusives for Truthful Cases	Unweighted Accuracy	Unweighted INC
AFMGQT (7-position)	Senter et al. (2008)	.758	.917	.212	.083	.030	.001	.849	.015
AFMGQT (7-position)	Nelson et al. (2012c)	.818	.364	.001	.333	.182	.303	.761	.242
AFMGQT (7-position)	Nelson and Handler (Accepted)	.780	.420	.040	.200	.140	.420	.814	.280
AFMGQT (ESS)	Nelson et al. (2011a)	.831	.616	.010	.175	.158	.208	.883	.183
AFMGQT (ESS)	Nelson and Blalock, (Accepted)	.511	.862	.211	.027	.277	.028	.839	.152
AFMGQT (ESS)	Nelson and Handler (Accepted)	.806	.639	.067	.131	.127	.229	.876	.178
Backster You-Phase (Backster)	Nelson et al. (2012a)	.943	.543	.009	.274	.048	.183	.828	.116
Backster You-Phase (Backster)	Nelson (2012a)	.668	.592	.019	.079	.313	.329	.927	.321
CIT (Lykken)	MacLaren (2001)	.815	.832	.185	.168	.001	.001	.823	.000
DLST/TES (7-position)	Research Division Staff (1995a)	.654	.676	.154	.206	.192	.118	.788	.155
DLST/TES (7-position)	Research Division Staff (1995b)	.833	.909	.167	.073	.000	.018	.880	.009
DLST/TES (7-position)	Nelson (2012b)	.910	.677	.037	.184	.053	.139	.874	.096
DLST/TES (7-position)	Nelson et al. (2012b)	.583	.940	.271	.020	.145	.039	.831	.092

(Continued)

Table 2 Summary of Validity Statistics for Studies Included in this Analysis—cont'd

Technique (Scoring System)	Study (Year)	Sensitivity	Specificity	False Negative	False Positive	Inconclusives for Deceptive Cases	Inconclusives for Truthful Cases	Unweighted Accuracy	Unweighted INC
DLST/TES (ESS)	Nelson and Handler (2012)	.917	.587	.036	.253	.047	.160	.831	.104
DLST/TES (ESS)	Nelson et al. (2012d)	.625	.950	.210	.040	.165	.010	.854	.088
DLST/TES (ESS)	Nelson (2012b)	.935	.730	.046	.195	.020	.075	.871	.048
DLST/TES (ESS)	Nelson et al. (2012b)	.665	.839	.207	.040	.126	.119	.859	.123
Federal You-Phase (7-position)	Nelson (2011)	.833	.417	.010	.138	.157	.444	.870	.301
Federal You-Phase (7-position)	Nelson et al. (Accepted)	.844	.730	.036	.171	.119	.097	.885	.108
Federal You-Phase (7-position)	Nelson (2011)	.813	.729	.050	.126	.090	.102	.897	.096
Federal You-Phase (ESS)	Nelson et al. (Accepted)	.859	.770	.027	.143	.145	.325	.906	.235
Federal ZCT (7-position)	Blackwell (1998)	.923	.448	.015	.295	.062	.257	.793	.159
Federal ZCT (7-position)	Krapohl and Cushman (2006)	.824	.560	.044	.180	.132	.260	.853	.196
Federal ZCT (7-position)	Honts et al. (2004) as reported in Honts in Grahnag (2004)	.917	.917	.001	.083	.083	.000	.958	.042

Appendix B Meta-analytic survey of validated polygraph techniques

Technique	Study								
Federal ZCT (7-pos. evidentiary)	Krapohl and Cushman (2006)	.792	.824	.122	.116	.086	.060	.872	.073
Federal ZCT (7-pos. evidentiary)	Nelson and Krapohl (2011)	.933	.667	.000	.233	.067	.133	.870	.100
IZCT (Horizontal)	Shurany and Chavez (2010)	.955	.900	.023	.001	.023	.100	.988	.061
IZCT (Horizontal)	Gordon et al. (2005)	.999	.800	.001	.001	.001	.200	.999	.100
IZCT (Horizontal)	Shurany (2011)	.999	.999	.001	.001	.001	.001	.999	.000
MQTZCT (Matte)	Matte and Reuss (1989)	.969	.914	.000	.001	.031	.086	.999	.059
MQTZCT (Matte)	Shurany et al. (2009)	.929	1.000	.071	.001	.000	.001	.964	.000
MQTZCT (Matte)	Mangan et al. (2008)	.978	1.000	.001	.001	.022	.001	.999	.011
MSU-MGQT (7-position)	Horvath (1988)	.900	.800	.100	.150	.000	.050	.871	.025
MSU-MGQT (7-position)	Horvath and Palmatier (2008)	.767	.700	.133	.067	.100	.233	.882	.167
RI-Screening (Global)	Krapohl et al. (2005)	.831	.634	.169	.366	.000	.000	.732	.000
RI-Screening (Global)	Krapohl and Rosales (2014)	.815	.370	.120	.530	.065	.100	.641	.083
Utah-RCMP/CPC (Utah)	Honts et al. (1985)	.895	.421	.001	.211	.105	.368	.833	.237
Utah-RCMP/CPC (Utah)	Driscoll et al. (1987)	.900	.900	.001	.001	.100	.100	.999	.100

(Continued)

Table 2 Summary of Validity Statistics for Studies Included in this Analysis—cont'd

Technique (Scoring System)	Study (Year)	Sensitivity	Specificity	False Negative	False Positive	Inconclusives for Deceptive Cases	Inconclusives for Truthful Cases	Unweighted Accuracy	Unweighted INC
Utah-RCMP/CPC (Utah)	Honts (1996)	.714	.818	.048	.001	.238	.182	.969	.210
Utah-DLC (Utah)	Honts and Raskin (1988)	.917	.846	.083	.001	.001	.154	.958	.077
Utah-DLC (Utah)	Horowitz et al. (1997)	.733	.867	.133	.133	.133	.001	.856	.067
Utah-PLC (Utah)	Kircher and Raskin (1988)	.880	.860	.060	.060	.060	.080	.935	.070
Utah-PLC (Utah)	Honts et al. (1987)	.800	.700	.001	.200	.200	.100	.889	.150
ZCT (ESS)	Blalock et al. (2009)	.773	.727	.122	.102	.104	.171	.870	.138
ZCT (ESS)	Handler et al. (2010)	.865	.881	.103	.089	.040	.039	.901	0.04
ZCT (ESS)	Nelson et al. (2008)	.749	.814	.154	.077	.097	.109	.872	.103
ZCT (ESS)	Nelson et al. (2011b)	.793	.930	.073	.001	.133	.070	.958	.102
ZCT (ESS)	Nelson and Krapohl (2011)	.833	.633	.001	.133	.167	.233	.913	.200

Table 3 Sample Sizes of Studies Included in this Analysis

Technique (Scoring System)	Study	Total N	N Deceptive	N Truthful	Total Scores	Deceptive Scores	Truthful Scores	Scorers
AFMGQT (7-position)	Senter et al. (2008)	69	33	36	69	33	36	1
AFMGQT (7-position)	Nelson et al. (2012c)	22	11	11	66	33	33	3
AFMGQT (7-position)	Nelson and Handler (Accepted)	69	33	36	100	50	50	1
AFMGQT (ESS)	Nelson et al. (2011a)	22	11	11	66	33	33	3
AFMGQT (ESS)	Nelson and Blalock (Accepted)	69	33	36	69	33	36	1
AFMGQT (ESS)	Nelson and Handler (Accepted)	100	50	50	100	50	50	1
Backster You-Phase (Backster)	Nelson et al. (2012a)	22	11	11	154	77	77	7
Backster You-Phase (Backster)	Nelson (2012a)	100	50	50	100	50	50	1
CIT (Lykken)	MacLaren (2001)	1,070	666	404	1,070	666	404	39
DLST/TES (7-position)	Research Division Staff (1995a)	94	26	68	94	26	68	3
DLST/TES (7-position)	Research Division Staff (1995b)	85	30	55	85	30	55	10
DLST/TES (7-position)	Nelson (2012b)	100	50	50	100	50	50	1
DLST/TES (7-position)	Nelson et al. (2012b)	49	25	24	98	50	48	2
DLST/TES (ESS)	Nelson and Handler (2012)	100	50	50	100	50	50	1
DLST/TES (ESS)	Nelson et al. (2012d)	49	24	25	49	24	25	1

(Continued)

Table 3 Sample Sizes of Studies Included in this Analysis

Technique (Scoring System)	Study	Total N	N Deceptive	N Truthful	Total Scores	Deceptive Scores	Truthful Scores	Scorers
DLST/TES (ESS)	Nelson (2012b)	100	50	50	100	50	50	1
DLST/TES (ESS)	Nelson et al. (2012b)	49	24	25	98	50	48	2
Federal You-Phase (7-position)	Nelson (2011)	100	50	50	100	50	50	1
Federal You-Phase (7-position)	Nelson et al. (Accepted)	22	11	11	220	110	110	10
Federal You-Phase (ESS)	Nelson (2011)	100	50	50	100	50	50	1
Federal You-Phase (ESS)	Nelson et al. (Accepted)	22	11	11	220	110	110	10
Federal ZCT (7-position)	Blackwell (1998)	100	65	35	300	195	105	3
Federal ZCT (7-position)	Krapohl and Cushman (2006)	100	50	50	1,000	500	500	10
Federal ZCT (7-position)	Honts et al. (2004) as reported in Honts in Grahnag (2004)	48	24	24	144	72	72	3
Federal ZCT (7-position evidentiary)	Krapohl and Cushman (2006)	100	50	50	1,000	500	500	10
Federal ZCT (7-position evidentiary)	Nelson and Krapohl (2011)	60	30	30	60	30	30	6
IZCT (Horizontal)	Shurany and Chavez (2010)	84	44	40	84	44	40	4
IZCT (Horizontal)	Gordon et al. (2005)	11	6	5	11	6	5	1
IZCT (Horizontal)	Shurany (2011)	84	36	48	84	36	48	3
MQTZCT (Matte)	Matte and Reuss (1989)	122	64	58	122	64	58	2

Appendix B Meta-analytic survey of validated polygraph techniques

Technique	Study							
MQTZCT (Matte)	Shurany et al. (2009)	57	28	29	57	28	29	4
MQTZCT (Matte)	Mangan et al. (2008)	140	91	49	140	91	49	1
MSU-MGQT	Horvath (1988)	20	10	10	40	20	20	2
MSU-MGQT	Horvath and Palmatier (2008)	30	15	15	60	30	30	1
RI-Screening (Global)	Krapohl et al. (2005)	100	59	41	100	59	41	1
RI-Screening (Global)	Krapohl and Rosales (2014)	100	50	50	400	200	200	4
Utah-RCMP/CPC (Utah)	Honts et al. (1985)	38	19	19	38	19	19	1
Utah-RCMP/CPC (Utah)	Driscoll et al. (1987)	40	20	20	40	20	20	1
Utah-RCMP/CPC (Utah)	Honts (1996)	32	21	11	32	21	11	1
Utah-DLC (Utah)	Honts and Raskin (1988)	25	12	13	25	12	13	1
Utah-DLC (Utah)	Horowitz et al. (1997)	30	15	15	30	15	15	1
Utah-DLC (Utah)	Kircher and Raskin (1988)	100	50	50	200	100	100	2
Utah-DLC (Utah)	Honts et al. (1987)	20	10	10	20	10	10	1
ZCT (ESS)	Nelson et al. (2008)	100	50	50	700	350	350	7
ZCT (ESS)	Nelson et al. (2011b)	100	50	50	250	150	100	25
ZCT (ESS)	Nelson and Krapohl (2011)	60	30	30	60	30	30	6
ZCT (ESS)	Blalock et al. (2009)	100	50	50	900	450	450	9
ZCT (ESS)	Handler et al. (2011)	100	50	50	1,900	950	950	19

tendency to either overestimate or underestimate the criterion accuracy of polygraph techniques in use today. There is little doubt that the establishment of requirements by the APA for criterion accuracy and inconclusive rates at certain levels may be both arbitrary and problematic in that it appears to place a premium for achievement of certain thresholds over the precision of polygraph accuracy estimates themselves. Continued inclusion of outliers discussed earlier, and for which the results are not likely replicable by independent researchers, may also be a problem. These limitations notwithstanding, this update serves to summarize the state of our present knowledge in the same way as the 2011 report anchored our knowledge at that time. As has been stated previously, nothing compels a reader to accept these conclusions as the only or final answer regarding polygraph validity. Readers are free to read the literature and reach their own conclusions. This summary is offered to assist in the identification of materials that may be considered useful and informative, and serves as both a resource for those who desire a convenient summary and as a point of comparison for others who face the need to investigate polygraph validity again at some point in the future.

Accuracy of a polygraph technique – or any human or instrumental method for deception detection or credibility assessment – will depend on the strength of relationship between observable human behavior or recordable human physiology and the criterion states of deception and truth-telling. Fundamentally, the prospect of deception detection rests on two footings: (1) that some epistemological difference exists between deception and truth-telling regarding the universe and reality in terms of physical things and physical events, and (2) that some linear, or at least describable, relationship exists between observable human behavior or recordable human physiology and the deceptive or truthful statements that a person may make about physical things and physical events as they exist in reality. If there is no epistemological difference between deception and truth-telling then credibility assessment through deception detection is not possible. Similarly, if there is no relationship between human behavior or human physiology and the deceptive or truthful statements a person may make about physical things and physical events in reality, then credibility assessment through deception detection is not possible. If there is some discernible relationship between human behavior or human physiology and the truthful or deceptive statements a person may make about physical reality, then deception detection is possible.

If credibility assessment and deception detection are possible, as they appear to be because observable or recordable relationships do exist, then the scientific challenge is to systematize the circumstances and quantify the rate or probability for which we can reasonably expect to be correct or incorrect in our assessments. The practical challenge for the polygraph profession will be to direct its attention and efforts to the practices with proven validity, and to divest the impulse to remain connected to traditions that may not be supported by evidence. This point deserves special consideration as the deliberate incorporation of unscientific or scientific ideas or practices into a repertoire of professional activity would be analogous to the difference between pseudoscientific and scientific lie detection. It will serve the long-term interests of scientific lie detection to continue to emphasize evidence-based practices and replicable research, and to divorce the profession from unscientific tradition. Although progress may appear to be slow within the polygraph profession, the 2011 report achieved the goal of advising the profession about the validation status of polygraph techniques in publication at that time. It is hoped that this brief update will be similarly useful.

Acronyms Used in Tables 1-3.

AFMGQT	Air Force Modified General Question Technique
CIT	Concealed Information Test
DLC	Directed-Lie Comparison question
DLST	Directed Lie Screening Test
ESS	Empirical Scoring System
IZCT	Integrated Zone Comparison Test
MQTZCT	Matte Quadri-Track Zone Comparison Test
MSU-MGQT	Michigan State University Modified General Question Technique
PLC	Probable-lie Comparison question
RCMP/CPC	Royal Canadian Mounted Police/Canadian Police College
RI	Relevant/Irrelevant screening test
TES	Test for Espionage and Sabotage
ZCT	Zone Comparison Technique

REFERENCES

Blackwell, J.N., 1998. PolyScore 3.3 and psychophysiological detection of deception examiner rates of accuracy when scoring examination from actual criminal investigations. Available at the Defense Technical Information Center. DTIC AD Number A355504/PAA. Reprinted in Polygraph 28 (2), 149–175.

Blalock, B., Cushman, B., Nelson, R., 2009. A replication and validation study on an empirically based manual scoring system. Polygraph 38, 281–288.

Driscoll, L.N., Honts, C.R., Jones, D., 1987. The validity of the positive control physiological detection of deception technique. Journal of Police Science and Administration 15, 46–50. Reprinted in Polygraph 16 (3), 218–225.

Gordon, N.J., Mohamed, F.B., Faro, S.H., Platek, S.M., Ahmad, H., Williams, J.M., 2005. Integrated zone comparison polygraph technique accuracy with scoring algorithms. Physiology and Behavior 87 (2), 251–254 (Same study is described in Mohamed, F. B., Faro, S. H., Gordon, N. J., Platek, S. M., Ahmad, H. and Williams, J.M., 2006.).

Handler, M., Nelson, R., Goodson, W., Hicks, M., 2010. Empirical Scoring System: A cross-cultural replication and extension study of manual scoring and decision policies. Polygraph 39, 200–215.

Honts, C.R., 1996. Criterion development and validity of the CQT in field application. Journal of General Psychology 123, 309–324.

Honts, C., Amato, S., Gordon, A., 2004. Effects of outside issues on the comparison question test. Journal of General Psychology 131 (1), 53–74.

Honts, C.R., Hodes, R.L., Raskin, D.C., 1985. Effects of physical countermeasures on the physiological detection of deception. Journal of Applied Psychology 70 (1), 177–187.

Honts, C., Raskin, D., 1988. A field study of the validity of the Directed Lie Control Question. Journal of Police Science and Administration 16 (1), 56–61.

Honts, C.R., Raskin, D.C., Kircher, J.C., 1987. Effects of physical countermeasures and their electromyographic detection during polygraph tests for deception. Psychophysiology 1 (3), 241–247.

Horowitz, S.W., Kircher, J.C., Honts, C.R., Raskin, D.C., 1997. The role of comparison questions in physiological detection of deception. Psychophysiology 34, 108–115.

Horvath, F.S., 1988. The utility of control questions and the effects of two control question types in field polygraph techniques. Journal of Police Science and Administration 16, 198–209.

Horvath, F., Palmatier, J., 2008. Effect of two types of control questions and two question formats on the outcomes of polygraph examinations. Journal of Forensic Sciences 53 (4), 1–11.

Kircher, J.C., Raskin, D.C., 1988. Human versus computerized evaluations of polygraph data in a laboratory setting. Journal of Applied Psychology 73, 291–302.

Krapohl, D.J., Cushman, B., 2006. Comparison of evidentiary and investigative decision rules: A replication. Polygraph 35 (1), 55–63.

Krapohl, D., Rosales, T., 2014. Decision accuracy for the Relevant-Irrelevant Screening Test: A partial replication. Polygraph 43 (1), 1–19.

Krapohl, D.J., Senter, S.M., Stern, B.A., 2005. An exploration of methods for the analysis of multiple-issue relevant/Irrelevant screening data. Polygraph 34 (1), 47–62.

MacLaren, V.V., 2001. A quantitative review of the guilty knowledge test. The Journal of Applied Psychology 86, 674–683.

Mangan, D.J., Armitage, T.E., Adams, G.C., 2008. A field study on the validity of the Quadri-Track Zone Comparison Technique. Physiology and Behavior 95 (1–2), 17–23.

Matte, J.A., Reuss, R.M., 1989. A field validation study of the Quadri-Zone Comparison Question Technique. Polygraph 18, 187–202.

Nelson, R., 2012a. Monte Carlo study of criterion validity of Backster You-Phase examinations. Polygraph 41 (1), 44–53.

Nelson, R., 2012b. Monte Carlo study of criterion validity of the Directed Lie Screening Test using the seven-position, three-position and Empirical Scoring Systems. Polygraph 41 (3), 241–251.

Nelson, R., 2011. Monte Carlo study of criterion validity for two-question zone comparison tests with the Empirical Scoring System, seven-position, and three-position scoring models. Polygraph 40 (2), 146–156.

Nelson, R., Blalock, B., Accepted. Extended analysis of Senter, Waller and Krapohl's AFMGQT examination data with the Empirical Scoring System and the Objective Scoring System, version 3. Polygraph.

Nelson, R., Blalock, B., Handler, M., 2011a. Criterion validity of the Empirical Scoring System and the Objective Scoring System, version 3 with the USAF Modified General Question Technique. Polygraph 40 (3), 172–179.

Nelson, R., Blalock, B., Oelrich, M., Cushman, B., 2011b. Reliability of the Empirical Scoring System with expert examiners. Polygraph 40 (3), 131–139.

Nelson, R., Handler, M., 2012. Monte Carlo study of criterion validity of the Directed Lie Screening Test using the Empirical Scoring System and the Objective Scoring System version 3. Polygraph 41 (3), 145–155.

Nelson, R., Handler, M., Accepted. Monte Carlo study of the United States Air Force Modified General Question Technique with two three and four questions. Polygraph.

Nelson, R., Handler, M., Adams, G., Backster, C., 2012a. Survey of reliability and criterion validity of Backster numerical scores of You-Phase exams from confirmed field investigations. Polygraph 41 (2), 127–135.

Nelson, R., Handler, M., Blalock, B. and Cushman, B., Accepted. Blind scoring of confirmed federal You-Phase examinations by experienced and inexperienced examiners: Criterion validity with the Empirical Scoring System and the seven-position model. Polygraph.

Nelson, R., Handler, M., Blalock, B., Hernández, N., 2012b. Replication and extension study of Directed Lie Screening Tests: Criterion validity with the seven- and three- position models and the Empirical Scoring System. Polygraph 41 (3), 186–198.

Nelson, R., Handler, M., Morgan, C., 2012d. Criterion validity of the Directed Lie Screening Test and the Empirical Scoring System with inexperienced examiners and non-naive examinees in a laboratory setting. Polygraph 41 (3), 176185.

Nelson, R., Handler, M., Morgan, C., O'Burke, P., 2012c. Short Report: Criterion validity of the United States Air Force Modified General Question Technique and Iraqi scorers. Polygraph 41 (1), 18–28.

Nelson, R., Krapohl, D., 2011. Criterion validity of the Empirical Scoring System with experienced examiners: Comparison with the seven-position evidentiary model using the Federal Zone Comparison Technique. Polygraph 40 (2), 79–85.

Nelson, R., Krapohl, D., Handler, M., 2008. Brute force comparison: A Monte Carlo study of the Objective Scoring System version 3 (OSS-3) and human polygraph scorers. Polygraph 37 (3), 185–215.

Research Division Staff, 1995a. A comparison of psychophysiological detection of deception accuracy rates obtained using the counterintelligence scope Polygraph and the test for espionage and sabotage question formats. DTIC AD Number A319333. Department of Defense Polygraph Institute. Fort Jackson, SC. Reprinted in Polygraph 26 (2), 79–106.

Research Division Staff, 1995b. Psychophysiological detection of deception accuracy rates obtained using the test for espionage and sabotage. DTIC AD Number A330774. Department of Defense Polygraph Institute. Fort Jackson, SC. Reprinted in Polygraph 27 (3), 171–180.

Senter, S., Waller, J., Krapohl, D., 2008. Air Force Modified General Question Test validation study. Polygraph 37 (3), 174–184.

Shurany, T., 2011. Polygraph Verification Test. European Polygraph 5 (5), 61–67.

Shurany, T., Chaves, F., 2010. Integrated Zone Comparison Technique and ASIT PolySuite algorithm: A field validity study. European Polygraph 4 (2), 71–80.

Shurany, T., Stein, E., Brand, E., 2009. A field study on the validity of the Quadri-Track Zone Comparison Technique. European Polygraph 1, 5–23.

APPENDIX

Confidential report

C1

Date: 8/15/2014

CLIENT:
Marshal Tucker
Tucker Law Firm
4321 Main Street
Anytown, SC, 22222

EXAMINEE:
NAME: JONES, Davey L.
DOB: 08/03/1967
TEST NO: 069951

The purpose of a polygraph examination is to determine an examinee's truthfulness to specific questions under consideration.

After executing a proper consent and release form, the above named individual, henceforth referred to as "the examinee" requested to undergo a polygraph examination. The completed release document has been incorporated into our files.

The polygraph test was administered according to the guidelines and procedures accepted and endorsed by the American Polygraph Association and in accordance with applicable South Carolina administrative codes.

THIS EXAMINER UNDERSTANDS THE RELEVANT ISSUE(S) TO BE: Did the examinee fire a weapon in the parking lot of the No Tell Motel which struck Dan L. Boone, causing his death on the night of 23 February 2013.

TESTING SITE: This examiner traveled to the Tucker Law Firm, 4321 Main Street, Anytown, SC to administer a polygraph examination to the examinee. The examination was conducted in a private office. The room was secure, quiet, private, and suitable for use.

PRETEST ADMISSIONS: No admission against self-interest were made by the examinee prior to the administration of the polygraph examination.

Prior to the administration of any polygraph test charts this examiner was provided a full understanding of the allegations against the examinee by his attorney. Based upon information made available to this examiner, the following recounts the circumstances requiring polygraph testing:

The examinee is accused of engaging in a verbal altercation with Mr. Dan L. Boone on the evening of 23 February 2013 while in the parking lot of the aforementioned motel. The verbal altercation became physical when Mr. Boone struck the examinee with his closed fist. The examinee is alleged to have withdrawn a 9 millimeter semi-automatic pistol from his pants pocket and shot Mr. Boone resulting in his death. The examinee denies that he possessed the weapon in question, asserting that Mr. Boone withdrew the weapon and pointed it at the examinee. In a subsequent struggle for the weapon, according to the examinee, the weapon discharged apparently striking Mr. Boone. The examinee denies that he ever pointed the weapon at Mr. Boone and further denies that he pulled the trigger causing the weapon to fire. He also denies having sole possession of the weapon at any time.

After a detailed discussion of allegations against the examinee, this examiner, in concert with the attorney developed the following relevant test questions:

> Relevant Question R5: **Did you point that pistol at that man that night in that parking lot?**
> Examinee response **"No"**
> Relevant Question R7: **Did you aim that weapon at that man in that parking lot that night?**
> Examinee response **"No"**
> Relevant Question R10: **Was that pistol in your possession at any time prior to the argument with that man that night?**
> Examinee response **"No"**

TEST PHASE

A Limestone computerized polygraph instrument recording thoracic and abdominal respiration, electrodermal activity, cardiovascular changes in pulse rate and blood pressure using a blood pressure cuff and a photoplethysmograph sensor (PPG) and a movement detection sensor was utilized to administer the examination. The Limestone system was calibrated and function tested prior to the examination to verify its proper operation. Three relevant issue polygraph test charts were then administered regarding the issue under consideration. Adequate physiological data was collected. The testing phase of the examination was concluded.

POSTTEST ADMISSIONS

The examinee was not subsequently questioned and made no additional statements or admissions against self-interest.

CONCLUSIONS AND RECOMMENDATIONS

A thorough examination of the polygraph test charts was conducted. A full review of the test charts collected indicates clear and consistent physiological criteria sufficient for evaluation in the relevant test questions presented. A numerical evaluation of the polygraph charts was conducted using both conventional numeric spot scoring rules (Department of Defense Polygraph Institute, 2006) and the Empirical Scoring System (ESS) (American Polygraph Association, 2011; Nelson and Handler, 2010, 2012; Nelson et al., 2011). There were sufficient artifact-free data present in the test charts collected to obtain criteria upon which to conduct a numeric evaluation and form a conclusion.

Using the Federal Scoring System 3-position scoring rules, the test data analysis score obtained of −6 exceeds the cut score of −3 for classification of **DECEPTION INDICATED** (Department of Defense Polygraph Institute, 2006).

Using the Empirical Scoring System (ESS), an evidence-based, normed, and standardized protocol for test data analysis, the grand total score of −9 equals or exceeds the required cut store of −4 for deceptive classifications. The level of statistical significance is calculated at $p = .006$, which exceeds the required alpha boundary ($\alpha = .05$). Normative data indicate that only a small portion (0.6%) of truthful persons are expected to produce a similar deceptive test score under normal circumstances. These results support the conclusion that there is **DECEPTION INDICATED** by the physiological responses to the test stimulus questions during this examination (American Polygraph Association, 2011; Nelson and Handler, 2010, 2012; Nelson et al., 2011).

CRITERION ACCURACY/PROBABILITY OF ERRORS

Event-specific examinations with $\alpha = 0.05$ for deceptive classifications and $\alpha = 0.05$ for truthful classifications can be expected to produce a false-positive error rate for which the 95% confidence interval is from 0.007 to 0.093, with an expected confidence interval of 0.007 to 0.093 for false negative errors when interpreted with an assumption of non-independent criterion variance (calculated using binomial approximation to the standard normal distribution using a nominal sample space of 100 cases). **The 95% confidence interval for unweighted mean decision accuracy is 0.907 to 0.993** (Nelson and Handler, 2010, 2012; Nelson et al., 2011).

Additional questions or discussion regarding this report are welcome. However, in the absence of any appropriate release, this "work product" will be discussed "only" with the client named on page one of this report. This examiner's confidence level in the validity of this test is high.

EXAMINER: MILTON O. WEBB, JR.
N.C. LICENSE NO: 378-P
TEST DATE: 15 August 2014

REFERENCES

Department of Defense Polygraph Institute, 2006. Test Data Analysis: DoDPI numerical evaluation scoring system.

American Polygraph Association, 2011. Meta-analytic survey of criterion accuracy of validated polygraph techniques. Polygraph 40 (4), 196–305. [Electronic version] Retrieved August 20, 2012, from, http://www.polygraph.org/section/research-standards-apa-publications.

Nelson, R., Handler, M., 2010. Empirical Scoring System. Lafayette Instrument Company.

Nelson, R., Handler, M., 2012. Using Normative Reference Data with Diagnostic Exams and the Empirical Scoring System. APA Magazine 45 (3), 61–69.

Nelson, R., Handler, M., Shaw, P., Gougler, M., Blalock, B., Russell, C., Cushman, B., Oelrich, M., 2011. Using the Empirical Scoring System. Polygraph 40. 67–78.

APPENDIX

Polygraph Examination Report

C2

Shaw Polygraph Services, Inc.
Professional Exams, Training & Consulting

1890 Star Shoot Parkway
Suite 170-366
Lexington, KY 40509
shawpolygraph@gmail.com

Polygraph Examination Report
Confidential

Examinee:	John Smith	**Photo:**
Purpose:	Criminal/Specific Issue	
Requester:	Somewhere Police Department	
Test Location:	Somewhere, KY	
Date of Exam:	January 31, 2015	
Final Call:	*No Deception Indicated*	

Examinee Data:

Race:	White (Non-Hispanic)	**Education:**	College Graduate	**DOB:**	4/16/1955
Sex:	Male	**Marital Status:**	Married	**Age:**	59

Purpose of Examination / Background:

The main issue under consideration for the polygraph examination was whether or not the examinee was telling the truth to the pertinent questions listed under the Test Phase section of this report.

On January 3, 2015, at approximately 2235 hours, Sarah Jones (wife of victim) reported to police that she had discovered the dead body of her husband, Allen Jones, lying in the driveway next to his car. She reported that she had been at her daughter's house throughout the evening babysitting her grandkids and found her husband in the driveway when she pulled into the driveway and her vehicle lights revealed his body and open car door.

Responding officers determined that Allen Jones was shot in the back 3 times. Upon further investigation and interviews by case detectives, it was learned that John Smith had previously loaned Allen Jones in excess of $10,000 to avoid foreclosure on his home. Sarah Jones confirmed that Mr. Smith was an acquaintance of her husband, but she had never had personal interactions with him.

During the detective's interview with Mr. Smith, Mr. Smith reported that he and Allen Jones were good friends and he was glad to have loaned him the money. He further commented that he had asked Allen Jones when he could repay the loan, but he never threatened his life. Mr. Smith denied shooting or having any knowledge about the death of Allen Jones and agreed to take a polygraph examination to prove the veracity of his statements.

Prior to the administration of the polygraph, this examiner reviewed pertinent case documents to include summary reports of each interview, the coroner's report and the initial responding officers' reports.

Pre-Test Interview:

On January 31, 2015, John Smith arrived and voluntarily submitted to a polygraph examination. The examinee read, completed and signed the Polygraph Consent & Release of Information Form.

In the opinion of the examiner, John Smith was suitable for polygraph testing. There were no known physical or psychological conditions that would preclude a valid polygraph examination.

During the pre-test interview Mr. Smith advised that he started loaning Allen Jones lump sums of money in late 2012 after Allen had been laid off from work. Allen was embarrassed to tell his wife about his troubles at work and asked Mr. Smith to help him out until he could figure things out. Mr. Smith commented that he had been frustrated with Allen's promises to pay him back and then not doing so, but he maintained he did not and would never make a threat against Allen's life over money.

Mr. Smith commented that there might have been other people Allen borrowed money from and perhaps those individuals were responsible for Allen's death. Smith made statements that he was angry he was even being considered as a suspect in this case as it was disparaging to his reputation and additionally felt it was a waste of time and money for everyone involved. He denied planning with anyone or participating in any way in the death of Allen Jones. He discussed possessing various firearms and being an avid hunter, but denied ever using one of his firearms against another person.

John Smith agreed to take a polygraph examination concerning these statements.

At the conclusion of the pre-test phase of the polygraph examination, the examiner discussed and thoroughly reviewed all the test questions with the examinee to ensure s/he completely understood each question before the onset of the testing phase of the examination.

Test Phase:

A Lafayette computerized polygraph system, model LX5000 was used for the collection of polygraph tests (test data). This instrument makes a continuous recording of autonomic responses associated with respiration, electrodermal activity, and cardiovascular functioning. The instrument also includes sensors designed to record peripheral behavioral activity and cooperation during the examination. A series of three charts were collected.

The examination technique consists of a combination of: 1) a polygraph testing protocol that conforms to evidence-based principles for target selection, test question construction, and test administration (the Event-Specific ZCT following the Utah Approach); and, 2) a test data analysis model (Empirical Scoring System) for which there exists a published and/or replicated body of at least two empirical studies that provide evidence of their diagnostic or screening accuracy for those dimensional aspects specified in the American Polygraph Association Meta-Analytic Report on Validated Techniques (APA, 2011).

Event-specific examinations consisting of three relevant questions that describe a known or alleged incident when scored with the ESS have been shown to provide a mean sensitivity rate of .817 (.706 - .927) and mean test specificity of .846 (.747 - .946). The mean false-negative error rate has been reported as .077 (.004 - .151), and the mean false-positive rate has been reported as .064 (.001 - .130). Unweighted decision accuracy for these exams has been reported as .921 (.866 - .977) with an estimated inconclusive rate of .098 (.039 - .157).

The following pertinent questions were asked during the polygraph examination.

1. Did you shoot Allen Jones?
   Answer: No

2. Did you participate in any way in the shooting of Allen Jones?
   Answer: No

3. Do you know for sure who shot Allen Jones?
   Answer: No

Examination Results

Global analysis of the physiological data revealed that it was of sufficient interpretable quality to complete a standardized numerical analysis of the test results. Analysis was performed using the following techniques:

Empirical Scoring System

Analysis of the polygraph tests using the Empirical Scoring System resulted in statistically significant numerical scores that support a conclusion of **No Deception Indicated** when Mr. Smith was answering the above listed questions. The statistical probability that Mr. Smith's pattern of data were produced by a person belong to a deceptive distribution is less than one chance in a hundred (p-value < .01) when compared to a validation sample used to produce the normative data and considered representative of the general testing population. In other words, the likelihood that Mr. Smith's response was produced by someone lying was less than 1%.

OSS3

Analysis of John Smith's test data using a computerized statistical algorithm, the Objective Scoring System, version 3, resulted in statistically significant scores indicative of **No Deception Indicated** to the pertinent questions. The statistical probability that John Smith's test data were produced by a deceptive person is approximately two percent (p-value <.024) or about 2 chances in 100.

It is the opinion of this examiner that Mr. Smith was being truthful during testing.

Post-Test Interview:

During the post-test phase of the exam, Mr. Smith was informed of the test results and the examination was concluded.

Signature of Examiner:

_____

Pamela K. Shaw • Shaw Polygraph Services, Inc.

Index

Note: Page numbers followed by *f* indicate figures and *t* indicate tables.

A

Admissibility, 207–221
Air Force Modified General Question Technique (AFMGQT)
  decision rules, 145, 165–166
  pretest, 142
  scoring, 144–145, 164–165
  test phase, 142–144, 143*t*, 144*t*
  versions of, 164, 164*t*, 165*t*
American Polygraph Association (APA), 319
American Society of Testing and Materials (ASTM), 266–267
Amputations/injuries
  cardiovascular, 232
  electrodermal, 232
  photoplethysmograph (PPG), 232
  pneumograph, 232
Anatomy and physiology
  cardiovascular system, 46–53, 47*f*, 48*f*, 49*f*, 50*f*, 51*f*, 52*f*
  integumentary system, 32–34, 32*f*
  nervous system, 34–44, 35*f*, 36*f*, 38*f*, 40*f*, 41*f*, 45*f*
  organization, 30–32, 31*f*
  respiratory system, 53–59, 53*f*, 54*f*, 56*f*, 57*f*, 58*f*
Ancient traditions, lie detection
  balance, 2
  Cófha, 3
  fire, 2
  hot oil, 3
  images, 3
  ordeals, 4
  poison, 3
  red-hot iron, 3
  rice, 3
  torture, 4
  trials by combat, 3–4
  water, 2–3
Army Zone Comparison Technique. *See* Federal Zone Comparison Technique (FZCT)
Arther Technique, 151–152
Asset forfeiture testing, 251–254
Autobiographical implicit association test (aIAT), 289–290
Autonomic nervous system (ANS), 39, 40, 42*f*

B

Backster Zone Comparison Technique, 22, 151–152
Base rate
  applicants, 195*t*
  assumptions, 194
  employees, 194*t*
  offenders, 194*t*
Behavior, observations of, 4–6
Berceau scientifique, 11*f*
Blood, 46
Blood vessels and circulation, 49–50, 50*f*, 51*f*
Boyle's law, 55
Brain, structure of, 37, 37*f*
Breathing
  lie detection instrumentation, 12, 13*f*
  regulation of, 55, 57*f*

C

Cardiograph scores, 113–114, 113*t*, 114*t*, 115*f*
Cardiovascular channel
  amputations/injuries, 232
  examinee, explaining of sensors, 83
  polygraph data, analysis of, 100–102, 101*f*, 102*f*, 103*f*
  tracing appearance, 91–93, 92*f*, 93*f*
Cardiovascular disorders
  heart attacks, 234
  heartbeat irregularities, 234
  respiratory blood pressure fluctuations (RBPFs), 234–235
Cardiovascular measures, in deception tests, 8–12, 10*f*, 11*f*
Cardiovascular system
  blood, 46
  blood vessels and circulation, 49–50, 50*f*, 51*f*
  cardiac output, influences on, 49*f*, 50
  heart, 46, 47, 47*f*
  heart conductive system, 47, 48*f*, 49, 49*f*
  microcirculation, 50*f*
  principal arteries, 51*f*
  sphygmomanomter, 52*f*
Concealed Information Test (CIT)
  advantages, 172–174
  analyzing, 180–182
  EDRs on, 182*f*

Concealed Information Test (CIT) *(Continued)*
    feature of, 174
    instrumentation, 177
    practices, 182
    principles, 175
    testing, 13–14, 178
Confidential report
    conclusions and recommendations, 337
    criterion accuracy, 337
    posttest admissions, 336
    pretest admissions, 335
    probability of errors, 337
    test phase, 336
Countermeasure question, 76
Credibility assessment tools, 277
Criterion-related validity, 186

D

Data collection
    sensor placement, 83–88
    sensors to examinee, 81–83
    tracing appearance, 88–93
Decision rules, definition, 96
Deterrence effect, 128
Differential salience (DS), 203–204
Directed lie comparison (DLC) questions, 73–75
Directed-Lie Screening Test (DLST)
    decision rules, 139–140, 140*t*
    directed lies, 137–138
    next steps, 140–141
    pretest interview, 137
    scoring, 139
    test phase, 138–139
Dwarfism, 235

E

Eccrine sweat gland activity, 33
EDA. *See* Electrodermal activity (EDA)
EDR. *See* Electrodermal response (EDR)
Electrodermal
    amputations/injuries, 232
    examinee, explaining of sensors, 82–83
    polygraph data, analysis of, 98–99, 99*f*
    scoring, 112–113, 113*t*
    sensor placement, 84–86, 85*f*, 86*f*
    tracing appearance, 89–90, 90*f*
Electrodermal activity (EDA), 13–15, 14*f*, 34, 96
Electrodermal response (EDR)
    definition, 96
    polygraph data, analysis of, 99, 99*f*, 100*f*
Empirical Scoring System (ESS), 108–109, 118–119

Employee Polygraph Protection Act (EPPA), 127
    authority of secretary, 310–311
    commerce, definitions, 309
    definitions, 309
    disclosure of information, 316–317
    effective date, 317
    Employee Polygraph Protection Act of 1988, 309
    employer, definitions, 309
    enforcement provisions, 311–312
    exemptions, 312–314
    law and agreements, 317
    lie detector, definitions, 309, 310
    lie detector, prohibitions, 310
    notice of protection, 310
    Secretary, definitions, 309
    use of exemptions, restrictions, 314–316
ERPs. *See* Event-related potentials (ERPs)
Ethics
    competence, 242
    ethical lapses, reasons for, 240–241
    examinee, 242
    external pressures, 240
    integrity, 242
    internal pressures, 240–241
    polygraph examiners, 239
    principles, 241–242
Event-related potentials (ERPs), 278–280
Eye tracking, 283–284

F

Fear of detection, 202
Federal Zone Comparison Technique (FZCT), 119–120, 120*t*
    decision rules, 159
    irrelevant questions, 158
    primary relevant questions, 157
    probable-lie comparison (PLC) questions, 157
    sacrifice relevant question, 157
    scoring rules, 159
    secondary relevant questions, 157
    symptomatic question, 157–158
    test phase, 158–159, 158*t*
Finger pulse amplitude (FPA), 96
Finger pulse line length (FPLL), 96
Foreign language interpreters
    interpreter, 254–255
    preparation, 255–256
    pretest interview, 257–258, 257*f*
    testing, 258–259, 259*f*
Franck plethysmograph, Verdin, 11*f*
Frontal cortex, 37–38

Frye, James Alphonso, 282
  to Daubert, 207–212
Functional magnetic resonance imaging (fMRI), 280–281
FZCT. *See* Federal Zone Comparison Technique (FZCT)

G

Guilt complex question, 77
Guilty Knowledge Test, 23

H

Hearing impairment
  interpreter, 236
  technology, 236–237
Heart, 46, 47, 47*f*
Heart conductive system, 47, 48*f*, 49, 49*f*
Hemispherical differentiation, 38, 38*f*
Hope/fear questions, 77

I

Information gain (IG), 197, 198*f*, 199*f*
Instrumentation, lie detection, 8, 9*f*
Integrated Zone Comparison Technique (IZCT), 151–152, 321
Integumentary system
  eccrine sweat gland activity, 33
  electrodermal activity (EDA), 34
  human skin, cross section of, 32–33, 32*f*
  skin conductance, 34
Interview route maps (IRM), 134–136, 135*f*
Introductory question, 76
Irrelevant questions, 64

J

Journal of Applied Psychology, 185
Journal of Forensic Sciences, 185

K

Keeler, Leonarde, 18, 20
Keeler Relevant/Irrelevant Technique, 151–152
Kymographion, Ludwig, 9*f*

L

Larson, John, 23
Laser Doppler vibrometry (LDV), 286–288, 288*f*
Law Enforcement Pre-Employment Technique (LEPET), 141
Leipzig, Carl, 9*f*
Less common questions, 76–78

Lie detection, history of
  analytic methods, 23–24
  ancient traditions, 2–4
  behavior, observations of, 4–6
  breathing, 12
  cardiovascular measures, 8–12
  electrodermal, 13–15
  evolution of techniques, 20–23
  first precedent in law, 15–16
  instrumentation, 8, 9*f*
  modern developments, 8–15
  modern instrumentation, 18–20
  multiple recordings, 17–18
  physiology, observations of, 6–7
The Lie Detector Test (Marston), 12

M

Marcy Technique, 151–152
Marey, Étienne-Jules, 12
Marey multichannel recorder, 9*f*
Marin Protocol, 266–271
Matte Quadri-Track Zone Comparison Technique (MQTZCT), 151–152, 321
Meta-analytic survey, 320, 322*t*, 323*t*, 327*t*
Michigan State University Modified General Question Technique (MSU-MGQT), 321
Microcirculation, 50*f*
Model Policy for Postconviction Sex Offender Testing, 248–249
Modifications of the Marston deception test (Larson), 25
Modified General Question Technique (MGQT), 141
Motion sensor
  examinee, explaining of sensors, 83
  sensor placement, 88, 88*f*
  tracing appearance, 90, 92*f*
Movement sensor, 106, 107*f*
MQTZCT. *See* Matte Quadri-Track Zone Comparison Technique (MQTZCT)
Multiple-issue and multiple-facet examinations, 117

N

National Center for Credibility Assessment (NCCA), 95
National Research Council (NRC), 190, 320–321
Nervous system
  autonomic nervous system (ANS), 39, 40, 42*f*
  brain, structure of, 37, 37*f*
  frontal cortex, 37–38
  hemispherical differentiation, 38, 38*f*
  neuron, structure of, 35–36, 36*f*
  organization of, 35*f*

Nervous system *(Continued)*
  parasympathetic division, 44, 45*f*
  plexuses, 41*f*
  spinal cord, 39, 40*f*, 41*f*
  sympathetic division, 42*f*, 43–44, 43*f*
  vagus nerve, 45*f*
Neuron, structure of, 35–36, 36*f*

O

Obesity, 237–238
Oculomotor Deception Test (ODT), 285–286, 286*f*
Ordeals, ancient traditions, 4
Organization, 30–32
  levels of, 31*f*

P

Paired testing, 266–271
Parasympathetic division, 44, 45*f*
PCSOT. *See* Postconviction Sex Offender Testing (PCSOT)
PDD. *See* Psychophysiological detection of deception (PDD)
Peak of Tension (POT)
  analyzing, 171–172, 172*f*, 173*f*, 174*f*, 175*f*
  approach, 18
  known solution (KSPOT), 168–170
  searching POT (SPOT), 6–7, 170–171
Photoplethysmograph (PPG)
  amputations/injuries, 232
  definition, 96
  examinee, explaining of sensors, 83
  polygraph data, analysis of, 115
  sensor placement, 86, 87*f*
  tracing appearance, 90, 91*f*
Physical conditions requiring accommodation
  amputations/injuries, 231–232
  blindness, 233
  cardiovascular disorders, 233–235
  dwarfism, 235
  hearing impairment, 235–237
  obesity, 237–238
  pregnancy, 238
  stuttering, 238–239
Physiology, observations of, 6–7
Pneumograph
  amputations/injuries, 232
  examinee, explaining of sensors, 82
  polygraph data, analysis of, 103–104
  scores, 110–112, 111*t*
  sensor placement, 83–84, 84*f*
  tracing appearance, 88–89, 89*f*

Polygraph
  accuracy of, 330
  characteristics, 276
  decision accuracy, 187*f*
  definitions, 309
  examination report, 339–341
  historical perspective, 1
Polygraph data, analysis of
  3-position scoring system, 108, 118
  7-position scoring system, 108, 118
  baseline rise, 104, 106*f*
  cardiograph scores, 113–114, 113*t*, 114*t*, 115*f*
  cardiovascular, 100–102, 101*f*, 102*f*, 103*f*
  chart interpretation, 97–98
  decision rules, 117–122
  definitions, 95–96
  electrodermal, 98–99, 99*f*
  electrodermal channel, scoring, 112–113, 113*t*
  electrodermal response (EDR) exemplars, 99, 99*f*, 100*f*
  Empirical Scoring System (ESS), 108–109, 118–119
  features, 97–98
  Federal Zone Comparison Technique (FZCT), 119–120, 120*t*
  global analysis, 122
  movement sensor, 106, 107*f*
  multiple-issue and multiple-facet examinations, 117
  photoplethysmograph (PPG), 115
  pneumograph, 103–104
  pneumograph scores, 110–112, 111*t*
  purposeful non-cooperation (PNC), 123
  Rank Order Analysis (ROA), 122, 123*f*
  Rank Order Scoring System, 115–117, 116*f*
  response windows, 109–110
  scoring rules, 109
  scoring systems, 107–117
  single-issue examinations, evidentiary, 121–122
  single-issue examinations: investigative, 119
  slowing, 104, 105*f*
  suppression, 104, 104*f*, 105*f*
  Utah Probable-Lie Test, 121
  vasomotor, 103, 103*f*
  "You Phase" ZCT, 120, 121*t*
Polygraph legal issues
  admissibility, 207–221
  Daubert v. Merrell Dow Pharmaceuticals, Inc., 211, 220
  general rule, 221
  interrogation, 221–223
  Kumho Tire Co. v. Carmichael, 212–213
  Lee v. Martinez, 216
  LeFevere v. State, 218

licensing, 227
Miranda considerations, 222–223
People v. Wheeler, 218
Postconviction Sex Offender Testing, 223–225
post-Daubert admissibility of, 212–217
sentencing, 219–220
State v. Dorsey, 215–216
stipulated polygraph evidence, 217–219
United States v. Piccinonna, 209
United States v. Scheffer, 212
workplace, 225–227
Polygraph screening
 adjudications, 132–133
 Air Force Modified General Question Technique (AFMGQT), 141–145
 Directed-Lie Screening Test (DLST), 136–141
 examination reports, 148
 pretest interviews, suggestions for, 134–136
 recording, 133
 Relevant/Irrelevant (RI) Screening Test, 145–148
 significant case tracking, 133
 successive hurdles, 129–130
 surveys, 133
 test results, 133–134
 test topics, 130–132
Polygraph theories
 differential salience, 203–204
 preliminary process theory (PPT), 204
 psychological set, 201–203
 relevant issue gravity (RIG), 203
Postconviction Sex Offender Testing (PCSOT), 224, 247–251
 instant offense, 249
 instant offense investigative, 249
 maintenance, 250–251
 prior allegation, 249
 sex offense monitoring, 250
 sexual history (I & II), 249–250
PPG. *See* Photoplethysmograph (PPG)
Pregnancy, 238
Preliminary process theory (PPT), 204
Premature ventricular contractions (PVCs), 101–102, 102f
Pretest interview
 acquaintance test, 156
 biographic information, 154–155
 consent form, 154
 examinee and examiner, 153–154
 polygraph, 155
 process, 154
 question introduction, 156
 rights advisement, 154
 suggestions for, 134–136
 test issues, 155–156
Primary relevant questions, 66–67
Probable-lie comparison (PLC) questions, 68–73
Psychological set, 201–203
Psychophysiological detection of deception (PDD), 29
Purposeful non-cooperation (PNC), 123
PVCs. *See* Premature ventricular contractions (PVCs)

R

Rank Order Analysis (ROA), 122, 123f
Rank Order Scoring System, 115–117, 116f
Recognition tests
 Concealed Information Test (CIT), 172–182
 Known Solution (KSPOT), 168–170, 171–172
 Peak of Tension (POT), 167–172, 172f, 173f, 174f, 175f
 Searching POT (SPOT), 170–171
Reid, John, 20–21
Reid Technique, 151–152
Relevant/Irrelevant (RI) Screening Test, 18, 78
 decision rules, 147–148
 pretest, 146
 scoring rules, 147
 test phase, 146–147, 147t
Relevant issue gravity (RIG), 203
Relevant questions, 65–68
Report of the Meta-analytic Survey of Validated Polygraph Techniques, 319
Report writing
 analyses and results, 245–246
 background, 243
 examination, 244
 examiners, 247
 identification, 243
 posttest statements, 247
 pretest, 244–245
 purpose, 244
 test phase, 245
Respiration line length (RLL), 96
Respiratory system
 Boyle's law, 55
 breathing, regulation of, 55, 57f
 inhalation and exhalation, 55, 56f
 larynx, 53–54, 54f
 oral cavity, 53–54
 respiration, negative feedback control of, 56, 58f
 respiratory pathway, 53
 respiratory structures, location of, 53, 53f
 speech and voice sounds, 53–54, 54f
Response onset window (ROW), 109
ROA. *See* Rank Order Analysis (ROA)

S

Saccadic eye movement, 283–285
Sacrifice relevant question, 75
Scientific issues
    base rates, 194–201, 194t, 195t
    decision rules, 191–193, 192f
    field studies, 189–190
    laboratory studies, 190–191
    polygraph theories, 201–204
    reliability, 188–189
    validity, 185–188
Scoring rules, definition, 96
Searching POT (SPOT), 170–171
Secondary relevant questions, 68
Sensor placement
    blood pressure cuff, 86–88, 87f
    electrodermal sensors, 84–86, 85f, 86f
    motion sensor, 88, 88f
    photoplethysmograph sensor, 86, 87f
    pneumograph sensors, 83–84, 84f
Sensors, explaining to examinee
    cardiovascular, 83
    electrodermal, 82–83
    general introduction, 82
    motion sensor, 83
    photoplethysmograph, 83
    pneumographs, 82
7-position scoring system, 108, 118
Sex offense monitoring, 250
Silent Answer Test (SAT), 260–261, 260f, 261f
Skin conductance (SC), 96
Skin potential (SP), 96
Skin resistance (SR), 96
Sphygmomanomter, 52f
Spinal cord, 39, 40f, 41f
Spot score, 96
Studies in Word Association (Jung, Carl), 13–14
Stuttering, 238–239
Successive hurdles, 129–130
Sympathetic division, 42f, 43–44, 43f
Symptomatic questions, 75–76

T

Test for Espionage and Sabotage (TES), 136
Test question construction (TQC)
    countermeasure question, 76
    crime involving identity theft, 64
    directed lie comparison (DLC) questions, 73–75
    fear of detection, 63
    guilt complex question, 77
    hope/fear questions, 77
    introductory question, 76
    irrelevant questions, 64
    laboratory study, 63
    less common questions, 76–78
    overall truth, 78
    polygraph testing, 61
    positive control, 78
    primary relevant questions, 66–67
    probable-lie comparison (PLC) questions, 68–73
    relevant questions, 65–68
    sacrifice relevant question, 75
    salience, 62–63
    secondary relevant questions, 68
    symptomatic questions, 75–76
    yes-no technique, 78
Thermal imaging, 281–282, 283f
3-position scoring system, 108, 118
TQC. *See* Test question construction (TQC)
Tracing appearance
    cardiovascular, 91–93, 92f, 93f
    chart, appearance of, 93, 93f
    electrodermal, 89–90, 90f
    motion sensor, 90, 92f
    photoplethysmograph, 90, 91f
    pneumograph, 88–89, 89f
Traumatic events, testing victims of, 271–273

U

Utah Probable Lie Test (UPLT)
    decision rules, 162–163
    four-question, 161t
    introductory question, 160
    irrelevant questions, 160
    mixed-issue, decision rules of, 163
    multiple-facet, decision rules of, 163
    PLC questions, 160
    relevant questions, 160
    sacrifice relevant question, 160
    scoring, 162
    single-issue, decision rules of, 163
    test phase, 160–162
    three-question format, 161t

V

Validity, 185–188
Vasomotor, polygraph data, analysis of, 103, 103f
Voice-based systems, 288–289
Volumetric glove, 10f

Y

Yes Test, 262–266, 263f, 264f, 265f, 266f
"You Phase" ZCT, 120, 121t

CPI Antony Rowe
Chippenham, UK
2018-12-10 15:24